VISUAL QUICKSTART GUIDE

FileMaker Pro 8

FOR WINDOWS AND MACINTOSH

Nolan Hester

Visual QuickStart Guide
FileMaker Pro 8 for Windows and Macintosh
Nolan Hester

Peachpit Press
1249 Eighth Street
Berkeley, CA 94710
(800) 283-9444
(510) 524-2178
(510) 524-2221

Find us on the Web at: www.peachpit.com

To report errors, please send a note to errata@peachpit.com

Peachpit Press is a division of Pearson Education

Editor: Nancy Davis
Production Coordinator: David Van Ness
Composition: David Van Ness
Cover Design: Peachpit Press
Indexer: Emily Glossbrenner
Proofreader: Liz Welch

ISBN: 0-321-39674-X

0 9 8 7 6 5 4 3 2 1

Printed and bound in the United States of America

To Mary, my true companion of the road,
especially during this past academic year
at MIT and Harvard.

Special thanks to:
Nancy Davis, David Van Ness, and Emily Glossbrenner, the unequalled team of colleagues who put the polish on this and every other book I write; Rick Aguirre for helping out with screenshots on some fat chapters early on; Liz Welch for her great catches amid my thickets of text; and Nancy Aldrich-Ruenzel for making this life of working anywhere possible.

Thanks also to the fellows, family, and staff associated with the Knight Science Journalism Fellowships at the Massachusetts Institute of Technology. They created our instant community away from home in Cambridge. It was a privilege to share with them a year of learning—not to mention rides on the T, brews at The Field, lobster at Woods Hole, and one very soggy trek around Costa Rica's Volcán Arenal.

In the final stretch, tunes by Cambridge's own *Tom Thumb and the Latter Day Saints* and radio broadcasts of the Red Sox pulled me through.

Table of Contents

Part I

Getting Started

Using FileMaker Pro 8

Welcome to the Visual QuickStart Guide for FileMaker Pro 8. If you've used earlier versions of FileMaker, you know how easy, flexible, and powerful the program is. If this is your first time using FileMaker, you're in for some pleasant surprises, including discovering how simple it is to share databases across a corporation or the Web.

Why FileMaker?

Anyone who's used FileMaker much will readily sing its praises. It's the most popular Macintosh database program, which explains why many folks assume it's a Mac-only program. In truth, it's also the second most popular stand-alone database program for Windows (Windows users account for 60 percent of the program's users). Anyone who hasn't used FileMaker may wonder what the fuss is all about. Three words—clean, flexible, simple—explain FileMaker's appeal:

- **The interface:** Unlike so many programs, FileMaker's interface—the menus, buttons, windows, and steps required to get work done—has grown simpler, not more complex over time. This simplicity, and the resulting consistency that appears across the program, make it easy for you to focus on your work instead of puzzling over the program itself.
- **Cross-platform consistency:** FileMaker works so consistently on Windows and Macs that your databases can move with you as you, and those using your databases, switch between the two platforms (**Figure 1.1**).

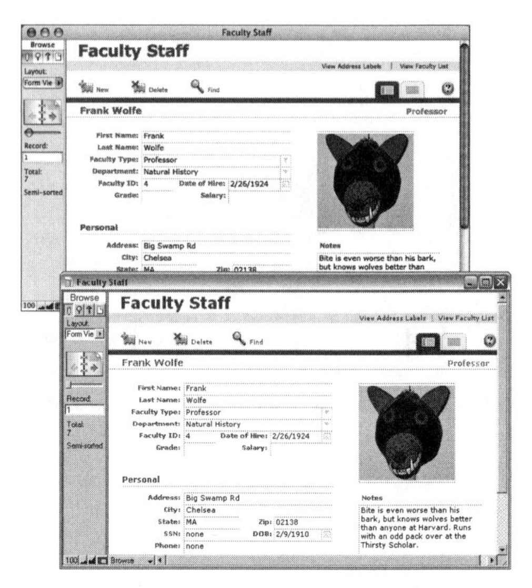

Figure 1.1 Windows or Mac: FileMaker works and looks almost identically on both operating systems.

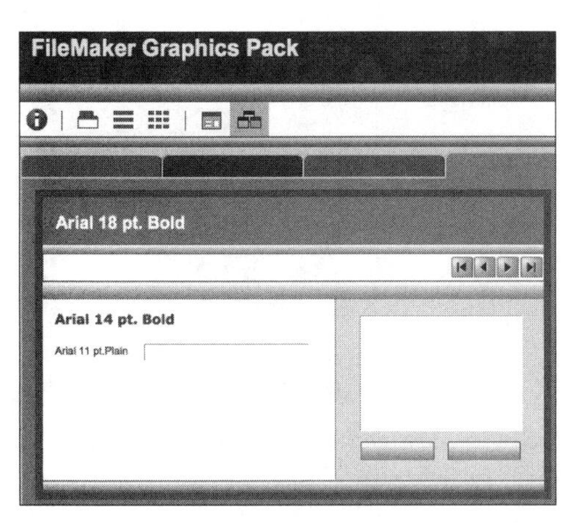

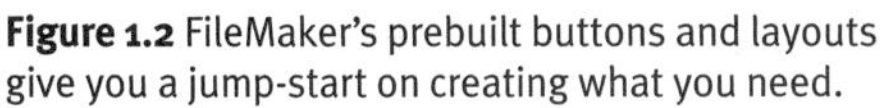
Figure 1.2 FileMaker's prebuilt buttons and layouts give you a jump-start on creating what you need.

- **Powerful yet simple:** Heavy-duty database programs are super: super powerful, super hard to learn. FileMaker isn't. Unlike, say Microsoft Access, you won't waste a week (or more) just learning the program. FileMaker gives you a jump-start by including pre-built buttons and layouts such as invoices and mailing labels (**Figure 1.2**). Most importantly, FileMaker can help you solve most of your problems on your own. Even if your firm has its own Information Technology department, that staff is probably already overtaxed. With FileMaker, you won't need IT's help as often—and when you do, they'll also save time using FileMaker's powerful behind-the-scenes features.
- **Plays well with others:** Thanks to its ongoing adoption of such standards as XML (Extensible Markup Language), and PDF (Portable Document Format), FileMaker acts as a data hub for moving information not just between Windows and Mac machines but across mixed-platform networks, the Web, and even with digital cameras and PDAs.

What's New in FileMaker 8?

If you're a brand-new FileMaker user, all of FileMaker 8 is new. FileMaker veterans will notice dozens of changes, big and small. Here's a quick rundown of FileMaker's most important changes:

New features and improvements

- **Seamlessly share with Excel and PDF files:** Being able to import Excel spreadsheets is not new. But version 8's ability to *export* to Excel now makes back-and-forth data sharing truly painless. Import Excel files directly into FileMaker without having to predefine your fields. When you're done working with that data in FileMaker, export it right back to Excel. Sweet. In the same easy sharing vein, the PDF Maker lets you instantly save any FileMaker data as a PDF document. For more information, see pages 226 and 228.
- **No more head scratching over relationships:** Creating relational databases, often a confusing process for beginners, became significantly easier in FileMaker 7 with its click-and-drag relationship graphs. Version 8 adds a small but very helpful improvement—now you can add notes to remind yourself and others why or how a particular relationship was created (**Figure 1.3**). For more information, see pages 131 and 136.

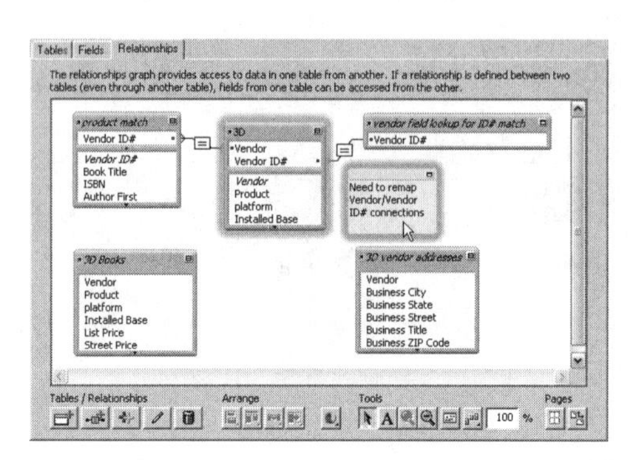

Figure 1.3 Add a note to a relationship graph to remind yourself and others how it's structured.

What's New in FileMaker 8?

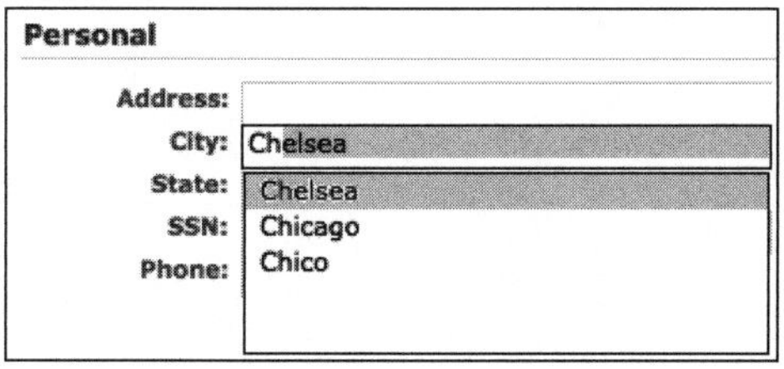

Figure 1.4 Type a few letters into a field and a drop-down list appears of likely items based on past entries.

- **Email almost anything instantly:** The new Fast Send feature lets you email just the data you want to share, whether it's a single field (even a picture) or multiple files (including Excel or PDF documents). For more information, see page 243.
- **Quickly create tabbed layouts:** FileMaker's new tabbed controls make it easy to group related items into a single screen—even if the original layout sprawls across several pages. For more information, see page 191.
- **Make fewer mistakes when entering data:** Type a few letters into a field and FileMaker's auto-complete feature offers a drop-down list of likely items, based on past entries for that particular field. Best of all, you can set it up in a couple of clicks (**Figure 1.4**). For more information, see page 100.
- **Instantly spot misspelled words:** You now can set FileMaker to instantly underline questionable words as you type. See page 80.

Using This Book

The key to this book, like all of Peachpit's Visual QuickStart Guides, is that word *visual*. As much as possible, the book uses illustrations with succinct captions to explain FileMaker's major functions and options. Ideally, you should be able to quickly locate what you need by scanning the page tabs, illustrations, and captions. Once you find a relevant topic, the text provides details and tips.

If you're new to FileMaker, you'll find it easy to work your way through the book chapter by chapter. By the final pages, you'll know FileMaker better than most of the folks who use it daily.

But if you've got an immediate FileMaker problem or question that you need answered right now, the book makes it easy for you to dive right in and get help quickly. For those of you who find even a QuickStart Guide too slow, consider jumping straight to pages 20–33, where FileMaker's menus and context-sensitive screens are explained with an extra serving of illustrations and screen shots.

One program, one book for Windows and Macintosh

FileMaker was one of the first programs that performed similarly whether you were using a Windows or Macintosh computer. In fact, the two versions are so similar now that anyone comfortable with FileMaker in general will find it relatively easy to pick up and move to FileMaker on the other platform—a real boon for anyone working in today's typical office with a mix of PCs and Macs. Still, there are some differences between FileMaker's Windows and Mac versions.

- Minor differences—slightly different menus, dialog boxes, window icons—are not highlighted in the text. I've alternated illustrations from both platforms when such differences aren't important to how FileMaker functions. But in many of the book's illustrations, you can't necessarily tell which platform is being used.
- Small but important differences between the versions are handled like so: "Under the Help menu, select FileMaker Help (Windows) or Show Balloons (Mac)."
- Major distinctions are highlighted with two icons:

  W This icon marks special instructions or features for the Windows version of FileMaker.

  M This icon marks special instructions or features for the Macintosh version of FileMaker.
- **Tips:** Signified by a ✔ in the margin, tips highlight shortcuts for performing common tasks or ways you can use your new FileMaker skills to solve common problems.

(continued on next page)

- **Italic words:** When italicized words appear in the book's text, you'll find the very same words on the FileMaker screen itself when you reach that step in the program. The italicized term might appear as a button or tab label, the name of a text window or an option button in a dialog box, or as one of several choices in a drop-down menu. Whatever the context, the italics are meant to help you quickly find the item in what can sometimes be a crowded screen. If the step includes an accompanying illustration, use it to help you find the item being discussed. For example: Select *Open an existing file* and click *OK*.

- **Code font:** When a word or words appear in `code font`, it's used to indicate the literal text you need to type into FileMaker. For example: In the text window, type `http://localhost` and press Enter. Web addresses are also in code font.

- **Menu commands and keyboard shortcuts:** Menu-based commands are shown as: File > Define Fields. Keyboard-based shortcuts (when available) are shown in parentheses after the first step in which they can be used. For example: (Ctrl L) means that you should press the Ctrl and L keys at the same time to switch to the Layout mode.

- **Cutouts in figures:** Sometimes a FileMaker menu or dialog box is so deep that it can be hard to fit on the page with all the other figures and still leave it large enough to read. In those cases, I cut out the middle or end of the figure to save some space and mark it with a white wavy line (**Figure 1.5**). Nothing critical to understanding the step is ever left out. And it sure beats running teeny, tiny figures.

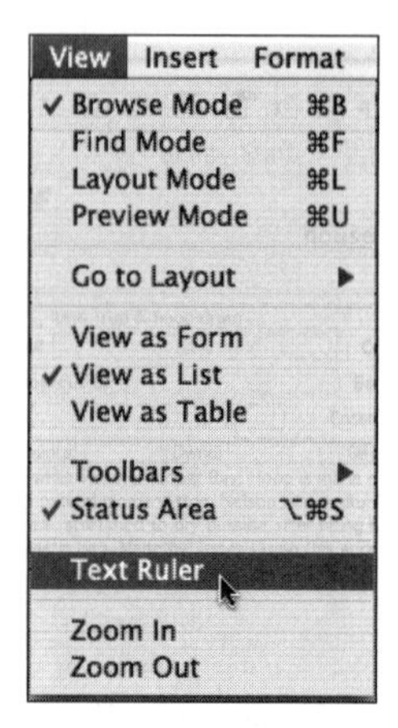

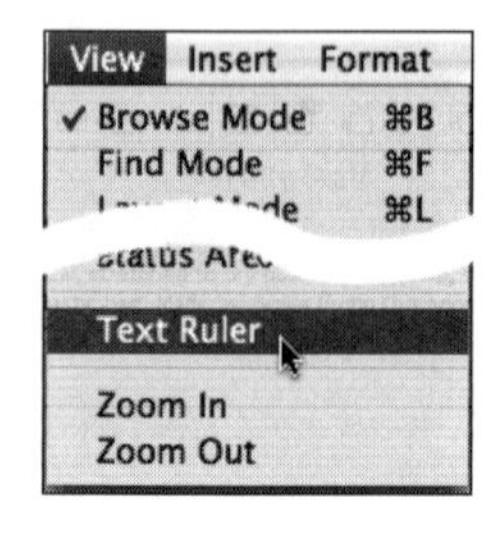

Figure 1.5 Sometimes the original dialog boxes or deep menus (left) will be snipped in the middle (right) to save space on the printed page.

Updates and feedback

For FileMaker updates and patches, make a point of checking FileMaker's Web site from time to time: `www.filemaker.com`

This book also has a companion Web site where you'll find examples from the book, and tips and tricks based on real-world tasks. So drop by `www.waywest.net/filemaker/` when you can. You're also welcome to write me directly at `filemaker@waywest.net` with your own tips or—heaven forbid—any mistakes you may have spotted.

Database Basics

If you're new to databases, this chapter covers some basic concepts that will help you start off on the right foot in tapping the power of databases. If you're already familiar with databases, you may want to skip ahead to *FileMaker Basics* on page 19.

While you might not think of them in this way, databases are everywhere: address books, cookbooks, television program listings, to-do lists scribbled on envelopes—examples abound. None of those examples involves a computer, but each illustrates a fundamental concept: databases *organize* information.

It slices! It dices!

An address book organizes information alphabetically. A cookbook organizes information by ingredient or by course. Television listings organize information by time and channel. To-do lists organize information by task and time. Each lets you find what you need precisely because of how the information is organized. A computer database is not so different except for one major advantage: it can quickly organize the *same* information in *multiple* ways.

In some ways, a database is like that late-night TV perennial, the Veg-o-Matic: It slices! It dices! It's ten kitchen tools in one! A database can slice the same basic information any number of ways: as address book entries, as mailing labels, as billing invoices—whatever's needed.

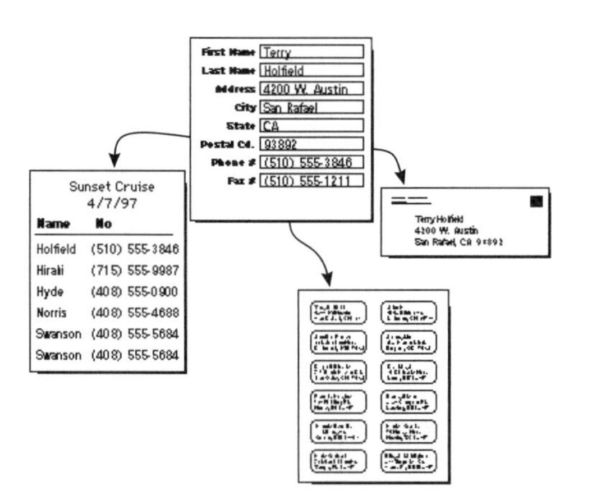

Figure 2.1 A database's real power comes from being able to display a single record's data in multiple ways.

Content vs. form

Understanding content versus form is the key to tapping the real power of any database. Do not confuse what a database contains (the content) with how it looks (the form). As important as data may be, it's not what gives a database its power. Instead, the power is in the program's ability to organize—and instantly reorganize—the display of that data (**Figure 2.1**).

Many people use spreadsheet programs to organize and analyze data. At times a spreadsheet is the best tool for such work, but a database often offers far more flexibility. Spreadsheet information, for example, is confined to rows and columns. Database programs like FileMaker can break free of that grid to display data as tables, lists, address labels, or in almost any form you need. Since FileMaker lets you drag data from Microsoft Excel and drop it right into a layout, making the switch couldn't be easier.

Tapping the power behind any database boils down to understanding and effectively using just a few items: fields, records, and layouts. Let's take a look at the role of each in a database program like FileMaker.

Anatomy of a Database

Databases often contain huge amounts of information, yet tiny pieces of that data can be fetched almost instantly. What's the secret? It's because everything within even the largest database is organized piece by piece into categories, or *fields* (**Figure 2.2**). Each field—the smallest unit within a database—contains information describing its contents. With that field information, the database can go to work. And by understanding the power of fields, so can you.

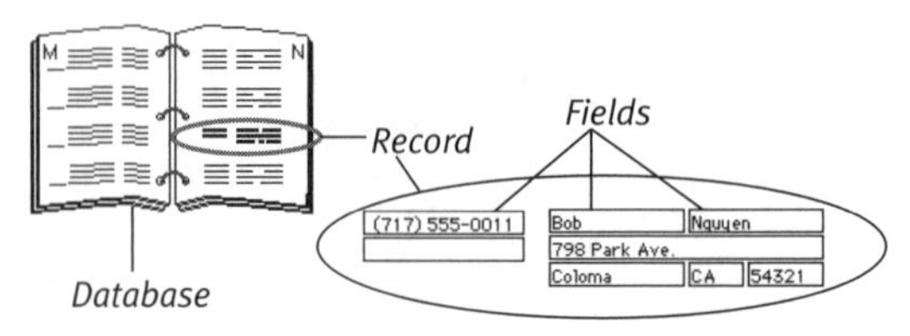

Figure 2.2 Every database organizes its information into individual records, which then contain fields for each bit of data.

The field—the smallest unit

Fields let a database keep track of what information goes where. Each field contains data but also carries a description, called a *field name*. The field name helps the database sort, sift, and manipulate without necessarily needing to deal directly with the data itself. It can be a bit confusing, but remember: fields, field names, and the data inside the fields are three different things (**Figure 2.3**).

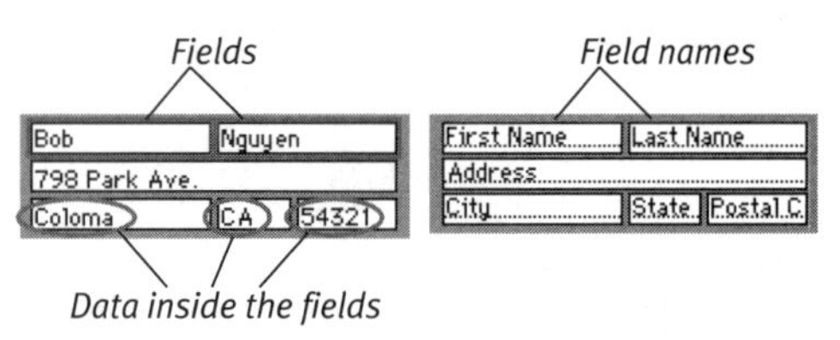

Figure 2.3 Each field contains data but also carries a description, called a field name, which makes it possible to quickly manipulate even a large database.

The more specific the fields you create within a database, the more powerful the database. Hang on to this idea as you learn more about FileMaker. For now here's an obvious example of why it's so important to make fields as specific as possible.

Though surely you wouldn't do this, imagine you've built an employee database with just one name field. With only a single name field, an alphabetical sort yields an immediate problem: Dennis Smith appears before Jennifer Norriz because D precedes J (**Figure 2.4**). Obviously that's not what you want. Creating two name fields lets you sort the last and first names alphabetically and independently (**Figure 2.5**). Obvious yes, but it's an idea that's easily forgotten in the heat of designing a new database. See Part III, starting on page 85, for more on defining and using fields with precision.

Name	Home Phone
Dennis Smith	205-555-9876
Jennifer Norriz	702-555-4688
Jeremy Smith	503-555-4655
John Winford	414-555-9987
Julie Davidson	415-555-0900
Michael St. Lorant	415-555-0143
Pamela Day	712-555-5245
Sonia Long	508-555-6899

Figure 2.4 Smith before Norriz: Having only *one* name field highlights the problem of not breaking fields into the smallest pieces possible. Figure 2.5 shows a better approach.

First Name	Last Name	Home Phone
Julie	Davidson	415-555-0900
Pamela	Day	712-555-5245
Sonia	Long	508-555-6899
Jennifer	Norriz	702-555-4688
Dennis	Smith	205-555-9876
Jeremy	Smith	503-555-4655
Michael	St. Lorant	415-555-0143
John	Winford	414-555-9987

Figure 2.5 By breaking data into smaller pieces, such as adding *two* name fields, you gain more control over your information. This concept is crucial to building powerful, yet precise, databases.

The record— grouping related fields

Put a bunch of fields together and you have what FileMaker calls a *record*. A single record contains related information about a single topic, person, or activity. In an address book, for example, the equivalent of a record would be the entry for one person. That entry or record would contain several related items: the person's name, address, and telephone number. As you already know, those three items are equivalent to fields in a database.

The database— a group of related records

Combine a bunch of records on a single topic (for example, customers), and you have a *database*. A database also can contain records on several related topics, such as customers, their addresses, invoices, and past orders. The ability to connect or relate *different* databases is what's meant by a *relational* database, like FileMaker.

One of the advantages of a relational database is that you can make such connections between databases without duplicating the information in each database. When you're dealing with thousands of records, this feature can save a lot of disk space—and lots of time.

The layout—one record, many forms

A *layout*, sometimes called a *view*, is simply a way to control how the information in a database is displayed. When you first begin building FileMaker databases, you may find yourself occasionally confusing records with layouts. Again, the difference boils down to content versus form: One record (content) can have many different layouts (forms) (**Figure 2.6**).

At its most basic, a record is *all* of the information for a single entry, while a layout shows a view of only the portion you need at the moment. Layouts also offer a way to hide everything you don't need at the moment. Let's go back to our paper address book example.

For each person in your book, you've probably listed their name, address, and phone number. If you're sending someone a birthday card, obviously you don't need to see their phone number. Similarly, if you want to call someone, you don't need their address. The paper address book shows you both. With databases, layouts enable you to show only what's relevant to the task at hand. So if you need mailing labels, you can take those address records and create layouts that only show the address. This notion of showing only what you need becomes especially important when you're working with a huge database containing dozens, or hundreds, of records and fields.

No matter whether you're using FileMaker or some other database program, these terms and concepts remain much the same. Now you're ready to delve into the particulars of FileMaker itself.

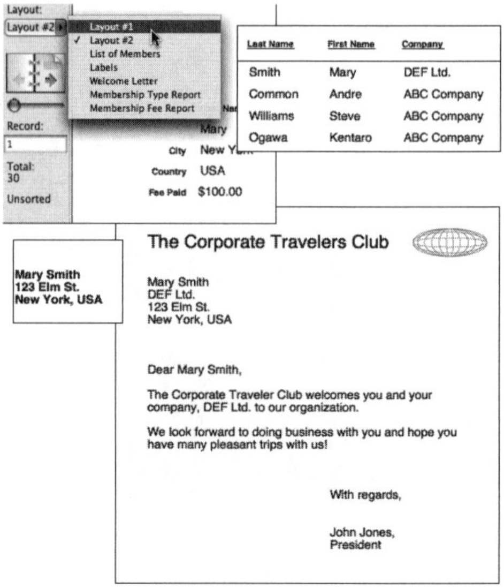

Figure 2.6 Using FileMaker's layout pop-up, the content of a single record can be displayed in many different forms, or layouts.

FILEMAKER BASICS

If you hate to read computer books, this chapter's for you. By taking a brief look at the menus assembled here and the explanations of how they and various commands work, you'll get a quick overview of FileMaker that will allow you to dive right in—if that's your style.

For readers who prefer a go-slow approach, this chapter's brief explanations also include page references to where in the book you'll find all the details you could want.

No matter which approach you prefer, this chapter provides a visual map for learning all of FileMaker's major functions.

FileMaker's Screen and Modes

When using FileMaker, you will always be working in one of four views or what it calls modes: Browse, Find, Layout, or Preview. Each mode handles a different set of tasks, so FileMaker's screen, menus, and their related options change from mode to mode. There are three ways to switch modes: the View menu, the mode tabs, or the pop-up menu (**Figure 3.1**).

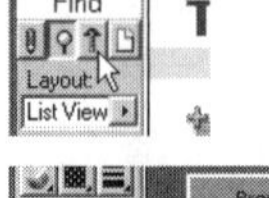

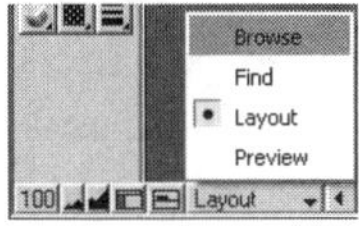

Figure 3.1 FileMaker offers three ways to switch modes: the View menu (top), the mode tabs in the main window's status area (middle), or the pop-up menu (bottom).

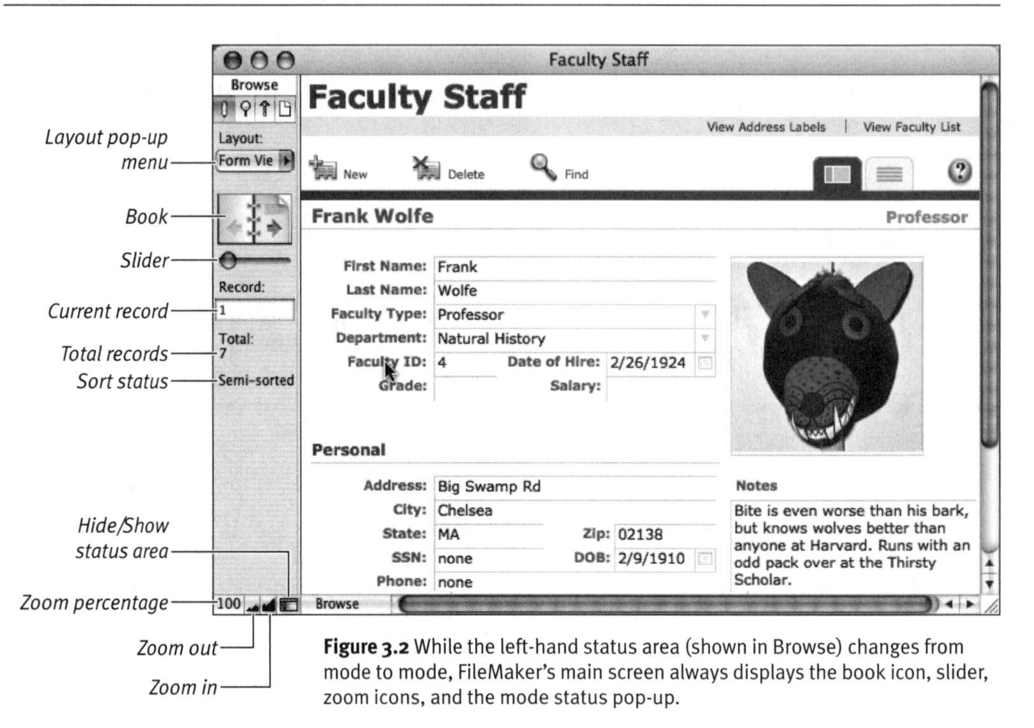

Figure 3.2 While the left-hand status area (shown in Browse) changes from mode to mode, FileMaker's main screen always displays the book icon, slider, zoom icons, and the mode status pop-up.

The FileMaker screen

Certain features of the FileMaker screen (**Figure 3.2**) remain constant: the book icon at the upper left, the status area along the left side (unless you elect to hide it), the Zoom-in and Zoom-out icons, and the status pop-up at the bottom of the screen, which lets you quickly choose your mode. As you switch from one view or mode to another, however, the left-hand status area displays a different set of tools and icons (**Figure 3.3**). The main record area also will change from mode to mode. For example, in Layout mode, the names of fields appear instead of the data itself.

Here's a quick rundown of the main elements of the FileMaker screen:

- **Layout pop-up menu:** Clicking your cursor on the box reveals all the layouts for the current record. For more on using Layout mode, see *Designing Layouts* on page 141.
- **Book:** This icon represents all the records in the current database. Clicking on the left and right pages of the book moves you forward or backward one record at a time. For more on using the book, see *Viewing Records* on page 41.
- **Slider:** Using your cursor to click on and drag the slider allows you to quickly jump forward or backward through a database's records. For more on using the slider, see *Viewing Records* on page 41.

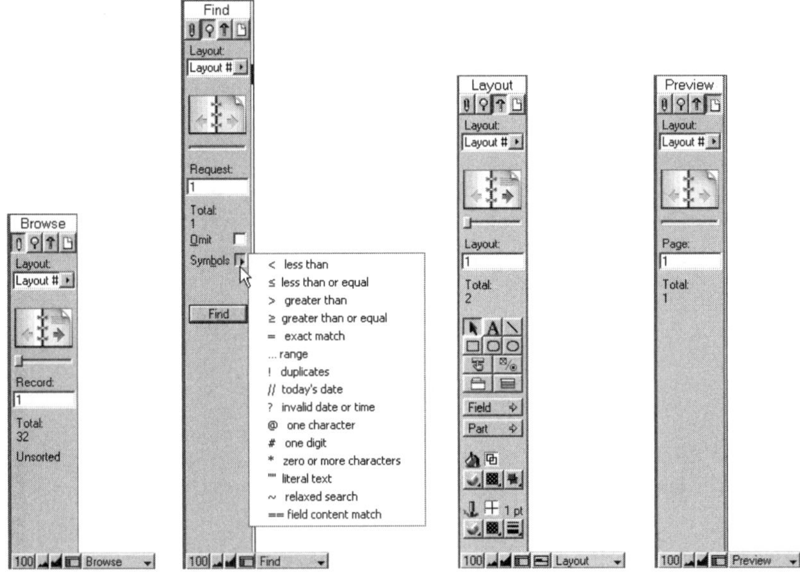

Figure 3.3 Tools and icons tailored to each mode appear in the left-hand status area as you switch among the modes (left to right): Browse, Find, Layout, and Preview.

- **Current record, Total records:** The current record number tells you where you are among all the database's records, which is represented by the Total records number. By clicking on the current record number, you can type in the number of a particular record you're seeking. See *Viewing Records* on page 41.
- **Sort status:** This simply tells you whether the records you're working with have been sorted or remain unsorted. For more on sorting records, see *Finding and Sorting Records* on page 49.
- **Status area:** Running along the left-hand side of your screen, the status area displays the icons and tools for whichever mode you're in (**Figure 3.3**). For more on each mode's tools and icons, see the next page.
- **Hide/Show status area:** Clicking on this icon allows you to hide or show the left-hand status area. This can be handy when you want to give the record itself as much screen space as possible.
- **Zoom percentage, Zoom in, Zoom out:** Clicking the Zoom-in or Zoom-out icon allows you to magnify or shrink your view of the current record. Clicking on the Zoom percentage box lets you toggle between the current magnification view and the 100 percent view. This makes it easy, for example, to jump between an extreme close-up view (400 percent) and a regular view (100 percent) in a single click instead of the multiple clicks required by the Zoom-in and Zoom-out icons.

Browse mode

Browse mode is the view where you'll spend most of your time if you're working with existing databases (**Figure 3.4**). Whenever you open a FileMaker database, it first appears in Browse mode. In Browse, you can view, sort, add, omit, and delete records. For more on using Browse mode, see *Viewing Records* on page 41 and *Finding and Sorting Records* on page 49.

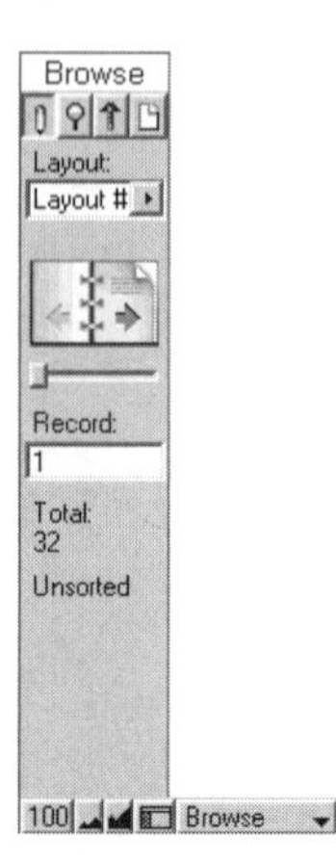

Figure 3.4 The status area for Browse mode appears to the left of the current record—though you can hide it if you want more screen space for the record.

Find mode

Find mode offers a powerful set of tools for locating individual records, or groups of records, within a database (**Figure 3.5**). In Find, you can search for records that match or don't match particular criteria based on text or mathematical values. For more on using Find mode, see *Finding and Sorting Records* on page 49.

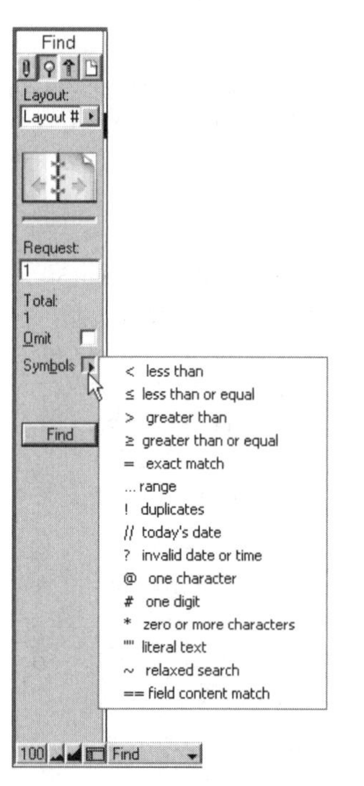

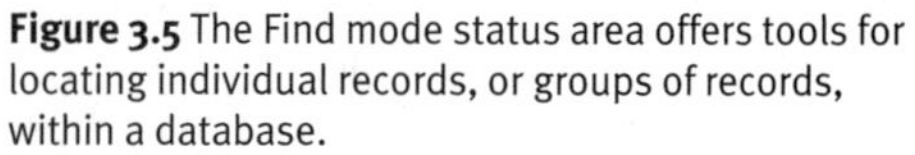

Figure 3.5 The Find mode status area offers tools for locating individual records, or groups of records, within a database.

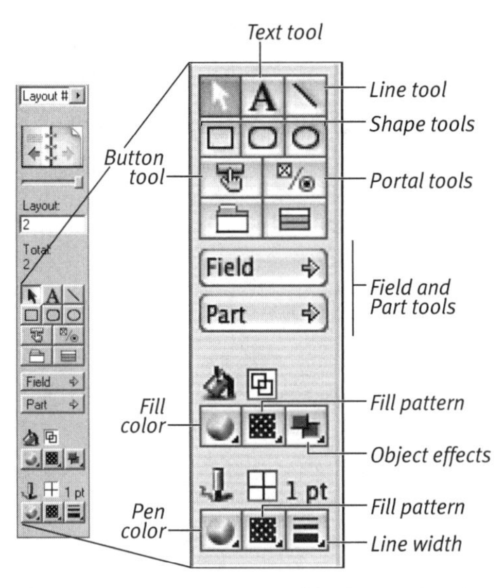

Figure 3.6 The most elaborate of the four modes, the Layout mode's status area contains tools to control the appearance of the records and record views you design.

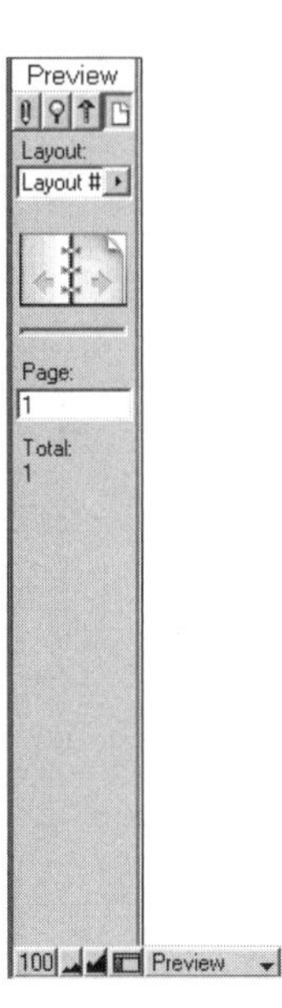

Figure 3.7 The *Preview* mode lets you control the appearance of printed FileMaker records.

Layout mode

Layout mode is where you design the appearance of the fields and records that display your data (**Figure 3.6**). In Layout, you can control every detail of fonts, field borders, button design—as well as the overall look of forms and entry screens. For more on using Layout mode, see *Creating and Designing Databases* on page 141.

Preview mode

Preview mode lets you control how your files look when printed (**Figure 3.7**). In Preview, you can set margins, get rid of unwanted gaps between fields, hide fields if you desire, and control how everything prints out, from reports to labels to envelopes. For more on using Preview mode, see *Printing*, on page 81.

FileMaker's Menus

This section provides a quick run-through of FileMaker's contextual menus, which change to reflect the mode you're in (**Figure 3.8**). Many of the menu commands and options are no different than those in any application: Open File, for example, is a fairly universal action. Some of the commands specific to FileMaker are highlighted on the following pages. Follow the page references for details on the various menu commands and options.

File Edit View Insert Format Layouts Arrange Scripts Window Help

File Edit View Insert Format Requests Scripts Window Help

File Edit View Insert Format Records Scripts Window Help

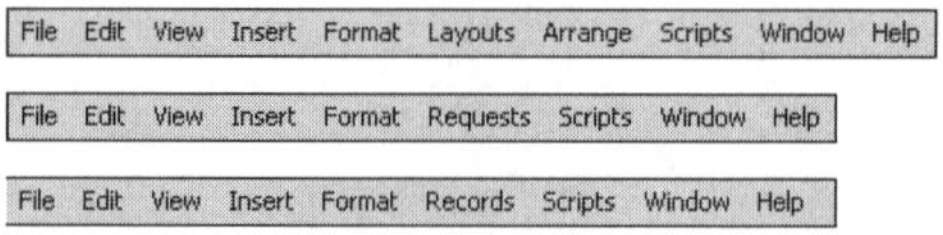

Figure 3.8 FileMaker's contextual menu bar changes depending on which mode you're in.

The File menu

As the name implies, all the commands within the File menu control actions related directly to file management (**Figure 3.9**). The File menu appears in all four FileMaker modes, with all its functions available.

- **New Database, Open, Open Remote, Open Recent, Close:** With the exception of Open Remote, these commands operate much as they do in most programs. The Open Remote command lets you open a FileMaker database shared over a network. See *Sharing* on page 243.
- **Define:** Use the Define drop-down menu to create fields, set options for entering data in them, and establish references to other files, tables, or value lists. See *Defining Fields* on page 93 and *Creating Relational Databases* on page 125. By defining accounts and privileges you can control which files can be seen on a network, who can see them, and which files can be shared; see *Sharing* on page 243.

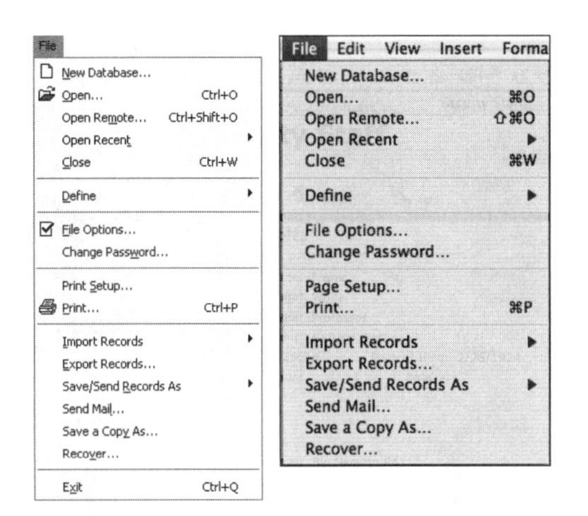

Figure 3.9 The File menu's commands are available in all four modes.

- **File Options, Change Password:** The File Options drop-down menu sets default layouts and scripts for a file. It also turns on FileMaker's new feature where potentially misspelled words are underlined as you type. See *Using Spell Check and Dictionaries* on page 73 and *Sharing* on page 243.
- **Print Setup/Page Setup, Print:** These commands operate much as they do in all programs. See *Printing* on page 81.
- **Import/Export Records, Save/Send Records As, Send Mail, Save a Copy As, Recover:** These commands help you convert other database files to the current FileMaker format and send your FileMaker information to others as email, Excel, or PDF files. For more on importing and exporting, see *Changing Formats* on page 225.
- **Exit/Quit:** Use this command to quit FileMaker. If you are running Mac OS X, you'll find the Quit command under the separate FileMaker Pro menu (**Figure 3.42**).

The Edit menu

Most of this menu's commands operate just as they do in other programs—except for a few explained below (**Figure 3.10**). The Edit menu appears in all four FileMaker modes, though not all its functions are available in every mode. (Dimmed items indicate functions not available within that mode.)

- W **Paste Special:** This command can be a tremendous time saver. Essentially, it lets you paste the contents of the clipboard into any FileMaker document.
- W **Object:** This command takes advantage of a standard Windows feature, OLE (Object Linking and Embedding), which allows you to cut and paste data from other applications. The great advantage of OLE is that the data is updated automatically within the FileMaker record whenever it's changed in the original application. See *Creating Layouts* on page 143.
- ◆ **Spelling** lets you set what dictionary checks the spelling of words. It does not control FileMaker's new check-as-you-type feature, which is set in the File menu. See *Using Spell Check and Dictionaries* on page 73.
- ◆ **Export Field Contents**, a new option in FileMaker 8, lets you export a single field's contents, which becomes very useful when combined with a related script step.
- ◆ **Preferences:** Setting FileMaker's preferences now will save you time later. To set preferences on the Mac, use the separate FileMaker Pro menu.

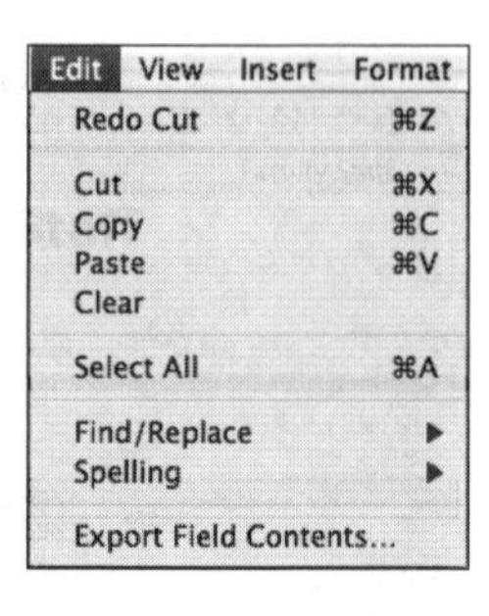

Figure 3.10 The Edit menu appears in all four modes, though not all functions are available in every mode.

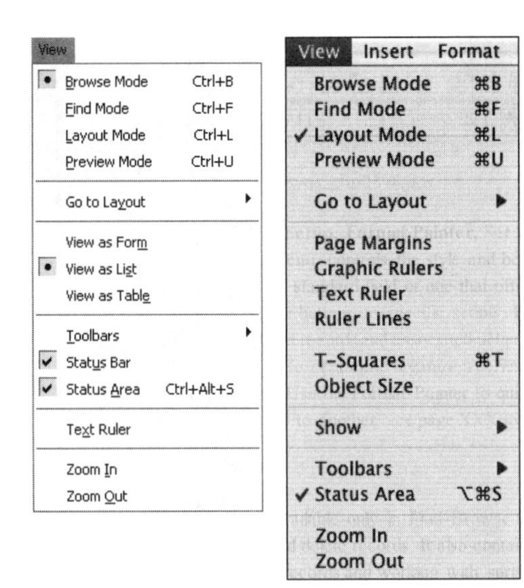

Figure 3.11 Depending on which mode you're in (Browse on the left, Layout on the right), the View menu's commands and functions change.

Insert
Picture...
QuickTime...
Sound...
File...
Object...
Current Date Ctrl+-
Current Time Ctrl+;
Current User Name Ctrl+Shift+N
From Index... Ctrl+I
From Last Visited Record Ctrl+'

Insert Format Records Scripts
Picture...
QuickTime...
Sound...
File...
Current Date ⌘-
Current Time ⌘;
Current User Name ⇧⌘N
From Index... ⌘I
From Last and Advance ⇧⌘'

Figure 3.12 Available only in Find and Layout modes, the Insert menu lets you quickly paste in a field, part, picture, sound, video, date, or user name.

The View menu

FileMaker operates in one of four modes: Browse, Find, Layout, or Preview. Each mode is used for a different set of tasks and, so, the options offered under the View menu change depending on which mode you're in (**Figure 3.11**). In each of the four contextual mode menus, however, the top section remains the same, allowing you to quickly switch to another mode.

The rest of the menu changes based on which mode you're in. For example, the Layout mode (right, **Figure 3.11**) includes Show and an extensive submenu.

The Insert menu

The Insert menu, available only in Find and Layout modes, offers a fast way to paste a field, part, object, button, portal, picture, sound, or video into a layout (**Figure 3.12**). It also enables you to paste in the date, time, a user name, an indexed item, or selected content of the previous record. For more information on inserts, see *Finding and Sorting Records* on page 49 and *Using Variable Fields* on page 164. For more on indexing, see *Storage options* on page 104.

The Format menu

The Format menu appears in all modes except Preview, but offers the most functions in Layout mode (**Figure 3.13**). The availability of the functions also varies depending on what you've selected within the current record. In general, the functions within the Format menu start at the character level and move toward the field level. See *Layout Formatting and Graphics*, on page 197.

- **Font** through **Text Color:** The top six functions control attributes *at the character level* within a selected field.
- **Text** through **Graphic:** The second group of functions controls attributes at the field level, that is, what *type* of content the field contains: text, numbers, a date, a time, or a graphic.
- **Field/Control** through **Button Setup, Format Painter, Set Sliding/Printing:** The Field/Control drop-down menu controls the style and behavior of the field *container*, that is, whether it's a standard field or one that offers a pop-up list or repeats itself. Button Setup links buttons to specific scripts. Portal Setup controls the appearance of related records and associated actions such as sorting. Use the new Tab Control Setup to create and organize a series of single-screen tabs displaying multiple fields. Use the Format Painter to quickly apply attributes from one layout object to another (see page 203).

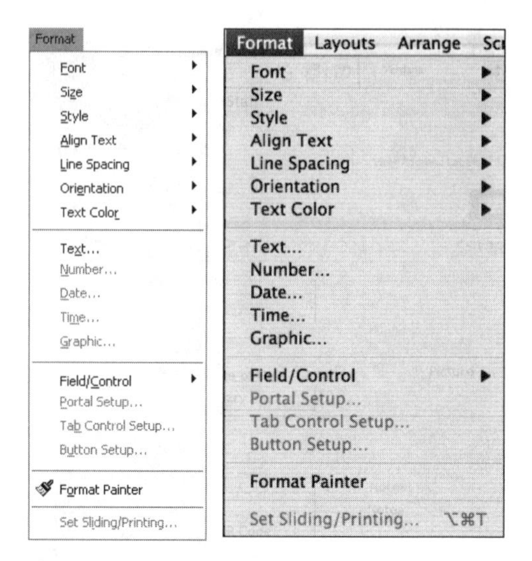

Figure 3.13 The Format menu appears in all modes except Preview, but offers the most functions in Layout mode.

Figure 3.14 Available only in Browse and Preview modes, the Records menu lets you create, duplicate, and delete records.

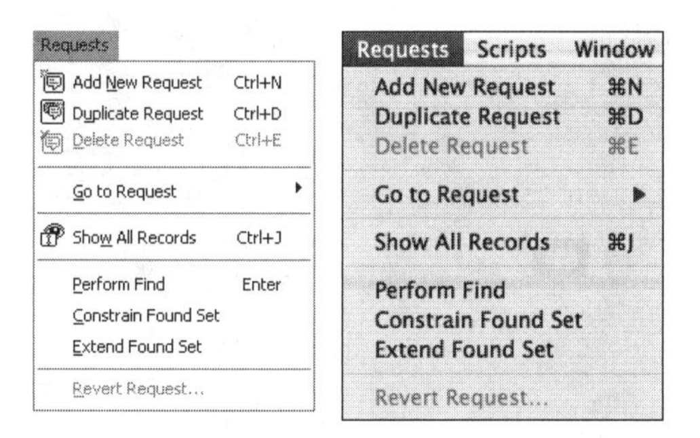

Figure 3.15 Available only in the Find mode, the Requests menu replaces FileMaker 4 functions found under the now-defunct Select menu.

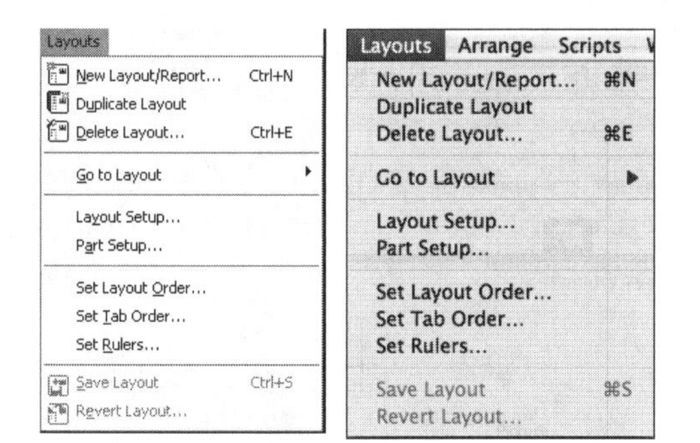

Figure 3.16 The Layouts menu, available only in Layout mode, lets you create, duplicate, and delete layouts.

The Records menu

The Records menu (**Figure 3.14**), available only in Browse and Preview modes, lets you create, duplicate, and delete records. It also contains commands for changing previous find requests for records and working with sorts of the records. In practice, you'll find yourself using the Records menu in tandem with the Requests menu, explained below. See *Finding and Sorting Records*, on page 49.

The Requests menu

The Requests menu (**Figure 3.15**), available only in Find mode, contains commands used for finding records. See *Finding and Sorting Records*, on page 49.

The Layouts menu

The Layouts menu (**Figure 3.16**), which naturally enough appears only in Layout mode, lets you create, duplicate, and delete layouts. It also lets you control which layouts will be visible in which modes. See *Creating Layouts* on page 143.

The Arrange menu

The Arrange menu (**Figure 3.17**), which appears only in Layout mode, lets you control the layering and grouping of objects as you design a layout. See *Creating Layouts*, on page 143.

The Scripts menu

Don't let this menu's unassuming appearance fool you (**Figure 3.18**). Choosing ScriptMaker will launch a powerful FileMaker feature that enables you to automate many of the program's operations. Existing scripts for the current file appear in the menu's second section.

The Window menu

This works much like the Window menu in most programs: The bottom half of the menu lists all currently open FileMaker databases, enabling you to arrange what's visible on your desktop (**Figure 3.19**).

The Help menu

FileMaker's Help menu has some of the best built-in help of any program (**Figure 3.20**). The *FileMaker on the Web* choice launches your Web browser and takes you to FileMaker's main support page, where you can register your copy, download program updates, and find out the latest on the product.

Figure 3.17 Use the Arrange menu, which appears only in Layout mode, to control the layering and grouping of objects as you design a layout.

Figure 3.18 Use the Scripts menu to launch ScriptMaker, which enables you to automate many of FileMaker's operations.

Figure 3.19 Use the Window menu to arrange multiple FileMaker databases on your desktop.

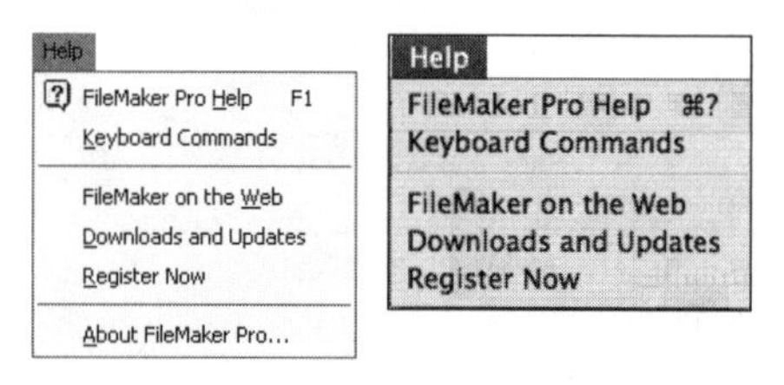

Figure 3.20 FileMaker's Help menu offers some of the best built-in help of any program.

FileMaker's Toolbars

By default, only the Standard toolbar appears when you launch FileMaker, though its appearance changes depending on which mode you're working in (**Figures 3.21–3.22**). FileMaker also includes a Text Formatting toolbar (**Figure 3.23**), which can be very handy when you're creating layouts and naming fields. The Arrange and Tools toolbars are available only in Layout mode (**Figures 3.24–3.25**).

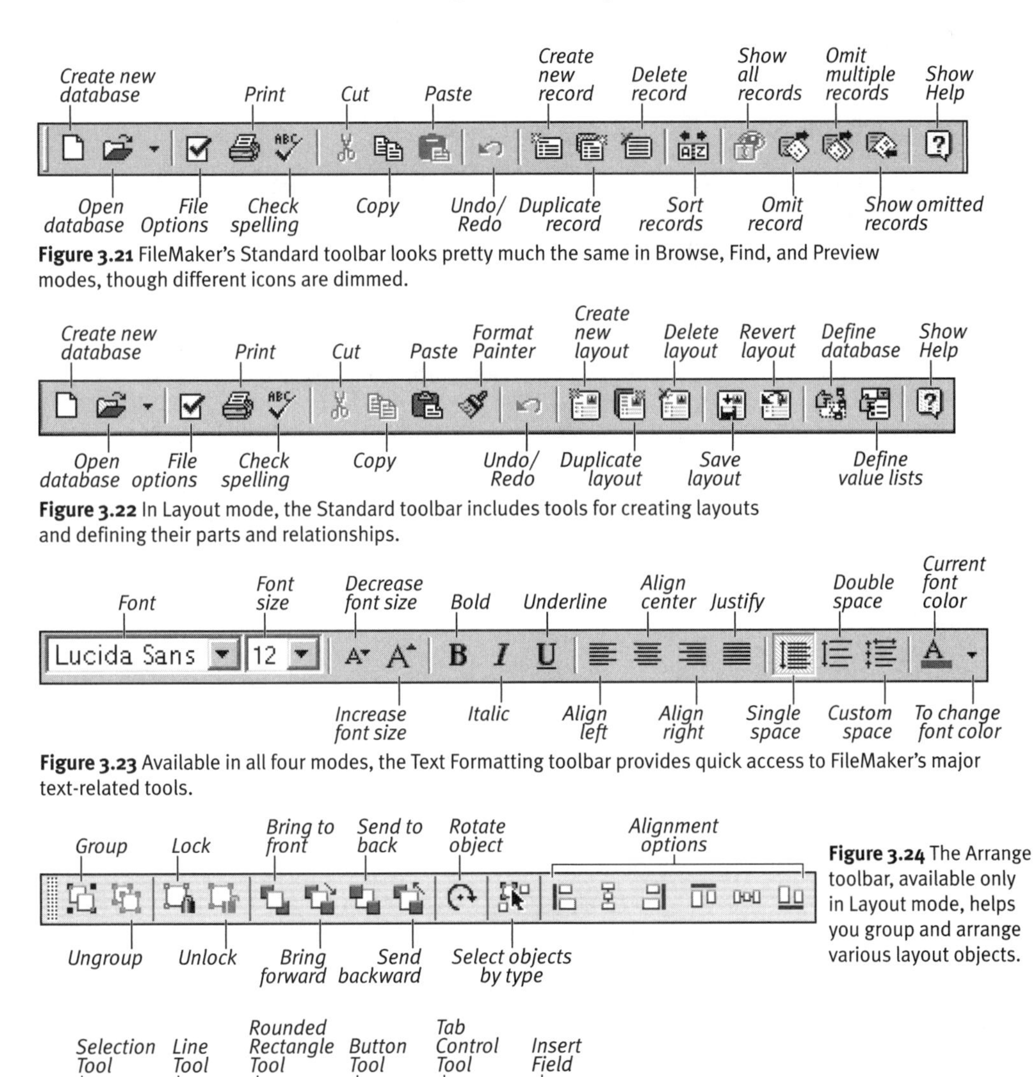

Figure 3.21 FileMaker's Standard toolbar looks pretty much the same in Browse, Find, and Preview modes, though different icons are dimmed.

Figure 3.22 In Layout mode, the Standard toolbar includes tools for creating layouts and defining their parts and relationships.

Figure 3.23 Available in all four modes, the Text Formatting toolbar provides quick access to FileMaker's major text-related tools.

Figure 3.24 The Arrange toolbar, available only in Layout mode, helps you group and arrange various layout objects.

Figure 3.25 The Tools toolbar, also only available in Layout mode, offers fast access to FileMaker's design tools.

To turn on/off toolbars:

1. Choose View > Toolbars and select a toolbar from the submenu to turn it on or off (**Figure 3.26**). Checked toolbars are already on; unchecked ones are off.

2. Release your cursor on the selected toolbar and by default, it will appear in the area below FileMaker's menu bar.

✔ Tip

■ The mode you're working in dictates which toolbars will be available: the Arrange and Tools toolbars cannot be turned on unless you're in Layout mode.

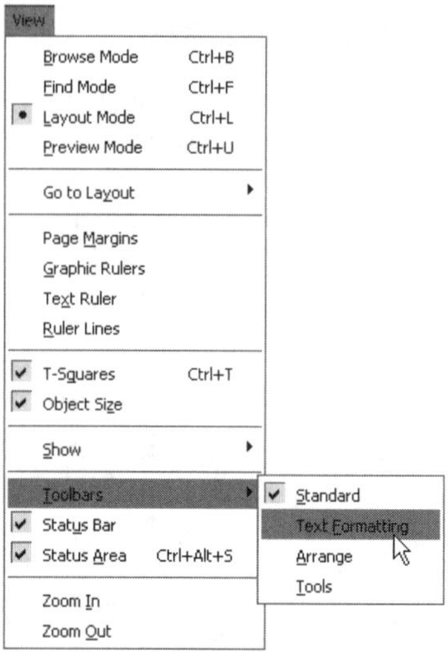

Figure 3.26 To turn toolbars on or off, choose View > Toolbars and make a selection from the submenu.

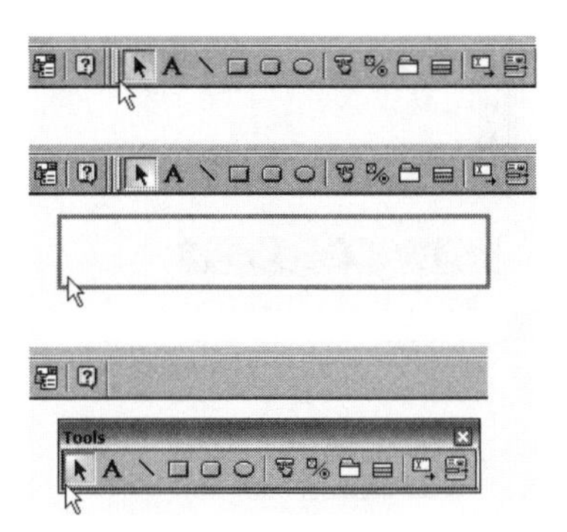

Figure 3.27 To move toolbars to your desktop, click on any toolbar's left edge (top), drag to the desktop (middle), and release your cursor (bottom).

Figure 3.28 To dock a toolbar below FileMaker's menu bar, click the toolbar's title (top), drag it toward the menu bar (middle), and release the cursor (bottom).

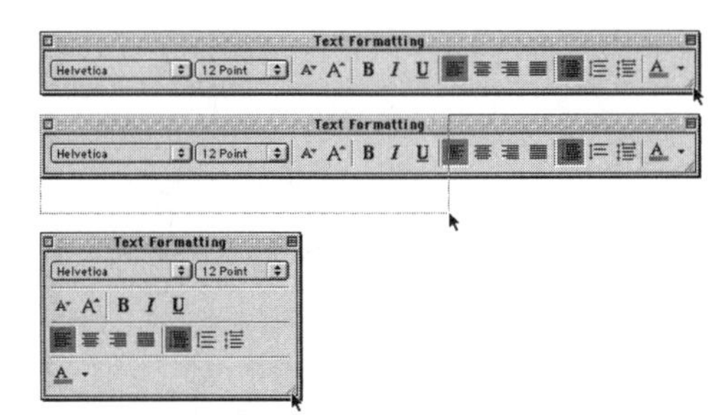

Figure 3.29 To resize a *freestanding* toolbar, click its outer edge (Windows) or lower-right corner (Mac) and drag the cursor to shrink or enlarge the toolbar.

Rearranging the toolbars

FileMaker makes it easy to rearrange the toolbars to suit your work setup. Sometimes it's easiest to have your activated toolbars "docked," that is, running horizontally across the top of FileMaker's main window. For some tasks, however, you may prefer to have a toolbar sitting out on the desktop itself. You also can resize toolbars when they're on your desktop.

To move toolbars to the desktop:

1. To move a docked toolbar (those running across FileMaker's main window), click your cursor on the vertical bar marking the toolbar's left-hand edge (top, **Figure 3.27**).
2. Continue pressing the cursor and drag the toolbar to a new spot on the desktop (middle, **Figure 3.27**).
3. Release the cursor and the toolbar will appear with its own title (bottom, **Figure 3.27**).

To dock toolbars in the main window:

1. To move a freestanding toolbar into a docked position below FileMaker's menu bar, click on the toolbar's title (top, **Figure 3.28**).
2. Continue pressing the cursor and drag the toolbar to the area just below the menu bar (middle, **Figure 3.28**).
3. Release the cursor and the toolbar will snap into place (bottom, **Figure 3.28**).

To resize freestanding toolbars:

- To resize a freestanding toolbar, click an outer edge (Windows) or its lower-right corner (Mac) and drag the cursor to shrink or enlarge the toolbar (**Figure 3.29**).

Opening, Closing, and Saving Files

Opening and closing files in FileMaker works like most programs. Unlike many programs, however, FileMaker automatically saves data as you enter it. If by habit, you type Ctrl S or ⌘ S, the Sort dialog box will appear. Just click *Done* and you'll be back to where you were with no harm done.

To open a file:

1. If you haven't started the FileMaker program, do so now by either choosing All Programs > FileMaker Pro from the Start menu (**Figure 3.30**) or double-clicking the *FileMaker Pro* icon in the FileMaker Pro 8 folder (Mac).
2. A dialog box will appear asking whether you want to create a new file using a template, create a new empty file, or open an existing file (**Figure 3.31**). Make your choice and click *OK*.
3. Depending on your choice in step 2, a dialog box will appear asking you to create and name a copy of the selected template (**Figure 3.32**), open an existing file, or create and name a new file.

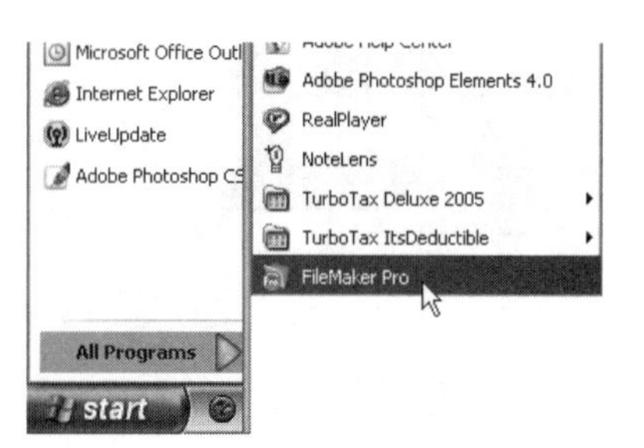

Figure 3.30 To launch FileMaker, navigate to the icon from the Start menu (Windows) or double-click its icon (Mac).

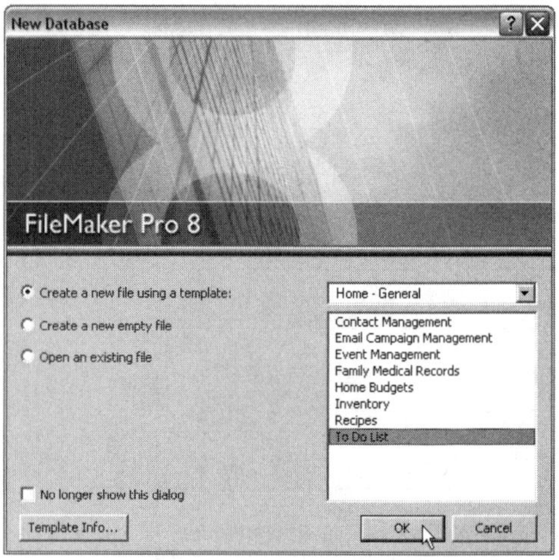

Figure 3.31 When FileMaker's opening dialog box appears, you may open a new template-based file, a new empty file, or an existing file.

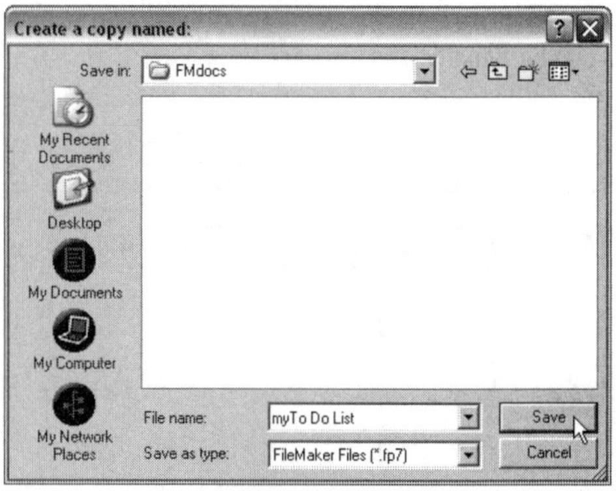

Figure 3.32 If you use one of FileMaker's templates, a dialog box will ask you to create and name a copy of the selected template.

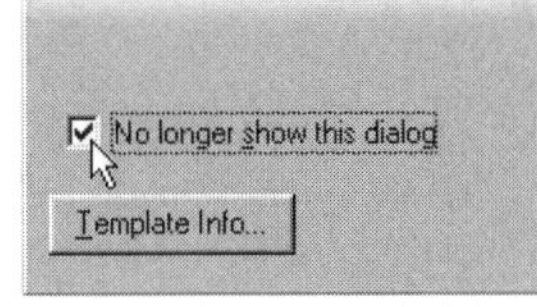

Figure 3.33 To skip FileMaker's opening dialog box, check the *No longer show this dialog* box.

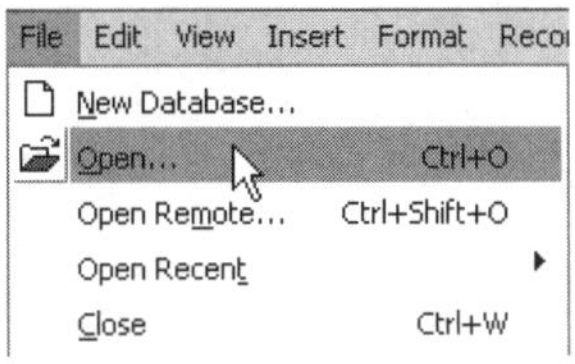

Figure 3.34 You also can open an existing file using the File menu.

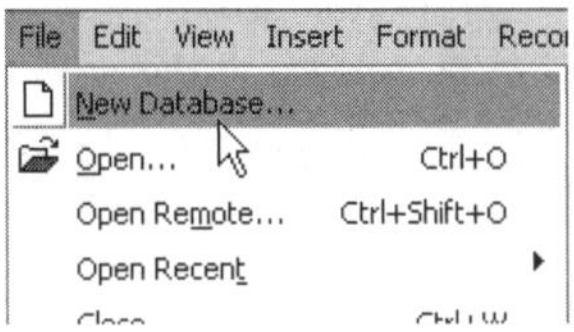

Figure 3.35 To create a new file, choose File > New Database.

✔ Tips

- If you'd rather not see the dialog box that asks whether you want to open a template, a new file, or an existing file every time you launch FileMaker, check the *No longer show this dialog* box (**Figure 3.33**). In the future, when FileMaker starts up, you can then go directly to the File menu.
- If you've turned off the opening dialog box (see the previous Tip), you still can open an existing file by choosing File > Open (**Figure 3.34**). Or use your keyboard: Ctrl O (Windows) or ⌘ O (Mac).

To create a new file:

◆ Choose File > New Database (**Figure 3.35**). A new database with no fields or records will appear.

Closing a file

Because FileMaker automatically saves your data, closing a file is simple. You can close a file several different ways.

To close a file:

- Choose File > Close (**Figure 3.36**). The keyboard equivalents are: Ctrl W (Windows) or ⌘W (Mac).

  or

  Click the close button in the record's upper-right corner (**Figure 3.37**) or click the FileMaker icon in the upper-left corner of the menu bar and choose Close (Ctrl 4) (**Figure 3.38**).

  Click the red button in the left corner of the record's title bar (**Figure 3.39**).

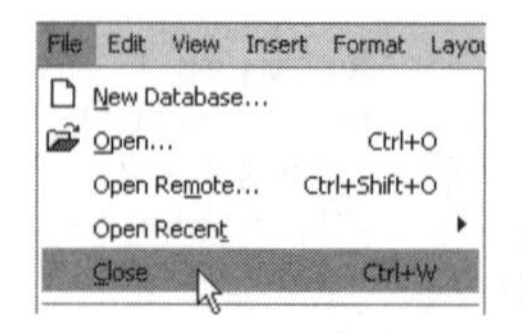

Figure 3.36 To close a file, choose File > Close.

Figure 3.37 To close a Windows FileMaker file, click the close button in the upper right of the document.

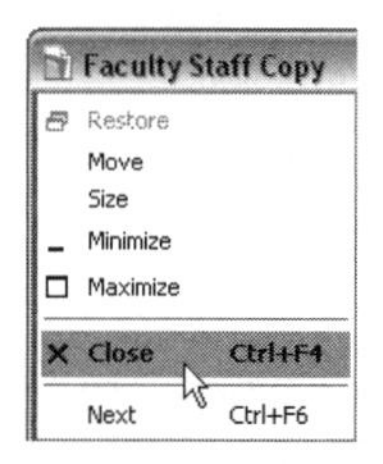

Figure 3.38 You also can close a Windows FileMaker file by double-clicking the FileMaker icon at the far left of the menu bar.

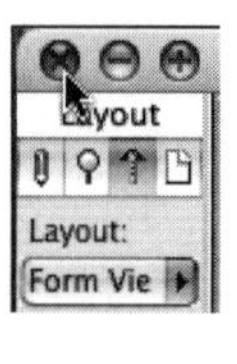

Figure 3.39 To close a Macintosh FileMaker file, click the close icon in the upper left of the document.

Saving files

Though FileMaker saves your work as you go, you may want to make a copy of a database right before making a lot of changes to the original.

To save a copy of a database file:

1. Choose File > Save a Copy As (**Figure 3.40**).

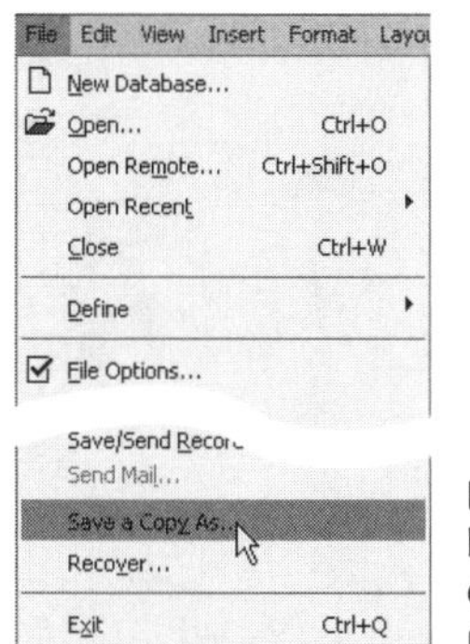

Figure 3.40 To make a backup copy of a record, choose *Save a Copy As* under the File menu.

2. When the dialog box appears, you can either accept the default name or type in a new name. Choose where you want to store the copy by navigating through the folder icons at the top of the dialog box. At the bottom of the dialog box (**Figure 3.41**), you also have the option to save the copy as a regular database file, a space-saving compressed file, or a clone. The clone option lets you save a database's layout, scripts, and field definitions but without any data.

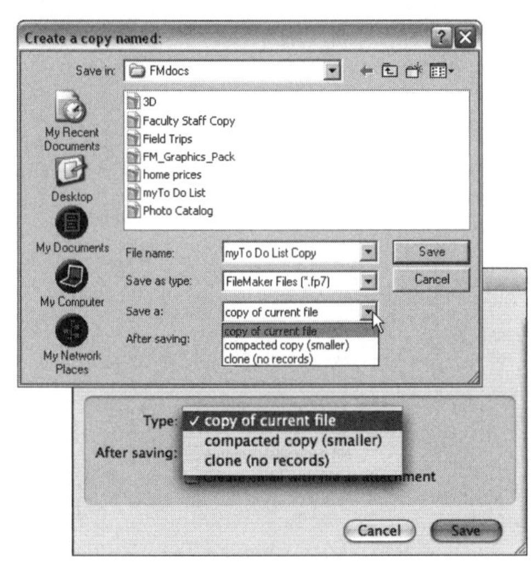

Figure 3.41 When making a backup copy, you can save it as a regular record, a compressed version, or a layout-only clone. Choose one and click *Save*.

3. Once you've picked your file name, destination, and file type, click *Save*.

To quit FileMaker:

- Choose File > Exit (Windows) or FileMaker Pro > Quit FileMaker Pro (Mac OS X) (**Figure 3.42**). The keyboard equivalents are: Ctrl Q (Windows) or ⌘ Q (Mac).

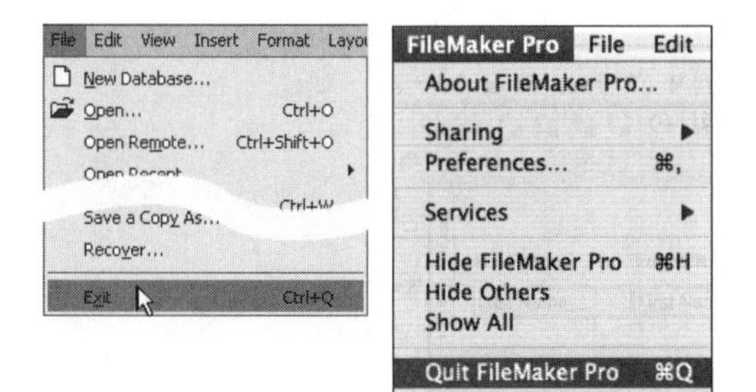

Figure 3.42 To quit FileMaker, choose File > Exit (left, Windows) or File > Quit FileMaker Pro (right, in Mac OS X).

✔ Tip

- If you don't quit FileMaker properly (for example, your machine crashes), the next time you open a FileMaker record the program will pause to run a consistency check. This takes only a moment, and then FileMaker is usually ready to go.

PART II

WORKING WITH EXISTING FILEMAKER DATABASES

Viewing Records

As eager as you might be to start creating your own database, the truth is you'll spend most of your time using FileMaker to view and modify existing records. Whether it's zipping through a big corporate health benefits database or working with your personal cookie recipes, knowing how to get around FileMaker records efficiently will save you lots of work over the long haul.

Opening a File

If you're working alone and this is your first time using FileMaker, you may not have any records to view. Never fear. To spare you the bother of having to create some records just for viewing, we'll be using some of the existing records that came with your copy of FileMaker. If you already have a FileMaker database to work with, feel free to use it.

By the way, when you first open a FileMaker file it automatically appears in Browse mode, which enables you to look at a record without worrying about the layout or how it'll print. For more on each of FileMaker's four modes, see page 19.

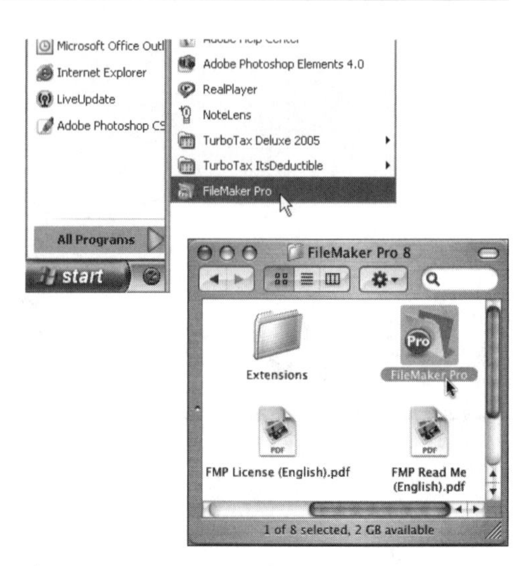

Figure 4.1 To launch FileMaker, use the Start menu (top, Windows) or double-click the icon in the application's folder (bottom, Mac).

To open a FileMaker database file:

1. If you haven't started the FileMaker program, do so now by either choosing Programs\FileMaker Pro from the Start menu (Windows) (top, **Figure 4.1**) or double-clicking the FileMaker Pro icon in the FileMaker Pro 8 folder (Mac) (bottom, **Figure 4.1**).
2. A dialog box will appear asking whether you want to create a *new* file using a template, create a new *empty* file, or open an *existing* file. Select *Open an existing file* and click *OK* (**Figure 4.2**).

Figure 4.2 When FileMaker's opening dialog box appears, choose *Open an existing file* and click *OK*.

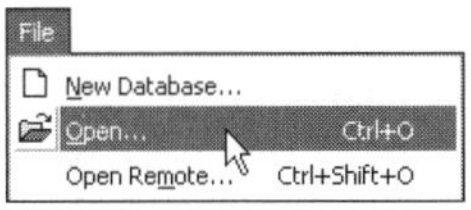

Figure 4.3 You also can open an existing file using FileMaker's File menu.

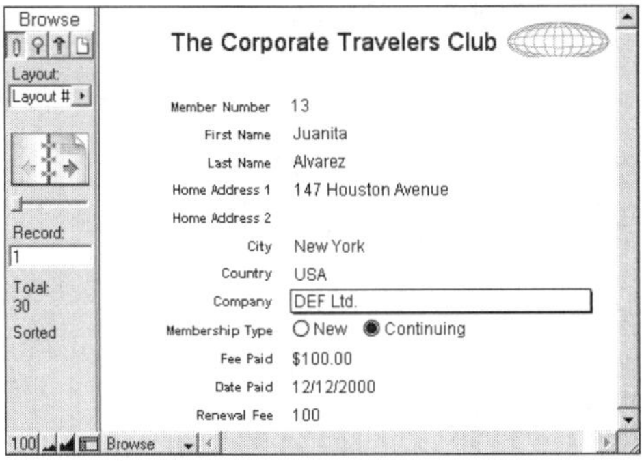

Figure 4.4 Download this chapter's example file, *SamplePeople.fp7*, from `www.waywest.net/filemaker/`.

3. If you've turned off the opening dialog box (see the first Tip on page 35), you still can open an existing file by choosing File > Open (**Figure 4.3**). Or use your keyboard: Ctrl O (Windows) or ⌘ O (Mac).
4. At this point, you can open a FileMaker file you may already have, in which case navigate your way through the dialog boxes to find it. If you don't have your own file, see the next step to open the example file featured in this chapter.
5. Use your Web browser to reach this book's companion Web site: `www.waywest.net/filemaker/` and click the Examples link. Then download the Chapter 4 file, which includes `SamplePeople.fp7`. Once you've downloaded and opened the Chapter 4 file, open `SamplePeople.fp7` by double-clicking it (**Figure 4.4**).

✔ Tip

- Don't be confused by fact that FileMaker 8 uses the same file ending as FileMaker 7: `.fp7`.

Viewing Multiple or Single Records

FileMaker lets you view records three different ways: as single records using the View as Form choice or as multiple records using the View as List or View as Table choice. Viewing one record at a time helps you see more detail within a particular record. Inspecting multiple records at the same time makes it easier to compare one to another.

To view multiple records:

- Our example, SamplePeople.fp7, opens showing just one record (**Figure 4.4**). To view several records at once, choose View > View as List or View > View as Table (**Figure 4.5**). Depending on your choice, the file will display as many individual records as your screen can accommodate (**Figure 4.6**) or display a table of records (**Figure 4.7**).

To view a single record:

- To view one record at a time, choose View > View as Form (**Figure 4.8**). The file will shift back to a view with only one record showing.

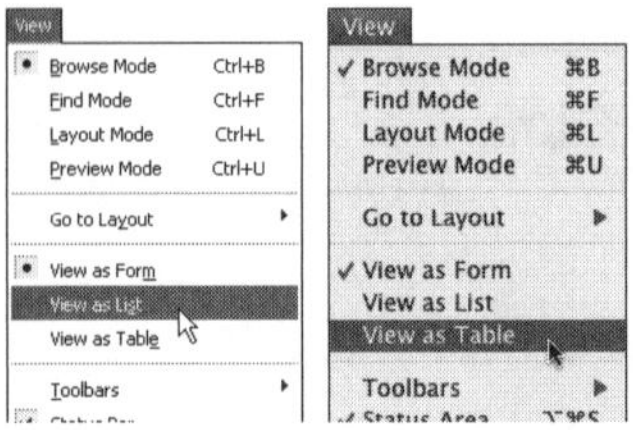

Figure 4.5 To see more than one record at once, choose View > View as List (left) or View > View as Table (right).

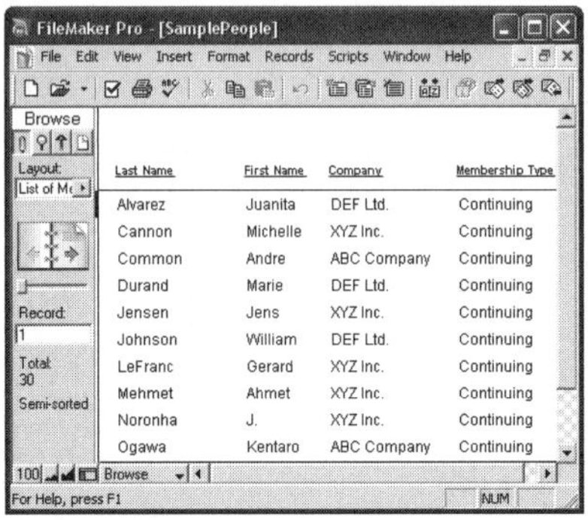

Figure 4.6 The View as List choice displays multiple records in the current layout, enabling you to compare one record to another.

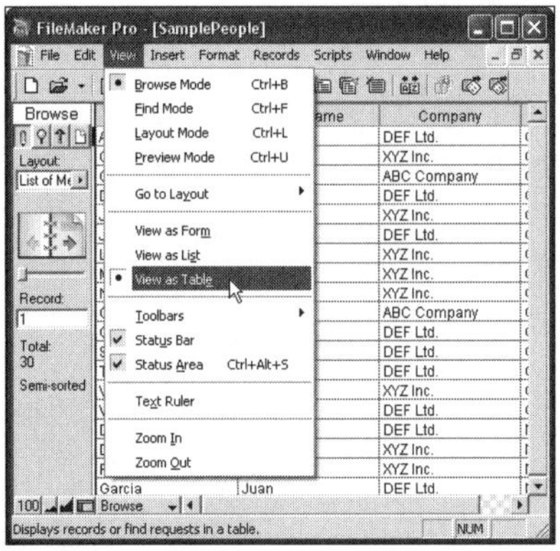

Figure 4.7 The View as Table choice uses a simple table layout to display as many records as your screen can accommodate.

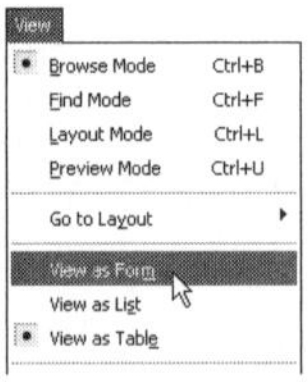

Figure 4.8 Choosing View > View as Form switches the file back to a single-record view.

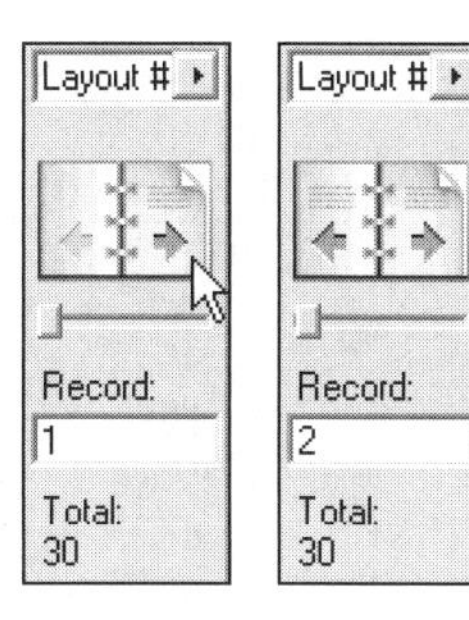

Figure 4.9 Click on the book pages to move forward or backward one record at a time.

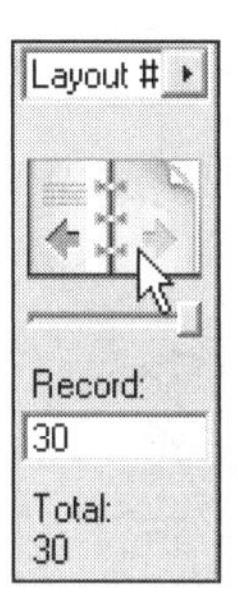

Figure 4.10 A blank page means you've reached the end of the record sequence.

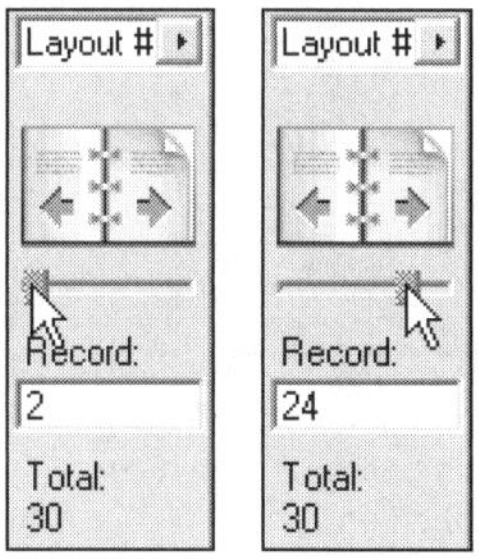

Figure 4.11 Jump ahead in the records by grabbing the slider and dragging it to the right. Dragging it to the left will let you move backward through the records.

Moving from Record to Record

FileMaker offers you three ways to quickly jump from record to record within any file. And, as with most things in FileMaker, you have several options within each view.

Navigating records in forms

◆ Click on the book icon's pages to move forward or backward—one record at a time. Click the right page to move forward in the sequence (**Figure 4.9**); click the left page to move back. A blank right or left page indicates there are no more records in that direction (**Figure 4.10**).

◆ To quickly skip ahead or back within the records, click and drag the book's slider. Dragging it to the right will skip you ahead in the sequence (**Figure 4.11**); dragging it to the left moves you back.

Navigating records in lists and tables

- You can use the book pages and slider in List or Table view as well (**Figures 4.12–4.13**).
- The List and Table views also allow you to skip from record to record simply by clicking anywhere within the records visible on your screen (**Figure 4.14**). This is especially handy when you need to change data in one field within each record. Clicking directly on that field highlights it, enabling you to begin entering your new data.

✔ Tip

- When you're working in List or Table view, a thin black bar just left of the records marks the current record (**Figure 4.13**).

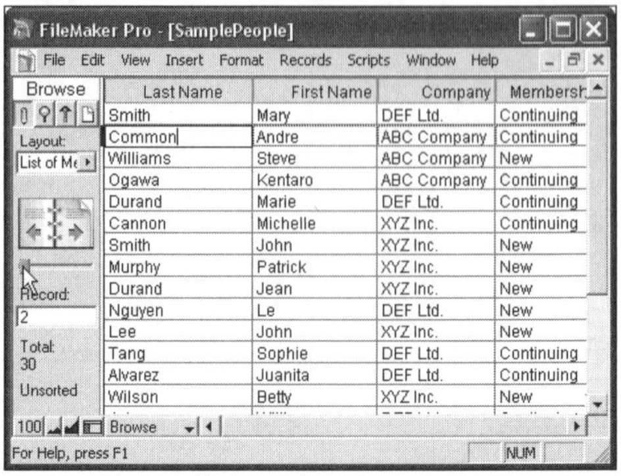

Figure 4.12 Dragging the slider works in the List and Table views as well. Just grab, drag, and ...

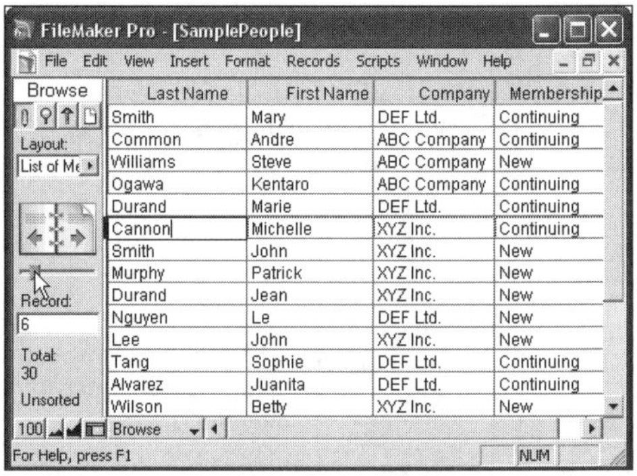

Figure 4.13 ... jump ahead in your records. Note how the black highlight in the thin bar left of the records now marks the Michelle Cannon entry.

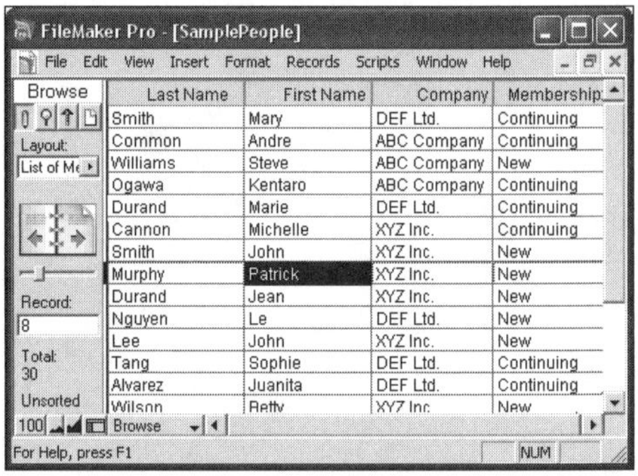

Figure 4.14 When in List or Table view, you can click directly on any field and it will become highlighted. Once highlighted, you can change a portion or all of the data within the field.

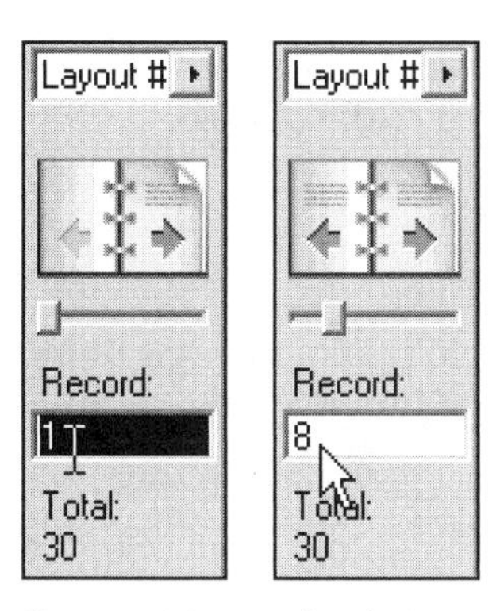

Figure 4.15 You can directly enter a record number by clicking the number just below the book or by pressing the Esc key. Type in a new record number, press Enter (Windows) or Return (Mac), and you're there.

Navigating directly by record number

◆ If you know the number of a particular record, you can go right to it by clicking on the current record number, typing in the desired number, and pressing Enter (Windows) or Return (Mac) (**Figure 4.15**). Pressing Esc automatically highlights the current record number, allowing you to work mouse-free. This method works in Form, List, or Table view.

Moving within a Record

Getting around within a single FileMaker record couldn't be easier, but as usual, there are several ways to do it.

Using your cursor to directly select a field works best when you need to change only a couple of items within a particular record. Using the Tab key generally works best when you're filling in new *blank* records or when you want to keep your hands on the keyboard. Both methods work in either Form or List View.

To move by direct selection:

◆ Double-click on any field you want to modify. Once the field becomes highlighted, type in your data (**Figure 4.16**). To reach another spot in the record, click your cursor on the desired field.

To move with the Tab key:

◆ After a record opens, press the Tab key to reach the first field. Continue pressing the Tab key until you reach the desired field. To move backward among the fields, press Shift Tab.

✔ Tips

- You can't tab to fields that contain calculations or summaries. But the contents of those fields are based on values set in other fields, so it's not really a problem. Just keep it in mind.
- FileMaker lets you set the tab order for all the fields in a record. Reordering the tabs is particularly handy if you need to reach only a few scattered fields within each record. For more on setting the tab order, see page 176.

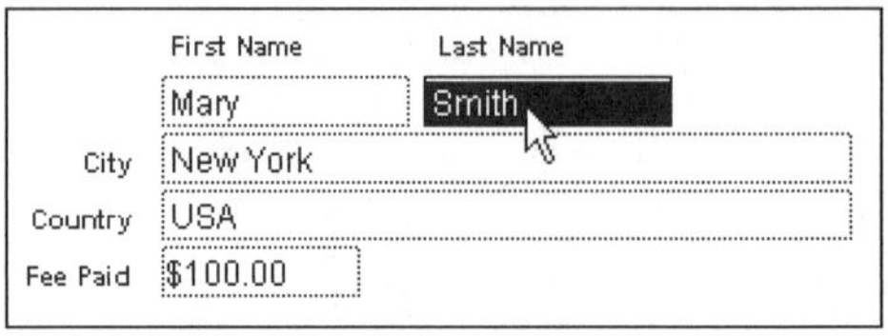

Figure 4.16 To enter data or modify a field, just double-click the field to highlight its contents. You can then type in your new data.

Finding and Sorting Records

Finding and sorting records are like two halves of the same process. Together, they give you the power to spotlight particular records in a particular order. That ability allows you to complete such mundane work as correcting entry errors as well as big-picture tasks like analyzing trends.

With Find you can hunt down a record that needs changing without having to go through the records one by one. While records normally are displayed in the order they were created, the Sort command lets you arrange the view to what best suits your needs. The new contextual sort feature, explained on page 67, makes sorting much easier to use.

Finding related field information in relational databases is covered in *Creating Relational Databases* on page 125.

Download the example database used in this section, home prices.fp7, at: `http://waywest.net/filemaker/`. (All FileMaker 8 files end with `.fp7`—the same suffix used by FileMaker 7.)

Finding Records

Understanding a few key terms—the Find request and the found set, along with *And* vs. *Or* searches—will make it easier to use FileMaker's Find features (**Figure 5.1**).

The Find Request: What FileMaker calls a *Find request* simply represents all the criteria entered for a particular search. Whether they're plain or fancy, all the field criteria associated with a single search represent one Find request.

The Found Set: FileMaker calls the records returned in any search the *found set*, which represents only the records activated by the current Find request. The rest of the file's records still exist but are not displayed and make up what FileMaker calls the *omitted set*. See *Omitting Records* on page 62 and *Deleting Records* on page 65.

Working with a found set allows you to focus on tailoring it for sorting, printing, exporting, etc. You can return to working with the full set of records in a file at any time. To do so, choose the *Show All Records* command under the Requests or Records menus. Or use your keyboard: Ctrl J (Windows) or ⌘ J (Mac).

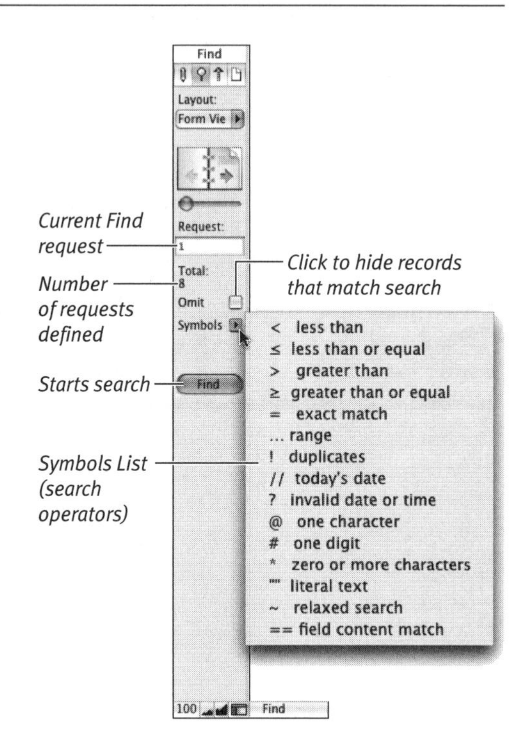

Figure 5.1 Switching to Find mode calls up search-related tools and buttons in FileMaker's left-hand status area.

Single- vs. Multiple-Criteria Searches: The single-criterion search is straightforward: You want to find every record containing a single item, such as the name Jones. Consequently, your Find request contains just one condition: find all instances of Jones in any field. That's why such searches are sometimes called simple searches. Multiple-criteria searches, on the other hand, can set any number of conditions and combine those conditions to broaden or narrow the number of instances found.

Any time you create a multiple-criteria search that looks for data that match *all* of your search criteria you're performing what's called a logical *And* search. If, for example, you create a Find request that asks for any records within a file where the city is San Francisco and the state is California, you're asking FileMaker to find records that contain San Francisco *and* California. Such *And* searches tend to narrow, or as FileMaker puts it *constrain*, your search since you're not just looking for records containing California but a smaller group within that group that also contains San Francisco.

Any time you create a multiple-criteria search that looks for data that match *any one* of your search criteria you're performing what's called a logical *Or* search. If, for example, you create a Find request for all records containing California *or* Arizona, FileMaker will find any records that match either value. Such *Or* queries tend to widen, or *extend*, your search.

Doing a Single-Criterion Search

If you need to find every instance of just a single item, use the single-criterion search.

To do a single-criterion search:

1. You can't search for information in a particular field unless you have a layout with that field in it. Switch to the layout of your database that contains the field or fields you want to search.
2. Once the correct layout appears, choose View > Find Mode (**Figure 5.2**). Or use your keyboard: Ctrl F (Windows) or ⌘ F (Mac). A blank version of the selected layout appears.
3. In our example we want to find all the houses on Pomona Avenue, so type Pomona into the Street Name field (**Figure 5.3**). Click the *Find* button in the mode status area along the left-hand side of the screen (**Figure 5.1**), or simply press Enter (Windows) or Return (Mac). (You can also choose Requests > Perform Find but using the keyboard is much easier.) Ten records appear that contain "Pomona" in the Street Name field (**Figure 5.4**). Notice that the left-hand mode status area shows the number of found records (10), along with the total record count (32).

✔ Tip

- Once you find a set of records, you can copy their data into another application, such as a spreadsheet, though FileMaker's field formatting will not be copied. Just use the Copy command: Ctrl C (Windows) or ⌘ C (Mac).

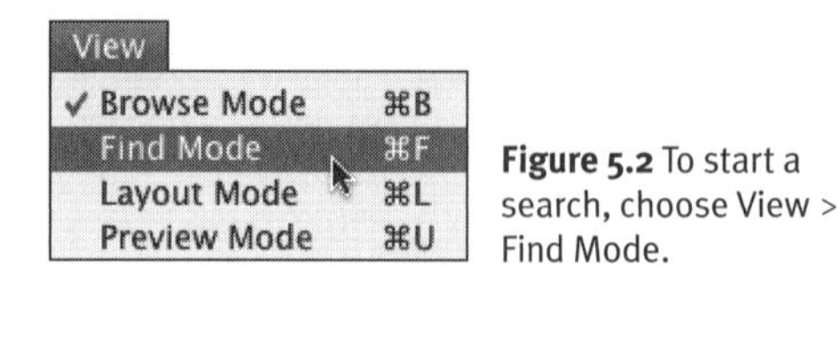

Figure 5.2 To start a search, choose View > Find Mode.

ST. JEROME REAL ESTATE

Sales Price | $/Sq.Ft | House Number | Street Name | Last Sold | Square Footage | Lot Size | Bed Rms

Pomona

Figure 5.3 Type into any field the data you're seeking.

Browse
Layout:
Layout #1
Record:
1
Found:
10
Total:
32
Unsorted

ST. JEROME REAL ES

Sales Price	$/Sq.Ft	House Number	Street Name	Last Sold	Square Footage
$180,000	$132	755	Pomona	5/27/97	1,363
$218,000	$195	145	Pomona	3/6/96	1,119
$228,500	$101	101	Pomona	8/15/97	2,265
$192,000	$207	215	Pomona	6/25/96	927
$230,000	$147	200	Pomona	5/22/97	1,567
$247,000	$172	220	Pomona	7/12/96	1,433
$291,000	$203	116	Pomona	9/6/96	1,432
$262,000	$174	138	Pomona	6/6/97	1,505
$211,000	$198	146	Pomona	4/16/96	1,067
$228,500	$101	11	Pomona	8/15/97	2,265

100 Browse

Figure 5.4 Once you click Find, FileMaker displays any records matching your search.

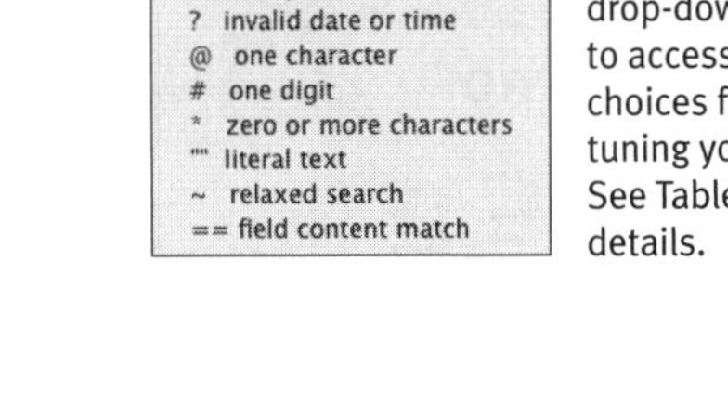

Figure 5.5 Click on the Symbols List drop-down menu to access 15 choices for fine-tuning your search. See Table 5.1 for details.

Searching with the Symbols List

Within Find mode, the Symbols List (a drop-down menu in the left-hand status area) offers 15 choices for quickly fine-tuning your search (**Figure 5.5**). Combined with the status area's *Omit* checkbox (for more information on Omit, see page 62), the Symbols List can be a major help when trying to find a series of records amid hundreds (**Table 5.1**).

Table 5.1

Using Find's Symbols/Operators Drop-down Menu

Use	To find	Type in field	Notes
<	Less than value to right of symbol	<200	
≤	Less than or equal to value to right	≤200	
>	Greater than value to right	>200	
≥	Greater than or equal to value to right	≥200	
=	Exactly value to right	=Pomona	Exact match and other values (e.g., will find Pomona Ave.)
...	A range of dates, times, numbers, text	... or .. (two periods)	Includes beginning and ending values; displays in A–Z, 1–10 order
!	Duplicate values	!	Finds any duplicate field entries—great for mailing lists
//	Today's date	//	
?	Invalid dates, times, or calculations	?	Finds format errors that can create calculation problems
@	One unknown or variable text character	@omona	A one-character search that will find Pomona and Romona
*	Zero or more unknown variable characters	P*a	No character limit: "P*a" finds Pomona but also Pia, Paula
" "	Text exactly as it appears	"Pomona"	Ignores letter case, so it will find "Pomona" and "pomona"
==	Field contents	=	Useful for finding empty fields

To use the Symbols List in a search:

1. Switch to the layout of your database that contains the field or fields you want to search. Choose View > Find Mode, or use your keyboard: Ctrl F (Windows) or ⌘ F (Mac). A blank version of the selected layout appears.
2. Click on the field you'll be searching. Now click on the Symbols drop-down menu in the left-hand mode status area and select the appropriate symbol or *operator* (**Figure 5.5**). (See **Table 5.1** for details on how each operator functions.) In this example, we want to find all the homes selling for less than $200,000. Select the first operator in the pop-up list, then type in 200,000 (**Figure 5.6**).
3. Click the *Find* button in the status area or press Enter (Windows) or Return (Mac). FileMaker then displays all the records meeting that criteria (**Figure 5.7**).

✔ Tips

- Use Find's Symbols list for multiple-criteria search requests, as well as for simple searches. (For more information on multiple-criteria searches, see page 69.)
- If your search request criteria include finding the current date, time, user name, an item from your index, or the last record, click on the field you'll be searching, choose *Insert*, and pick any command between *Current Date* and *From Last Record*. (For information on indexing, see *Storage options* on page 104.)
- The Symbols List also includes *...range*, which you can use to search for records that contain items between two values (**Figure 5.8**).

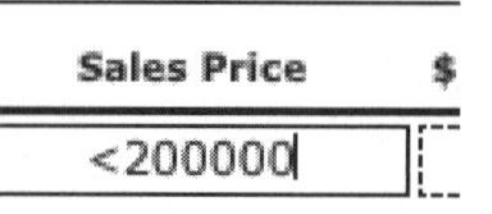

Figure 5.6 Combining data you type in directly (200,000) with the drop-down menu's symbols (<) lets you quickly define a search for all entries of less than 200,000.

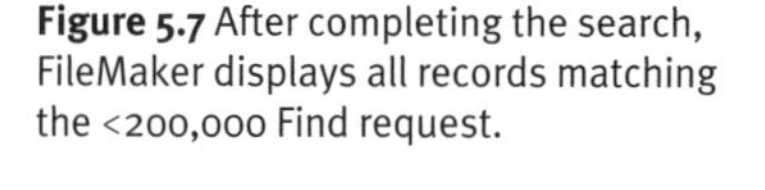

Sales Price	$/Sq.Ft	House Number	Street Name
$192,000	$207	215	Pomona
$183,000	$215	11	San Carlos
$166,000	$177	12	Carmel
$187,000	$174	7415	Fairmont
$152,000	$169	227	Carmel
$173,000	?	217	Ashbury
$185,000	$155	140	Ashbury
$173,000	$166	244	Ashbury
$183,000	$215	11	San Carlos
$191,000	$165	309	Carmel

Figure 5.7 After completing the search, FileMaker displays all records matching the <200,000 Find request.

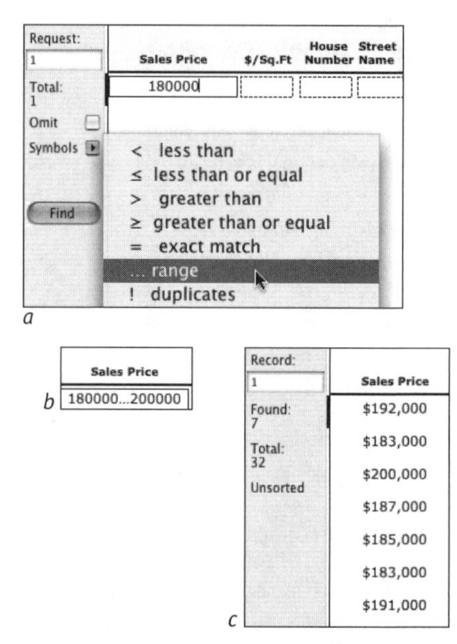

Figure 5.8 Use the Symbols List's *...range* choice (a) to insert an ellipsis between two values (b) to find every instance between those values (c).

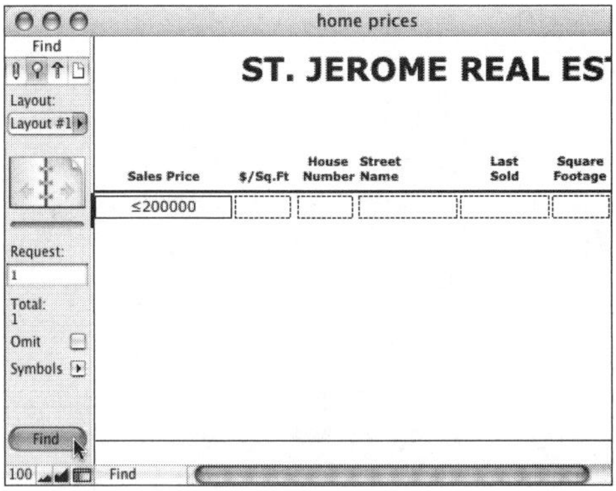

Figure 5.9 A multiple-criteria search begins just like a single-criterion search: Type in your search term and click the *Find* button or press Enter or Return.

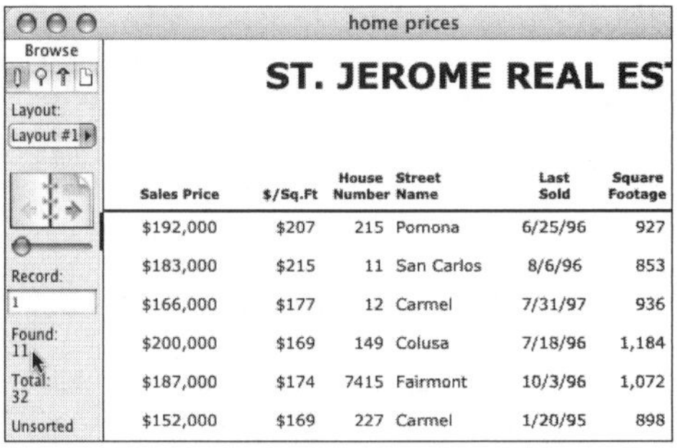

Figure 5.10 In this example, 11 records match the first search criteria: houses costing $200,000 or less.

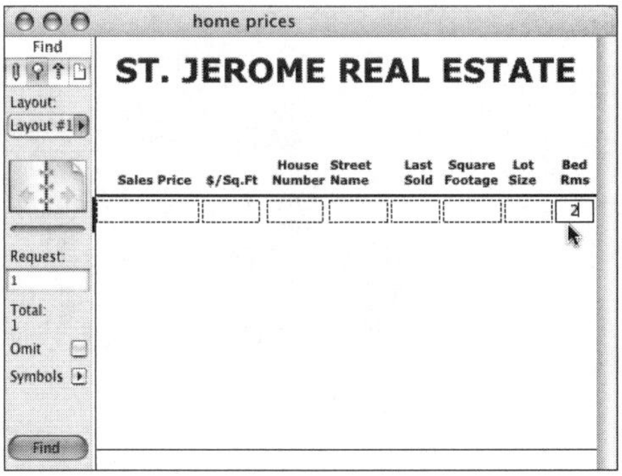

Figure 5.11 Switch back to Find mode and type your second criteria into any field. Do not press the *Find* button.

Doing Multiple-Criteria Searches

While constructing multiple-criteria searches takes more time than single-criterion searches, they enable you to cast a customized, fine-mesh net for exactly what you're seeking.

To narrow a search using multiple criteria:

1. Choose View > Find mode or use your keyboard: Ctrl F (Windows) or ⌘F (Mac). Type what you're seeking into the relevant field. Click the *Find* button or press Enter or Return (**Figure 5.9**). The records matching your first criteria appear in Browse mode (**Figure 5.10**).
2. Switch back to Find mode and type your second search criteria into another blank field (**Figure 5.11**).

(continued)

3. Choose Requests > Constrain Found Set (**Figure 5.12**). FileMaker searches through the first found set and displays only records that also meet your second criterion, thereby narrowing or *constraining* your search (**Figure 5.13**).

✔ Tips

- The Constrain Found Set approach isn't necessary if you are searching for multiple criteria in *different* fields. In those cases, you can just choose View > Find Mode and enter your multiple criteria (**Figure 5.14**). Click the *Find* button in the mode status area, or press Enter (Windows) or Return (Mac), and you're done.
- If nothing in the database matches one of your search criteria, FileMaker tells you and gives you the chance to revise your search by clicking *Modify Find* (**Figure 5.15**).

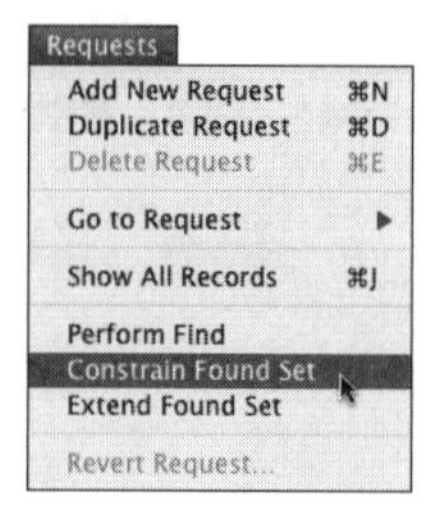

Figure 5.12 Instead of clicking the *Find* button, choose Requests > Constrain Found Set.

Browse
Layout:
Layout #1
Record:
1
Found:
8
Total:
32
Unsorted

ST. JEROME REAL ESTATE

Sales Price	$/Sq.Ft	House Number	Street Name	Last Sold	Square Footage	L Si
$192,000	$207	215	Pomona	6/25/96	927	4
$183,000	$215	11	San Carlos	8/6/96	853	4
$166,000	$177	12	Carmel	7/31/97	936	4
$200,000	$169	149	Colusa	7/18/96	1,184	3
$187,000	$174	7415	Fairmont	10/3/96	1,072	4
$152,000	$169	227	Carmel	1/20/95	898	
$185,000	$155	140	Ashbury	12/19/97	1,197	4

Figure 5.13 FileMaker searches through the first 11 records and narrows, or *constrains*, the results to the eight houses that also meet the two-bath criteria.

Sales Price	$/Sq.Ft	House Number	Street Name	Last Sold	Square Footage	Lot Size	Bed Rms
≤200000							2

Figure 5.14 If you are searching for multiple criteria in *different* fields, you can do a one-step find and skip the Constrain Found Set command.

No records match this set of find requests.

Cancel   Modify Find

Figure 5.15 If no records match your request, click *Modify Find.*

Figure 5.16 Type what you're seeking into the relevant field, then click the *Find* button or press Enter or Return.

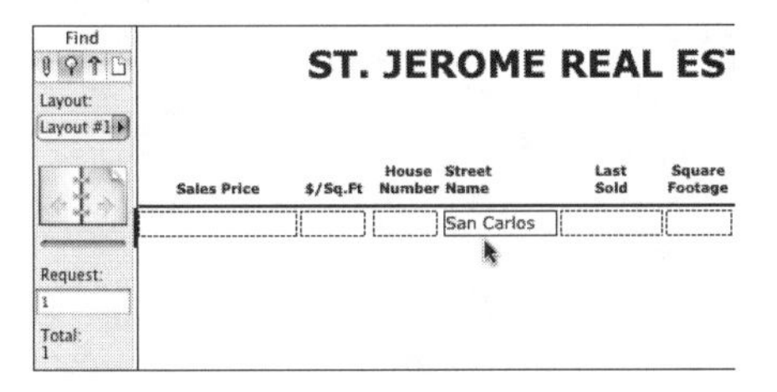

Figure 5.17 The records matching your first criterion appear.

Figure 5.18 Back in Find mode, type your second search criterion into any blank field.

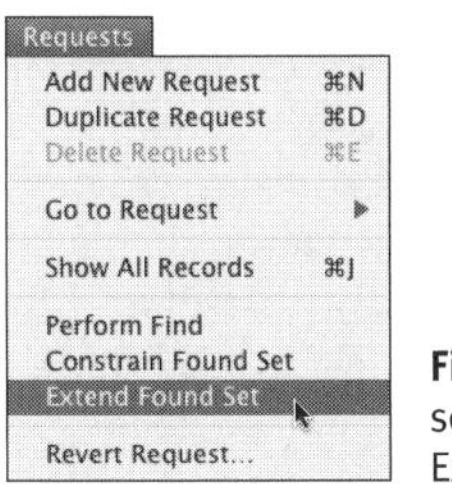

Figure 5.19 To broaden the search, choose Requests > Extend Found Set.

To broaden a search using multiple criteria:

1. Choose View > Find Mode or use your keyboard: Ctrl F (Windows) or ⌘ F (Mac). Type what you're seeking into the relevant field. Click the *Find* button or press Enter or Return (**Figure 5.16**). The records matching your first criteria appear in Browse mode (**Figure 5.17**).
2. Switch back to Find mode and type your second search criteria into another blank field, or in this example, the *same* field used in the first find (**Figure 5.18**).
3. Choose Requests > Extend Found Set (**Figure 5.19**). The newfound set includes all records that meet your first criterion *or* the second criterion, thereby broadening or *extending* your search (**Figure 5.20**).

✔ Tip

- Previous versions of FileMaker accomplished the same thing using the Add New Request command, but many users found that approach confusing. If you still prefer that method, however, just remember to *not* hit Enter or Return after you type in your first search criteria. Instead, you choose Requests > Add New Request, type what you're seeking into a duplicate set of the fields used in the first request, and then click the *Find* button or press Enter (Windows) or Return (Mac).

Figure 5.20 The newfound set includes all records that meet your first criterion *or* the second criterion, *extending* your search.

Modifying Find Requests

The new Constrain and Extend found set commands make it much easier to change your find request as you work. FileMaker offers several other useful commands for altering or modifying your most recent Find request. Most reside under the Requests menu (**Figure 5.21**), except for Modify Last Find, which appears under the Records menu.

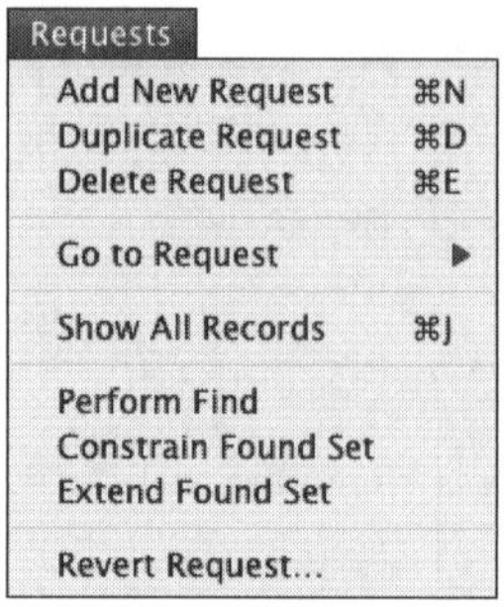

Figure 5.21 Commands for altering or modifying your most recent Find request reside under the Requests menu, but can be selected *only* if you're in Find mode.

To modify your previous Find request:

1. Make sure you are in the layout you want. If necessary, use the layout drop-down menu to select the right one.
2. Since you are modifying a previous Find, you will already be in Browse mode, so choose Records > Modify Last Find (Ctrl R in Windows or ⌘R on the Mac) (**Figure 5.22**).
3. When the form appears, modify your request and click *Find* or press Enter (Windows) or Return (Mac).

Figure 5.22 If you want to change a search but already are in Browse mode, choose Records > Modify Last Find.

Figure 5.23 To duplicate a Find request, choose Requests > Duplicate Request.

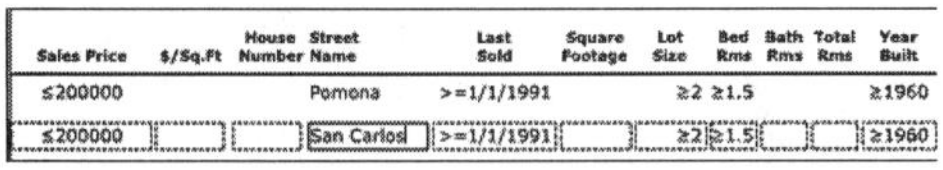

Figure 5.24 The Duplicate Request command saves time if you only need to change a few of the previous Find request's criteria.

To duplicate (and then change) a Find request:

1. Switch to the layout you want.
2. If you've typed in your first request but are still in Find mode, choose Requests > Duplicate Request (Ctrl D in Windows or ⌘D on the Mac) (**Figure 5.23**).

   If you've already performed the Find and now are in Browse mode, first choose Records > Modify Last Find (Ctrl R in Windows or ⌘R on the Mac) (**Figure 5.22**), and then choose Requests > Duplicate Request (Ctrl D in Windows or ⌘D on the Mac) (**Figure 5.23**).
3. A duplicate of your first request appears (**Figure 5.24**). You can then alter the appropriate fields—saving yourself a bit of time.
4. Repeat the steps until you've duplicated (and then changed) all the requests you need. Click *Find*, or press Enter (Windows) or Return (Mac).

To delete a Find request:

1. Switch to the layout you want.
2. If you've typed in a request but are still in Find mode, use the book icon to click to the Find request you want to delete (**Figure 5.25**).

   If you've already performed the Find and now are in Browse mode, first choose Records > Modify Last Find (Ctrl R in Windows or ⌘R on the Mac). Now use the book icon to click to the Find request you want to delete (**Figure 5.25**).
3. Choose Requests > Delete Request (**Figure 5.26**). Or use your keyboard: Ctrl E (Windows) or ⌘E (Mac). The selected request will be deleted (**Figure 5.27**).

✔ Tip

- You can delete as many Find requests as you like—until there's just one left, which you cannot delete.

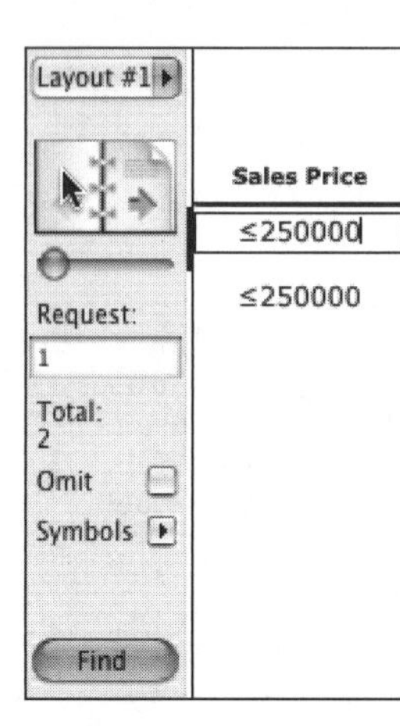

Figure 5.25 If you want to delete a particular request and are still in Find mode, use the book to reach it.

Requests
Add New Request ⌘N
Duplicate Request ⌘D
Delete Request ⌘E
Go to Request
Show All Records ⌘J
Perform Find
Constrain Found Set
Extend Found Set
Revert Request...

Figure 5.26 Once you find the request, choose Requests > Delete Request.

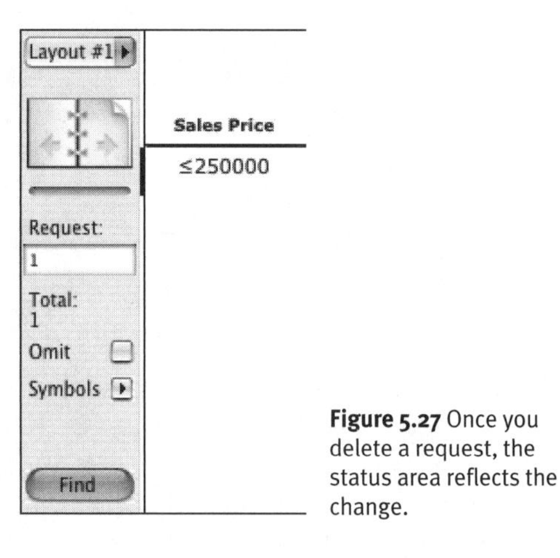

Figure 5.27 Once you delete a request, the status area reflects the change.

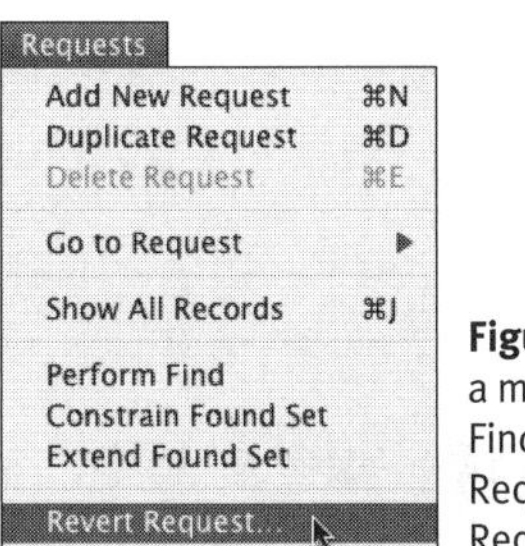

Figure 5.28 If you make a mistake in creating a Find request, choose Requests > Revert Request.

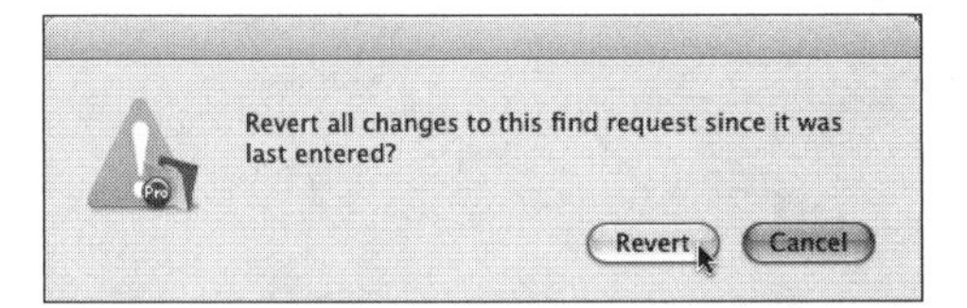

Figure 5.29 Choosing Requests > Revert Request triggers an alert dialog box. Click *Revert* to correct a mistake or *Cancel* to leave things as they are.

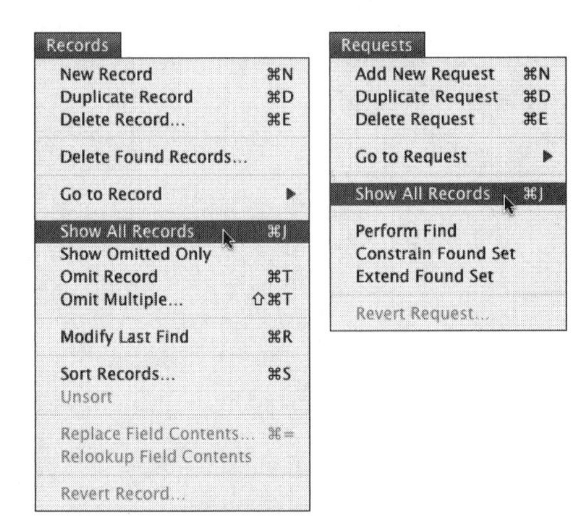

Figure 5.30 To find all your records, choose Records > Show All Records if you are in Browse mode (left) or Requests > Show All Records if you're in Find mode (right).

Reverting Requests

This command lets you correct entries *while* you're creating a Find request. It does not return you to where you were before you performed a Find. But it will let you start fresh on building the current Find request—no matter how many fields you've already filled in within that request.

To revert a request:

1. You must be in Find mode, filling out a Find request. When you make a mistake, choose Requests > Revert Request (**Figure 5.28**).
2. When the warning dialog box appears, click *Revert* (**Figure 5.29**). All the fields within that Find request become blank, allowing you to start fresh.

To find all records:

- If you are in Browse mode, choose Records > Show All Records (left, **Figure 5.30**). If you're in Find mode, choose Requests > Show All Records (right, **Figure 5.30**). The keyboard command is the same in either mode: Ctrl J (Windows) or ⌘ J (Mac).

Omitting Records

Omitting records does not delete them from your database but simply hides them from view. In that sense, omitted records are the reverse of the *found set* generated by a Find request. When you perform a Find, the records *not* shown are what FileMaker calls the *omitted set*. Used with the Find and Sort commands, the Omit command allows you to quickly make a selection and then *invert* it by finding all the records *not* in that selection.

To omit one record:

1. In Browse mode, select the record you want to omit.
2. Choose Records > Omit Record (**Figure 5.31**). Or use your keyboard: Ctrl T (Windows) or ⌘ T (Mac).

✔ Tip

- When you omit records, you're essentially narrowing, or constraining, the found set. Some FileMaker users find that a helpful concept. If that sets your head spinning, then forget it: It's just another way of looking at things.

Figure 5.31 To hide a record from view, select it, then choose Records > Omit Record. Omitting records does not delete them but simply tucks them out of sight.

To omit more than one record:

1. In Browse mode, select the first record of the group you want to omit.
2. Choose Records > Omit Multiple (**Figure 5.32**). Or use your keyboard: Shift Ctrl T (Windows) or Shift ⌘ T (Mac).
3. A dialog box appears asking how many records you want to omit. In our real estate example, we sorted the records to place together the six Ashbury records we want to omit (**Figure 5.33**). Since we'd selected the first Ashbury record in Step 1, we enter 6 and click the *Omit* button (**Figure 5.34**). The Ashbury records have been omitted—not deleted, just hidden. The "Found: 26" and "Total: 32" in the left-hand status area confirm that six records have been omitted (**Figure 5.35**).

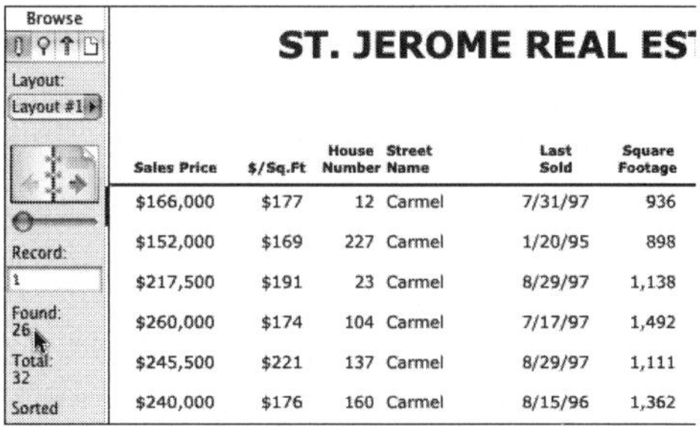

Figure 5.32 Choosing Records > Omit Multiple hides a group of records —starting with the first one you select.

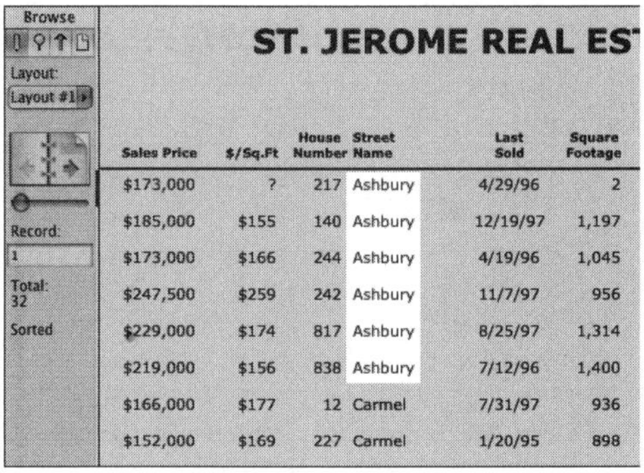

Figure 5.33 In the example, the far-left thin black bar indicates the first of the six Ashbury records that will be omitted.

Figure 5.34 When the Omit Multiple dialog box appears, type in the number of records you want to hide, then click *Omit*.

Figure 5.35 All six Ashbury records have been hidden. The *Found: 26* and *Total: 32* in the left-hand status area confirm that six records have been omitted.

To bring back omitted records:

- Remember: Omitting a record does not delete it but simply removes it from the found set. To bring it back, choose Records > Show Omitted Only (**Figure 5.36**). The six records omitted in our previous example appear and are now the found set (**Figure 5.37**). The *previous* found set of 26 records is now omitted. It takes some getting used to, but the Find Omitted command's back-and-forth toggle nature becomes very handy when used with the Find and Sort commands.

Figure 5.36 Because omitted records are only hidden, choosing Records > Show Omitted Only restores them to view.

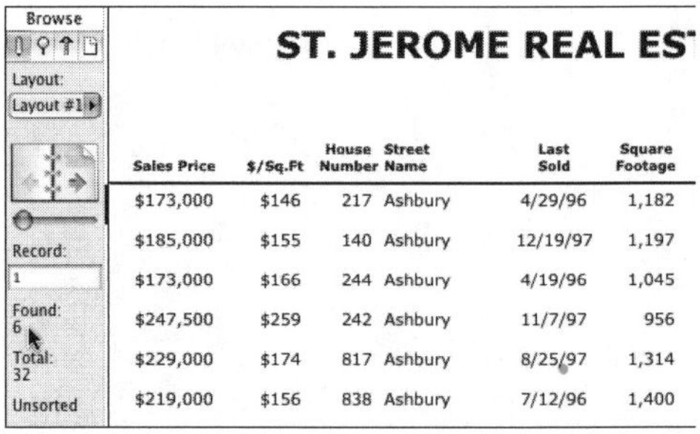

Figure 5.37 The six previously hidden records return to view after choosing Show Omitted.

✔ Tip

- Whenever you select the Show Omitted command it will display any records not already on the screen—even if you have every single record displayed. In that case, the Show Omitted command will display *no* records. Choose Show Omitted again and up pop *all* the records. When you think about it, it makes sense.

File Edit View Insert Format Records Scripts Window

home prices

ST. JEROME REAL

New Record ⌘N
Duplicate Record ⌘D
Delete Record... ⌘E
Delete Found Records...
Go to Record
Show All Records ⌘J
Show Omitted Only
Omit Record ⌘T
Omit Multiple... ⇧⌘T
Modify Last Find ⌘R
Sort Records... ⌘S
Unsort
Replace Field Contents... ⌘=
Relookup Field Contents
Revert Record...

$/Sq.Ft	House Number	Street Name	Last Sold
$146	217	Ashbury	4/29/96
$155	140	Ashbury	12/19/97
$166	244	Ashbury	4/19/96
$259	242	Ashbury	11/7/97
$174	817	Ashbury	8/25/97
$156	838	Ashbury	7/12/96

Figure 5.38 First select the record you want to delete (in this case the first record on the left), then choose Records > Delete Record.

Figure 5.39 FileMaker presents a warning dialog box to make sure you really want to delete a record. If you're sure, click *Delete*.

ST. JEROME REAL ESTATE

Sales Price	$/Sq.Ft	House Number	Street Name	Last Sold	Square Footage	Lot Size	Bed Rms
$173,000	$146	217	Ashbury	4/29/96	1,182	2	5
$185,000	$155	140	Ashbury	12/19/97	1,197	4922	2
$173,000	$166	244	Ashbury	4/19/96	1,045	3852	3
$247,500	$259	242	Ashbury	11/7/97	956	3852	2
$229,000	$174	817	Ashbury	8/25/97	1,314	4000	2

Figure 5.40 The record selected in Figure 5.38 disappears after the Delete command is invoked.

Deleting Records

Unlike the Omit command, which just hides records, the Delete command really does zap records and all the data inside them. Once you delete them, they're gone: no undo, no going back. To play it safe, consider making a backup copy of a file before you embark on a record-deleting session.

Think about this for a second. First create a copy of the file—just in case. If you're only looking to start with a fresh empty version of the layout, consider creating a clone of the existing database. Cloning gives you an empty database but does so by copying an existing database's layout without touching the original.

To delete a single record:

1. In Browse mode, select the record you want to delete. In our real estate example, we've selected an unwanted blank record. Choose Records > Delete Record or use your keyboard: Ctrl E (Windows) or ⌘E (Mac) (**Figure 5.38**).
2. As a safeguard against accidentally deleting a record, FileMaker presents a warning dialog box (**Figure 5.39**). If you're sure, click the *Delete* button. The selected record is then deleted (**Figure 5.40**).

To delete a group of records:

1. Use the Find or Omit Multiple command to select a group of records to delete.
2. Once you've selected the group of records, choose Records > Delete Found Records (**Figure 5.41**). (To keep you from accidentally invoking the command, it has no keyboard equivalent.) As a second safeguard, FileMaker presents a warning dialog box that notes how many records are about to be deleted (**Figure 5.42**). If you're sure, click the *Delete All* button.

To delete all records in a database:

1. If you truly want to delete all the records, choose Show All Records from the Requests or Records menus (Ctrl J in Windows or ⌘ J on the Mac).
2. Choose Records > Delete All Records (**Figure 5.43**).
3. Again, FileMaker presents a warning dialog box asking if you really want to delete that many records (**Figure 5.44**). Remember: There's no undo for this command. If you're sure, click the *Delete All* button.

Figure 5.41 To delete a group of records, select them, and then choose Records > Delete Found Records.

Figure 5.42 To keep you from accidentally deleting a group of records, FileMaker asks for confirmation of the number selected. If you're sure, click *Delete All*.

Figure 5.43 To delete all records in a database, choose Records > Delete All Records.

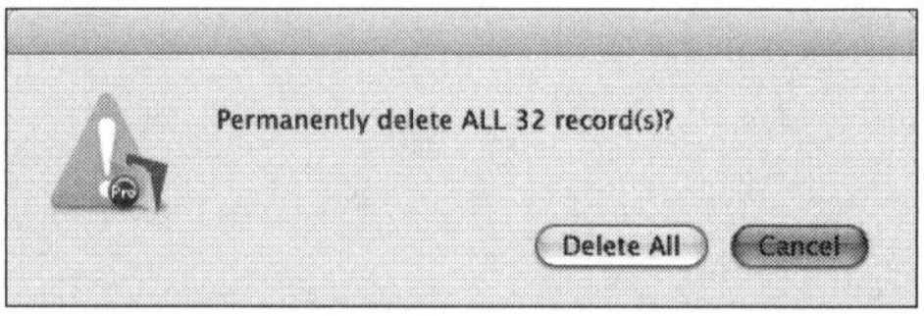

Figure 5.44 To keep you from accidentally wiping out your database, FileMaker presents an alert dialog box.

Table 5.2

How FileMaker Sorts What		
CONTENT	ASCENDING	DESCENDING
Text	A to Z	Z to A
Numbers	1–100	100–1
Time	6:00–11:00	11:00–6:00
Dates	1/1/98–12/1/98	12/1/98–1/1/98
	Jan. 1–Dec. 1	Dec. 1–Jan. 1

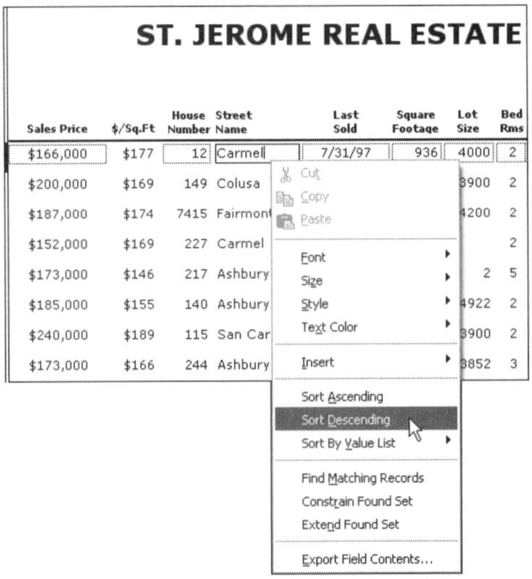

Figure 5.45 Right-click (Windows) or Control-click (Mac) on any field and use the drop-down menu to make your sorting choice.

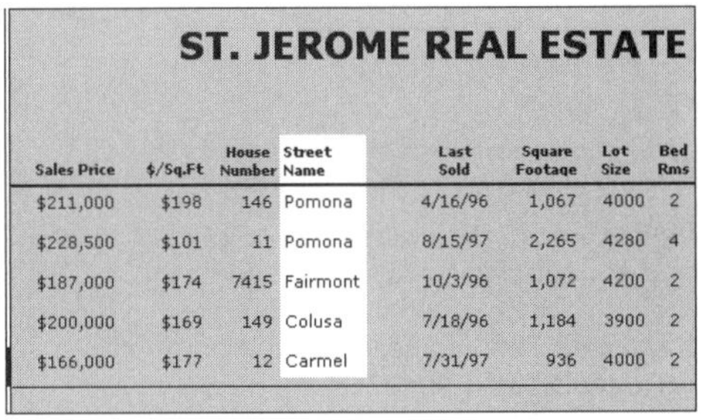

Figure 5.46 After you run a contextual sort, the records are rearranged in descending order by street name.

Sorting Records

FileMaker stores records in the order they were created but that's no reason for you to work with them in that somewhat random order. By running a sort, you can rearrange the order for browsing, printing, or updating. FileMaker uses the found set concept discussed on page 50 to search through select fields and then arrange the records as you desire.

You can sort records using single or multiple criteria, just like finding records. FileMaker's new contextual sort feature makes single-criterion sorts so simple that you'll probably use it far more often than the actual Sort command. No matter which way you trigger a single-criterion sort, you can arrange your records in one of three ways: ascending order, descending order, or a custom order based on a value list you create. If, like me, you can hardly keep right and left straight, let alone what's ascending and descending, *How FileMaker Sorts What* (**Table 5.2**) should help.

To run a contextual sort:

- While in Browse mode, right-click (Windows) or Control-click (Mac) on any field and use the drop-down menu to choose Sort Ascending, Sort Descending, or Sort By Value List (**Figure 5.45**). If you choose Sort By Value List, pick an item from the secondary drop-down menu. The records will be resorted based on your choice (**Figure 5.46**).

To run a single-criterion sort:

1. Use any combination of the Find, Omit, and Delete commands to first narrow your selection of records for sorting. Of course, you can always sort the entire file.
2. Choose Records > Sort Records (**Figure 5.47**). Or use your keyboard: Ctrl S (Windows) or ⌘ S (Mac).
3. The Sort Records dialog box appears (**Figure 5.48**). On the left side is a list of the fields in your file. Select the field you want to sort with by clicking on an item in the left list, then click the *Move* button in the middle to place it in the right-hand window.
4. By default, the field will be sorted in ascending order. If you want to change the *type* of sort, first click the field in the right-hand list, then click on the appropriate radio button (*Ascending*, *Descending*, or *Custom*) in the lower-left area of the Sort Records dialog box (**Figure 5.49**). See *To set (or reset) a custom sort order* on page 71.
5. Click the *Sort* button in the middle of the dialog box or simply press Enter (Windows) or Return (Mac). If you want to adjust the results, choose Records > Sort Records again or use your keyboard: Ctrl S (Windows) or ⌘ S (Mac).

✔ Tip

- The Sort order will remain in place until you perform a new sort.

Figure 5.47 To run a sort, choose Records > Sort Records.

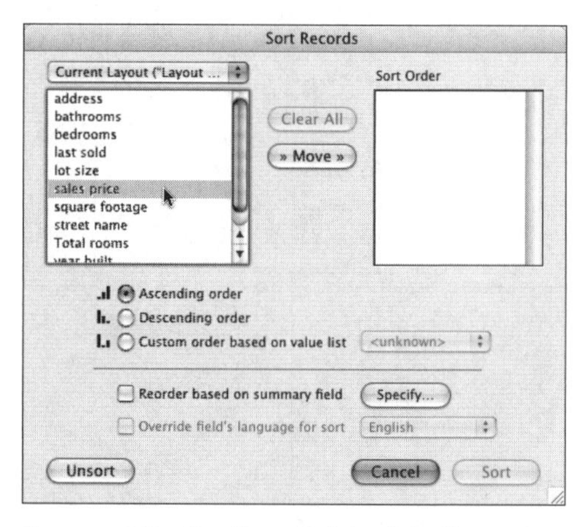

Figure 5.48 The Sort Records dialog box allows you to control which fields are sorted, the type of sorting used, and the order in which the sort occurs.

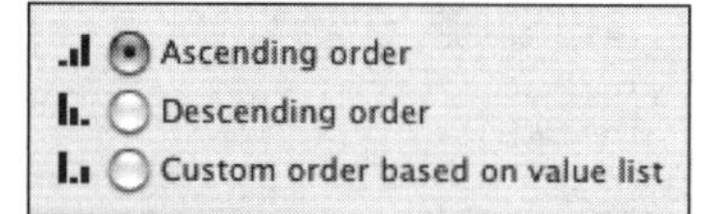

Figure 5.49 After you've selected a field, you can change the *type* of sort by clicking the appropriate radio button (*Ascending*, *Descending*, or *Custom*) in the lower-left area of the Sort Records dialog box.

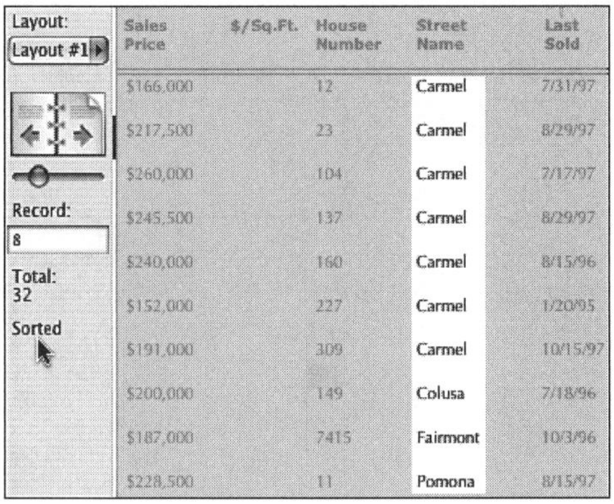

Figure 5.50 By controlling the sort order within the Sort Records dialog box, all Carmel homes appear first (with their house numbers in ascending order), followed by all the Pomona homes.

Running Multiple-Criteria Sorts

A multiple sort allows you to precisely arrange the order of your database records. When you sort more than one field at once, the precedence is based on the order in the Sort Records dialog box. Fields listed first in the box's right-side list will take precedence over fields listed later. Looking at our real estate example, if the Street field is listed before the Number field the records will be first sorted by the street name (A to Z) and then by the address number (1 to 100) (**Figure 5.50**).

To run a multiple-criteria sort:

1. Use any combination of the Find, Omit, and Delete commands to first narrow your selection of records to sort. Of course, you can always sort the entire file.
2. Choose Records > Sort Records (**Figure 5.47**). Or use your keyboard: Ctrl S (Windows) or ⌘ S (Mac).
3. The Sort Records dialog box appears (**Figure 5.48**). Select the left-side field name you want to first sort by. Click the *Move* button in the middle to place the field name in the right-hand *Sort Order* list.

(continued)

4. Continue selecting field names on the left side and placing them in the right side by using the *Move* button. Remember: Their relative precedence is set top to bottom. If you need to change the right-side order, click and hold your cursor over the double arrow just left of the field name and then drag up or down. The field name will move, altering the sort order precedence (**Figure 5.51**).

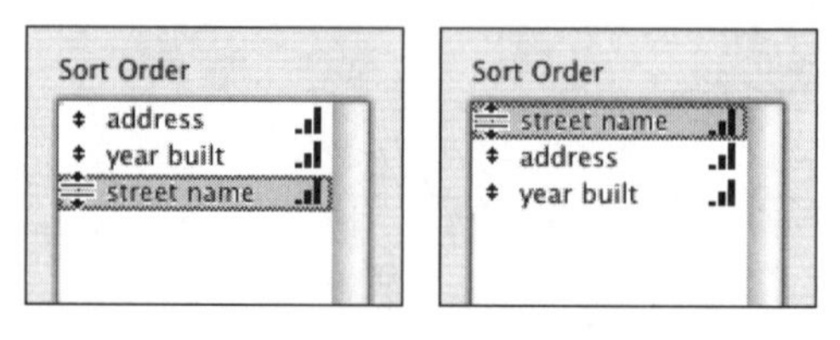

Figure 5.51 To change the sort order, use your cursor to drag the selected field name up or down in the order.

5. Pick the *type* of sort (*Ascending*, *Descending*, or *Custom*) for each right-side field name by clicking on the name, then clicking on the appropriate radio button in the lower-left area of the Sort Records dialog box.

6. When you're ready, click the *Sort* button or simply press [Enter] (Windows) or [Return] (Mac). The records appear in the sorted order. If you need to adjust the sort order, choose Records > Sort Records again or use your keyboard: [Ctrl][S] (Windows) or [⌘][S] (Mac).

   Since you can unsort with the click of a button, feel free to experiment a bit to get a full sense of how different sorts work.

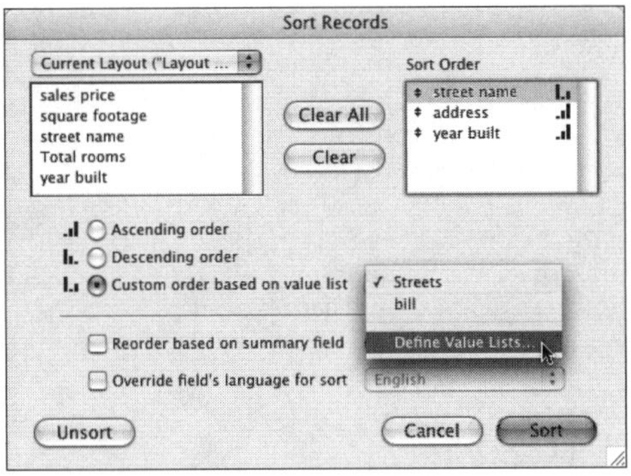

Figure 5.52 Click the radio button labeled *Custom order based on value list*, wait for the pop-up menu to appear, and choose *Define Value Lists*.

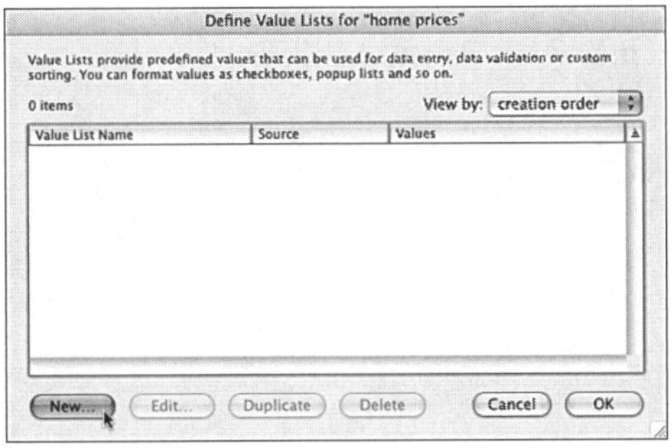

Figure 5.53 When the Define Value Lists dialog box appears, click *New*.

Setting Sort Orders

The custom sort order is determined by a *value list*. Such lists—and their order—are typically created when fields are first being defined (see *Defining Fields* on page 93). However, you can change the order of a value list—and thereby the custom sort order—any time.

To set (or reset) a custom sort order:

1. Choose Records > Sort Records or use your keyboard: Ctrl S (Windows) or ⌘S (Mac).
2. The Sort Records dialog box appears (**Figure 5.52**). If the field name for which you want to create a custom sort order is already listed in the right-side list, click on it there and go to step 3.

   If the field name for which you want to create a custom sort order has not yet been selected and moved to the right side, click on its name in the left-side list. Now click the *Move* button, which places the field's name in the right-side list.
3. By default, the field's sort type is Ascending. To change the type to a custom order, click the radio button labeled *Custom order based on value list*, wait for the pop-up menu to appear, and choose *Define Value Lists* (**Figure 5.52**).
4. When the Define Value Lists dialog box appears, click *New* (**Figure 5.53**).

(continued)

5. When the Edit Value List dialog box appears, type an easy-to-recognize name into the Value List Name box, then type each of your custom values into the right-side box in the exact order you want them sorted (**Figure 5.54**). When you're done, click *OK*.

6. When the Define Value Lists dialog box reappears, click *OK*.

7. When the Sort Records dialog box reappears, click Sort to apply your Custom order. The records will sort out in the order of the names in the Streets value list (**Figure 5.55**).

✔ Tip

- Once you've defined a value list, you can quickly reach it with a right-click (Windows) or Control-click (Mac) on any field (**Figure 5.56**).

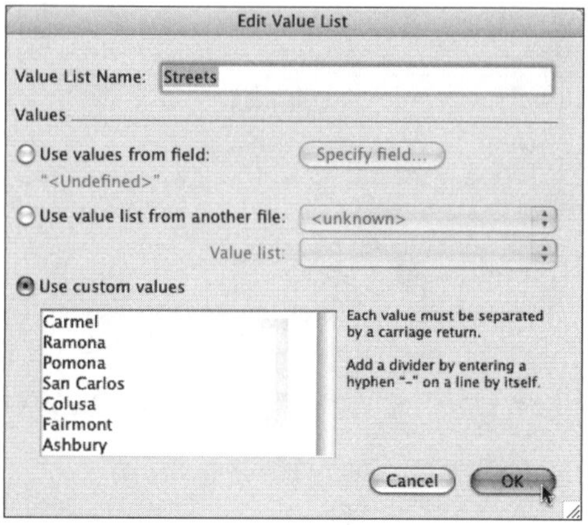

Figure 5.54 Use an easy-to-recognize word for your Value List Name, then type your custom values in the right-side box in the exact order you want them sorted. When you're done, click *OK*.

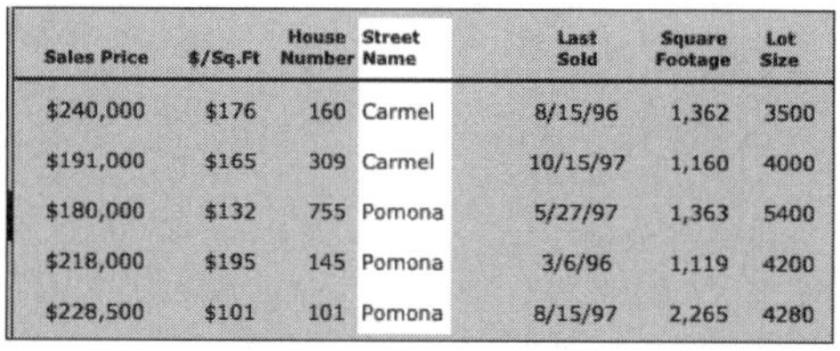

Figure 5.55 Once you run the custom sort, the record sequence mirrors the order of the value list.

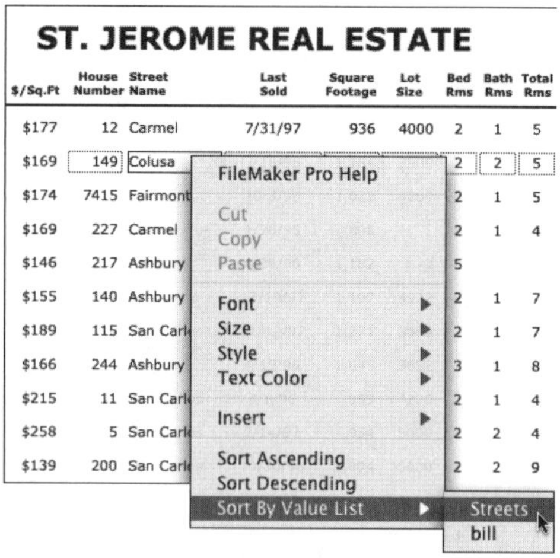

Figure 5.56 If you've already defined a value list, it's just a right-click (Windows) or Control-click (Mac) away.

Using Spell Check and Dictionaries

6

By default, FileMaker automatically checks spellings against two dictionaries: a main dictionary based on your computer's language setting and a user-defined dictionary that's created automatically and named `User.upr`. Since the main dictionary contains 100,000 words and your default user dictionary can hold up to 32,000 words, this combo works fine in almost all situations.

Sometimes, however, you may want to create a special user dictionary for occasional use. Examples might include a dictionary of trademarks or medical terms. This requires two separate actions: first you create the new user-defined dictionary and then you select it. Each FileMaker database can be linked to its own user dictionary. This allows you to link a medical database to a user medical dictionary or link a music-oriented database to a user dictionary of performing artists' names. Once that file-to-dictionary link is made, you need not specify it again.

You can use these same steps to switch your *main* dictionary from one language to another. User dictionaries are built either by adding words one by one or by importing an existing file of special terms created in another application, such as Microsoft Word.

To check spelling:

1. When you have a record or layout to spell check, choose Edit > Spelling. The submenu then offers you the choice of checking the spelling of only what you've already highlighted (*Check Selection*), the entire record currently on your screen (*Check Record*), or the records browsed in the current session (*Check All*) (**Figure 6.1**). Choose one and release your cursor and the Spelling dialog box appears.
2. If the dictionary says the selection is spelled correctly, click *Done* (top, **Figure 6.2**). If FileMaker suspects that the word is misspelled, it displays one or more possible replacement words (bottom, **Figure 6.2**). Click the one you prefer—or type in your own choice—then click the *Replace* and *Done* buttons.
3. If the word isn't in FileMaker's dictionary because it's a formal name or special term, you can click *Ignore All* or *Learn*, and then click *Done* when that button appears. Clicking *Learn* adds the word to your *current user dictionary*. If you are not already using a special dictionary for this file, FileMaker automatically adds the word to `User.upr`, your default special user dictionary, which resides inside the folder where you installed FileMaker.

✔ Tip

- If the field or file you're spell checking is password protected or access to it is otherwise restricted, you won't be able to change a misspelling.

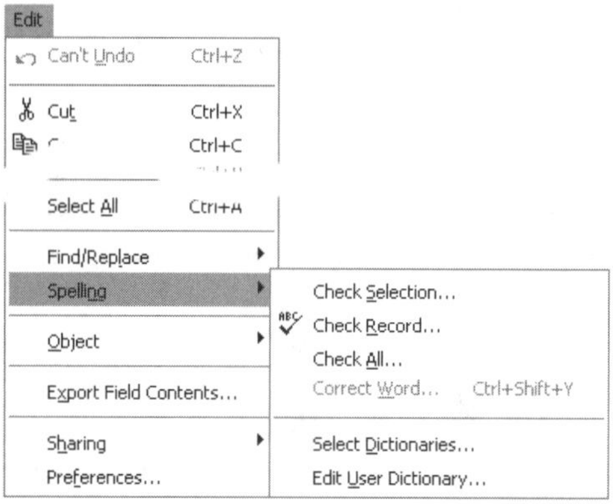

Figure 6.1 Found under the Edit menu, the Spelling submenu offers you three spelling selection choices.

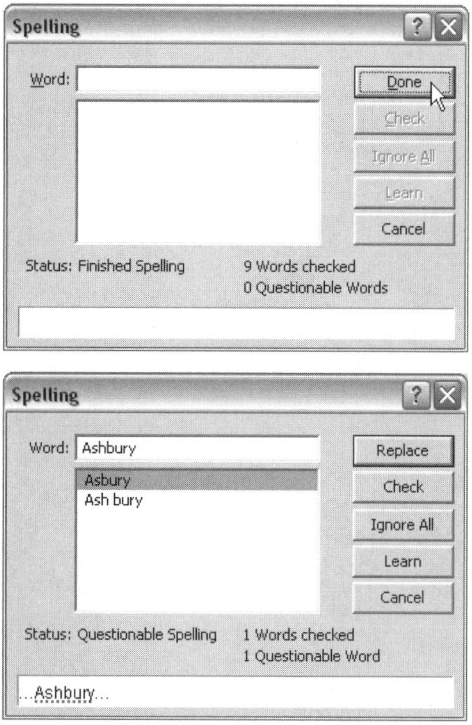

Figure 6.2 The Spelling dialog box, which changes depending on whether the selection is spelled correctly (top) or seems questionable (bottom), offers five options including seeing the word in context.

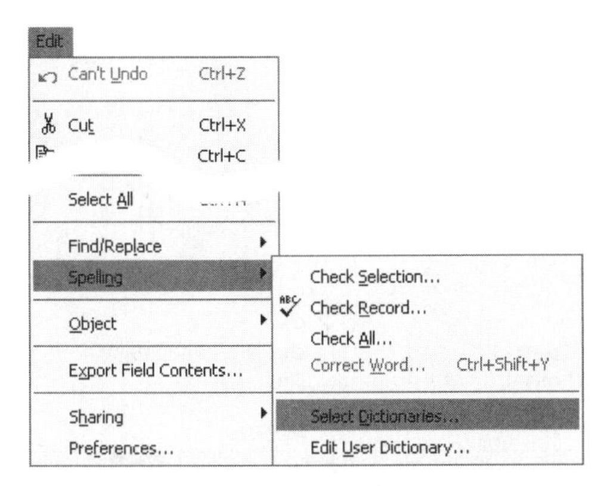

Figure 6.3 To create or select a dictionary, choose Edit > Spelling > Select Dictionaries.

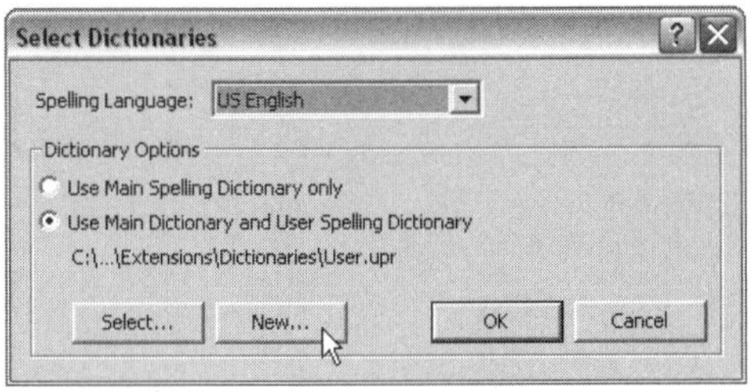

Figure 6.4 To create additional user dictionaries, click *New* in the Select Dictionaries dialog box.

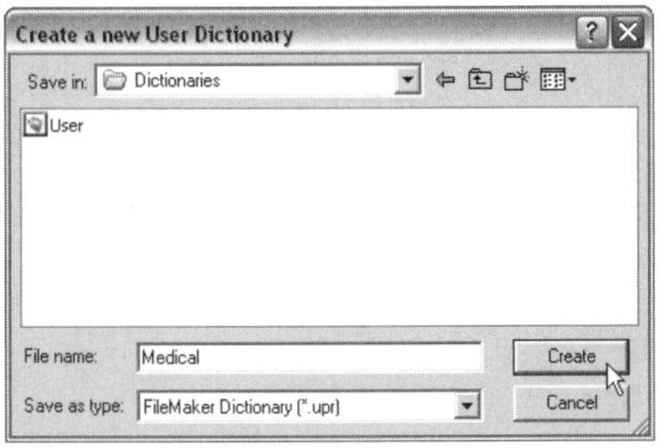

Figure 6.5 Give any additional user dictionary an easy-to-remember name, such as *Medical* for a special medical dictionary.

To create additional user dictionaries:

1. Choose Edit > Spelling > Select Dictionaries (**Figure 6.3**).
2. In the dialog box that appears, click *New* (**Figure 6.4**). When the Create a new User Dictionary dialog box appears, navigate to `...\FileMaker Pro 8\Extensions\Dictionaries\` and type in an easy-to-remember name for your new dictionary, such as *Medical* for a special medical dictionary (**Figure 6.5**). Once you're done, click *Create*.
3. When the Select Dictionaries dialog box reappears, the just-created special dictionary will be activated, along with the main dictionary (**Figure 6.6**). Click *OK* to close the dialog box.

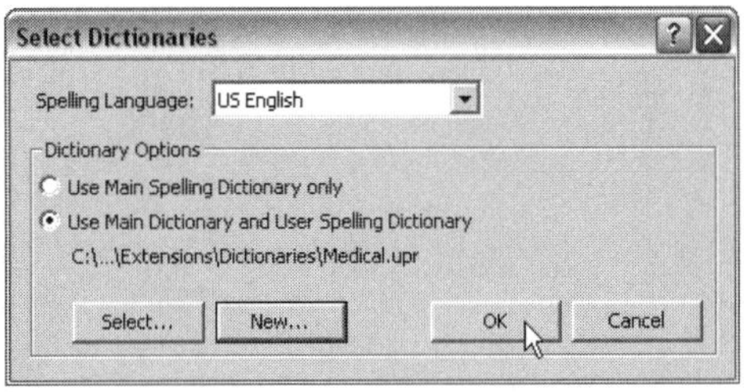

Figure 6.6 When the Select Dictionaries dialog box reappears, click *OK*.

To switch spelling language:

1. Choose Edit > Spelling > Select Dictionaries (**Figure 6.3**).
2. In the dialog box that appears, click the *Spelling Language* drop-down menu and choose another language (**Figure 6.7**).
3. To apply your new choice and close the dialog box, click *OK* (**Figure 6.8**).

✔ Tip

- Occasionally, you may want to check words only against the *main* dictionary and not use any *user* dictionaries. To do so, choose Edit > Spelling > Select Dictionaries. Within the dialog box that appears, click the *Use Main Spelling Dictionary only* button, and click OK to apply the choice and close the dialog box.

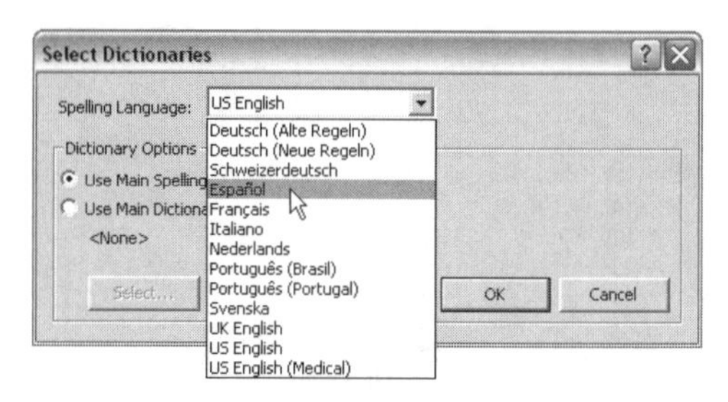

Figure 6.7 To switch to another language, make a choice from the drop-down menu.

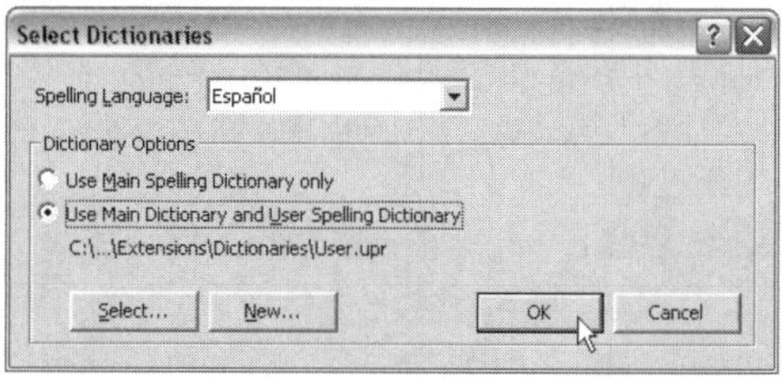

Figure 6.8 To apply your new language choice and close the dialog box, click *OK*.

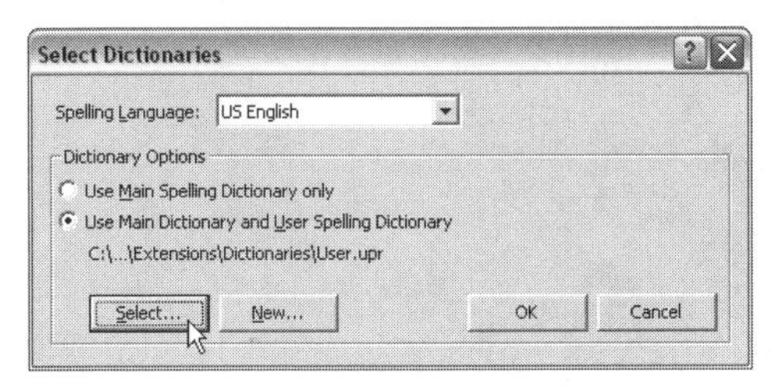

Figure 6.9 To switch user dictionaries, click *Select*.

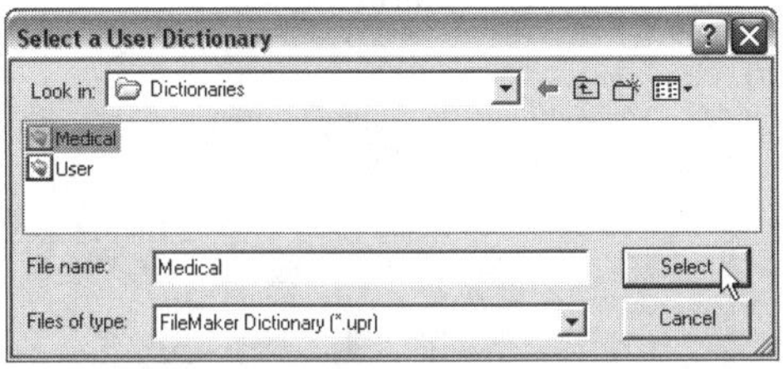

Figure 6.10 Click on the name of the dictionary you want to use and click *Select*.

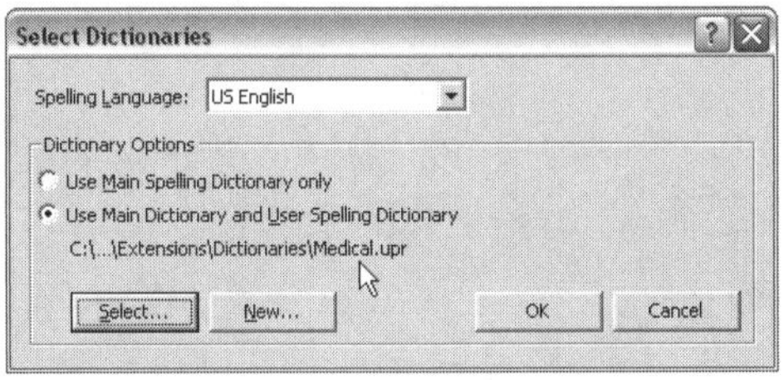

Figure 6.11 The newly selected user dictionary will be listed as active in the Select Dictionaries dialog box.

To select or switch user dictionaries:

1. Choose Edit > Spelling > Select Dictionaries (**Figure 6.3**).
2. In the dialog box that appears, click *Select* (**Figure 6.9**).
3. If you previously created a user dictionary, FileMaker will open the Dictionaries folder automatically; otherwise navigate to `...\FileMaker Pro 8\Extensions\Dictionaries\`. Click on the dictionary you want to use and click *Select* (**Figure 6.10**).
4. When the Select Dictionaries dialog box reappears, the dictionary you chose will be listed as the active user dictionary (**Figure 6.11**). Click *OK* to close the dialog box.

Editing User Dictionaries

Editing a dictionary lets you add and remove words one by one or import an existing text file of special terms you've created in another application (Microsoft Word in our example).

To edit a user dictionary:

1. First make sure you've selected the right dictionary to edit. (See *To select or switch user dictionaries* on the previous page.) Choose Edit > Spelling > Edit User Dictionary (**Figure 6.12**).
2. When the dictionary's dialog box appears, type the word you want to add into the *Entry* text box, then click *Add* (**Figure 6.13**). To remove words, navigate through the list within the lower text box, click on the word you want removed, and click *Remove*. You can continue adding or removing words one by one until you're done. If you've already built a list of special terms in another application, you can use this dialog box to import them as a text file (see *To import or export a text file* on the next page.)
3. When you're done editing the dictionary, click *OK* to close the dialog box.

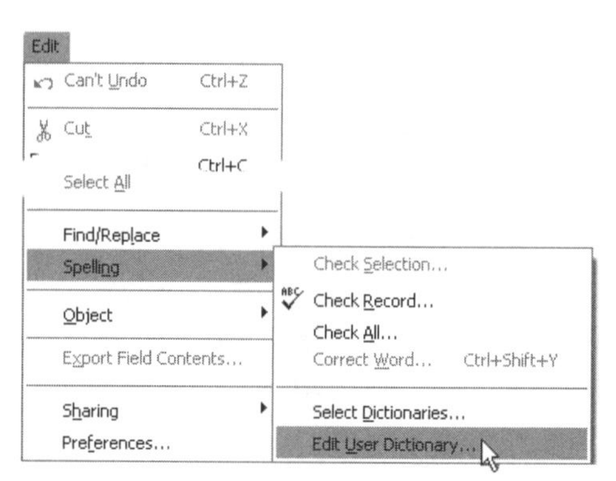

Figure 6.12 To change dictionary entries, choose Edit > Spelling > Edit User Dictionary.

User Dictionary
Entry
Fairmont
Add
User Dictionary
Ashbury
Remove
Import...
Export...
OK
Cancel

Figure 6.13 Within the User Dictionary dialog box, type in the word you want, then click *Add*. (Choose *Remove* to delete selected words from the dictionary.)

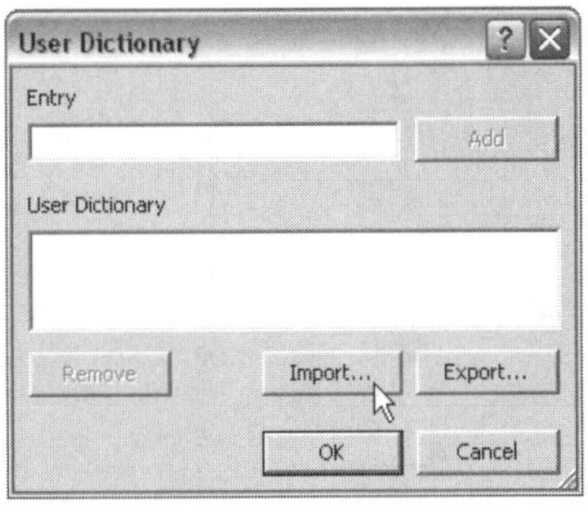

Figure 6.14 To import (or export) a file of special terms, click *Import* or *Export*.

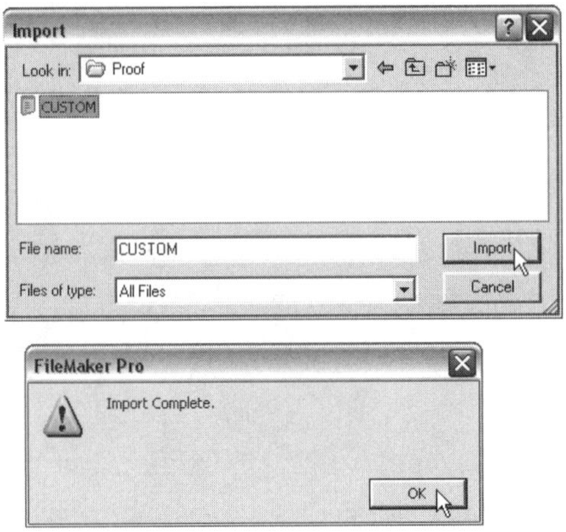

Figure 6.15 Navigate to the file you want to import (here it's a Microsoft Word dictionary) and click *Import* (top). When an alert dialog box confirms that the import is finished, click *OK* (bottom).

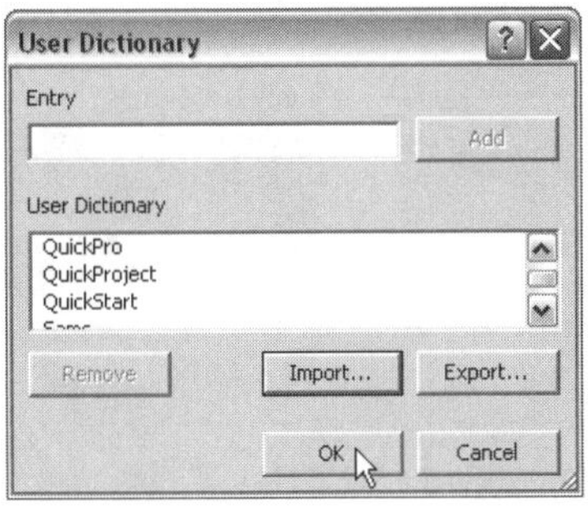

Figure 6.16 The imported file's words are added to the FileMaker dictionary. Click *OK* to close the dialog box.

To import or export a text file:

1. Within FileMaker, choose Edit > Spelling > Edit User Dictionary (**Figure 6.12**).
2. When the dictionary's dialog box appears, click *Import* or *Export* when the buttons appear (**Figure 6.14**). (Click *Export* if you want to use a FileMaker dictionary in another application.)
3. Navigate to the file you want to import (a Microsoft Word dictionary in our example). Once you find it, click *Import* (top, **Figure 6.15**). When the alert dialog box appears, confirming that the import or export is finished, click *OK* to close the dialog box (bottom, **Figure 6.15**).
4. The file's words will be added to your user dictionary (**Figure 6.16**). Click *OK* to close the dictionary dialog box.

Handling misspelled words

When you're creating new records, FileMaker can help reduce errors by highlighting words that may be misspelled. FileMaker also offers options for changing questionably spelled words without running a spell check on the entire database.

To highlight misspelled words:

1. Within FileMaker, choose File > File Options (**Figure 6.17**).
2. When the File Options dialog box appears, click the *Spelling* tab (**Figure 6.18**). If you want FileMaker to simply underline questionable words in red, select the checkbox. If you want a more obvious warning, select *Beep on questionable spellings* or (in Windows) *Flash menubar on questionable spellings.*
3. Click *OK* to apply the setting and close the dialog box.

To correct highlighted words:

1. When FileMaker highlights a word as misspelled, right-click (Windows) or Control-click (Mac) the word (**Figure 6.19**).
2. When the drop-down menu appears, choose *Suggested Spellings* and then either pick a suggestion or choose *Ignore All* or *Learn Spelling*. Release the cursor and the choice will be applied.

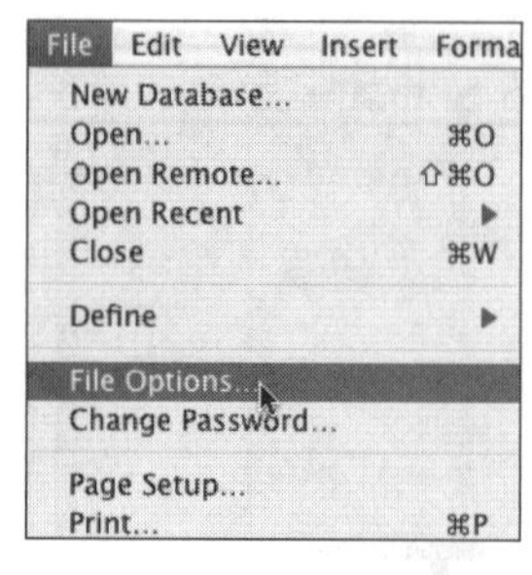

Figure 6.17 To set a FileMaker database to highlight misspelled words, choose File > File Options.

Figure 6.18 To simply underline questionable words in red, select the checkbox. If you want a more obvious warning, select *Beep on questionable spellings* or (bottom in Windows) *Flash menubar on questionable spellings*.

Figure 6.19 To correct a highlighted word, right-click (Windows) or Control-click (Mac) the word, choose *Suggested Spellings*, and make a choice in the sub-menu.

Printing

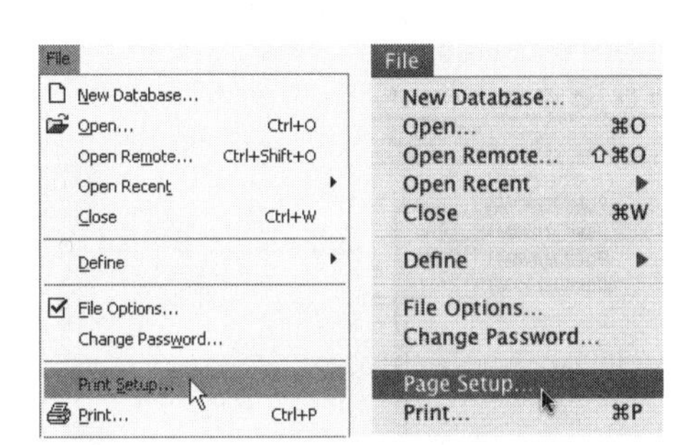

Figure 7.1 To change your printer, choose File > Print Setup (Windows) or Page Setup (Mac).

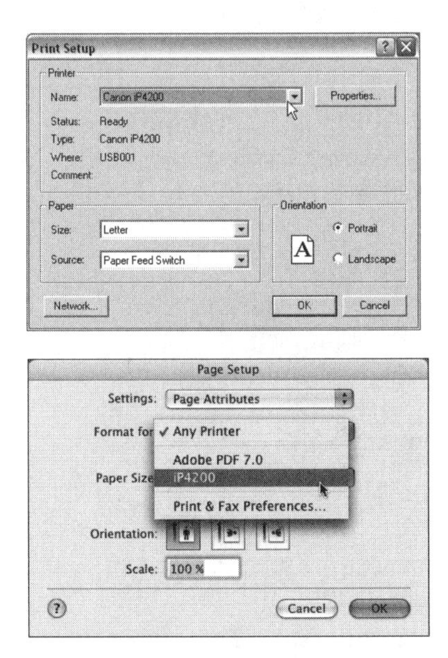

Figure 7.2 Use the drop-down menu of connected printers to select another printer.

In general, printing in FileMaker is not too different from printing in your other applications. But there are a few twists worth considering, so read on.

To change the default printer:

- Choose File > Print Setup (Windows) or File > Page Setup (Mac) (**Figure 7.1**). When the setup dialog box appears, select a new printer using the drop-down menu (**Figure 7.2**). Make sure your page margins are correct by checking the *Paper/Paper Size* and *Orientation* settings. When you're done, click *OK*.

✔ Tip

- This is necessary only if you want to use a *different* printer for FileMaker files than your regular printer. Otherwise, just choose File > Print and FileMaker will automatically use the settings of your default printer.

To show layout margins:

- Switch to Layout mode (Ctrl L in Windows, ⌘ L on the Mac), and choose View > Page Margins (**Figure 7.3**). The page margin is marked by a gray boundary, while the edge of the paper is marked by a darker boundary (**Figure 7.4**).

To set layout margins:

1. First, make sure you have the right paper size selected by choosing File > Print Setup (Windows) or File > Page Setup (Mac) and selecting your paper as necessary using the drop-down menus.
2. Switch to Layout mode (Ctrl L in Windows, ⌘ L on the Mac), and choose Layouts > Layout Setup (**Figure 7.5**).
3. When the Layout Setup dialog box appears (**Figure 7.6**), select the *Use fixed page margins* checkbox and use the four number-entry boxes to adjust your *Top*, *Bottom*, *Left*, and *Right* margins. Check *Facing Pages* to account for a narrower inside margin if you'll be printing on both sides of the paper.
4. Click *OK*.

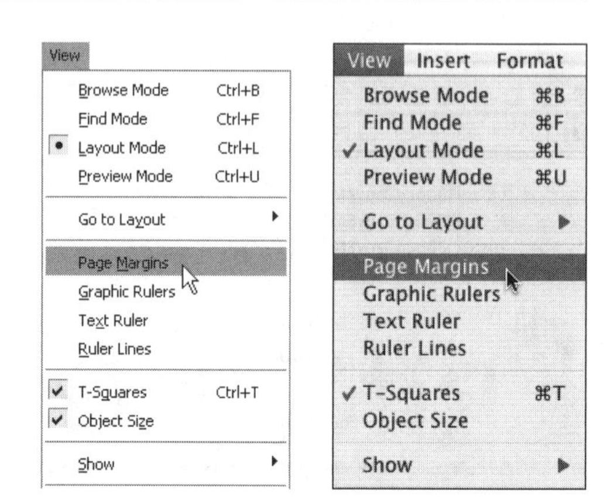

Figure 7.3 Check your margins by switching to Layout mode and choosing View > Page Margins.

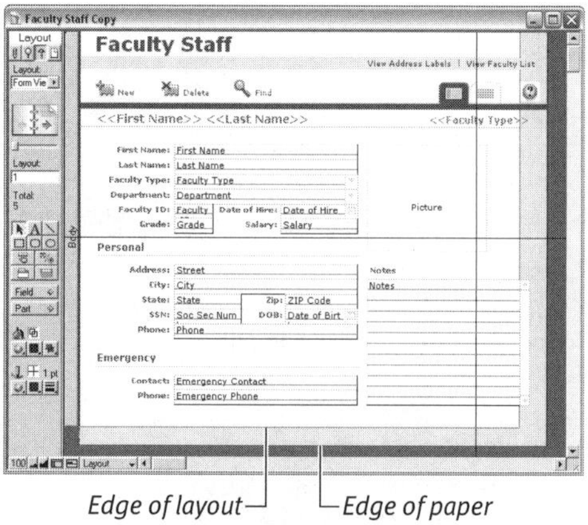

Edge of layout *Edge of paper*

Figure 7.4 A gray boundary marks the layout's edge; a darker boundary the paper's edge.

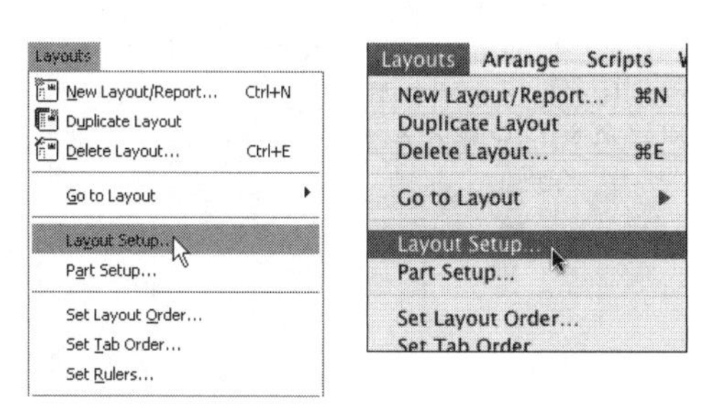

Figure 7.5 Choose Layouts > Layout Setup to change margins.

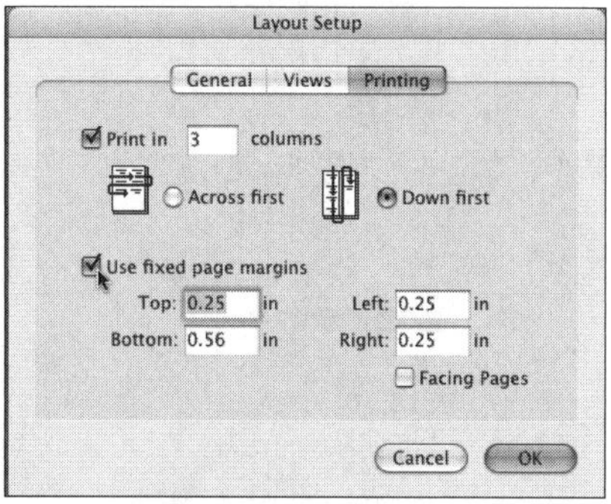

Figure 7.6 Select *Use fixed page margins* and enter new numbers to adjust your *Top*, *Bottom*, *Left*, and *Right* margins.

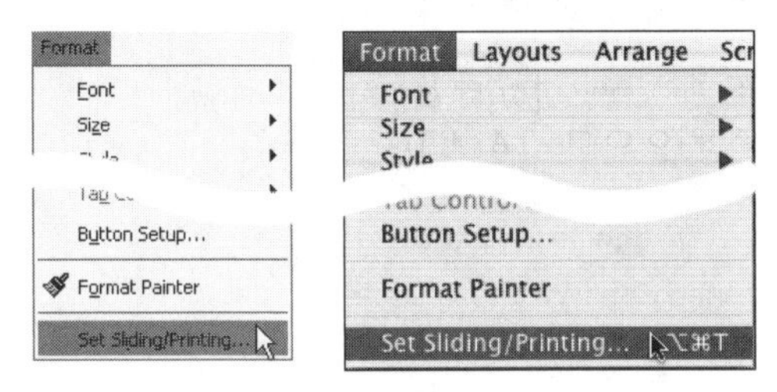

Figure 7.7 The problem with fixed field size printouts: Giving *Beauregard* enough room makes *Al* space out.

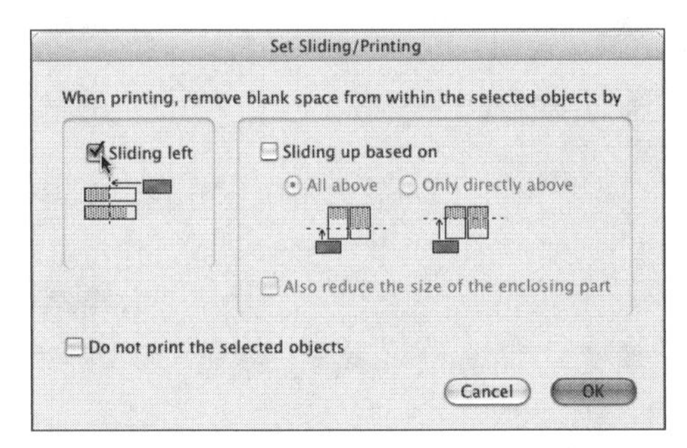

Figure 7.8 To remove unwanted space in fields or parts, choose Format > Set Sliding/Printing.

Figure 7.9 Within the Set Sliding/Printing dialog box, check *Sliding left* to close horizontal gaps or *Sliding up based on* to close vertical gaps in fields or parts.

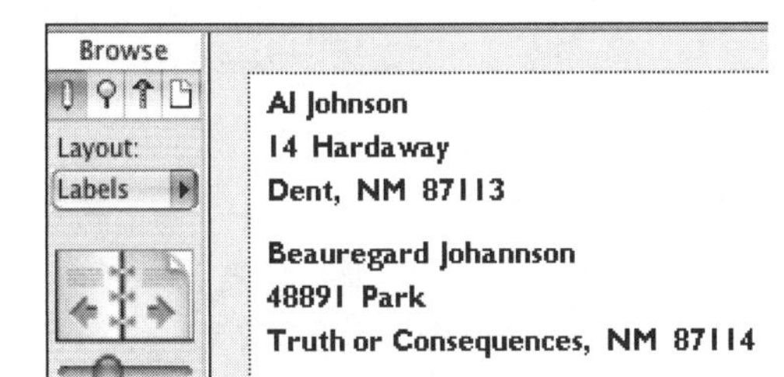

Figure 7.10 With sliding activated, the field size printouts match their entries.

Removing Unwanted Space

Data varies: some runs long, some short (**Figure 7.7**). To eliminate wasted field space, create a neater printout—and keep Al and Beauregard happy—you want to use a feature FileMaker calls "sliding." With sliding, FileMaker automatically closes up unused space either to the left or above any fields you select. The great thing about sliding is that FileMaker only applies it when necessary. If you have a field with a long text entry, it gets the room it needs.

To remove unwanted spaces:

1. Switch to Layout mode (Ctrl L in Windows, ⌘ L on the Mac).
2. Use the Pointer Tool to select all the fields you want to make sure are closed up properly. Choose Format > Set Sliding/Printing (Option ⌘ T on the Mac, no Windows equivalent) (**Figure 7.8**).
3. When the Set Sliding/Printing dialog box appears, check the *Sliding left* box (**Figure 7.9**). (Check *Sliding up based on* to control vertical spacing in a layout, especially within layout *parts.*) Click *OK.*
4. Switch to Preview Mode (Ctrl U in Windows, ⌘ U on the Mac) to see the change (**Figure 7.10**).

✔ Tips

- Sliding can be applied to objects, along with layout items that aren't in a field, such as lines you've placed in a layout for visual effect. In both cases, just select the item and apply sliding using the Format menu.
- Sliding only works on the body; headers and footers won't slide. Instead, see *To resize a part* on page 169.

To preview a printout:

- Choose View > Preview Mode (Ctrl U in Windows, ⌘U on the Mac) to see if your printout will be just as you want it (**Figure 7.11**).

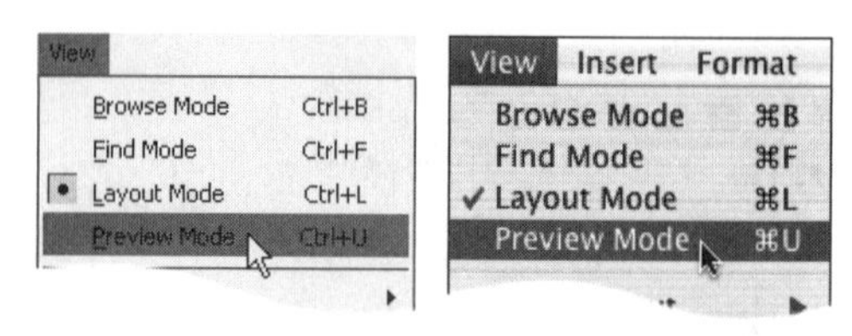

Figure 7.11 Before printing, you can choose View > Preview Mode or use your keyboard: Ctrl U (Windows) or ⌘U (Mac).

To print:

1. Switch to the layout you want to print from and run any needed Find Requests or Sorts. Choose File > Print (Ctrl P in Windows, ⌘P on the Mac).
2. When the Print dialog box appears:

   [W] Use the Print drop-down list (**Figure 7.12**) to determine whether you print all the records being browsed (the found set), only the current record, or a blank record with the fields showing.

   [M] Use the drop-down menu to choose *FileMaker Pro* (**Figure 7.13**). When the FileMaker settings appear in the lower portion of the Print dialog box (**Figure 7.14**), use the radio buttons to choose whether you print all the records being browsed (the found set), only the current record, or a blank record with the fields showing. A drop-down menu for the blank record option lets you choose whether you want fields in blank records printed as formatted, with boxes, or with underlines.
3. Once you've set your other choices (print range and number of copies), click *OK* (Windows) or *Print* (Mac).

Figure 7.12 In Windows, the Print drop-down list lets you choose which FileMaker records you print.

Figure 7.13 Use the Print dialog box's drop-down menu to reach the FileMaker settings.

Figure 7.14 When the FileMaker settings appear in the lower portion of the Print dialog box, use the radio buttons to control which FileMaker records print.

✔ Tip

- Printing out a script can be a terrific way to troubleshoot any problems that you can't quite find. Sometimes you see on paper what you can't see on the screen.

Part III

Creating Databases

Planning Databases

The time you spend in this little chapter with nothing more than a notepad and your thoughts will save you hours of frustration later at the keyboard. Here's the secret to successful databases: they're not really about data, they're about people and how they work together. It might seem odd, but the data itself shouldn't dictate the database design. Instead, let an organization's processes among its people and groups drive the design.

Start with basic questions: Where does the group's information come from? Who knows what? Who needs what? Why is it done that way? And, most importantly, what does the group *wish* the database could do? Obviously, a mere database cannot solve every problem—and you don't have forever to finish the job. But by taking time upfront to talk to users about their needs, the organization's structure, and its information flow, you'll build a better database.

Even organizations that don't already have a database still have information flows, whether it's hidden in paper memos, electronic spreadsheets, or the brains of those folks you find in every office who seem to know where everything's kept. Now, let's start small and keep it simple. So, step away from the computer. That's right...nice and slow...

The Process: Start to Finish

Step 1—Make a rough pass: To start, stay focused on the problem you want to solve. For example, "I want to track orders of my products from customers." Put another way, ask yourself, "What are the connections (or relations) among those items?" In this case, customers place orders for products and, so, orders contain specific products for specific customers. Now, let's grab a pencil—and eraser—to generate some lists based on that statement.

Those three broad categories serve as starting points for creating three related—but separate—databases. The specific bits of information you might track, such as addresses, the status of orders, and product descriptions, naturally become the individual fields you'll list within the appropriate database. As your rough list of fields and possible databases grows, draw some boxes and arrows to sketch out how you might organize the data (**Figure 8.1**).

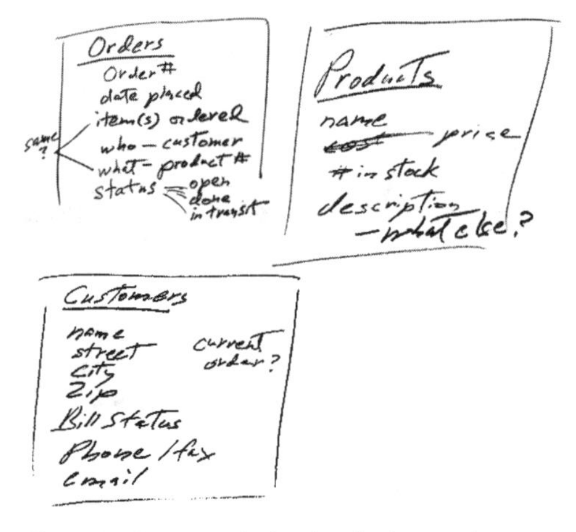

Figure 8.1 Use a rough sketch to brainstorm how you might organize your data.

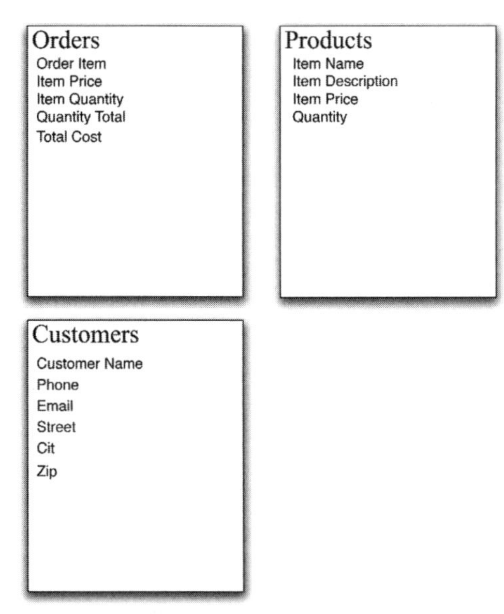

Figure 8.2 Create a cleaned-up list of possible fields and databases, then gather comments from users.

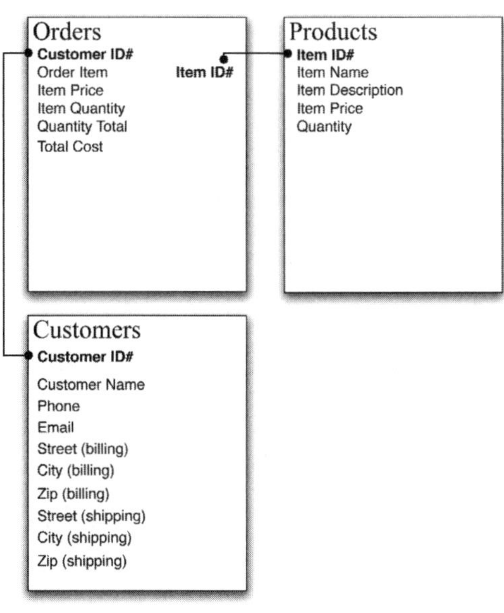

Figure 8.3 Refine your list of fields based on user comments and add match fields to link the related databases.

Step 2—Get comments, refine formal list: Clean up your rough sketch and use the result to start gathering comments and reactions from possible users (**Figure 8.2**). The goal here is to see if you've overlooked any necessary fields or databases, and showing your own list will help others focus on what's missing. Maybe someone wants a picture for each product. In our example, someone suggested using separate fields for billing and shipping addresses. What else is missing?

Based on everyone's comments, as you refine the list, you'll find that most fields naturally fall into *one* of the possible databases. If you find people asking that the *same field* appear in *several* databases, that's usually a sign that you need to link the databases using what FileMaker calls a *match field*. For example, customer names naturally go in the Customers database but you also might want each record in the Orders database to show who placed the order. Match fields let you create a *relation* between the databases so that you can display customer names within the Orders database without duplicating data already in the Customers database. These *relational databases* keep everything speedy without bulking up any single database with extraneous data. So, in our example list of needed fields, we've added a *Customer ID#* match field to link the Customers database and the Orders database (**Figure 8.3**). Similarly, we've added an *Item ID#* match field to link the Orders database and the Products database.

Step 3—Define fields and relationships: Once you've settled on a list of necessary fields and databases, you'll use FileMaker to define the fields, including those match fields (**Figure 8.4**). Hold off touching your computer just yet. The details of defining fields are explained in *Defining Fields* on page 93.

The Define Database dialog box, the same one you'll use to define your fields, includes a tab for defining your other databases. That makes it easy to switch among the databases as you continue defining fields (**Figure 8.5**). To link the related databases, you then switch to the Define Database dialog box's Relationships tab. Using its click-and-drag tools, you draw lines between your match fields and, presto, you create a set of relational databases (**Figures 8.6–8.7**). The details are explained in *Creating Relational Databases* on page 125.

The best part of the process is that FileMaker doesn't lock you into figuring it all out upfront. At any time, you can go back and add more fields, databases, and links. Don't bog down trying to think of everything right now. Instead, consider the layouts you'll need to clearly organize all that data.

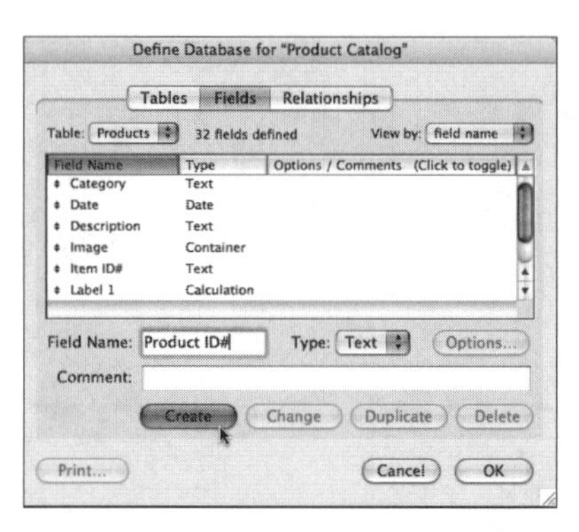

Figure 8.4 Once you have a list of necessary fields and databases, you create them using the Define Database dialog box.

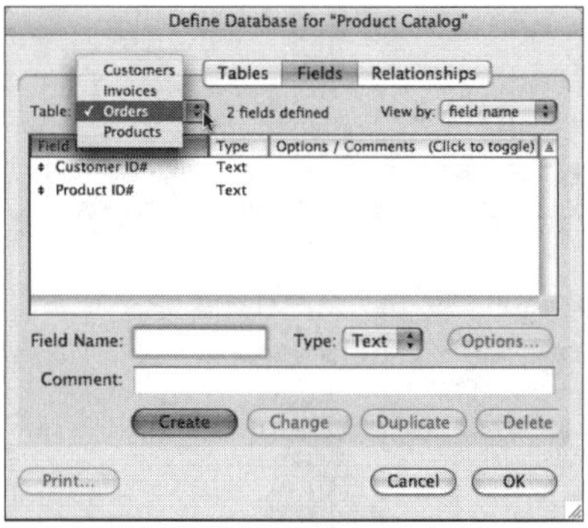

Figure 8.5 The Define Database dialog box lets you easily switch between defining fields and defining databases.

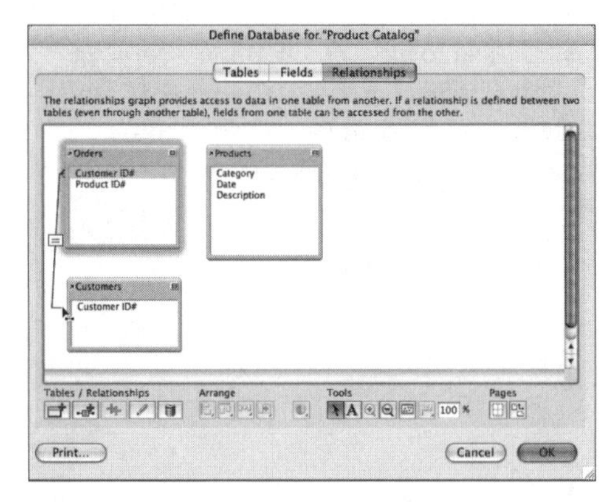

Figure 8.6 The Relationships tab lets you use click-and-drag tools to draw connections between your match fields.

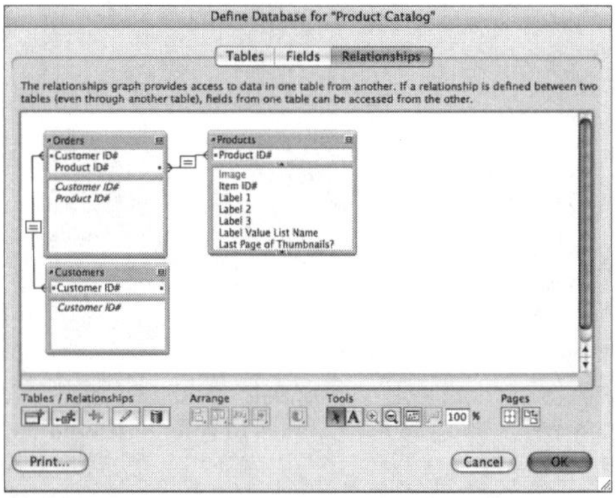

Figure 8.7 FileMaker makes it easy to create and understand the relational links among your databases.

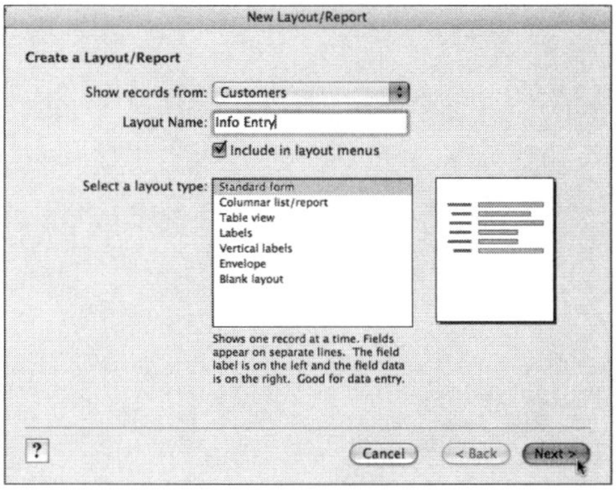

Figure 8.8 Use the New Layout/Report dialog box to choose among basic layout forms.

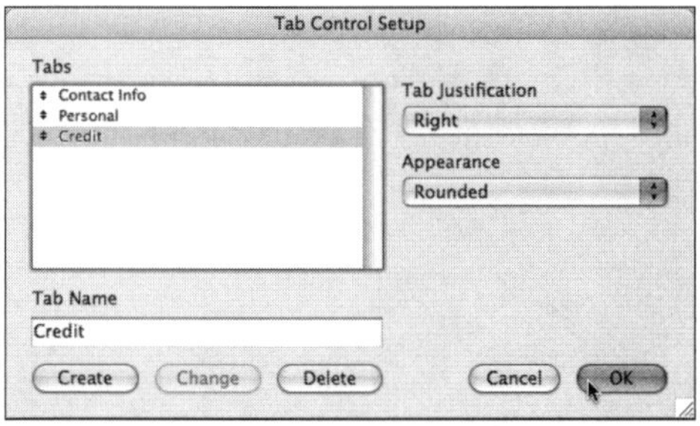

Figure 8.9 Use the Tab Control Setup dialog box to quickly generate a list of layout tabs.

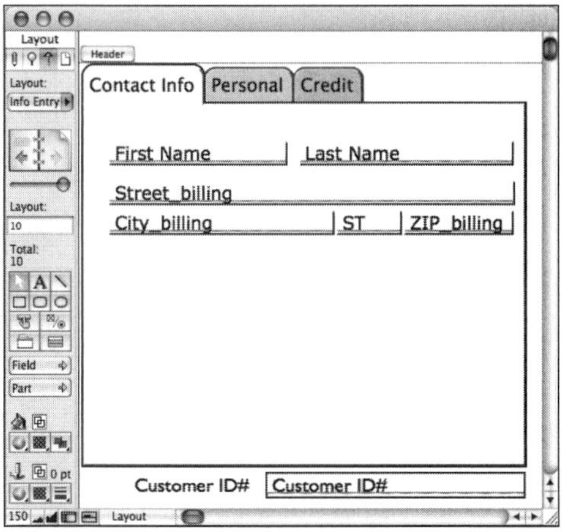

Figure 8.10 Tabbed layouts make it easy to store lots of information in an at-a-glance design.

Step 4—Create layouts: In general, you'll want to create a separate layout for each major task: entering customer data, printing mail labels, generating order invoices, etc. Also consider creating different layouts for each type of user. Sales folks, for example, probably need to see different data than accountants.

A good place to start is FileMaker's Standard form layout, which lends itself to capturing most of the basic information you'll need for each particular database, such as customer data (**Figure 8.8**).

FileMaker's new tabbed layouts make it easy to tuck database clutter out of sight so that users can focus on the information they need (**Figures 8.9–8.10**). See *Creating Layouts* on page 143. To make layouts easy on the eyes and easy to understand, see *Layout Formatting and Graphics* on page 197. For more information on using lookups and portals to link related databases, see *Creating Relational Databases* on page 125.

Step 5—Review once more, then populate: Before you begin adding information to the still-empty database (called populating it), run your design by key users for one last look. After making any adjustments, your new relational database is ready to start accepting information record by record or by importing existing data. See *Changing Formats* on page 225.

Remember: Like a Web site, a database is never really finished. Inevitably, you and its users will find ways to improve it and expand its usefulness. For now, at least, step back and give everyone time to settle into using your new database.

9

DEFINING FIELDS

Before you can start adding information to a database, you need to create the fields that will contain the information. Creating the fields is a two-step process: you define the fields by giving them names and then set options for what kind of data can be added to those fields. Controlling the *appearance* of your database is covered separately in *Creating Layouts* starting on page 143.

Choosing a Field Type

FileMaker's eight different types of fields are assigned using the *Type* drop-down menu in the Define Database dialog box (**Figure 9.1**). For step-by-step instructions on using this dialog box, see *To define a field* on page 96. (See *Storage options* on page 104 for information about global fields.) But first, here's a quick rundown on the best uses for each field type:

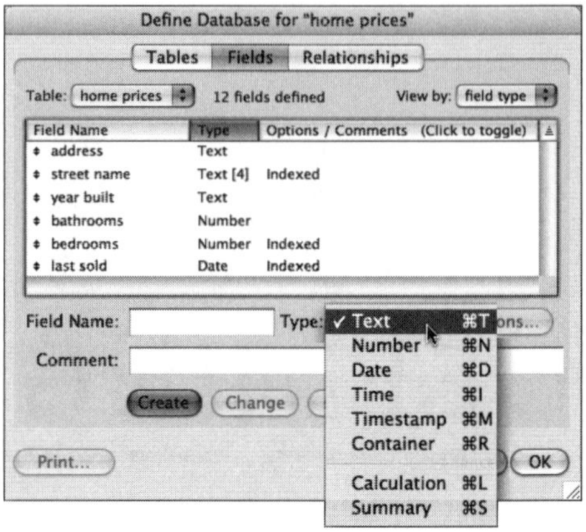

- **Text:** A text field can contain up to 1 billion characters (letters, symbols, and numbers as text). Text fields can be sorted (usually A–Z or Z–A) and used in formulas. Even items that might not at first blush seem to be text sometimes should be placed in text fields. For example, telephone numbers usually contain non-numeric hyphens or slashes, and so are best made into text fields.
- **Number:** A number field can contain up to 800 characters (numbers or other characters, which will not be treated as numbers). Number fields can be sorted (1–100 or 100–1) and used in formulas for calculations and summary fields. Also used for Boolean values (0, 1) to represent true/false or yes/no.
- **Date:** Can contain only dates in the format of 1/1/1975 and 12/28/2008. They can be sorted (earliest-latest or latest-earliest) and used in formulas for calculations and summary fields. Be sure to use four digits for years. For more, see *Validation options* on page 102.
- **Time:** Can only contain the hours, minutes, and seconds of a time. Time fields can be sorted (earliest-latest or latest-earliest) and used in formulas for calculations and summary fields.

Figure 9.1 Choose your field type using the *Type* drop-down menu in the Define Database dialog box.

- **Timestamp:** Contains a specific date and time and can be used as a reference point in calculations.
- **Container:** Holds graphics, photos, sounds, movies, QuickTime multimedia files, or Object Linking and Embedding (OLE) objects (Windows only), or documents (PDFs, Microsoft Word or Excel files). Container fields cannot be sorted, but can be used in formulas for calculations and summary fields. While container fields cannot contain text or numbers, you can create—and sort—related text or number fields to describe a container field's contents. See *Understanding Formulas* on page 114 and *Using Calculation and Summary Fields* on page 119.
- **Calculation:** These fields display the results of calculations made using other fields and so cannot have values typed directly into them. The result can be text, a number, date, time, timestamp, or container. With the exception of summary functions, calculation fields operate on data *within single records*. See *Using Calculation and Summary Fields* on page 119.
- **Summary:** Like calculation fields, summary fields cannot have values entered directly into them. Instead, they display summary values based on other fields in the database. In general, summary fields operate on data *from a group of records*. See *Using Calculation and Summary Fields* on page 119.

Defining and Changing Fields

As you create fields for your database, you'll need to assign names and field types (for example, text or number), then choose how they will be displayed. The following steps cover most field types. For information on defining calculation and summary fields, see pages 119 and 124.

To define a field:

1. To create a field, choose File > Define > Database (**Figure 9.2**). Or use your keyboard: Ctrl Shift D (Windows) or Shift ⌘ D (Mac).
2. When the Define Database dialog box appears, the *Fields* tab is selected automatically. Type the name of your first field in the *Field Name* text box (**Figure 9.3**).
3. Choose the type of field you want from the dialog box's *Type* drop-down menu (**Figure 9.4**). For more on deciding which field type best suits your needs, see *Choosing a Field Type* on page 94.
4. Once you click the *Create* button, the name of your new field appears in the center window of the Define Database dialog box (**Figure 9.5**).
5. At this point, you can repeat the steps to create another field. Or you can further define your field by highlighting its name in the center window of the Define Database dialog box and then clicking the *Options* button. See *Setting Field Entry Options* on page 98.
6. When you've finished creating fields (you can always add more later), click *OK* to close the dialog box. FileMaker then displays the created fields in Browse mode. To dress up a field's appearance and layout, see *Creating Layouts* on page 143.

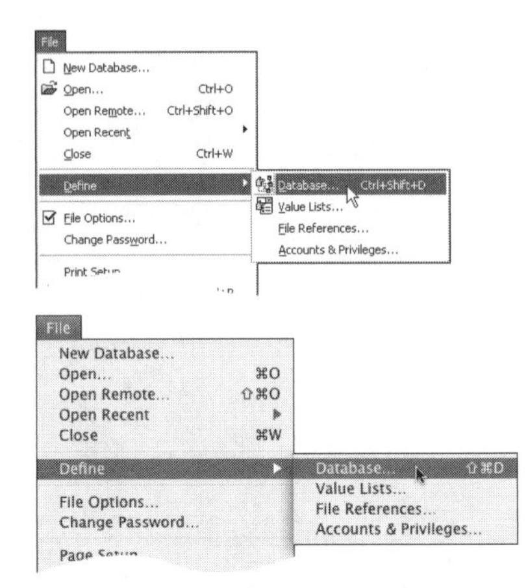

Figure 9.2 To create a field, choose File > Define > Database.

Figure 9.3 Assign a name to a new field within the Define Database dialog box.

✔ Tip

- In naming your fields, FileMaker prevents you from using any of the symbols or words it needs to calculate functions: , (comma), +, *, /, ^, &, =, >, <, (,), ", ;, :, AND, OR, XOR, NOT. You also cannot use words that are the names of FileMaker functions, such as *Status*, *Count*, or *Sum*. One last thing: Don't start a file name with a period or a number.

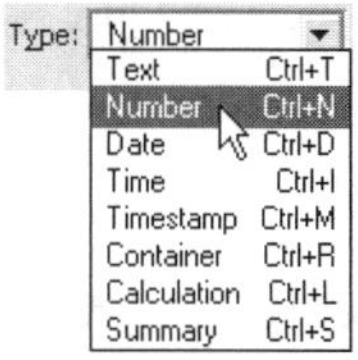

Figure 9.4 The *Type* drop-down menu in the Define Database dialog box offers a choice of eight field types.

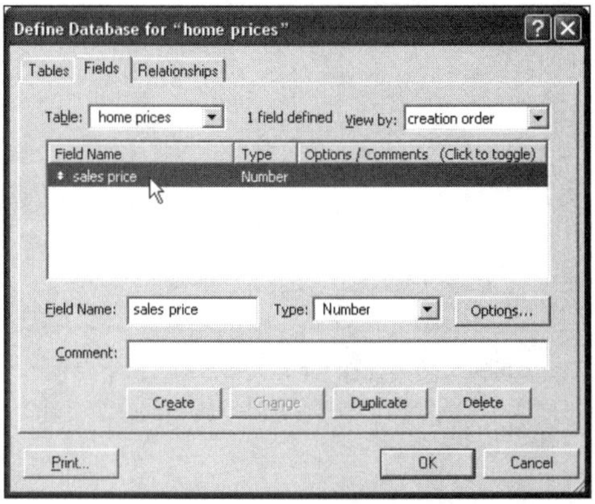

Figure 9.5 Once you create a field, its name appears in the list of fields within the Define Database dialog box.

To delete or add a field:

1. Choose File > Define > Database (Ctrl Shift D in Windows, Shift ⌘ D on the Mac) to open the Define Database dialog box where the *Fields* tab is automatically selected (**Figure 9.3**).
2. To *delete* a field, click on its name in the center window, then click the *Delete* button. When the warning dialog box appears, again click *Delete*.

   To *add* a field, type the new field's name into the Field Name text box, make a selection from the *Type* drop-down menu, and click the *Create* button.
3. When you're ready, click *OK* to close the dialog box.

To change a field's name or type:

1. Choose File > Define > Database (Ctrl Shift D in Windows, Shift ⌘ D on the Mac) to open the Define Database dialog box where the *Fields* tab is automatically selected (**Figure 9.3**).
2. To change the *name* of a field, click on its name in the center text window and type a new name into the *Field Name* text window.

   To change a field's *type*, highlight the field in the center text window, then find and select your new type choice in the *Type* drop-down menu.
3. Click *OK* to close the dialog box.

Setting Field Entry Options

FileMaker's Options dialog box offers several powerful tools for speeding data entry and ensuring it meets certain standards. If more than one person will be entering data into the database, these options can reduce keyboard mistakes and problem-generating format variations. The options can be set while you're defining fields—or added later.

FileMaker lets you customize your field entries for three general areas: Auto-Enter, Validation, and Storage. See page 100 (Auto-Enter), page 102 (Validation), and page 104 (Storage options). (Furigana is a Japanese-only option.)

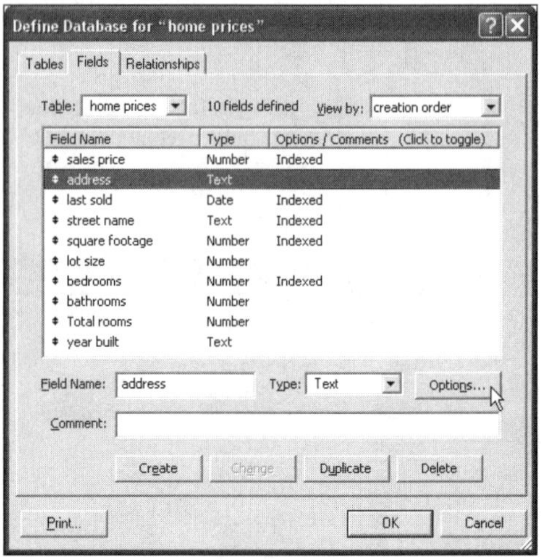

To set field entry options:

1. Whether you want to set entry options for a new field or add them to an existing field, the steps are the same: Choose File > Define > Database. Or use your keyboard: Ctrl Shift D (Windows) or Shift ⌘ D (Mac).
2. In the center window of the Define Database dialog box, select a field, then click the *Options* button (**Figure 9.6**). Or use the shortcut: double-click in the list on the field you want.

Figure 9.6 Double-click the field whose entry options you want to modify or click the *Options* button.

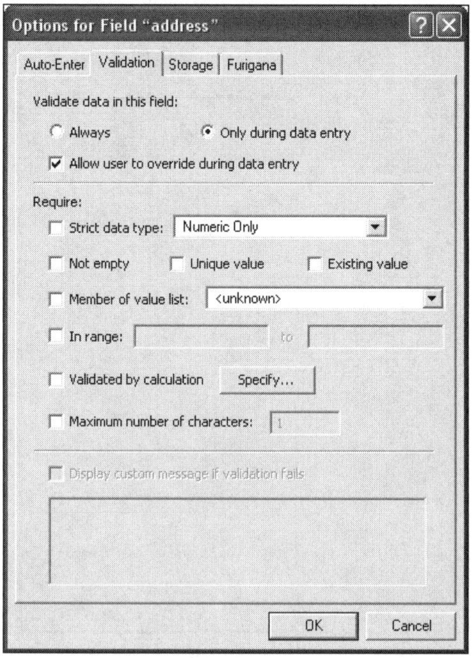

Figure 9.7 The tabs in the Options dialog box control the Auto-Enter, Validation, and Storage settings. (Furigana is a Japanese-only option.)

Figure 9.8 To switch among the Auto-Enter, Validation, and Storage settings, just click a tab.

3. When the options dialog box appears, make your selections. Of the three functions handled by the dialog box (*Auto-Enter*, *Validation*, and *Storage*), only one appears at a time (**Figure 9.7**). Click any of the tabs to reach the desired function (**Figure 9.8**). Once you're done, click *OK* to close the dialog box.
4. The Define Database dialog box reappears. If you want to set entry options for another field, repeat steps 2 and 3. Once you're ready, click *OK* to close the dialog box.
5. Though you've changed the entry options for a field, its *display* remains the same until you change the layout.

Auto-Enter options

Follow steps 1–3 in *To set field entry options* on page 98 to reach the Auto-Enter options (**Figure 9.9**). Here's how each functions:

- **Creation:** Use the first checkbox and its related drop-down menu (**Date, Time, Timestamp, Name, Account Name**) to have the date or time when a record is created or modified entered automatically (**Figure 9.10**). It can also automatically enter the name of the person who originally created the record or the name of the person who most recently changed the record. Your choice here must conform with the type of field you've created: If you've already defined the field type as Date, the *Creator Name* and *Modifier Name* choices won't be available.
- **Modification:** Use this option and its related drop-down menu as you would the *Creation* options above.
- **Serial number:** Use this option and its related radio buttons and text window to generate a unique number for every record in a database. It's particularly useful for invoices and other records that need one-of-a-kind identifiers. Once you've checked the *Serial number* box, you can then use the *next value* box to set the starting number for the next record. Starting numbers can include text at the front, such as A100 or Bin10. Use the *increment by* box to control whether the serial numbers increase in steps of 1, 2, 5, 10, or whatever.
- **Value from last visited record:** This checkbox can save you a bit of keyboarding if you're creating a series of records where some of the fields need to contain the same value.

Figure 9.9 The Auto-Enter panel's eight checkboxes control the automatic entry of values into selected fields.

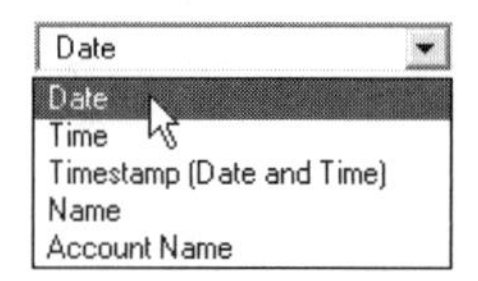

Figure 9.10 The Auto-Enter drop-down menu triggers the entry of dates, times, or names related to when a field is created or modified.

- **Data:** Use this checkbox and the related text window to have a bit of text or a number automatically appear in a particular field.
- **Calculated value:** Use this checkbox and the *Specify* button to automatically enter the results of any formula you choose. See *Using Calculation and Summary Fields* on page 119.
- **Looked-up value:** Use this checkbox and the *Specify* button to enter a value from another database. See *Creating Relational Databases* on page 125.
- **Prohibit modification of value during data entry:** This checkbox only becomes active if you've checked one of the previous boxes. Use it to ensure that a field's data isn't improperly changed. See the *Strict, Display custom message* choices under Validation options.

Validation options

Follow steps 1–3 in *To set field entry options* on page 98 to reach the Validation options (**Figure 9.11**). These options ensure that data entered in the fields you select is correctly formatted.

- **Strict data type:** Use this checkbox and its related drop-down menu to automatically create a Numeric Only, 4-Digit Year Date, or Time of Day type of field. The 4-Digit Year Date choice, which uses the format 2000 instead of 00, is intended to avoid Y2K problems. If FileMaker encounters a 2-digit year date, it uses this rule: numbers in the 90–99 range are converted to 1990–1999; numbers in the 00–10 are converted to 2000–2010.
- **Not empty, Unique value, Existing value:** Use the first checkbox to make sure a field isn't skipped during data entry. The other two checkboxes work in opposing ways—*Unique* ensures that a record contains a one-of-a-kind value while *Existing* ensures that the value is the *same* as that of another field.
- **Member of value list:** Use this checkbox and its related drop-down menu to present the user with a predefined list of entry choices. Value lists may be the single best tool in speeding data entry and preventing typos in records. See *Using Value Lists* on page 107.

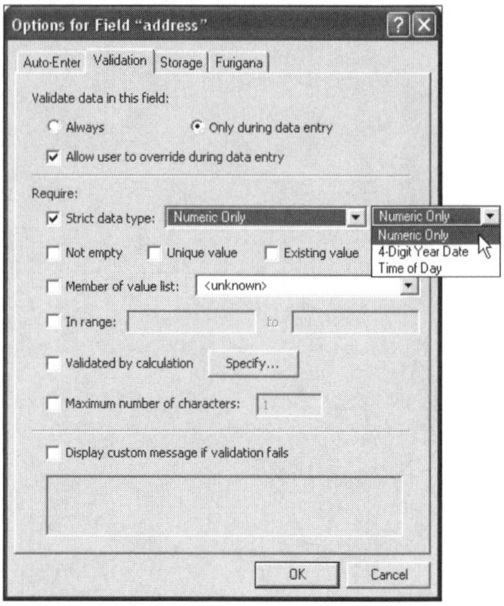

Figure 9.11 The Validation panel's checkboxes ensure that data entered into selected fields is correctly formatted.

- **In range:** Use this checkbox to ensure that the data entered falls within the range of the text, numbers, dates, or times you specify in the two entry boxes.
- **Validated by calculation:** Use this checkbox and the *Specify* button to double-check a value against a chosen formula.
- **Maximum number of characters:** Use this checkbox and the text window to control how many characters will be displayed.
- **Display custom message if validation fails:** This checkbox controls what users see if the data they enter doesn't meet the criteria you've already set in the Validation dialog box. Create a custom message in the text window below the checkbox that explains why the entry was not accepted—and what users might do to conform to the field's requirements. The message can contain up to 255 characters.

Storage options

FileMaker's storage options include creating global or indexed values. A global storage field (previously known as global fields) contains a single value used for every record in a file. That value can be text, a number, date, time, or container. Typical uses include displaying boilerplate text or a company logo within each record. Global field values can be used in formulas for calculations and scripts. Since global fields appear in every record, they cannot be used to find records within a database.

Indexing creates an alphabetical (or numeric) list of all the values in the selected field, greatly speeding any search for records—once the index is created. But indexing also increases your database's size, eating up hard drive space. For that reason, FileMaker gives you field-by-field control of which, if any, fields are indexed. Indexing can also be used to store results for calculation fields. (See *To store calculation results* on page 123.) Manually setting which fields should be indexed is no longer really necessary, however, since FileMaker can now automatically generate an index when—and only when—you do something that would be speedier with an index, such as a find request.

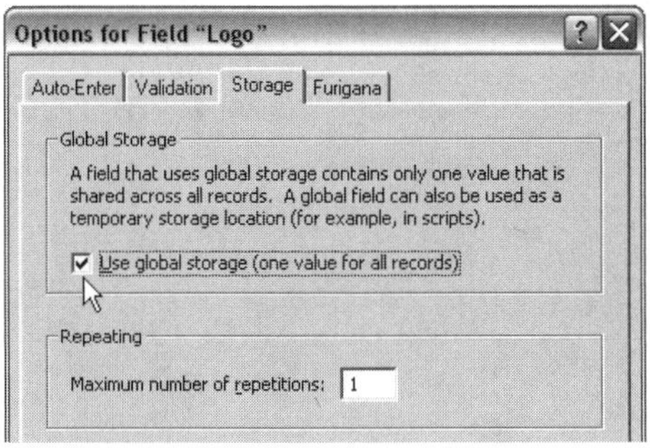

Figure 9.12 In the Options dialog box, click the *Storage* tab and check *Use global storage*.

To create global storage fields:

1. Choose File > Define > Database (Ctrl Shift D in Windows, Shift ⌘ D on the Mac).
2. When the Define Database dialog box appears, the *Fields* tab is automatically selected. Use the *Table* drop-down menu to select a table, then type a name into the *Field Name* text box.
3. Make a choice from the *Type* drop-down menu, then click *Create*. The name of your new field is added to the list of field names.
4. Select the new name in the list and click the *Options* button. When the Options dialog box appears, click the *Storage* tab and check *Use global storage* (**Figure 9.12**).
5. Click *OK* to close the Options dialog box, then click *OK* to close the Define Database dialog box to apply the change.

To set indexing:

1. Choose File > Define > Database ([Ctrl][Shift][D] in Windows, [Shift][⌘][D] on the Mac).
2. When the Define Database dialog box appears, the *Fields* tab is automatically selected. Select a field to index from the center list and click *Options*.
3. In the *Indexing* section, select *All*. (**Figure 9.13**) (Ignore the *Minimal* setting.) If necessary, reselect which language the index will use from the bottom drop-down menu.
4. Click *OK* to close the Options dialog box and the Define Database reappears. If you want to set indexing for another field, repeat the steps. When you're finished, click *OK* to close the dialog box.

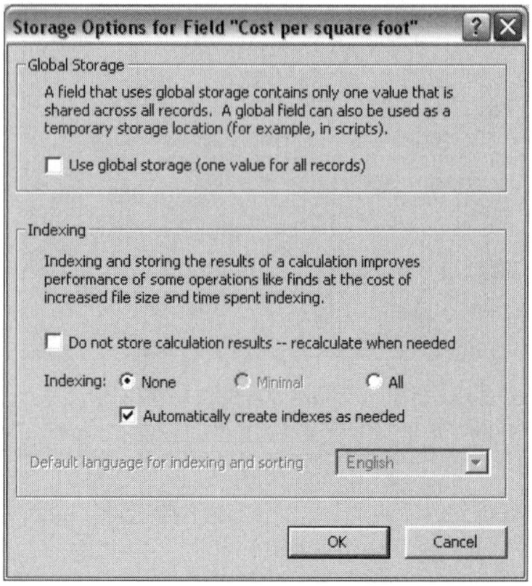

Figure 9.13 In the *Indexing* section, select *All* to set indexing for the selected field.

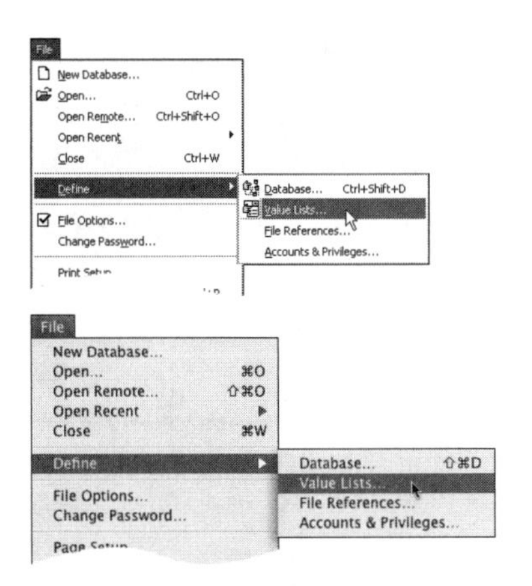

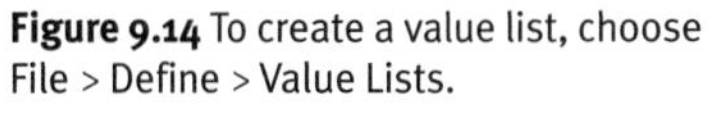

Figure 9.14 To create a value list, choose File > Define > Value Lists.

Figure 9.15 When the Define Value Lists dialog box appears, click *New* to create a new list or *Edit* if you want to change an existing value list.

Figure 9.16 When the Edit Value List dialog box appears, *Use custom values* will be selected, so type your values into the text box, and click *OK*.

Using Value Lists

By offering users a predefined list of field entry choices, value lists save lots of time and aggravation. The more people you have entering data into a database, the more important value lists become in maintaining record consistency and accuracy. Don't worry about locking yourself in: Like so many things in FileMaker, value lists can be altered any time. A quick-and-dirty explanation for formatting value lists is included in this section, but you'll want to read *Creating Layouts* on page 143 to get a fuller sense of your formatting options for value lists. While value lists often are created at the same time you create a field, they exist independently of any particular field and can be created at any time.

To define a custom value list:

1. Choose File > Define > Value Lists (**Figure 9.14**).
2. When the Define Value Lists dialog box appears, click *New* to create a new list or *Edit* if you want to change an existing value list (**Figure 9.15**).
3. When the Edit Value List dialog box appears, a generic name appears in the *Value List Name* text box and the *Use custom values* radio button will be selected. Type in a distinctive name for your new value list, then click inside the blank text box to enter the custom values you want (**Figure 9.16**). (You can also create a value list using values from another field or database. See *To define a value list using another field or database* on page 109.)

(continued)

4. Type in your first value, then press Enter (Windows) or Return (Mac) to begin a new value. When you're done adding values to the list, click *OK* to close the dialog box. To create another value list, repeat steps 2 and 3.

5. When you've finished creating lists, click *OK* to close the Define Value Lists dialog box (**Figure 9.17**). Though you've made the field into a value list, its *display* will not change until you change the layout. See *To format a value list field* on page 110 for a quick rundown. Also see *Creating Layouts* on page 143.

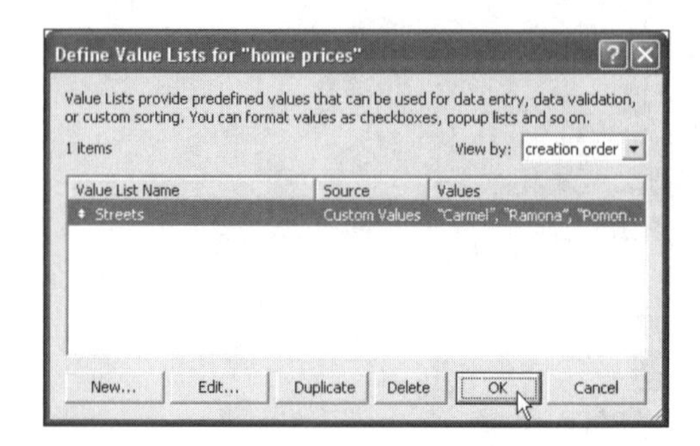

Figure 9.17 When you've finished defining your value lists, click *OK* to close the dialog box.

✔ Tip

- If you have a long list of entries for a value list, you can make it easier to read by typing in some hyphens, *, # (or whatever) on a line of their own, then pressing Enter (Windows) or Return (Mac) to start a new line with a new value.

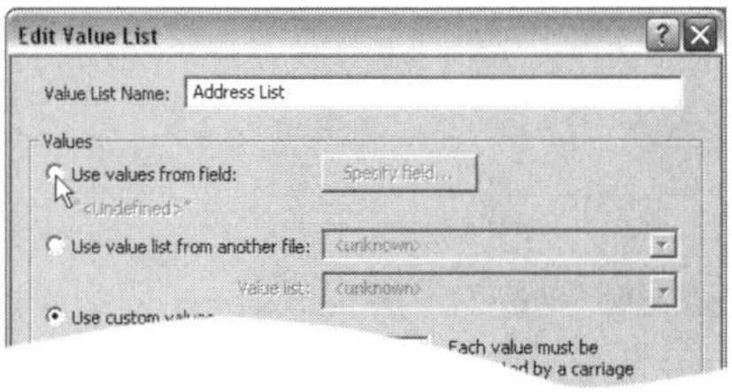

Figure 9.18 When the Edit Value List dialog box appears, select the first radio button, *Use values from field*.

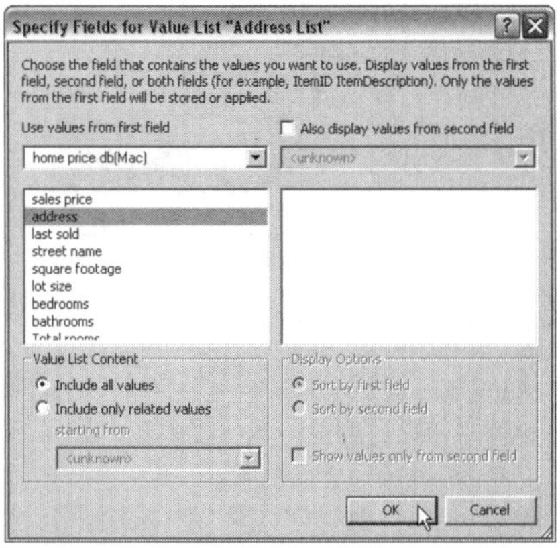

Figure 9.19 In the Specify Fields for Value List dialog box, use the top-left drop-down menu to select the database you're already using and then pick a field in the list below.

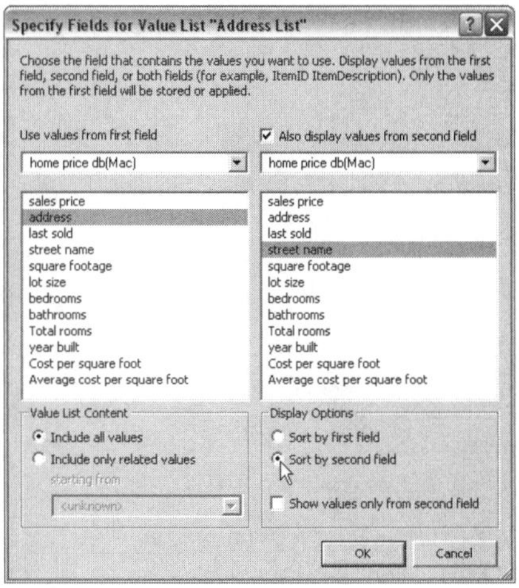

Figure 9.20 You can add to the value list by checking *Also display values from second field*.

To define a value list using another field or database:

1. Choose File > Define > Value Lists.
2. When the Define Value Lists dialog box appears, click *New* to create a new list or *Edit* if you want to change an existing value list.
3. When the Edit Value List dialog box appears, select the first radio button, *Use values from field* (**Figure 9.18**).
4. When the Specify Fields for Value List dialog box appears, use the top-left drop-down menu to select the database you're already using and then pick a field in the list that appears below it (**Figure 9.19**).
5. If you like, you can add to the value list by checking *Also display values from second field* (**Figure 9.20**). Pick a field in the list that appears in the right list and, if you like, use the *Display Options* panel to set how the list will be sorted.
6. Once you've made your choices, click *OK* to close the dialog box, then click *OK* a second time when the Edit Value List dialog box reappears.

✔ Tips

- You also can create a value list based on another *database*. In step 3, select the second radio button, *Use value list from another file*, and then use the related drop-down menu to navigate your way to the file you want and open it. When a new dialog box appears listing all of that database's fields, select the ones you want to use and click *OK*.
- You'll need to switch to Layout mode to format how you want the value list to appear. See the following page, *To format a value list field*, for a quick rundown. See *Creating Layouts* on page 143.

To format a value list field:

1. If you haven't already defined your value list, see *To define a custom value list* on page 107. When you're ready to format a field, switch to Layout mode (Ctrl L for Windows, ⌘ L on the Mac). Select the field you want to format by clicking on it.
2. Choose Format > Field/Control > Setup (**Figure 9.21**). The Field/Control Setup dialog box appears (**Figure 9.22**).
3. Use the *Display as* drop-down menu to select which style you want for your value list: Drop-down List, *Pop-up Menu, Checkbox Set*, or *Radio Button Set* (**Figure 9.23**).
4. Depending on your choice in step 3, the *Control Style* section of the Field/Control Setup dialog box may include two checkboxes to make your value list formatting more flexible for the user. Both options can work as double-edged swords so consider whether you want to give users that flexibility or whether you'd prefer to limit entries to what's in the value list.

   Choose *Include "Other..." item to allow entry of other values* if you want to let users enter a value that's *not* in your value list. This formatting option can be added to every value list format except the pop-up menu. If the user picks the *Other...* choice, a dialog box opens, allowing the user to add another value.

   Choose *Include "Edit..." item to allow editing of value list* if you want to let users change the choices in your value list. This choice can only be used for the pop-up menu format. If the user picks the "*Edit...*" choice, a dialog box opens allowing the user to change an existing value or add more values to the list.

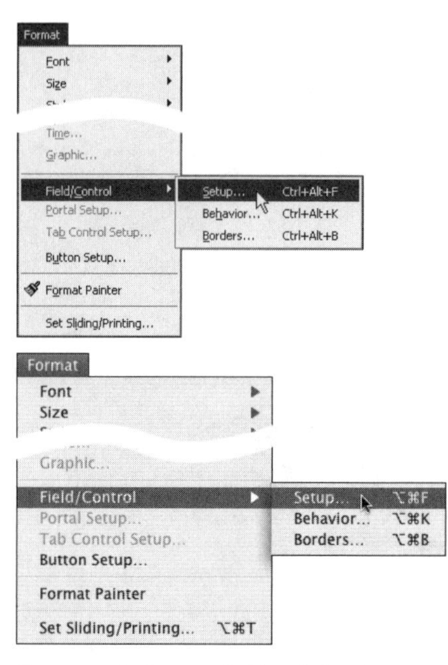

Figure 9.21 To format a field, switch to Layout mode, then choose Format > Field/Control > Setup.

Figure 9.22 Use the Field/Control Setup dialog box to control the *appearance* of the value list.

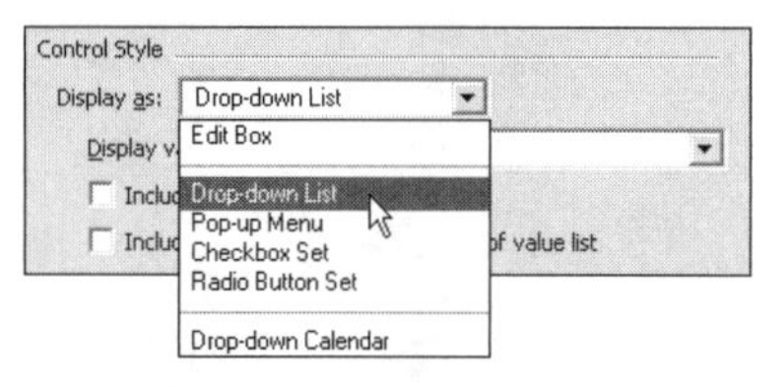

Figure 9.23 Use the *Display as* drop-down menu to select your value list's style.

5. When you're done making your selections, click *OK* at the bottom of the Field/Control Setup dialog box. Switch to Browse mode (Ctrl B for Windows, ⌘ B on the Mac) and your field appears with its new formatting.

✔ Tip

- Which value list style best suits your needs? The pop-up menu option simply shows a blank field—with no clue that it holds multiple choices—unless the user clicks on it. That's handy if you don't have much screen space or want a clean, simple look. The checkbox and radio button options let the user immediately see all the choices for the field. Checkboxes allow multiple selections, while radio buttons only allow one selection at a time.

Using Repeating Fields

If you have databases created before early 2004, they might contain repeating fields, which can accommodate more than one value. For old databases, the information below remains useful. But now that FileMaker is fully relational, it's much simpler to create multiple tables and just connect them, as explained in *Creating Relational Databases* on page 125.

To define a repeating field:

1. Choose File > Define > Database (Ctrl Shift D in Windows, Shift ⌘ D on the Mac). When the Define Database dialog box appears, double-click the name of the field you want to define as repeating (**Figure 9.24**).
2. When the Options for Field dialog box appears, click the *Storage* tab, and enter a number in the *Maximum number of repetitions* box (**Figure 9.25**). Click *OK* to close the dialog box.
3. The Define Database dialog box reappears; click *OK* to close the dialog box. Though you've now defined the field as repeating, its *display* will not change until you change the layout. See *To format a repeating field* on the next page for a quick rundown. See *Creating Layouts* on page 143.

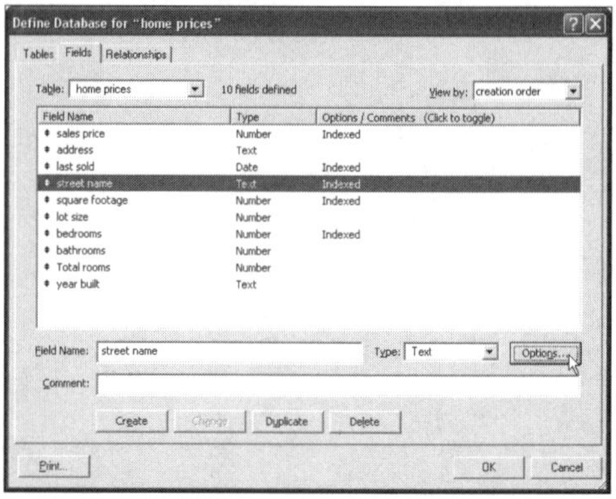

Figure 9.24 To *define* a repeating field, double-click the field's name in the Define Database dialog box or select it and click *Options*.

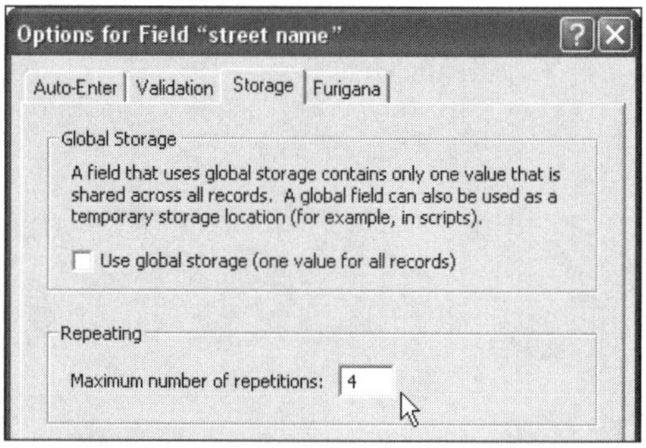

Figure 9.25 Enter a number in the *Maximum number of repetitions* box.

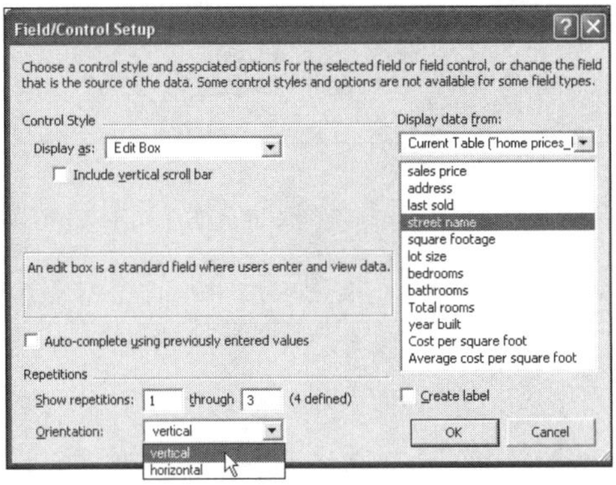

Figure 9.26 Within the box's *Repetitions* section, make a choice from the Orientation drop-down menu.

To format a repeating field:

1. Switch to Layout mode (Ctrl L for Windows, ⌘ L on the Mac). Select the field you want to format by clicking on it.
2. Choose Format > Field/Control > Setup and the Field/Control Setup dialog box appears. Within the box's *Repetitions* section, make a choice from the Orientation drop-down menu (**Figure 9.26**). Choosing *vertical* stacks the fields; *horizontal* places them side by side. Click *OK* to close the dialog box.
3. FileMaker returns you to the Layout view of the field and the rest of the record. Switch to Browse mode (Ctrl B for Windows, ⌘ B on the Mac) to see the new format.

✔ Tip

- In the above example, the repeating fields appear as a drop-down list, but you can use the Style section's pop-up menu to have them appear in any of the other three formats. The pop-up menu format works best for repeating fields, however, since the checkbox and radio button options will produce a blizzard of boxes and circles.

Understanding Formulas

Formulas are used in two kinds of FileMaker fields: calculation fields and summary fields. For the most part, formulas used in calculation fields operate on data in the *current* record. Formulas used in summary fields operate on data from *more than one* record.

Beneath a sometimes-confusing raft of terms and definitions, formulas are simple. Using a set of specific instructions, formulas take data from one or more fields, calculate or compare or summarize it, and then display the results. That's it. The twist comes in that word *specific*: Formulas must be constructed in a set order, or syntax. Mess up the syntax and the formula won't work properly, if at all.

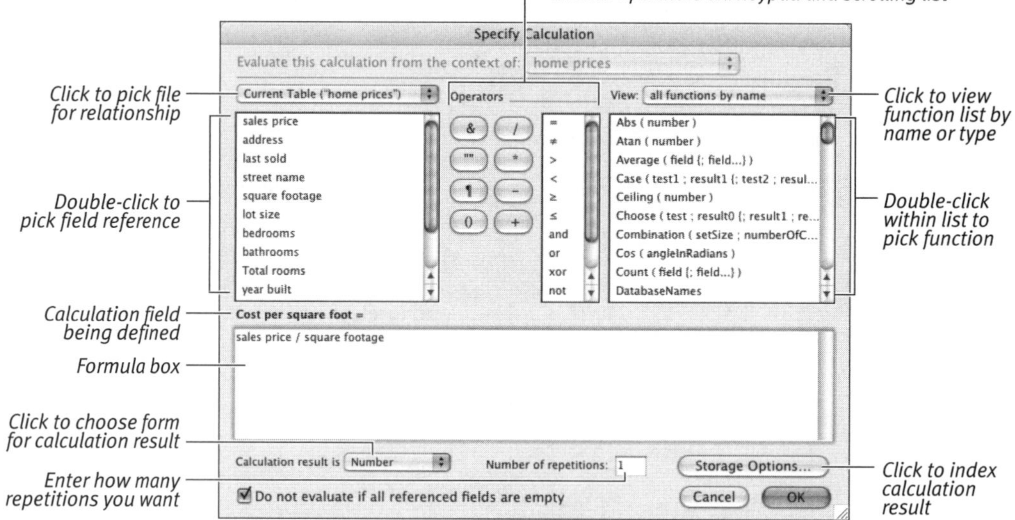

Figure 9.27 Within the Specify Calculation dialog box, formulas are built in the center formula box using pieces taken from (upper left to right) the field reference list, the keypad and scrolling list of operators, and the functions list.

Syntax and the parts of a formula

You'll build most of your formulas within the Specify Calculation dialog box (**Figure 9.27**), which will go a long way in helping keep your syntax straight. The dialog box works like a construction kit with tools to let you assemble the necessary field references, constants, operators, and functions. Once the formula is run, it spits out results, whose form you also control. Before you start, however, take a moment to understand some of the key terms used in formulas.

Field References: A field reference directs a formula to use the value in the field it's named after. The left-hand list within the Specify Calculation dialog box displays all the field references in the selected database.

Constants: As the name implies, a constant is a *fixed* value used in a formula. It remains the same from record to record. A string of text, a number, a date, or a time can all be constants. Each of these types of constants must be typed in a particular format for the formula to recognize which type of constant it represents. For more on the required formats, see **Table 9.1**, *Constants*.

Table 9.1

Constants

For This Type Data	Remember To	Examples
Text	Enclose text in quotes (")	"Welcome to FileMaker" "94530-3014"
Number	Do not include currency symbols or thousand separators (, or ;)	80.23 450000
Date	Use the value as parameter of the Date function or the TextToDate function.	Date(3,13,1998) TextToDate("03/13/1998")
Time	Use the value as parameter of the Time function or the TextToTime function.	Time(10,45,23) TextToTime ("10:45:23")

Expressions: An expression is simply a value or any computation that produces a value. Expressions can contain field references, constants, and functions, and can be combined to produce other expressions. See **Table 9.2**, *Expression Examples*.

Operators: Operators enable a formula to compare the contents of two (or more) fields. Insert operators into your formulas using your keyboard or the keypad and scrolling list within the Specify Calculation dialog box (**Figure 9.28**). Operators combine expressions and resolve what operation should be performed on the expressions. For example, the addition sign, +, is simply an operator that combines the value appearing before it with the value appearing after it: Subtotal + Tax.

Mathematical and text operators are used with—surprise—numbers and text. Comparison operators compare two expressions and return a result of True or False, in what is known as a Boolean expression. Logical operators compare two or more conditions, such as whether the Cost field is more than $200,000 (the first condition) *and* the Square footage field is less than 1,000 (the second condition). See **Tables 9.3–9.6**.

Table 9.2

Expression Examples

Type of Expression	Example
Text constant	"FileMaker"
Number constant	80.23
Field reference	Cost per square foot
Function	TextToDate
Combination of expressions	(Price/House Size)*0.10

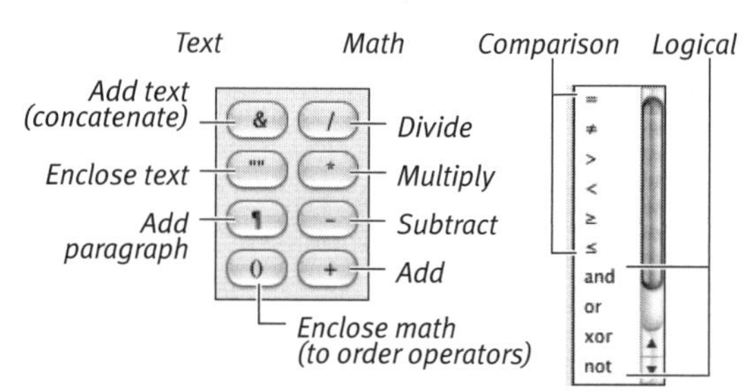

Figure 9.28 Build formulas using the keypad and scrolling list, which contain text, math, comparison, and logical operators.

Table 9.3

Mathematical Operators (see Figure 9.28)

Symbol	Name	Definition	Examples
+	Addition	Adds two values	2+2, Subtotal+Sales Tax
–	Subtraction	Subtracts second value from first	2–1, Total–Discount
*	Multiplication	Multiplies value	Subtotal*Sales Tax
/	Division	Divides first value by second	Total/Units
^	Exponentiation	Raises first value to power of second	(A2 + B2) returns A^2B^2
( )	Precedence	Expressions inside parentheses evaluated first	(5*20)/5

Table 9.4

Text Operators (see Figure 9.28)

Symbol	Name	Definition	Examples
&	Concatenation	Appends the text string on right to end of text string on left	"AAA" & "BBB" returns "AAABBB"
" "	Text constant	Marks beginning and end of text constant. Quotes with no text between them indicate a blank space. Text in formula without quotes is interpreted as a field name or function name. To mark a quote mark within a text constant, precede it with another quote mark.	"Welcome to FileMaker" returns as Welcome to FileMaker " " returns an empty (null) value "Welcome to our "favorite" place" returns as Welcome to our "favorite" place
¶	Return marker	Inserts a paragraph return in a text constant	"Welcome to¶FileMaker" returns Welcome to FileMaker

Table 9.5

Comparison Operators (see Figure 9.28)

Symbol	Name	Definition	Examples
=	Equal to	True when both items are equal	4=5 returns False 4=4 returns True
≠ or <>	Not equal to	True when the items are not equal	4≠5 returns True 4≠4 returns False
>	Greater than	True when value on left exceeds value on right	4>5 returns False 5>4 returns True
<	Less than	True when value on left is less than value on right	4<5 returns True 5<4 returns False
≥ or >=	Greater than or equal to	True when value on left is greater than or equal to value on right	4≥5 returns False 5≥5 returns True
≤ or <=	Less than or equal to	True when value on left is less than or equal to value on right	5≤4 returns False 4≤4 returns True

Table 9.6

Logical Operators (see Figure 9.28)

Symbol	Definition	Examples
AND	True only when both values are true: True when true AND true False when true AND false False when false AND false	Cost per square foot <200 AND Bedrooms≥2
OR	True when either value is true: True when true OR true True when true OR false False when false OR false	Cost per square foot <200 OR Bedrooms≥2
XOR	True when either, but not both, of values is true: False when true AND true True when false AND true False when false AND false	Cost per square foot <200 XOR Bedrooms≥2
NOT	Changes value within parentheses from false to true, or true to false: False when NOT (true) True when NOT(false)	NOT Cost per square foot >200

Using predefined formulas (functions)

A function is simply a *predefined* formula with a set name, such as *TextToDate*. Functions perform a particular calculation and return a single value. FileMaker comes with more than 150 functions. All those functions are available via the right-hand list within the Specify Calculation dialog box, but scrolling through the whole list for one function would be a bother. Instead, use the top-right drop-down menu to display handier portions of the list (**Figure 9.29**). Try several choices to see which set of functions best suits your needs (**Figure 9.30**).

Functions have three parts: the predefined function, the parameters used by the function, and a set of parentheses enclosing the parameter. In almost all cases, FileMaker functions follow this syntax, or order:

Function name(*parameter*)

For example: TextToDate(*time*) or Average(*field*)

The parameter (the value within the parentheses) can be a field reference, a constant, an expression, or another function. Sometimes a function needs more than one parameter, in which case you'll separate each parameter from the next parameter with a comma or semicolon:

Average (*field1, field2, field3*)

In this example, field1, field 2, and field3 are just placeholders for the actual field reference you'd place into the formula.

Calculation Results: Once the formula runs, it displays the calculation as a result. The result can take several forms—text, number, date, time, or container—which you control via the Specify Calculation dialog box. See *To change the display of calculation results* on page 122.

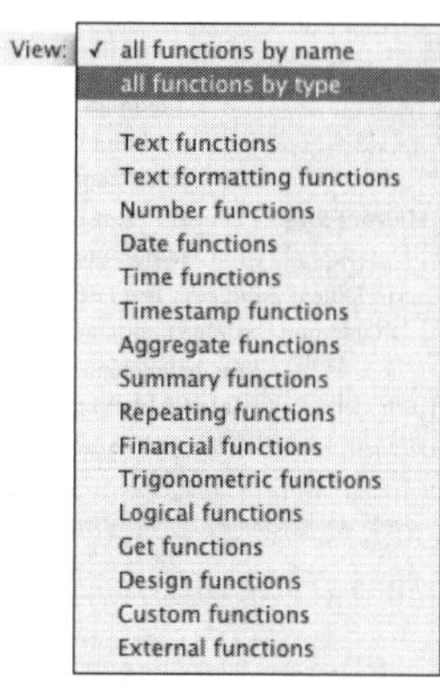

Figure 9.29 Use the Specify Calculation dialog box's View drop-down menu to fine-tune your view of FileMaker's 150+ built-in functions.

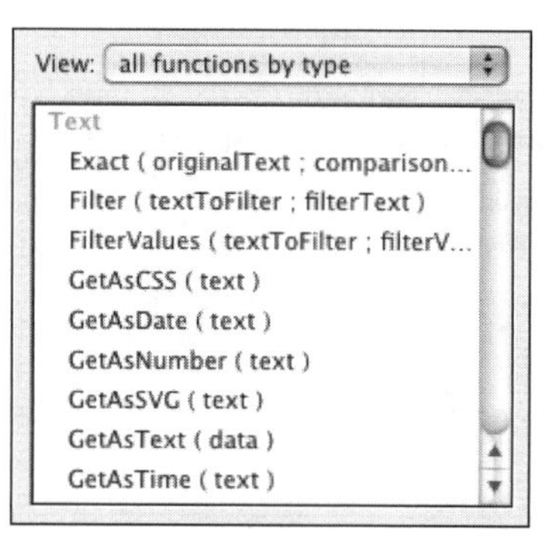

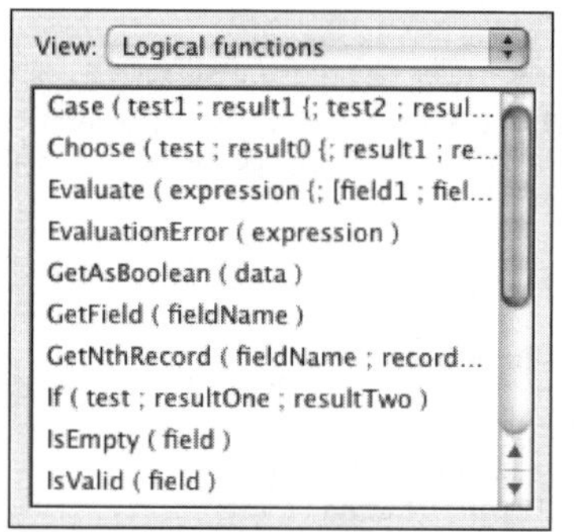

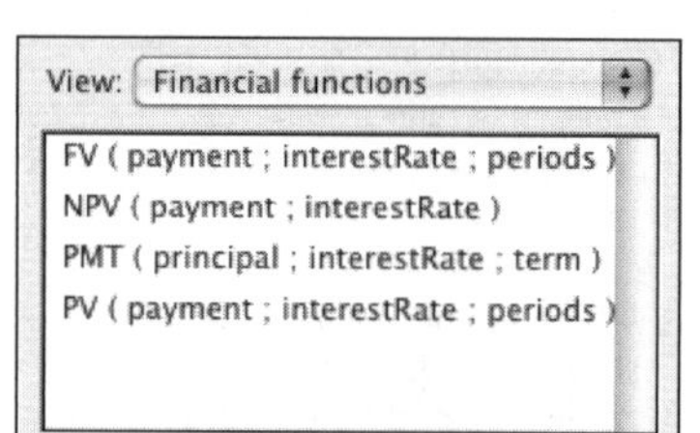

Figure 9.30 The View pop-up menu helps you quickly find the function you need.

Figure 9.31 Once you create a new field, select *Calculation* from the *Type* drop-down menu and click *Create*.

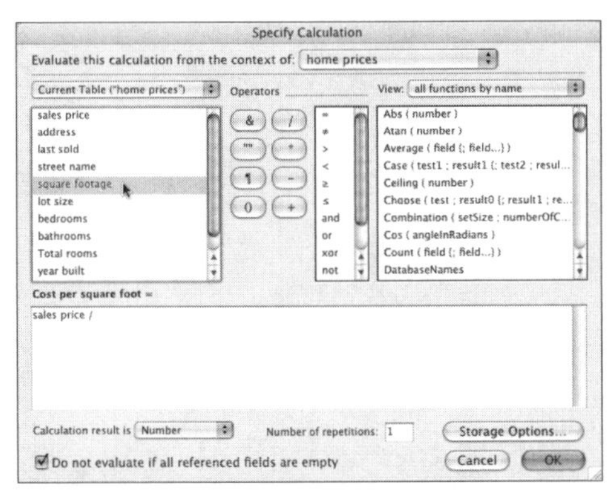

Figure 9.32 Use the Specify Calculation dialog box to create your formula, then click *OK*.

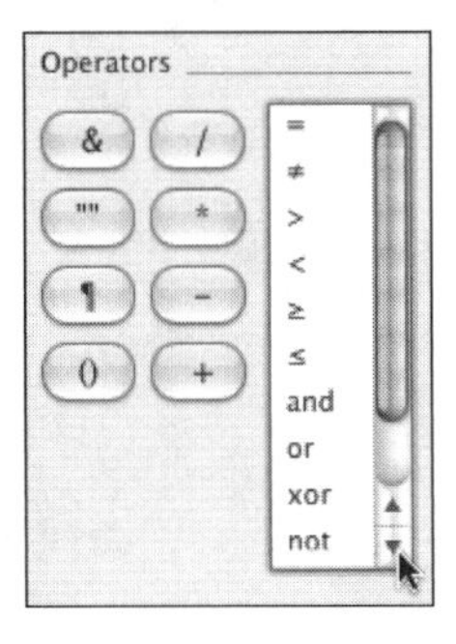

Figure 9.33 The Specify Calculation dialog box's formula operators are controlled by the keypad and the scrolling window.

Using Calculation and Summary Fields

You cannot enter anything directly into a calculation or summary field. Instead, the fields store and display the results of calculations you build via the Specify Calculation dialog box or the Options for Summary Field dialog box.

Formulas used to define a calculation field can be as basic or as complex as you need and will seldom use every tool available in the Specify Calculation dialog box. Our first example walks through a very simple formula.

To define a calculation field:

1. To create a calculation field, choose File > Define > Database (Ctrl Shift D in Windows or Shift ⌘ D on the Mac).
2. When the Define Database dialog box appears, type into the Field Name text box the name of your field.
3. Select *Calculation* from the *Type* drop-down menu, then click *Create* (**Figure 9.31**).
4. The Specify Calculation dialog box, where you define a formula for the selected field, appears. The simple *Cost per square foot* example uses just two field references and a single symbol: (*sales price/square footage*).

   Add the *sales price* field reference by double-clicking its name within the list (**Figure 9.32**). Now click the division symbol (/) in the symbols keypad (**Figure 9.33**). Back in the left-side list, double-click the *square footage* field reference. (For information on using the *Storage Options* button in the Specify Calculation dialog box, see *To store calculation results* on page 123.)

(continued)

5. Once you're finished building the formula, click *OK* to close the dialog box.
6. When the Define Database dialog box reappears, click *OK* to close that dialog box.

✔ Tips

- Instead of mouse-clicking on the symbols keypad within the Specify Calculation dialog box, you can use their equivalents on your keyboard.
- Selecting the *Do not evaluate if all referenced fields are empty* checkbox keeps FileMaker from performing a calculation unless the field referenced by the formula has a value—saving some otherwise wasted time.

To edit a formula:

1. To reach the Specify Calculation dialog box and edit a formula, choose File > Define > Database (Ctrl Shift D in Windows, Shift ⌘ D on the Mac). When the Define Database dialog box appears, double-click on the name of the calculation field whose formula you want to change.

2. The Specify Calculation dialog box shows the formula in the center box. If you want to start fresh, double-click on the formula, then press Delete or simply click on the first piece of the new formula (usually a field reference).

   To edit individual parts of the formula, highlight that piece, and then click the replacement field reference, operator, or function.

3. When you've finished editing the formula, click *OK*, then click *OK* when the Define Database dialog box reappears.

✔ Tip

- If you ever change the name of a field, you don't need to manually edit the formulas that reference that field. FileMaker automatically updates the field references in formulas to reflect any field name changes.

To change the display of calculation results:

1. First create a calculation field and build a formula for it. (See *To define a calculation field* on page 119.) Now click the *Calculation result is* pop-up menu (**Figure 9.34**).

   By default, FileMaker displays the results of a calculation as a number, which is what's needed in most cases. However, there are formulas that may need to be displayed as text, a time, a timestamp, or even a container. Make your selection and release the cursor.

2. Click *OK*. When the Define Database dialog box reappears, click *OK* to close the dialog box.

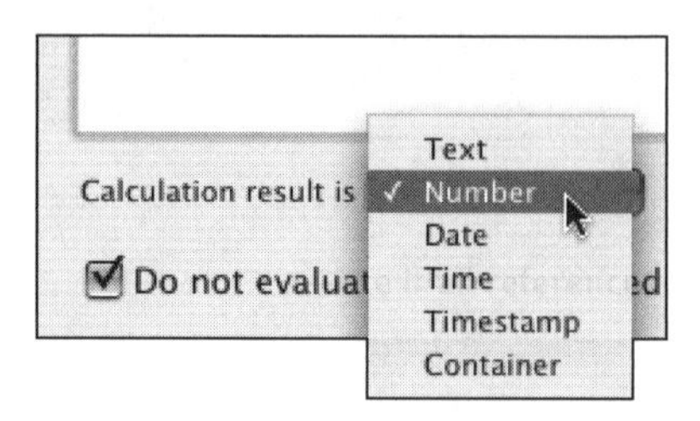

Figure 9.34 Use the *Calculation result is* pop-up menu in the Specify Calculation dialog box to control how the results are displayed.

To repeat a calculation field:

1. Choose File > Define > Database (Ctrl Shift D in Windows, Shift ⌘ D on the Mac).

2. Within the Define Database dialog box, double-click on the name of the calculation field you want to repeat. When the Specify Calculation dialog box appears, just enter a number in the *Number of repetitions* text window near the bottom of the dialog box. Click *OK*.

3. When the Define Database dialog box reappears, click *OK* to close the dialog box. Remember: The appearance of a repeating field doesn't change until you format it. See *To format a repeating field* on page 113.

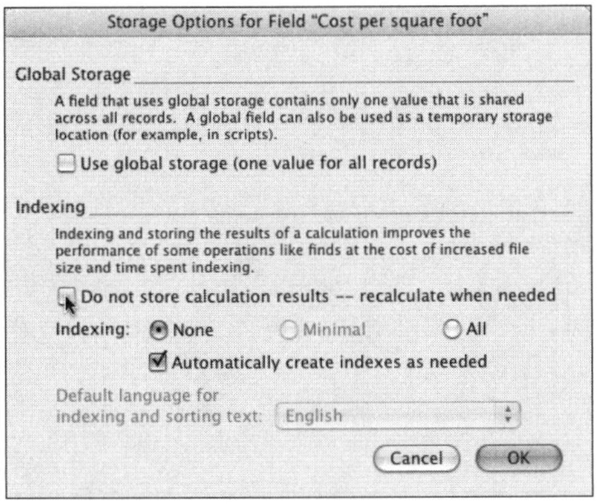

Figure 9.35 Use the checkbox in the Storage Options dialog box to control whether to store a calculation result or calculate it only when needed.

Storing calculation results

Storing calculation results carries the same tradeoffs as indexing any other field: It speeds finding records but also increases your database's size. FileMaker offers a decent compromise, however, by giving you the option of only performing a calculation (and, so, storing the result) when it's needed, such as when you're printing or browsing that particular field and record.

Unless you tell it otherwise, FileMaker automatically stores calculations except those from summary fields, as well as those that depend on another calculation already marked as unstored.

To store calculation results:

1. First create a calculation field and build a formula for it. (See *To define a calculation field* on page 119.) If you already have a calculation field defined, choose File > Define > Database (Ctrl Shift D in Windows, Shift ⌘ D on the Mac).
2. When the Define Database dialog box appears, double-click on the name of the calculation field whose results you want to store or index. The Specify Calculation dialog box appears with the formula in the center box. Click the *Storage Options* button.
3. The Storage Options dialog box appears (**Figure 9.35**). To keep a result from being stored, select *Do not store calculation results—recalculate when needed.*
4. Click *OK*. When the Define Database dialog box reappears, click *OK* to close the dialog box.

To define a summary field:

1. Choose File > Define > Database (Ctrl Shift D in Windows, Shift ⌘ D on the Mac).
2. When the Define Database dialog box appears, type into the *Field Name* text box the name of your summary field. Select *Summary* from the *Type* drop-down menu. Click the *Options* button (**Figure 9.36**).
3. When the Options for Summary Field dialog box appears, choose which type of summary you want performed from the left-hand list, and select which field you want summarized from the scrolling list in the center (**Figure 9.37**, **Table 9.7**). You can also modify several of the summary types by selecting the checkbox just below the scrolling list, whose function varies in response to which type you've chosen. See **Table 9.7**, *Summary Field Types.*
4. Click *OK*. When the Define Database dialog box reappears, click *OK* to close the dialog box.

✔ Tip

- Formatting summary fields varies depending on which summary part you use to display them. See *Creating Layouts* on page 143.

Figure 9.36 To define a Summary field, click that choice in the *Type* area of the Define Database dialog box, then click *Create*.

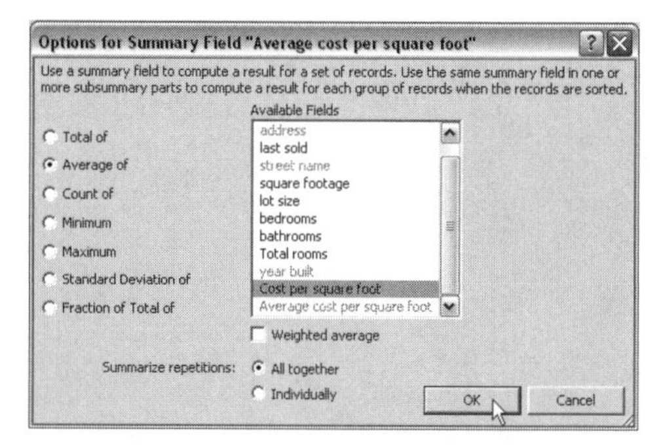

Figure 9.37 Use the Options for Summary Field dialog box to select a summary action. The *Weighted average* checkbox modifies many of the left-hand options.

Table 9.7

Summary Field Types (see Figure 9.37)

Name	Definition	Option Via Checkbox	To Fine Tune Option:
Total of	Totals values in selected field	Running total	
Average of	Averages values in selected field	Weighted average	Pick a field for averaged values
Count of	Counts how many records contain a value for field	Running total	
Minimum	Finds lowest number, or earliest time or date, for field	none	
Maximum	Finds highest number, or latest time or date, for field	none	
Standard Deviation of	Calculates standard deviation from mean of values in field	by population	
Fraction of Total of	Calculates the ratio of field's value to total for all values in field	Subtotaled	Pick a field for subtotaled values

Creating Relational Databases

Creating relational databases is a multi-step process, which you begin by adding *match fields* (sometimes called *key fields*) to each set of source and destination files. The match fields enable you to take the second step of *creating the relationship* (or *link*), which simply acts as a pointer from the destination file to the source file. In the final step, you then *define the relationship* between the files by specifying what fields you actually want used in creating lookups and portals between them. Additionally, you can define relationships for specific layouts, which give your databases tremendous flexibility.

For example, in this chapter we create match fields in the source and destination files using identity numbers. The match fields then let us link different source and destination files. Each relationship includes only one destination file and one source file. But you can create multiple relationships because the same file can be the destination for some data and the source of other data. Whether you're dealing with a table, file, record, or field, the *source* is where the data comes *from*. In contrast, the *destination* is where the data goes *to*. For a bit of lingo help, see **Table 10.1**, *Too Many Terms for Some Simple Ideas*.

The examples in this chapter are based on three database files: *productsEG,* which lists product descriptions and prices; *customersEG,* which lists all the contact information for each customer; and *ordersEG,* which uses information from both databases, plus its own information, to generate order lists and cost totals for those orders (**Figure 10.1**). To put all that information in a single database file would be unwieldy. By dividing it into three files, each database remains compact and simple to use, which is what relational databases are all about. As you read the rest of the chapter, refer back to **Figure 10.1** to see how these three relational files put relationships, match fields, lookups, and portals to use. If you want to use these same databases to follow along, you'll find them at `www.waywest.net/filemaker/`.

Table 10.1

Too Many Terms for Some Simple Ideas

FileMaker Term	What It Means
destination file, table, record, or field *current* *master* *target*	The file, table, record, or field you copy data *to*
source file, table, record, or field *related* *originating*	The file, table, record, or field you copy data *from*
relationship *link* *join expression*	connection between tables or files, using *match* (or *key*) *fields*

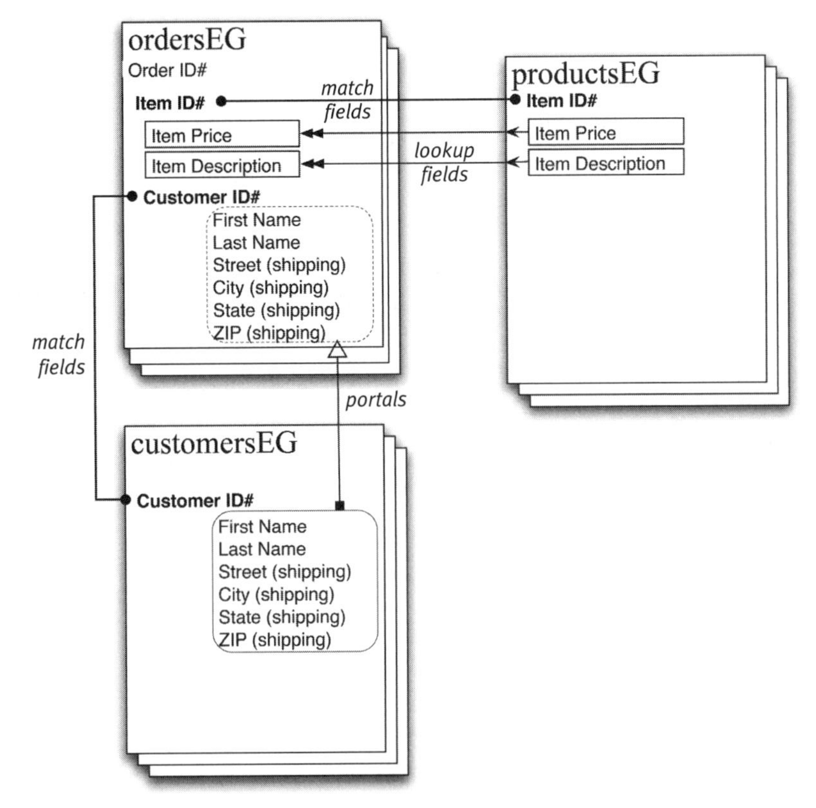

Figure 10.1 How three related files connect: The *ItemID#* match fields link the files *productsEG* to *ordersEG*, allowing the *Item Price* and *Item Description* fields to be copied using lookup fields. The *CustomerID#* match fields link *customersEG* to *ordersEG*, making the multiple-record portal of customer information appear within *ordersEG*.

Creating Match Fields

As first discussed on page 89, you need to create match fields in your source and destination files *before* you can define their relationship using a link. As our match field, we'll use an automatically generated serial number in the source file and an identically named field in the destination field. (For more information on using the Auto-Enter option, see page 100.) By the way, once the two files are linked, you can display *any* field stored in the *source* file within your *destination* file (not just the match fields).

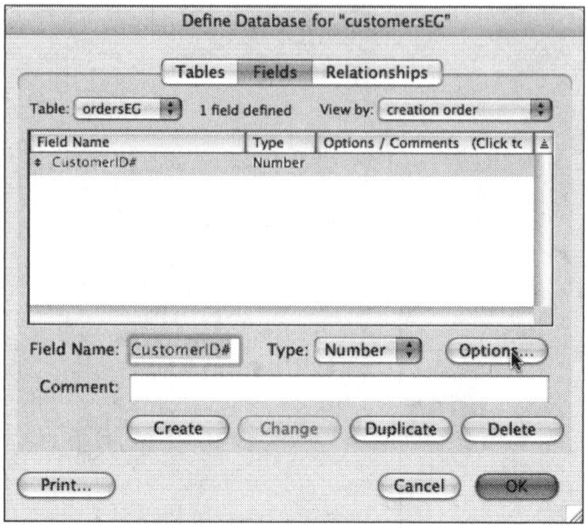

Figure 10.2 In the *Field Name* text window, enter a name that makes it obvious that this will act as a match field.

To create match fields in a source file/table:

1. Open the source file (*customersEG* in our example), then choose File > Define > Database (Ctrl Shift D in Windows, ⌘ Shift D on the Mac).
2. When the Define Database dialog box appears, click the *Fields* tab. In the *Field Name* text window, enter a name that makes it obvious that this will act as a match field. (In our example, we use *CustomerID#*.) Select *Number* from the *Type* drop-down menu and click the *Options* button (**Figure 10.2**).

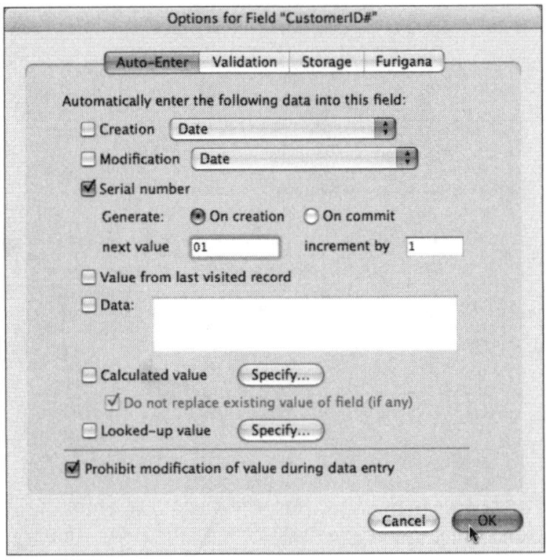

Figure 10.3 Click the *Auto-Enter* tab, then select *Serial number* and *On creation*.

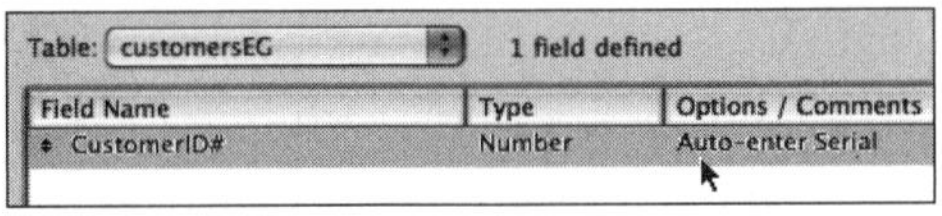

Figure 10.4 When the Define Database dialog box reappears, the Options column lists your auto-enter choices.

3. When the Options dialog box appears, click the *Auto-Enter* tab, then select *Serial number* and *On creation* (**Figure 10.3**). To guard against this number being accidentally changed later, select *Prohibit modification of value entry during data entry*. (It's up to you whether to use the *next value* or *increment by* choices. In our example, we've set the *next value* so our very first record will have a Customer ID# of 01.) Click *OK* to close the dialog box.

4. When the Define Database dialog box reappears, the Options column lists your auto-enter choices (**Figure 10.4**). Click *OK* to apply the choices and close the dialog box.

✔ Tip

- You don't have to create match fields while defining the relationships between files, as done in this chapter. If you plan ahead, you could create them when first defining fields, as explained in Chapter 9. Any records generated before the field was created, however, will have to be filled manually using the Replace Field Contents command (Ctrl+= in Windows, ⌘+= on the Mac).

To create a match field in a destination file/table:

1. Open the destination file (*ordersEG* in our example), then choose File > Define > Database (Ctrl Shift D in Windows, ⌘ Shift D on the Mac).
2. When the Define Database dialog box appears, click the *Fields* tab (**Figure 10.5**). In the *Field Name* text window, enter the exact same name you used for the match field in the source file. (In our example, that's *CustomerID#*.) Select *Number* from the *Type* drop-down menu but do not click the *Options* button. Instead, click *OK* to close the Define Database dialog box. You're now ready to link the match fields by creating a relationship (see the next page).

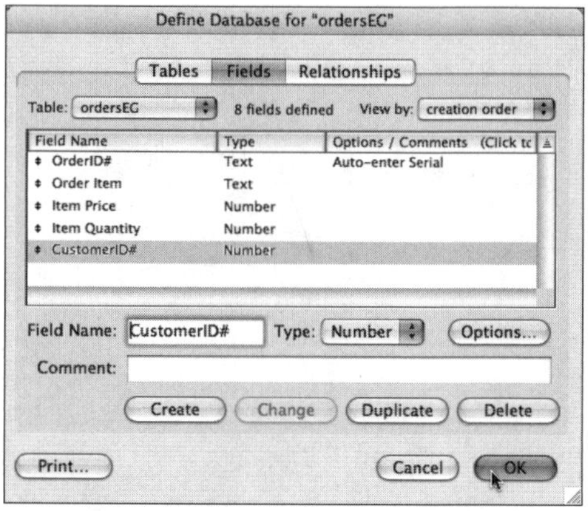

✔ Tip

- In step 2, there's no need to open the Options dialog box because the value for the match field will come from the source file/table.

Figure 10.5 In the *Field Name* text window, enter the exact same name you used for the match field in the source file.

Creating Relationships (Links)

FileMaker's click-and-drag interface in the Define Database dialog box makes this so much easier than it was in earlier versions. The dialog box includes a full set of tool buttons (**Figure 10.6**). But in most cases your cursor and a double-click are all you need. Remember: With these steps you're creating a relationship, which is what *links* two files or tables together. Picking which fields from one file to *display* in the other requires adding a lookup field or portal, covered on pages 136 and 139.

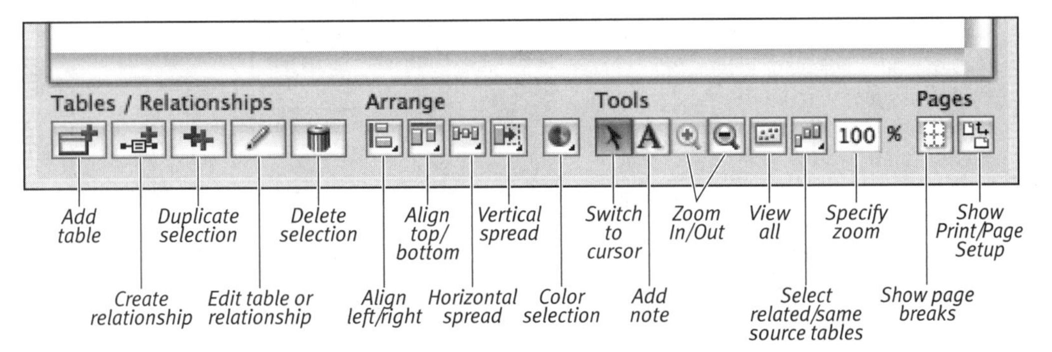

Figure 10.6 The Relationships tab of the Define Database dialog box includes a full set of tools for working with relationships.

To create a relationship:

1. Open the destination file (*ordersEG* in our example) and choose File > Define > Database (Ctrl Shift D in Windows, ⌘ Shift D on the Mac).
2. When the Define Database dialog box appears, click the *Relationships* tab and the open database appears as a box listing its fields (**Figure 10.7**).
3. Click the Add table button ( ) and when the Specify Table dialog box appears, use the *File* drop-down menu to choose *Add File Reference* (**Figure 10.8**). (See the first Tip on next page.)
4. Use the Open File dialog box to navigate to the other database with which you want to create a relationship (**Figure 10.9**). Double-click the database, and it is added to the Specify Table dialog box (**Figure 10.10**). An identically named table (what FileMaker calls a *table occurrence*) is created (*customersEG* in our example). Click *OK* to close the Specify Table dialog box.

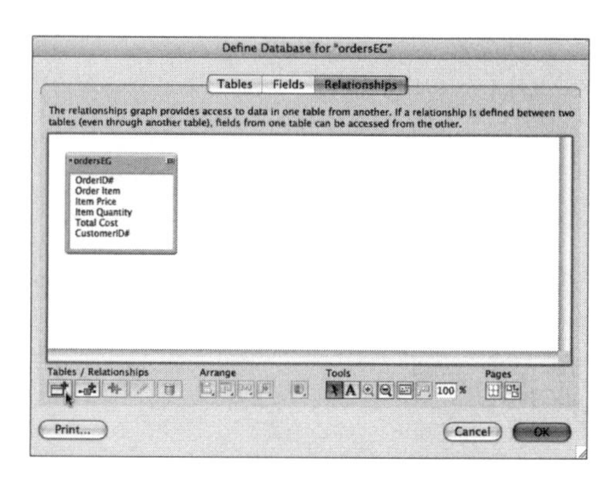

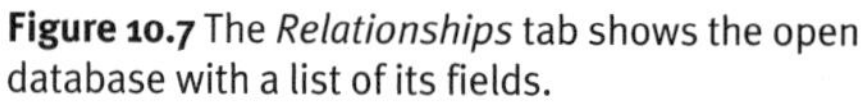

Figure 10.7 The *Relationships* tab shows the open database with a list of its fields.

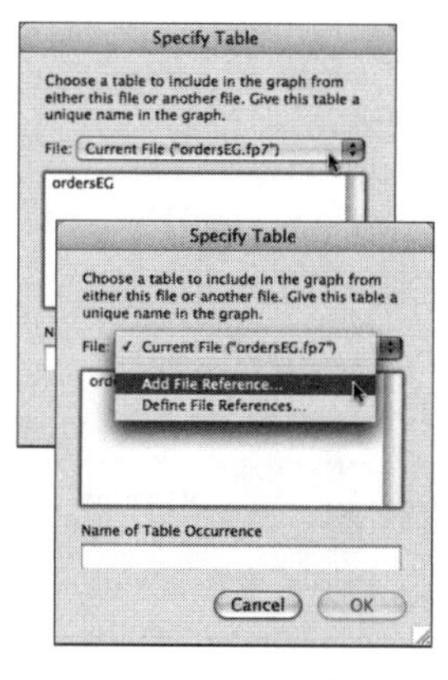

Figure 10.8 Use the *File* drop-down menu in the Specify Table dialog box to choose *Add File Reference*.

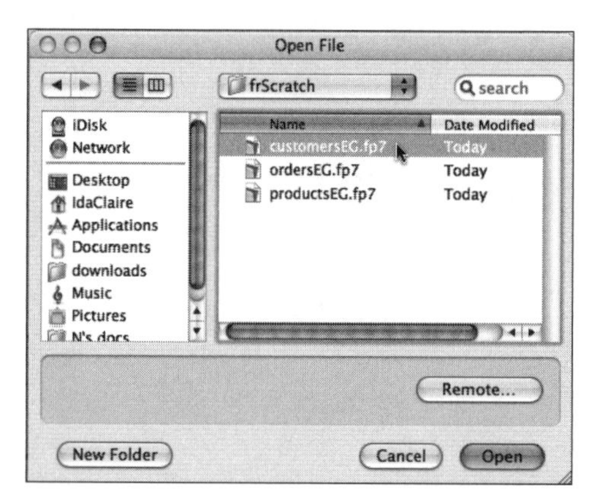

Figure 10.9 Use the Open File dialog box to navigate to the other database with which you want to create a relationship.

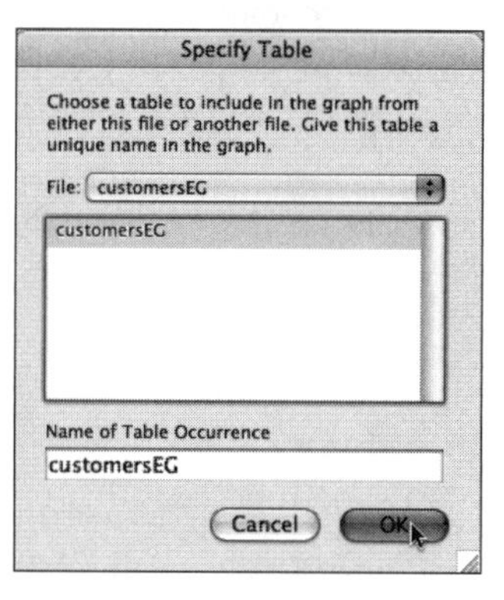

Figure 10.10 Once you open the other database, it's added to the Specify Table dialog box.

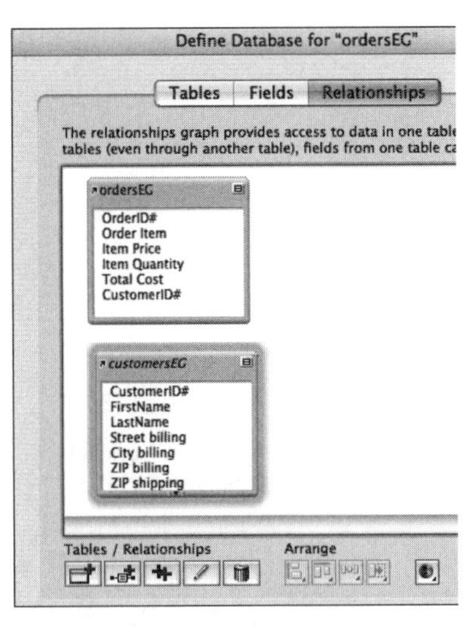

Figure 10.11 When the *Relationships* tab reappears, the second database appears with all its fields listed.

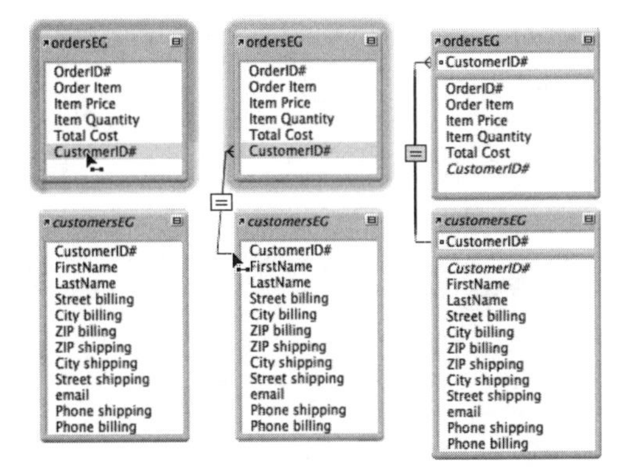

Figure 10.12 Link the match fields by clicking on the destination file's match field (*CustomerID#* in *ordersEG*) and dragging your cursor to the identically named match field in the source file (*customersEG*).

5. Repeat steps 3 and 4 if you need to create additional relationships with any other external database.

6. When the *Relationships* tab view of the Define Database dialog box reappears, the second database is included (**Figure 10.11**). Its title is italicized (*customersEG* in our example) to indicate that this is an external file rather than another occurrence of the first database.

7. Finally, to link the match fields, click on the destination file's match field (*CustomerID#* in *ordersEG* in our example) and drag your cursor to the identically named match field in the source file (*CustomerID#* in *customersEG* in our example) (left and middle, **Figure 10.12**). Release the cursor and FileMaker links the two match fields and lists them at the top of each box (right, **Figure 10.12**).

8. Click *OK* to close the Define Database dialog box.

✔ Tips

- In step 3 if you were creating a relationship between two tables in the *same* database, the other table would be listed automatically in the *File* drop-down menu—eliminating the need to select *Add File Reference*.
- When would you want to create a relationship between two tables in the same database? A typical case might be where you have self-contained data that fits tidily with the related main table, such as a table of zip codes. But for databases that you expect to contain many records and many fields—such as our example databases for orders, customers, and products—it's best to create separate but related databases.

Editing relationships

Suppose in the previous steps, you accidentally connected the wrong fields. Editing the relationship is easy, so you can change the relationship any time.

To change or edit relationships:

1. If necessary, reopen the Define Database dialog box by choosing File > Define > Database (Ctrl Shift D in Windows, ⌘ Shift D on the Mac).
2. When the Define Relationships dialog box appears, the *Relationships* tab is selected automatically (assuming you used the same tab when you last opened the dialog box). Click the Edit table button ( ) or double-click the box astride the line connecting the two fields (**Figure 10.13**).
3. When the Edit Relationship dialog box appears, you can select a new field on the left or right, as well as the = drop-down menu between the lists to change the mathematical operator (**Figure 10.14**). When you're done, click *OK* to close the dialog box and apply the change.

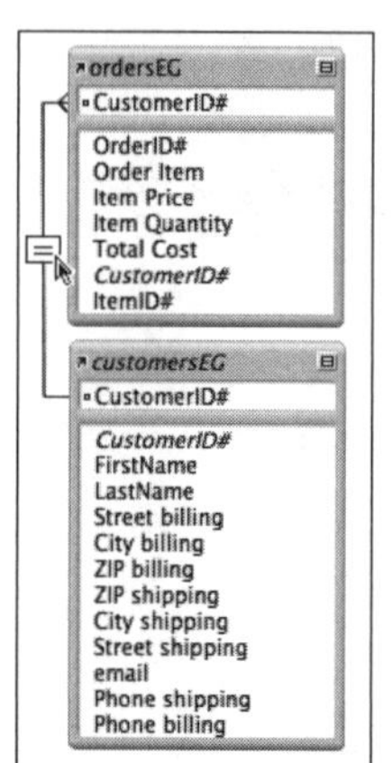

Figure 10.13 To change or edit a relationship, double-click the mathematical operator astride the line connecting the files.

Figure 10.14 Use the Edit Relationship dialog box to select a new field on the left or right, or click the = drop-down menu to change the mathematical operator. (See **Table 10.2** for details about the bottom options.)

✔ Tips

- The *Duplicate* and *Delete* choices within the Edit Relationship dialog box work similarly to duplicating or deleting fields or records: Duplicate a relationship to save time in creating a variation of an existing relationship; delete relationships you no longer need.
- For details on the options at the bottom of the dialog box, see **Table 10.2**, *Edit Relationship Options.*
- In step 3, using the equals operator (=) is critical for creating *match* fields. But the does not equal operators (≠, <, ≤, >, ≥, or X) can be very useful in creating relationships between *other* fields.

Table 10.2

Edit Relationship Options*

Check Box Named	To
Allow creation of records in this table using this relationship	Automatically create a record in the *source* file if you enter data in *destination* file's portal or related field that meets match field criteria. Press Tab to activate.
Delete related records in this table when a record is deleted in the other table	Automatically delete records in *source* file when you delete data in *destination* file's portal or *source* field that meets match field criteria. Press Tab to activate.
Sort records	Sort related records before they're displayed in current file. Click *Specify* to set sort order.

*Options set in Edit Relationship dialog box.

Defining Relationships

When you define relationships, you do so by using *lookups* or *portals*. Lookup fields *copy* data from a source database into a destination database, where it remains unchanged unless you update it manually. Portals do not copy data, but simply *display* it in the destination file by, in effect, using a window back to the source file (hence the name, portal). For that reason, portals require less storage space since the data is stored in only one file. The portal is also "live" so that any change in the linked data is automatically reflected. Sometimes, you don't want a live connection. Take, for example, an order where you want to preserve an item's cost *at the time of the sale*. A portal showing an item's cost would display an ever-changing price, which could change even after the order was filled. In that case, a lookup would be better. But, when you want to have the most up-to-date data displayed, such as a customer's contact information, use a portal.

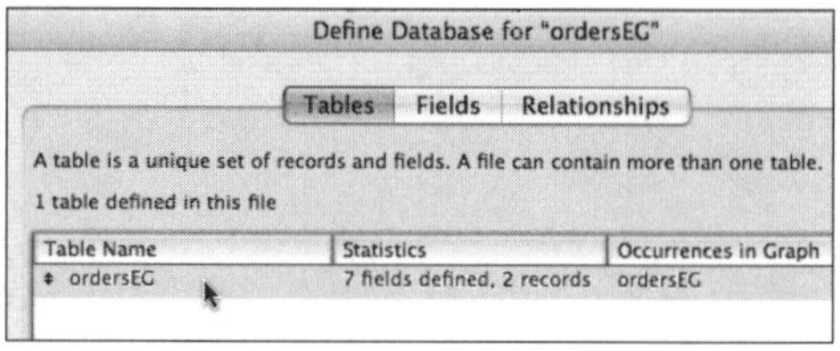

To define a lookup:

1. Open the database you want to use as the destination file (*ordersEG* in our example). In either Browse or Layout mode, choose File > Define > Database (Ctrl Shift D in Windows, ⌘ Shift D on the Mac).

2. When the Define Database dialog box appears, click the *Tables* tab, and select the same file (**Figure 10.15**).

3. Now click the dialog box's *Fields* tab (**Figure 10.16**). In the *Field Name* text window, type in a new field with exactly the same name as the field you want to look up in the source file (in our example, *Item Price* from the *productsEG* file). Select *Number* from the *Type* drop-down menu and click *Create*.

Figure 10.15 When the Define Database dialog box appears, click the *Tables* tab, and select the destination file.

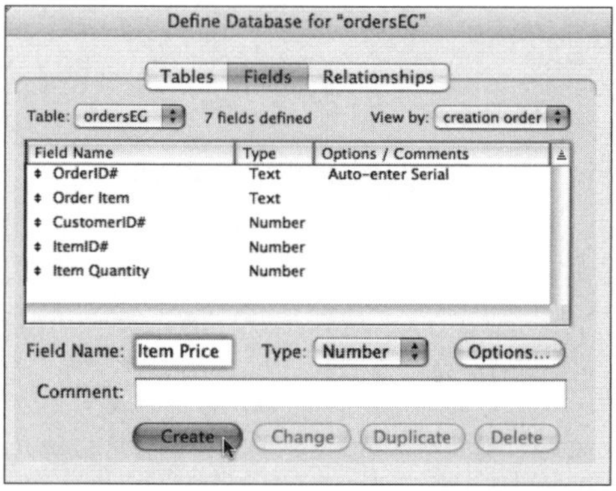

Figures 10.16 In the *Field Name* text window, type in a new field with exactly the same name as the field you want to look up in the source file.

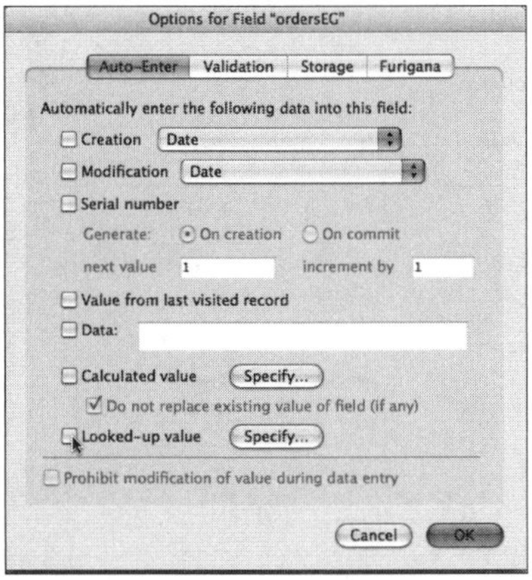

Figures 10.17 When the Options dialog box appears, select *Looked-up value* and click the *Specify* button.

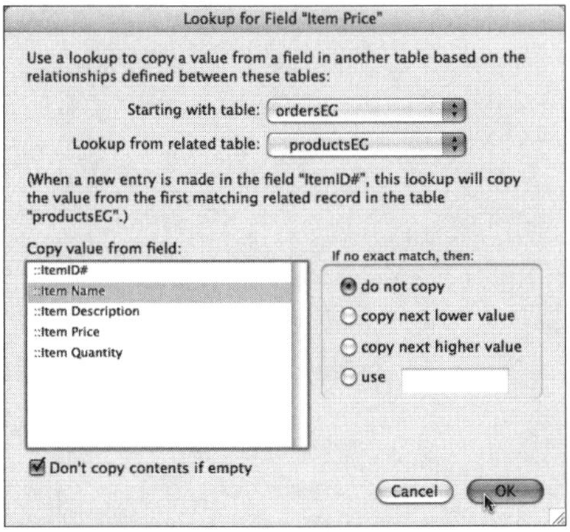

Figure 10.18 Use the *Lookup from related table* drop-down menu to select the source file, then select your source fields in the left-hand list.

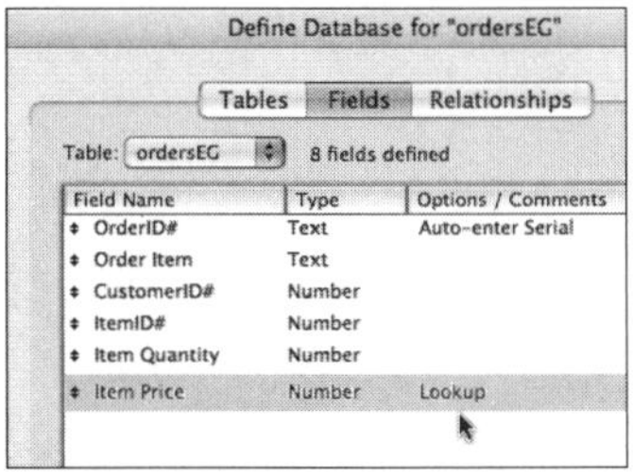

Figure 10.19 The field within the *destination* field (*Item Price*) will have a *Lookup* to the *source* file.

4. Click the *Options* button and when the Options dialog box appears, select *Looked-up value* and click the *Specify* button (**Figure 10.17**).

5. When the Lookup for Field dialog box appears, use the *Lookup from related table* drop-down menu to select the source file (*productsEG* in our example) (**Figure 10.18**).

6. In the left-hand *Copy value from field*, select the source field you want to use (*Item Name* in our example). Leave the default selections *Don't copy contents if empty* and *If no exact match then: do not copy* as they are. Click *OK* to close the dialog box.

7. When the Options dialog box reappears, click *OK* again. Finally, when the Define Database dialog box for your destination file reappears, the field within the destination field (*Item Price*) will have a *Lookup* to the source file (**Figure 10.19**).

(continued)

8. Repeat to add as many lookup fields as you need. Click *OK* to close the dialog box.
9. Since you already linked the two files using a match field, once you also add the lookup fields to a *layout* in the destination file, you can switch to Browse mode, enter a CustomerID#, press Tab, and FileMaker automatically looks up the other fields and copies them from the source file (**Figure 10.20**).

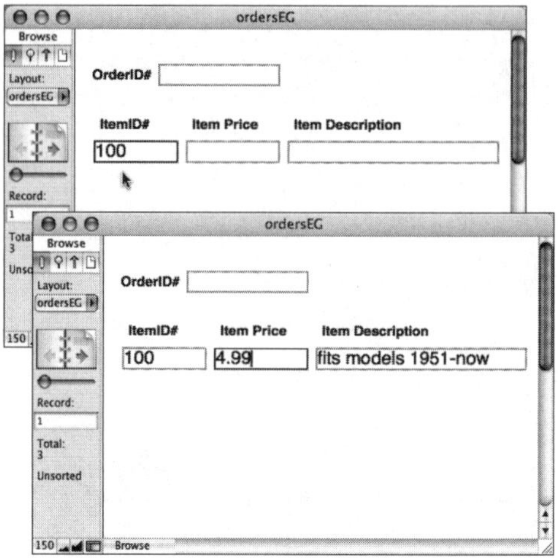

Figure 10.20 In Browse mode, enter a CustomerID#, press Tab, and the other fields are copied from the source file.

✔ Tips

- In step 3, it helps to have the source file open and visible on your screen to ensure that you enter the exact name of the source field in the destination file's Define Database dialog box.
- In step 5, the source file appears in the drop-down menu because you've already defined its relationship to your destination file. If your lookup requires another file that you haven't yet linked to the destination file, select *Define Relationships* from the drop-down menu.
- Once you've defined a relationship, you can create lookups from the destination file to any number of source files. Simply repeat the above steps except that in step 3, you create a new field named after another source file and field.

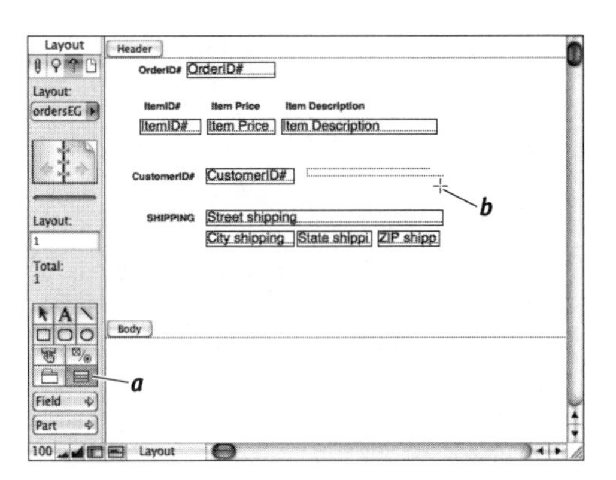

Figure 10.21 Click the Portal Tool (a) and drag the pointer (b) to shape the portal to the size needed.

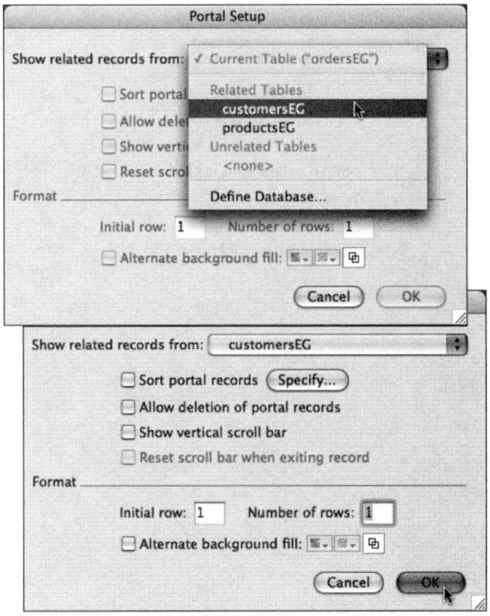

Figure 10.22 When the Portal Setup dialog box appears, use the pop-up menu to choose the source file that contained your match field.

To define a portal:

1. Open the database you want to use as the destination file and switch to Layout mode (Ctrl L in Windows, ⌘ L on the Mac).
2. Assuming you're still working with the default layout (otherwise, select your intended layout in the pop-up menu), click the Portal Tool (a, **Figure 10.21**). Click in the layout and drag the pointer until the portal reaches the general shape and size you want (b, **Figure 10.21**). Release the cursor.
3. When the Portal Setup dialog box appears, use the pop-up menu to choose the source file that contained your match field (**Figure 10.22**). (In our example, we use *customersEG*.) Click *OK* to close the dialog box. (If you have not linked the files previously, choose File > Define > Database and see *To create a relationship* on page 132.)

(continued)

4. When the Add Fields to Portal dialog box appears, click items in the *Available fields* list (Shift-click to select multiple items), then click *Move* (top, **Figure 10.23**). Once you're satisfied with your new list of *Included fields*, click *OK* to close the dialog box (bottom, **Figure 10.23**).

5. The labels of the fields being used appear in the layout's portal (**Figure 10.24**). You can style and format this field as you would any other. (See *Formatting and Graphics in Layouts* on page 197.)

6. Switch to Browse mode (Ctrl B in Windows, ⌘B on the Mac) and the data for those linked fields appears in the portal. In our example, the customer's name, which is stored in the *customersEG* file, now appears in the *ordersEG* file (**Figure 10.25**).

✔ Tips

- In step 3 (**Figure 10.22**), you can use the *Format* panel's text windows and checkbox to choose how many rows (record listings from the related file) you want to appear in the portal. You can change these Format options later if need be.
- You can create portals to *different* source files in the *same* destination layout. This would allow you, for example, to display the billing status for a customer within your orders layout.
- If the portal data is cut off at the end, switch back to Layout mode and click-and-drag the corner of the field to expand the view.

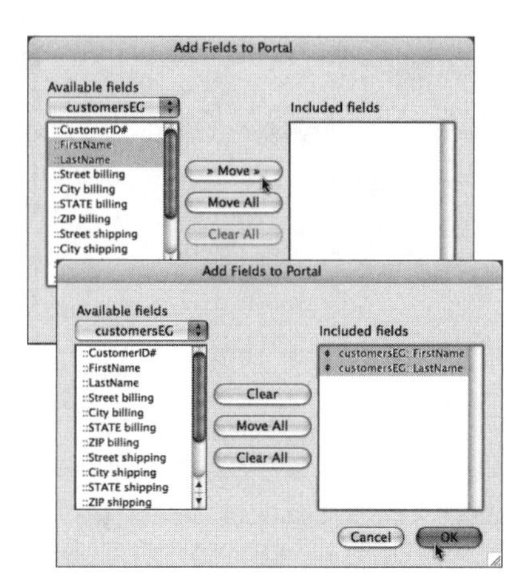

Figure 10.23 In the Add Fields to Portal dialog box, select items in the *Available fields* list and move them into your new list of *Included fields*.

Figure 10.24 The labels of the fields being used appear in the layout's portal.

Figure 10.25 Switch to Browse mode and the data for those linked fields appears in the portal.

Part IV

Designing Layouts

Creating Layouts

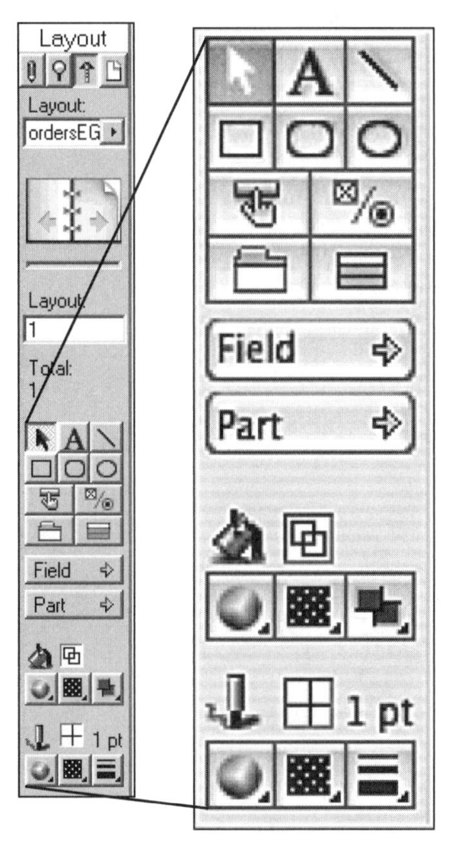

Figure 11.1 All the tools for creating layouts reside in the left-hand status area when you're in Layout mode.

FileMaker's layouts allow you to vary the *appearance* of your data without changing the data itself. This gives you the freedom to create layouts tailored to specific tasks and users. Workers entering orders will find it easier to use a layout that mirrors the sequence of information they get from customers. Sales managers may prefer layouts that help them spot what's selling well. Day-to-day tasks need a different layout than big-picture analysis demands. Remember: You need not show all of a database in a layout. In fact, the more you can pare down a layout to just the essential information, the easier it will be to use.

The Layout status area (**Figure 11.1**) runs down the left side of your screen when you're in Layout mode. The status area includes all the tools you'll need for adding text, graphics, fields, and parts to a layout and then applying colors, patterns, and lines to make them attractive.

You don't necessarily need to start from scratch to create layouts: FileMaker includes dozens of built-in templates. Some you may want to use as is, others may provide a starting point for creating your own custom layouts. For more information, see page 147.

Choosing a Layout Type

When you first define fields in a database, FileMaker by default generates a *standard* layout, which lists the fields and their labels in the order they were created (**Figure 11.2**). You're free to modify that default layout any way you like. Or you may save yourself some trouble in generating a new layout by choosing from the predefined layout types built into FileMaker. Also consider how your layout may be improved using FileMaker's new tabbed controls, which let you organize information into file-folder-styled tabs. See *Using Tabbed Layouts* on page 191.

Use the New Layout command to create standard, columnar, table, label, envelope, and blank layouts. For information on label and envelope layouts, see *Using Label and Envelope Layouts* on page 157.

Here's a quick comparison of each layout type:

Standard: Nothing fancy here. This layout displays all the database's fields in the order they were created. The field labels for each field appear just *left* of the fields (**Figure 11.3**). It includes a blank header and footer.

Columnar list/report: This layout places the database's fields in a row across a single page. The labels for the fields appear in the header *above* the body of the record (**Figure 11.4**). (The footer is blank.) You determine the order of the fields when creating the layout or you can go back and rearrange them any time. Columnar lists and reports make it easier to compare one record to another or to squeeze multiple records onto the same screen.

Figure 11.2 When you first define fields, FileMaker by default generates a standard layout with fields and labels listed in the order they were created.

Figure 11.3 The Standard layout displays fields and their labels in the order they were created.

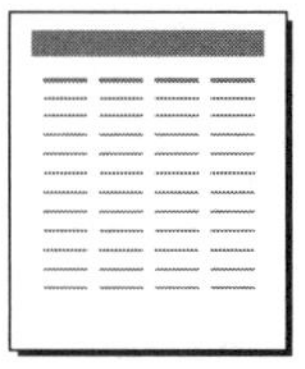

Figure 11.4 The Columnar list/report layout places fields in a single row across the page.

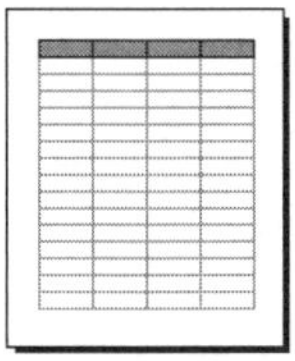

Figure 11.5 The Table view is automatically generated and helps you inspect multiple records on a single screen.

Figure 11.6 The Labels layout handles dozens of preset mailing label styles.

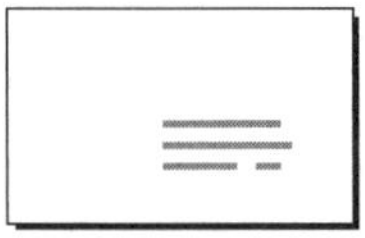

Figure 11.7 The Envelope layout takes the hassle out of generating addressed envelopes.

Figure 11.8 The Blank layout is exactly that—a blank slate if you want to start from scratch.

Table view: This isn't actually a layout as FileMaker usually defines the term (**Figure 11.5**). Instead it is an automatically generated view of your data that is very useful for seeing and sorting multiple records on a single screen. For details on using tables, see page 44. For details on controlling the layout setup for tables, see page 156.

Labels: Use this layout only for labels: you can't enter data into it directly (**Figure 11.6**). The dialog box that appears lets you choose from dozens of pre-set Avery label styles. For more information, see *To create a label layout* on page 157. (The new *Vertical labels* option is useful for Asian characters.)

Envelope: This layout is tailored for printing on regular business envelopes and includes main and return address areas (**Figure 11.7**). Like the labels layout, it's not used for entering data directly. It includes a header and body but no footer. For more information, see *To create an envelope layout* on page 157.

Blank: This layout is entirely blank—nothing appears in the header, body, or footer (**Figure 11.8**). If you want to start with a clean slate and only add fields as you're ready, this is the layout for you.

Working with Layouts

Because label and envelope layouts behave a tad differently than most layouts, they're covered separately on pages 157–160.

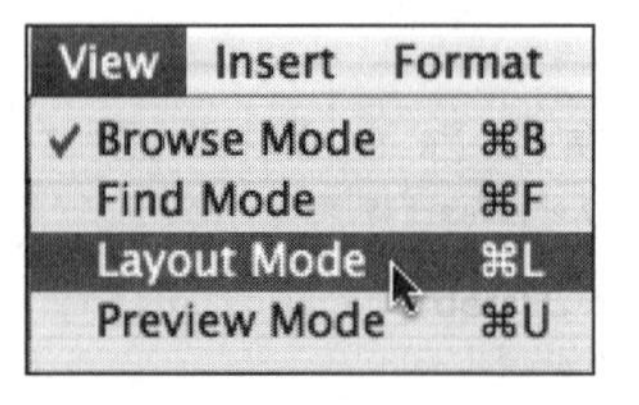

Figure 11.9 To switch to Layout mode, choose View > Layout Mode.

To switch to layout mode:

- Choose View > Layout Mode (**Figure 11.9**).

or

- Use your keyboard: Ctrl L, in Windows, ⌘ L on the Mac.

or

- Click on the T-square button at the top of the tool panel (top, **Figure 11.10**) or the status mode pop-up at the bottom of your screen (bottom, **Figure 11.10**) .

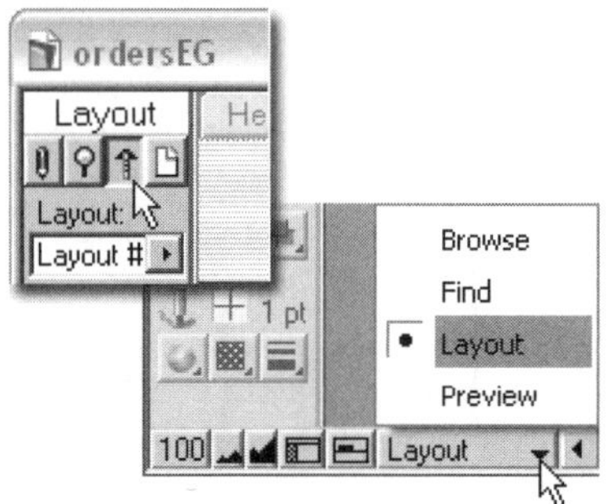

Figure 11.10 You also can switch to Layout mode by clicking the T-square button at the top of the tool panel (top) or the pop-up at the bottom of the status area (bottom).

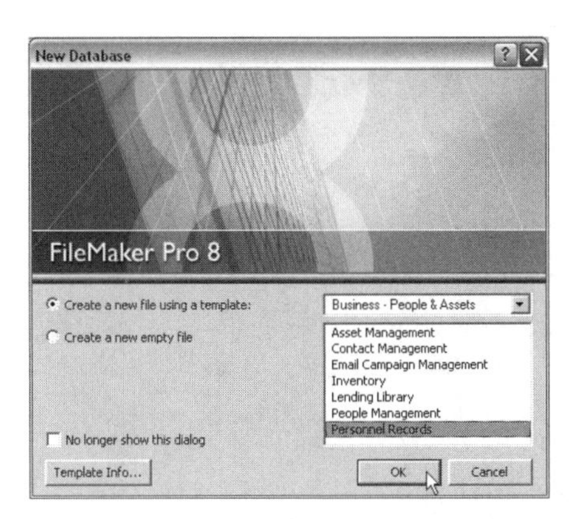

Figure 11.11 To create a template-based file, select *Create a new file using a template*, pick a template from the list, and click *OK*.

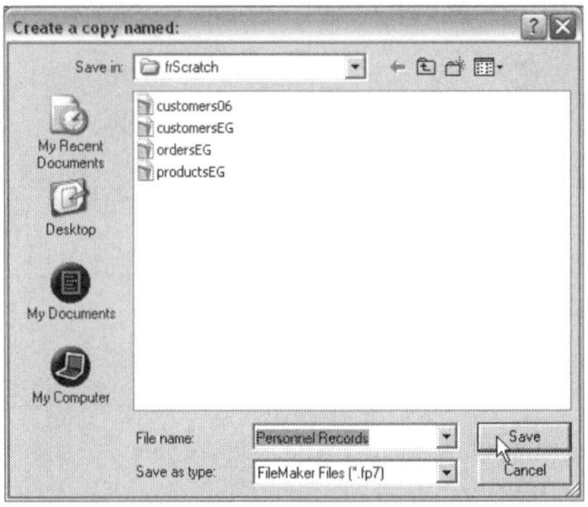

Figure 11.12 Use the create a copy dialog box to navigate to where you want to store the file and give it a distinctive name.

Figure 11.13 A copy of the template appears, ready for you to modify as needed.

Creating template-based layouts

Why reinvent the wheel when FileMaker has rounded up a terrific collection of templates into what it calls Starter Solutions? These templates are empty databases using pre-built layouts, which you can easily customize using the information in this chapter and Chapters 12 and 13.

To create a template-based layout:

1. Choose File > New Database.
2. When the New Database dialog box appears, select *Create a new file using a template*, select a template in the right-side list, and click *OK* (**Figure 11.11**). (If this dialog box doesn't appear, see the first Tip on the next page.)
3. When the dialog box for creating a copy appears (**Figure 11.12**), navigate to the folder where you want to store the file. By default, FileMaker gives the file the same name as the original template but it'll be less confusing if you use a distinctive name. Click *Save*.
4. A copy of the template appears in its default layout, ready for you to modify as needed (**Figure 11.13**).

(continued)

✔ Tips

- In step 2, if you don't see the dialog box in **Figure 11.11**, choose Edit > Preferences (Windows) or FileMaker Pro > Preferences (Mac), select the *General* tab and check *Show templates in New Database dialog box* (**Figure 11.14**). Click *OK* to close the Preferences dialog box and start again with step 1.
- In step 2, if you want to know more about a particular template before using it, click *Template Info*. A detailed description of the selected template—with the option of seeing information on all the templates—appears in a separate window (**Figure 11.15**). If you find a template you want to use, click *New Database* and resume with step 3.

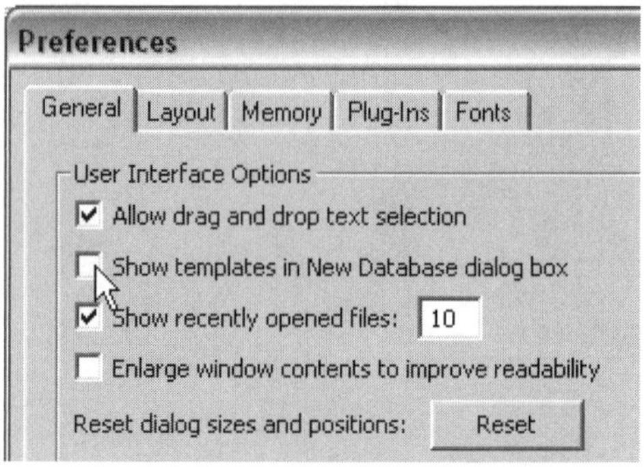

Figure 11.14 If you don't see the dialog box in **Figure 11.11**, open FileMaker's Preferences dialog box, select the *General* tab and check *Show templates in New Database dialog box*.

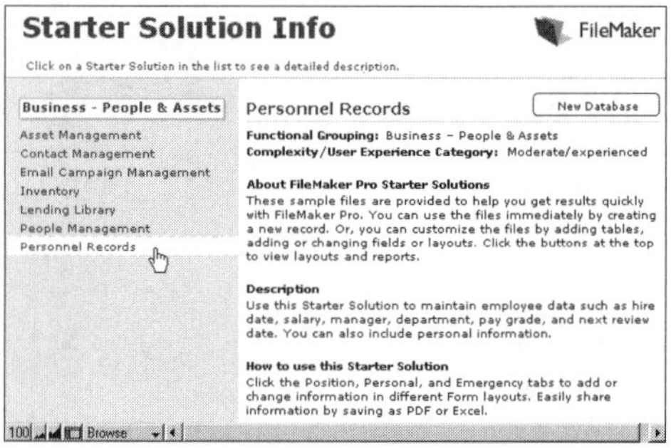

Figure 11.15 Click any item in the left-side list to see information on how to use that template. Once you find an appropriate template, click *New Database*.

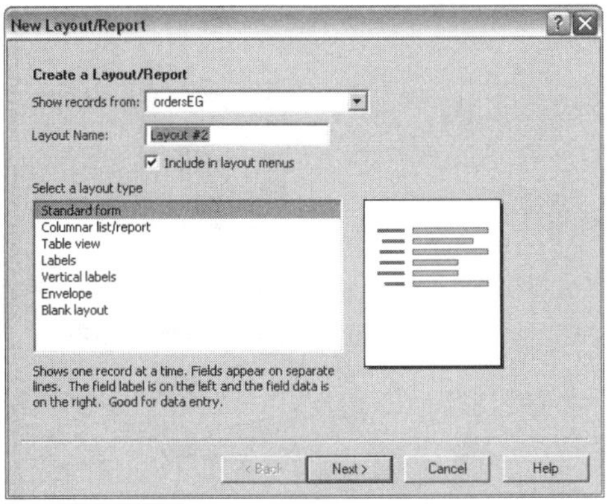

Figure 11.16 In the Create a Layout/Report portion of the New Layout/Report dialog box, give your layout a name, choose one of seven types, and click *Next.*

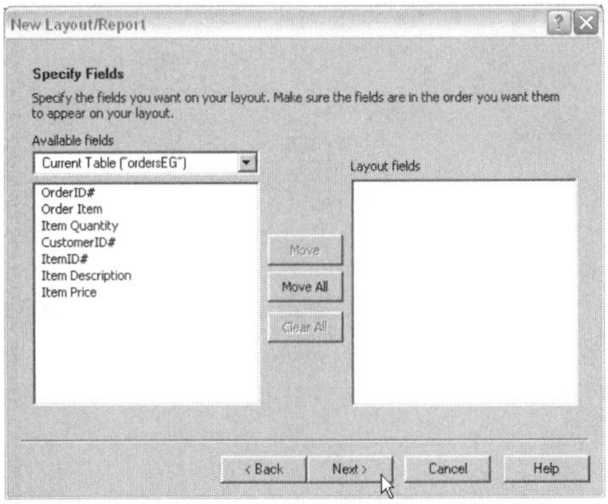

Figure 11.17 Highlight the fields in the left-hand list that you want to appear in the layout and use the *Move* or *Move All* button to place them in the right-hand list.

Creating a new layout

FileMaker now includes a set of three screens within the New Layout/Report dialog box that walks you through the process. For Windows users, this Wizard-style guide will be old hat.

To create a new layout:

1. Switch to Layout mode (Ctrl L in Windows, ⌘ L on the Mac). Choose Layouts > New Layout/Report (Ctrl N in Windows, ⌘ N on the Mac).
2. When the Create a Layout/Report portion of the New Layout/Report dialog box appears, type a name into the *Layout Name* text box (**Figure 11.16**). By default, FileMaker assigns each new layout a generic name (e.g., *Layout #2*), but it's best to give it an easy-to-recognize name. Choose one of the seven layouts in the left-side *Select a layout type* text box (a preview appears to the right), and click *Next.*
3. When the Specify Fields screen appears (**Figure 11.17**), highlight the fields in the left-hand list that you want to appear in the layout and use the *Move* or *Move All* button to place them in the right-hand list. Or double-click on fields in the left list and they will automatically appear to the right. When you're done, click *Next.*

(continued)

4. When the Select a Theme screen appears, make a choice in the left-side *Layout themes* list and a preview appears to the right (**Figure 11.18**). When you're done, click *Finish*.

   The new layout appears on your screen (**Figure 11.19**). If you're happy with the layout, switch to Browse (Ctrl B in Windows, ⌘B on the Mac) and begin entering data. More likely, however, you'll want to further format the layout. For more information, see *Formatting Fields or Objects* on page 203.

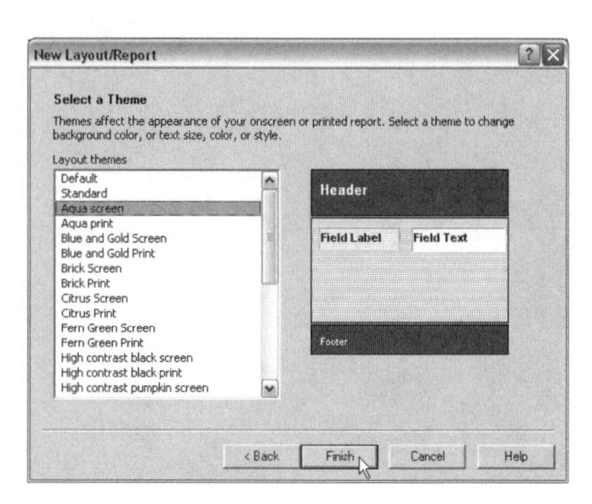

Figure 11.18 Pick a theme on the left and a preview appears on the right.

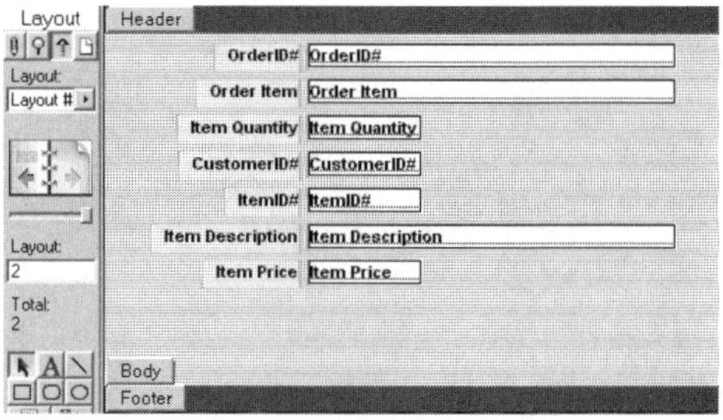

Figure 11.19 Once you make your choices in a series of dialog boxes, the new layout appears on your screen.

✔ Tips

- By default, FileMaker activates the *Include in layout pop-up menu* checkbox in the New Layout/Report dialog box (**Figure 11.16**). It's best to leave it checked to ensure that this layout appears in your layout's pop-down menu.
- As you create more layouts, click on the pop-down menu above the book icon to quickly switch to the layout you need to use.

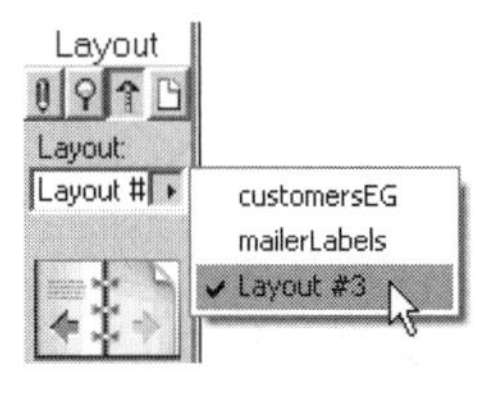

Figure 11.20 Select the layout you want to rename by clicking it in the Layout pop-down menu.

To rename a layout:

1. Make sure you're in Layout mode (Ctrl L in Windows, ⌘ L on the Mac), then select the layout you want to rename by clicking it in the pop-down menu just above the book icon (**Figure 11.20**).
2. Choose Layouts > Layout Setup.
3. When the Layout Setup dialog box appears, make sure the *General* tab is selected, type in the new name, and click *OK* (**Figure 11.21**). The layout pop-down menu now displays the renamed layout (**Figure 11.22**).

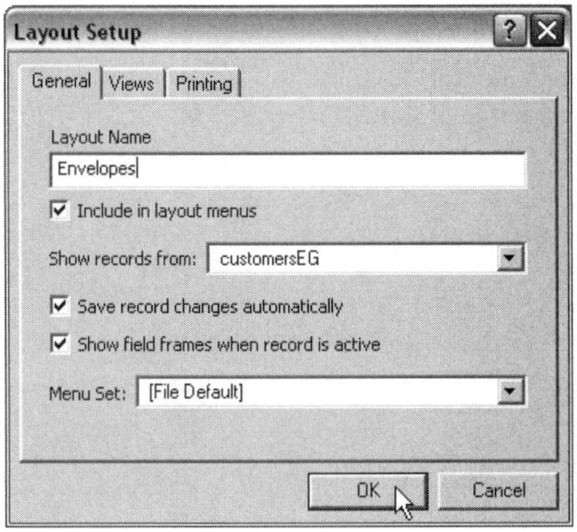

Figure 11.21 Type the new layout name inside the *Layout Name* text box and click *OK*.

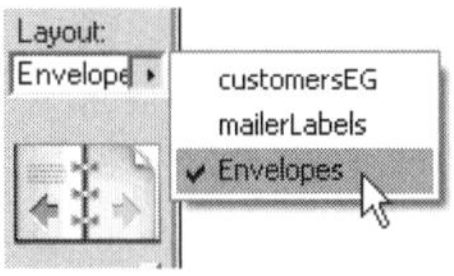

Figure 11.22 The new name appears in the pop-down menu of available layouts.

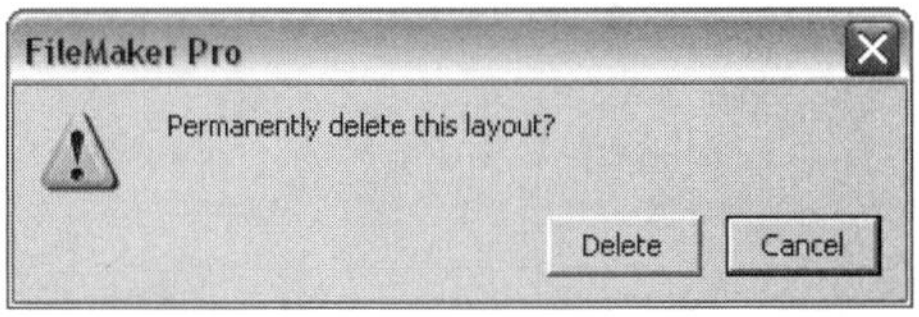

To delete a layout:

1. Make sure you're in Layout mode (Ctrl L in Windows, ⌘ L on the Mac), then select the layout you want to rename by clicking it in the pop-down menu just above the book icon (**Figure 11.20**).
2. Once the layout appears onscreen, choose Layouts > Delete Layout (Ctrl E in Windows, ⌘ E on the Mac).
3. A warning dialog box appears. If you're sure, click *Delete* (**Figure 11.23**). The layout disappears onscreen, replaced by the next layout listed in the pop-down menu.

Figure 11.23 Still sure you want to get rid of the layout? Then click *Delete*.

Duplicating a layout

This procedure will save you some time if you want to design a new layout based on elements in an existing layout.

To duplicate a layout:

1. Make sure you're in Layout mode (Ctrl L in Windows, ⌘ L on the Mac). Select the layout you want to duplicate by clicking on it in the pop-down menu just above the book icon.
2. Choose Layouts > Duplicate Layout. (There are no keyboard equivalents.) The duplicate layout appears onscreen and will be listed in the layout pop-down menu as a copy of the layout you selected. If you want to give the duplicate layout a more distinctive name, see *To rename a layout* on the previous page.

To choose a layout view:

- Make sure you're in Layout mode (Ctrl L in Windows, ⌘ L on the Mac). Click on the pop-down menu just above the left-hand book and release your cursor on the layout of your choice (**Figure 11.24**).

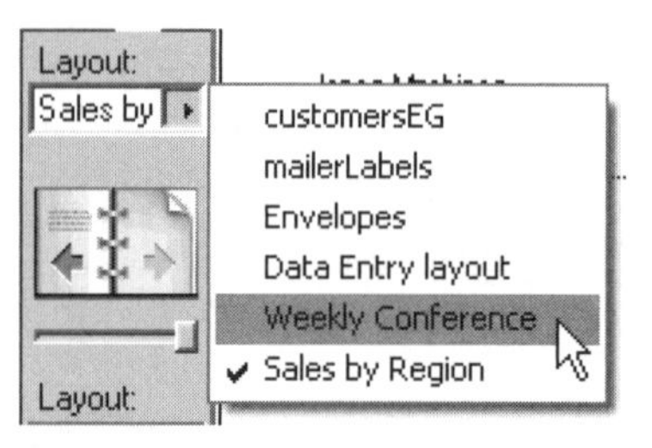

Figure 11.24 To choose among your existing layouts, use the pop-down menu just above the book icon.

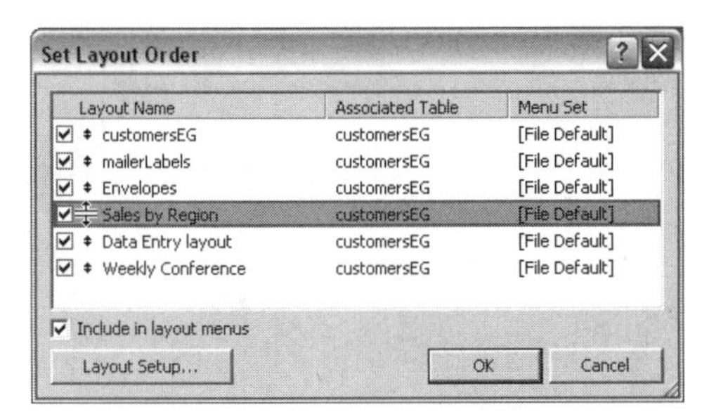

Figure 11.25 Click and drag to reorder layouts listed within the Set Layout Order dialog box.

To reorder the layout pop-down menu:

1. Make sure you're in Layout mode (Ctrl L in Windows, ⌘ L on the Mac). Choose Layouts > Set Layout Order.
2. When the Set Layout Order dialog box appears, click on the layout name you want to reorder. Keep your cursor down and a double arrow appears (**Figure 11.25**). While holding down the cursor, drag the layout name to the place you want it listed in the order. Release the cursor. Repeat this step to further rearrange the layout order.
3. Once you're satisfied with the order, click *OK*. The layout pop-down menu now reflects the new order.

✔ Tips

- If you've set up a database for multiple users, only the host will be able to reorder the list—and only when filesharing for the database is turned off.
- The *Menu Set* feature (**Figure 11.25**) is only available in FileMaker Pro 8 Advanced, a more expensive version with more features.
- Hurray for the new *Layout Setup* button within the Set Layout Order dialog box: Just click and up pops the Layout Set dialog box for on-the-fly changes.

Putting layouts in the pop-down menu

FileMaker's default is to automatically include layouts in the pop-down menu via the checkbox within the New Layout/Report dialog box (**Figure 11.26**). If you want to tidy up the list by excluding some layouts—or you mistakenly excluded a layout from the list—the steps are the same.

To exclude or include layouts in the layout pop-down menu:

1. Make sure you're in Layout mode (Ctrl L in Windows, ⌘ L on the Mac). Choose Layouts > Set Layout Order.
2. In the Set Layout Order dialog box a column of checkboxes runs down the left side. To *exclude* a layout from the pop-down menu, uncheck the box by clicking it. To *include* a layout, click the box again (**Figure 11.27**).
3. When you're satisfied, click *OK*.

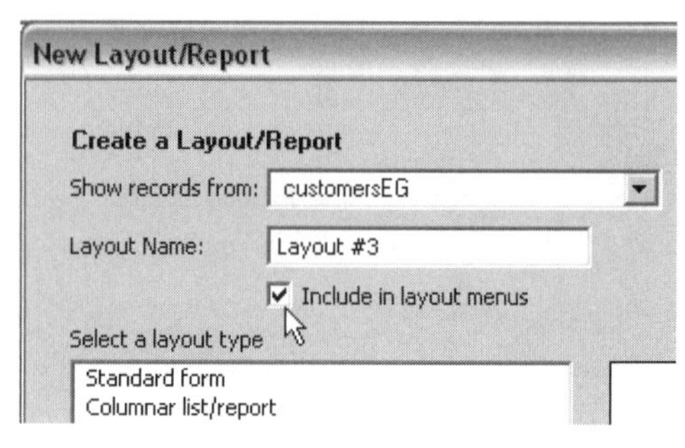

Figure 11.26 So easy to miss: The *Include in layout pop-up menu* checkbox within the New Layout/Report dialog box determines which layouts *initially* appear in the pop-down menu.

Set Layout Order

Layout Name	Associated Table	Menu Set
☑ customersEG	customersEG	[File Default]
☑ mailerLabels	customersEG	[File Default]
☑ Envelopes	customersEG	[File Default]
☑ Sales by Region	customersEG	[Standard FileM...
☐ Data Entry layout	customersEG	[File Default]
☐ Weekly Conference	customersEG	[File Default]

Include in layout menus

Layout Setup... OK Cancel

Figure 11.27 Click the boxes to control which layouts appear in the revised pop-down menu of layouts. Checked layouts will appear; unchecked will not.

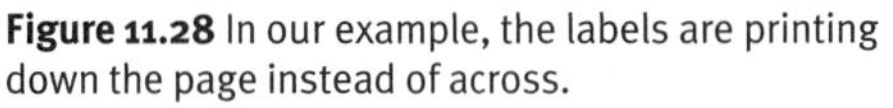

Figure 11.28 In our example, the labels are printing down the page instead of across.

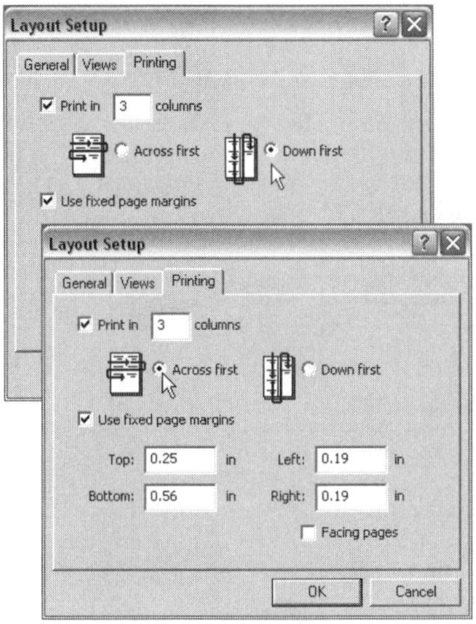

Figure 11.29 Click the *Printing* tab in the Layout Setup dialog box, then select one of two radio buttons to change the orientation.

Figure 11.30 Switch to Preview mode to see the effects of your choices.

Changing the general layout setup

Use this to change how layout columns print and to change a layout's page margins.

To change the general layout setup:

1. In our example, the labels are printing down the page instead of across (**Figure 11.28**). Pick the layout you want to change by selecting it via the pop-down menu.
2. Choose Layouts > Layout Setup.
3. Within the Layout Setup dialog box click the *Printing* tab. In our example, the *Down first* radio button is selected (top, **Figure 11.29**). To change the orientation, select the *Across first* button (bottom, **Figure 11.29**).
4. When you're done, click *OK* and switch to Preview mode to see the effects of your choices (**Figure 11.30**).

✔ Tips

- Select *Use fixed page margins* and use the four number-entry boxes if you want to use different margins from your printer's default settings.
- Use the *Facing pages* checkbox if you'll be printing on both sides of the page. This places the narrower, inside margin on the left of odd-numbered pages and on the right of even-numbered pages.

Changing the table view setup

Use this to change the setup of the table view. You also can use it to limit a user's view of the database as a list, form, or table.

To change the table view:

1. Pick the layout you want to change by selecting it via the pop-down menu just above the left-hand book.
2. Choose Layouts > Layout Setup.
3. When the Layout Setup dialog box appears, click the *Views* tab, and then click the *Properties* button (**Figure 11.31**).
4. When the Table View Properties dialog box appears, use the checkboxes to set whether the table will display a grid, a header or any other parts, and column headers (**Figure 11.32**). You also can use the *Rows* checkbox and its adjacent text windows to fine-tune the height of the table rows.
5. Once you've made your choices, click *OK* and switch to Browse mode to see the effects of your choices.

✔ Tip

- In step 3, if you uncheck any of the three views, that choice will be dimmed (and, so, not available) in the View menu within the Browse mode (**Figure 11.33**).

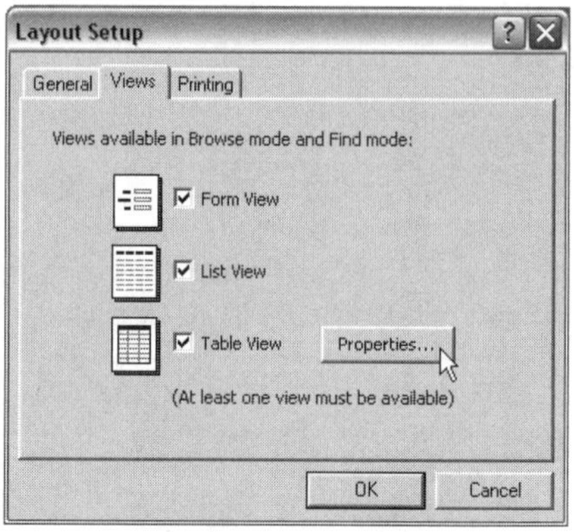

Figure 11.31 Use the *Views* tab of the Layout Setup dialog box to control which views are available in Browse mode or click *Properties* to set the details of the *Table View*.

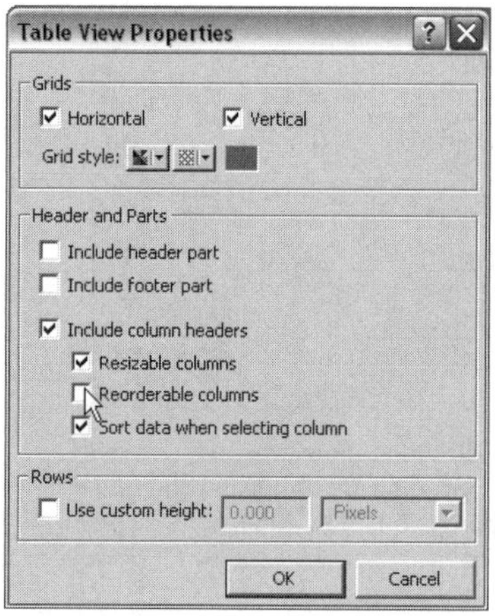

Figure 11.32 The Table View Properties dialog box offers precise control over how the table appears.

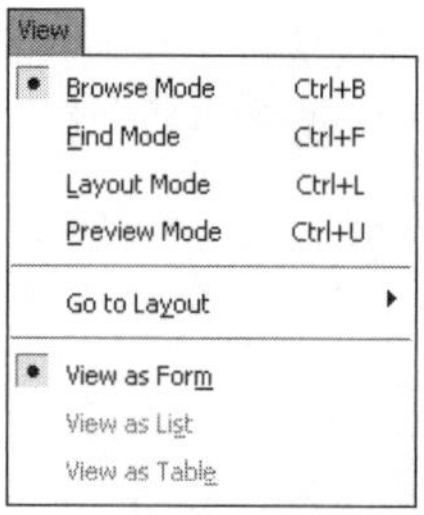

Figure 11.33 Based on your choices in step 3, some choices will be dimmed in the View menu.

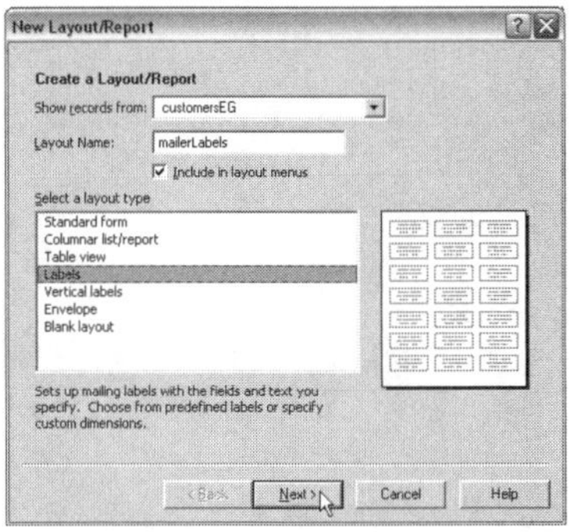

Figure 11.34 When the New Layout/Report dialog box appears, choose *Labels* in the left-side list and click *Next*.

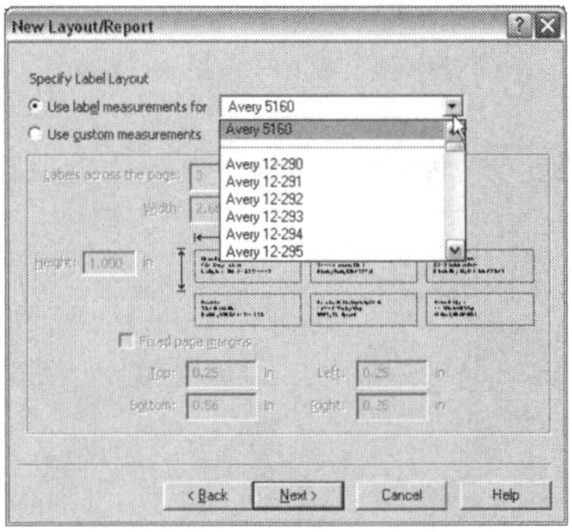

Figure 11.35 Use the label setup screen to choose a preset Avery-based label size or create a custom size.

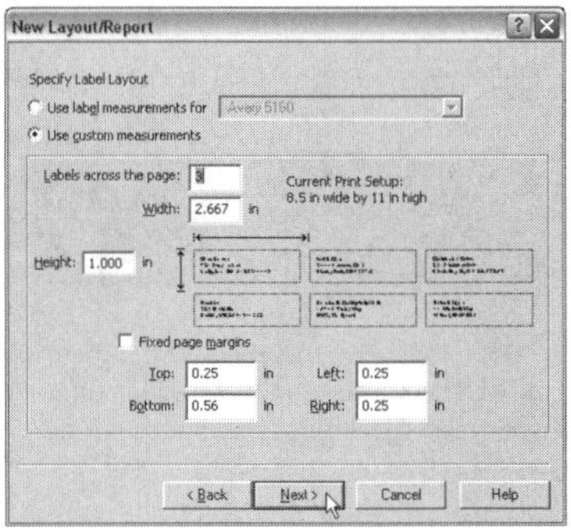

Figure 11.36 Choosing the *Use custom measurements* button lets you adjust the label's width and height, and set how many labels fit across the page.

Using Label and Envelope Layouts

FileMaker makes generating labels and addressing envelopes easy—and a real boon for what sometimes can be an inconvenient process. For more information on using other, standard layouts, see *Working with Layouts* on page 146.

To create a label layout:

1. Switch to Layout mode (Ctrl L in Windows, ⌘L on the Mac), then choose Layouts > New Layout/Report (Ctrl N in Windows, ⌘N on the Mac).
2. When the Create a Layout/Report screen of the New Layout/Report dialog box appears, type a name into the *Layout Name* text box. Choose *Labels* in the left-side *Select a layout type* list and click *Next* (**Figure 11.34**).
3. The next dialog box gives you the choice of using one of several dozen preset Avery-based label sizes or creating a custom-size label (**Figure 11.35**).
4. To use an Avery-based label, leave the *Use label measurements for* radio button selected and use the pop-down menu to choose the appropriate Avery size based on the labels you're using. By the way, even non-Avery label packages usually list an Avery-equivalent stock number.
5. To create a custom size, select the *Use custom measurements* radio button, then use the *Labels across the page*, *Width*, and *Height* boxes to configure your label's size (**Figure 11.36**).
6. Click *Next*.

(continued)

7. When the Specify screen appears, make a selection in the Available Fields list and click the *Add Field* button (**Figure 11.37**). Selected fields appear in the lower window surrounded by « » brackets. The brackets act as placeholders for data.

8. To place a field on a new line, press Enter (Windows) or Return (Mac). To insert punctuation marks, space between the fields, or additional text, just use your keyboard.

9. To remove a mistake, select the entry in the lower box and press Delete. To start over, click on the dialog box's *Clear All* button. To further format the layout, see *Formatting Fields or Objects* on page 203.

10. When you're done, click *Next*. One final dialog box appears (**Figure 11.38**), giving you a choice of switching to Preview mode to see how the labels will print or staying in Layout mode to continue tweaking its appearance. Make your choice and click *Finish*. The chosen view appears, which in our example is the Layout view (**Figure 11.39**).

✔ Tip

- In step 7, thanks to FileMaker's improved relational database features, you're not limited to just using fields from the current file or table (**Figure 11.37**). Instead, you have the option of using the *Available fields* drop-down menu to add fields from any related file or table.

Figure 11.37 Use the Specify screen to choose the fields you want displayed.

Figure 11.38 Once you're done setting up the layout, you can switch to Preview mode to see how the labels will print, or stay in Layout mode.

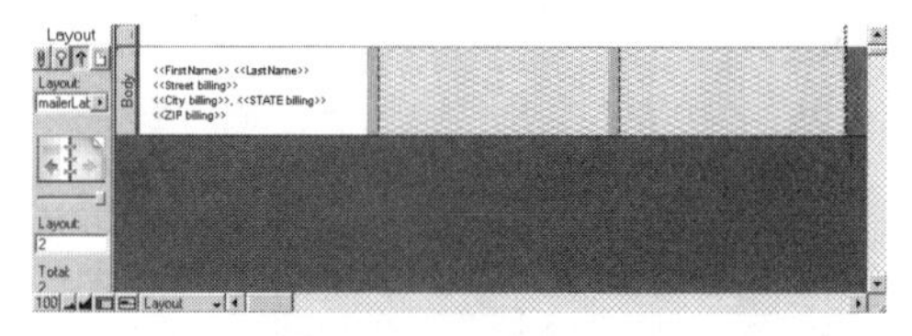

Figure 11.39 The layout for the label appears once you close the Specify Label Contents screen. Click on and drag the vertical marker to adjust the label's width.

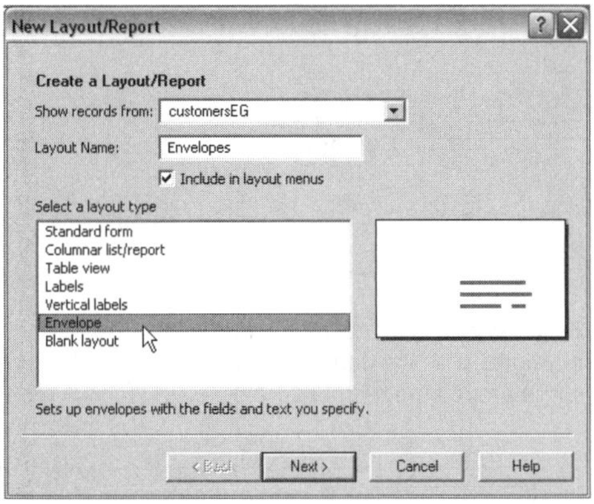

Figure 11.40 When the New Layout/Report dialog box appears, name the layout and choose *Envelope* in the left-side list.

To create an envelope layout:

1. Switch to Layout mode (Ctrl L in Windows, ⌘L on the Mac), then choose Layouts > New Layout/Report (Ctrl N in Windows, ⌘N on the Mac).

2. When the Create a Layout/Report dialog box appears, type a name into the *Layout Name* text box. Choose *Envelope* in the left-side *Select a layout type* list and click *Next* (**Figure 11.40**).

3. When the Specify dialog box appears, double-click on the fields in the upper-left list that displayed or select each one in the list and click the *Add Field* button (**Figure 11.37**). Selected fields appear in the lower window surrounded by « » brackets. The brackets act as placeholders for data.

   To place a field on a new line, press Enter (Windows) or Return (Mac). To insert punctuation marks, space between the fields, or additional text, just use your keyboard.

   To remove a mistake, select the entry in the lower box and press Delete. To start over, click on the dialog box's *Clear All* button. To further format the layout, see *Formatting Fields or Objects* on page 203.

4. When you're done, click *Next*. One final dialog box appears (**Figure 11.38**), giving you a choice of switching to Preview mode to see how the envelopes will print or staying in Layout mode to continue tweaking its appearance. Make your choice, click *Finish* and the layout appears in the chosen mode. For more information on printing, see *Printing* on page 81.

To create an envelope return address:

1. Once you've created an envelope layout, be sure you're still in Layout mode. Select the layout using the pop-down menu just above the book icon.
2. Select the Type tool from within the Layout mode's status area, then click within the envelope layout's *header*.
3. Type in the return address, using the text options under the Format menu. For more on formatting *individual* blocks of text, see *Formatting Fields or Objects* on page 203. For more on *database-wide* text defaults, see *To set formatting defaults* on page 200.
4. Click on and drag the double arrow between the header and body to close up the empty space around the return address (**Figure 11.41**).
5. Choose Preview from the Mode menu (Ctrl U in Windows, ⌘U on the Mac) to double-check your envelope layout before you print it (**Figure 11.42**).

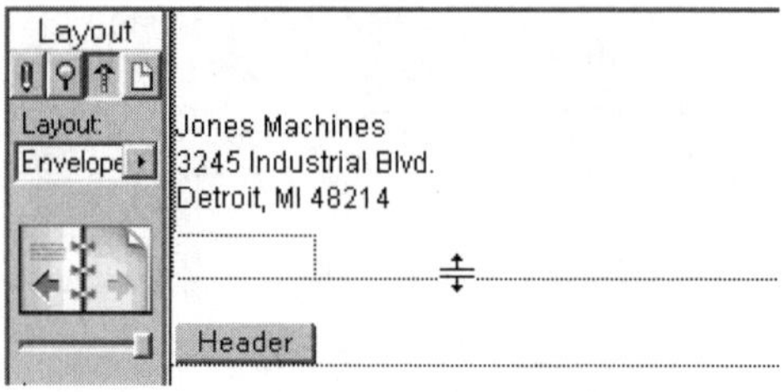

Figure 11.41 After creating a return address for an envelope, drag the double arrow to close up empty space around the return address.

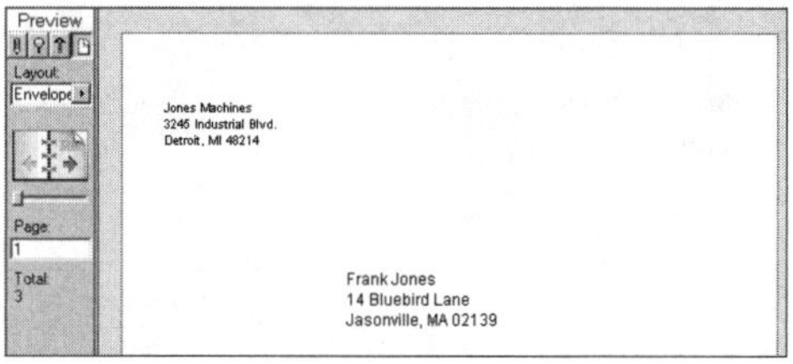

Figure 11.42 Use the Preview command (Ctrl U in Windows, ⌘U on the Mac) to double-check the envelope's appearance before printing.

Creating Form Letter Layouts

Form letters—standard letters containing bits of customized information—are easy to create using FileMaker's merge fields. By creating a layout that's mostly text with a few judiciously placed merge fields, you can create a customized letter for your customers:

> Dear Ms. Rose,
>
> Spring is in the air and as a long-time customer, you'll want to take advantage of our annual spring flower sale.
>
> All bedding plants are 20 percent off, garden tools are discounted by 15 percent, and turf builders are reduced by 30 percent. But the savings don't stop there! You'll find hundreds of items on sale.
>
> For preferred customers like yourself, the doors open at 10 a.m. on Thursday, May 18. The sale starts for the general public at 10 a.m. on Friday, May 19.
>
> Sincerely,
>
> James Green

In FileMaker, which uses << and >> to mark merge fields, the letter looks like this:

> Dear <<courtesy title.>> <<last name>>,
>
> Spring is in the air and as a long-time customer, you'll want to take advantage of our annual spring flower sale.
>
> All <<spring purchase #1>> are <<discount-spring purchase #1>> off, <<spring purchase #2>> are discounted by <<discount-spring purchase #2>>, and <<spring purchase #3.>> are reduced by <<discount-spring purchase #3>>. But the savings don't stop there! You'll find hundreds of items on sale.
>
> For preferred customers like yourself, the doors open at 10 a.m. on Thursday, May 18. The sale starts for the general public at 10 a.m. on Friday, May 19.
>
> Sincerely,
>
> <<sales staff name>>

If you resist the urge to drown customers with frequent mailings, form letters with merge fields can be a powerful tool.

To create a form letter with merge fields:

1. Open the database from which the data will be drawn and switch to Layout mode (Ctrl L in Windows, ⌘ L on the Mac).
2. Choose Layouts > New Layout/Report (Ctrl N in Windows, ⌘ N on the Mac). When the New Layout/Report dialog box appears (**Figure 11.43**), type a name into the *Layout Name* text box, choose *Blank layout* within the *Select a layout type* area, and click *Finish*.
3. When the new layout appears, select the Type tool from the left-hand Layout status area and begin typing in your letter. When you reach the spot where you want the first merge field to appear (**Figure 11.44**), choose Insert > Merge Field (Ctrl M in Windows, Option ⌘ M on the Mac).

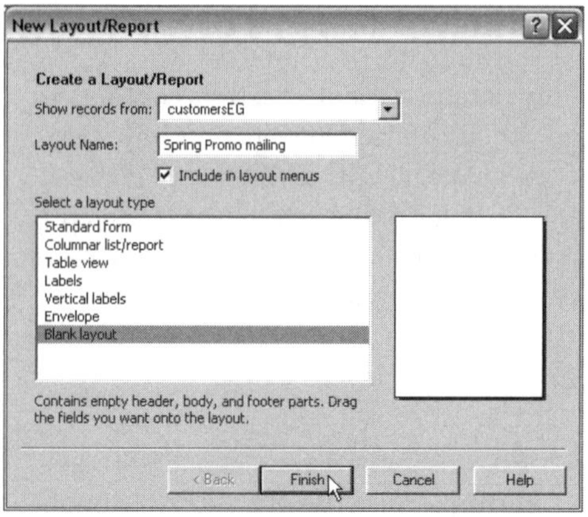

Figure 11.43 To create a form letter, choose *Blank layout* when selecting a new layout.

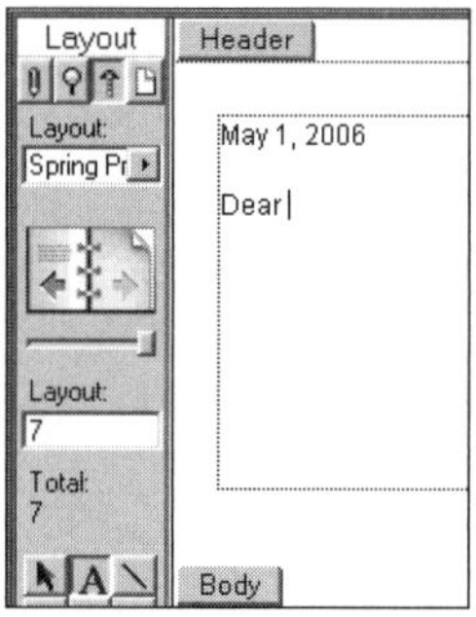

Figure 11.44 Click your cursor where you want a merge field to appear, then choose Insert > Merge Field (Ctrl M in Windows, Option ⌘ M on the Mac).

Figure 11.45 When the Specify Field dialog box appears, double-click on the field you want as a merge field.

Figure 11.46 Once you place a merge field in a layout, a pair of << >> mark its boundaries.

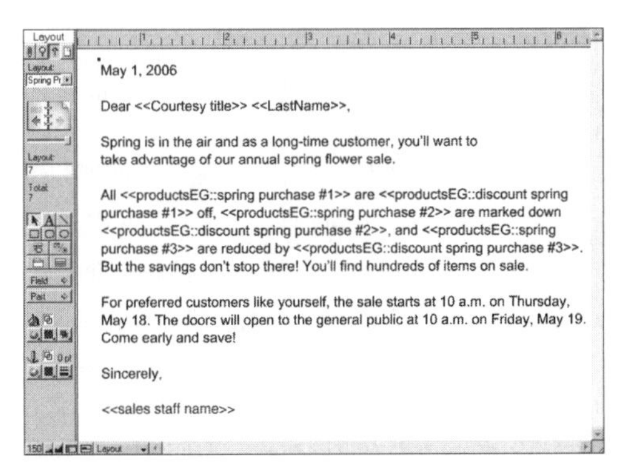

May 1, 2006

Dear <<Courtesy title>> <<LastName>>,

Spring is in the air and as a long-time customer, you'll want to take advantage of our annual spring flower sale.

All <<productsEG::spring purchase #1>> are <<productsEG::discount spring purchase #1>> off, <<productsEG::spring purchase #2>> are marked down <<productsEG::discount spring purchase #2>>, and <<productsEG::spring purchase #3>> are reduced by <<productsEG::discount spring purchase #3>>. But the savings don't stop there! You'll find hundreds of items on sale.

For preferred customers like yourself, the sale starts at 10 a.m. on Thursday, May 18. The doors will open to the general public at 10 a.m. on Friday, May 19. Come early and save!

Sincerely,

<<sales staff name>>

Figure 11.47 The final form letter shows where each merge field's contents will be inserted once you switch to Browse mode.

4. When the Specify Field dialog box appears, double-click on the field you want to appear in the letter (**Figure 11.45**). A merge field appears within the form letter layout (**Figure 11.46**).

5. Continue typing the letter, adding additional merge fields as you need them until you're done (**Figure 11.47**). To see what the form letter will look like, switch to Browse mode. To format the letter's fonts and other text attributes, see *Formatting Fields or Objects* on page 203. To set the letter's margins and prepare it for printing, see *Printing* on page 81.

✔ Tip

- Thanks to FileMaker's improved relational abilities, it's easy to create merge fields pulling from any related file or table. For example, in **Figure 11.47**, all the merge fields in the second paragraph come from the productsEG file instead of customersEG, the source of the first merge fields. FileMaker marks such related file merge fields with :: (a double colon) to remind you of the external source. (For details, see *To create a relationship* on page 132.)

Using Variable Fields

FileMaker's Insert menu includes a great feature that lets you insert field data that is automatically updated. There are two types of fields in the Insert menu: fixed and variable (**Figure 11.48**). Fixed data field—Current Date, Current Time, and Current User Name—paste information that is current *at the time it is entered.* Once pasted into a file, the data remains fixed and is not updated. In contrast, the variable fields—Date Symbol, Time Symbol, User Name Symbol, Page Number Symbol, and Record Number Symbol—are updated *when the file is viewed or printed.*

These variable fields are particularly handy for form letters because a letter can be prepared in advance, yet contain the dates and times reflecting the time when it's actually printed out. This trick, by the way, need not be confined to form letters. Use it in any layout where you need updated information to appear—including onscreen forms.

To insert a variable field:

1. Make sure you're in Layout mode (Ctrl L in Windows, ⌘ L on the Mac), select the Type tool from within the Layout mode's status area, and click in the layout where you want the variable data to appear.
2. Choose Insert and then the variable field type you want: Date Symbol, Time Symbol, User Name Symbol, Page Number Symbol, or Record Number Symbol (**Figure 11.48**). Release your cursor and a placeholder symbol is inserted (**Figure 11.49**). For more on what appears in the layout, especially the placeholder symbols, see **Table 11.1**.

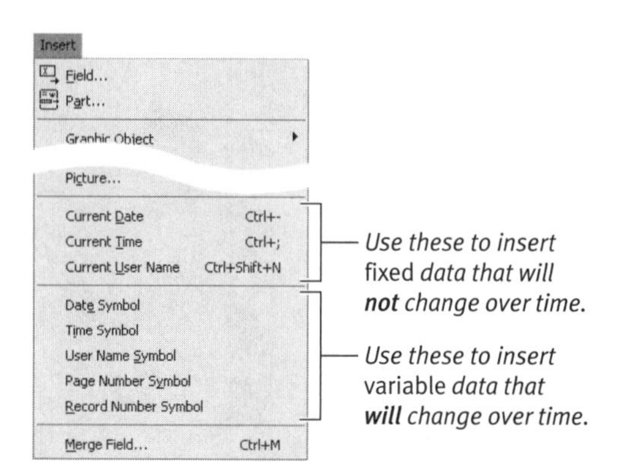

Figure 11.48 The Insert menu contains two types of fields: fixed and variable.

//

Dear <<Courtesy title>> <<LastName>>,

Spring is in the air and as a long-time customer, take advantage of our annual spring flower sale.

Figure 11.49 When you choose Insert > Date Symbol, a double forward slash (//) acts as a placeholder within the layout.

Table 11.1

Variable Field Symbols

To Use	Choose Insert And:	Inserts (Symbol
Fixed date	Current Date	Date at time field created
Fixed time	Current Time	Time at time field created
Fixed user name	Current User Name	Name of person creating field
Variable date	Date Symbol	Placeholder (//)
Variable time	Time Symbol	Placeholder (::)
Variable name	User Name Symbol	Placeholder (II)
Variable page	Page Number Symbol	Placeholder (##)
Variable record	Record Number Symbol	Placeholder (@@)

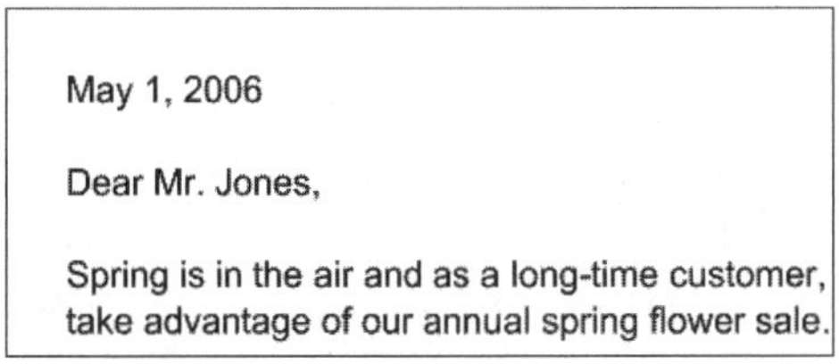

May 1, 2006

Dear Mr. Jones,

Spring is in the air and as a long-time customer, take advantage of our annual spring flower sale.

Figure 11.50 When you switch from Layout to Browse mode, the date symbol is replaced by the *current* date, which will be continually updated.

3. Return to Browse mode and the placeholder is updated to reflect the most current data (**Figure 11.50**).

✔ Tip

- The formatting for dates, times, and numbers inserted with variable fields is controlled like any other date, time, or number field. For example, you can have dates appear as 5/6/2008 or May 6, 2008. For more information, see *Formatting and Graphics in Layouts* on page 197.

Working with Parts

In most cases, the functions of the various layout parts are obvious from their names: header, body, and footer. Summary parts work a bit differently than other layout parts. Since summary fields gather information from across several records, they cannot appear within the body of an individual record. That's where the various kinds of summary parts come in by providing a way to display this cross-record data. *Grand summary* parts summarize information for all the records being browsed. *Subsummary* parts do the same for a group of records, based on the break field you designate within the Part Definition dialog box.

Title header: This special type of header appears only at the top of the page or first screen. It can also be used as a title page. Each layout can only contain one title header.

Header: Use for field titles or column headings in columnar layouts (**Figure 11.51**). It appears at the top of every page or screen. Each layout can only contain one header.

Leading grand summary: Use this type of summary part to display summary information at the *beginning* of the group of the records being browsed.

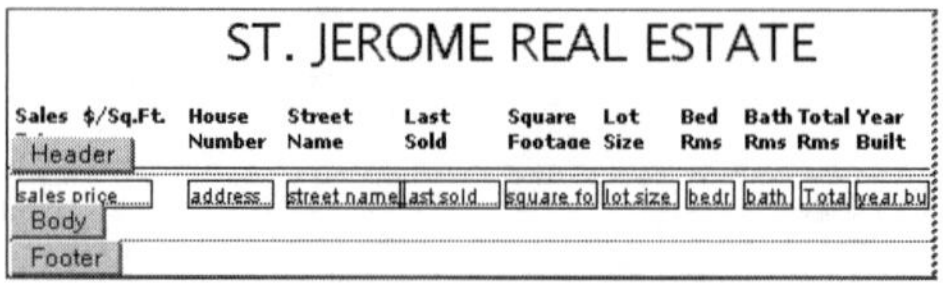

Figure 11.51 Used in a columnar layout, a header part enables you to run field titles across the top for more than one row of records.

Body: Use for the bulk of your data, including graphics. The body appears for each record in the database. Each layout can only contain one body.

Subsummary: Use this type of summary part to display summary information for the group of records specified by the break field.

Trailing grand summary: Use this type of summary part to display summary information at the *end* of the group of the records being browsed.

Footer: Use for dates or page numbers. The footer appears at the bottom of each page or screen. Each layout can contain only one footer.

Title footer: This special type of footer appears only at the bottom of the *first* page or screen. Each layout can only contain one title footer.

To add a layout part:

1. Make sure you're in Layout mode (Ctrl L in Windows, ⌘ L on the Mac). Choose Layouts > Part Setup.
2. When the Part Setup dialog box appears, click *Create* (**Figure 11.52**).
3. Within the Part Definition dialog box, select the type of part you want to create from the eight choices (**Figure 11.53**).
4. If you're creating a subsummary part, you'll also need to select from the right-hand list which field (also known as a break field) you'd like the records to sort by.
5. The Part Definition dialog box also allows you to control where and how pages will break. Check the appropriate box or boxes. Click *OK*.
6. When the Part Setup dialog box reappears, click *Done* and the new part appears in the layout.

✔ Tip

■ If you're clear about the purpose and placement of layout parts, you can add a part directly by clicking on the Part button in the left-hand Layout status area and dragging the resulting part to where you want it (**Figure 11.54**).

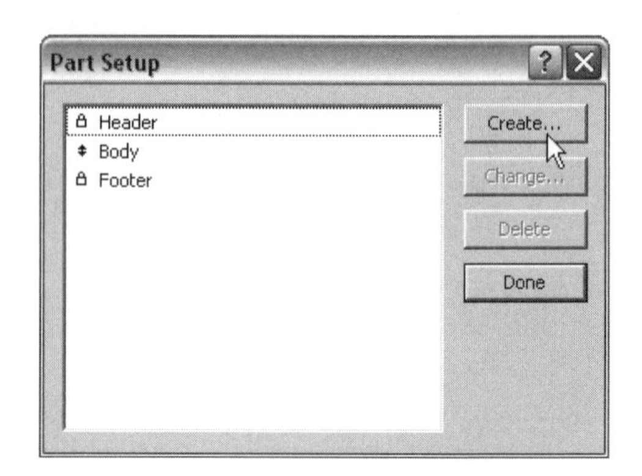

Figure 11.52 Click *Create* when the Part Setup dialog box appears.

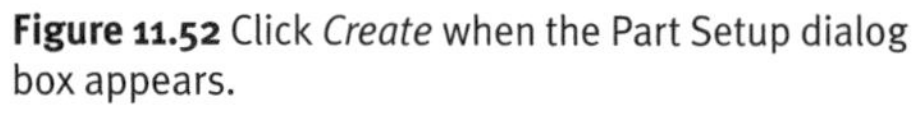

Figure 11.53 The Part Definition dialog box offers eight choices.

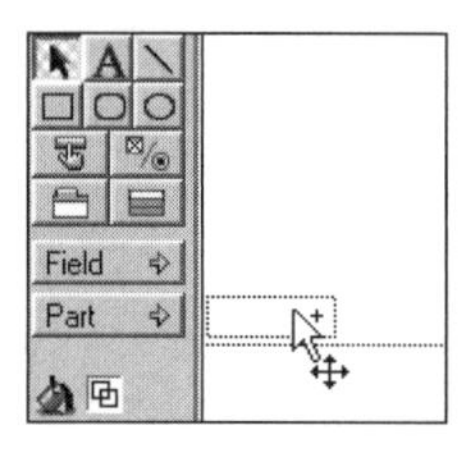

Figure 11.54 The *Part* button within the Layout status area lets you add a part by clicking and dragging directly within the layout.

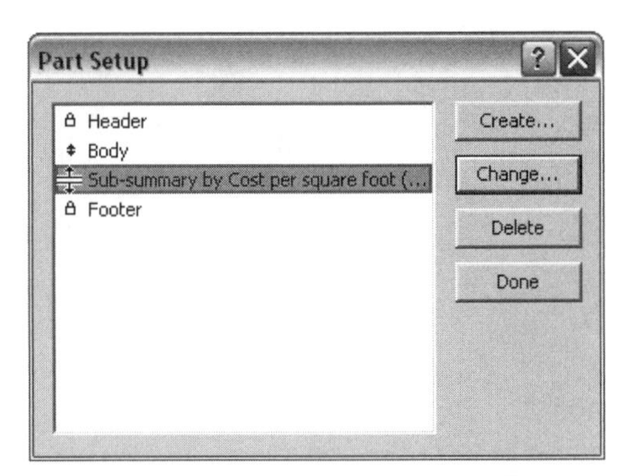

Figure 11.55 Reorder parts by clicking and dragging them within the Part Setup dialog box.

Figure 11.56 To resize a part, click and drag on the dotted line separating one part from another.

To delete a part:

1. Make sure you're in Layout mode (Ctrl L in Windows, ⌘ L on the Mac). Choose Layouts > Part Setup.
2. Within the Part Setup dialog box, select the part you want eliminated and press Delete. If you've selected a part that contains objects, you'll get a warning dialog box. If you're sure, click Delete.

To reorder parts:

1. Make sure you're in Layout mode (Ctrl L in Windows, ⌘ L on the Mac). Choose Layouts > Part Setup.
2. Click on the part you want to move, hold the cursor down, and drag the part to a new position in the order (**Figure 11.55**).
3. Click *Done*. The part appears in the new position.

To resize a part:

◆ Make sure you're in Layout mode (Ctrl L in Windows, ⌘ L on the Mac). Click on the dotted line separating one part from another and drag it to make the part larger or smaller (**Figure 11.56**).

✔ Tip

■ Resizing one part doesn't change the size of any other parts in the layout. Instead, the size of the entire layout will grow or shrink accordingly.

Changing a Part's Type and Options

FileMaker's Part Definition dialog box (**Figure 11.57**) does more than simply let you change a part's type. It also gives you control over where a page breaks in relation to a particular part and whether the pages are renumbered after that part. The page break and renumbering options are particularly useful when creating forms from which you may want to print out one record per page (**Table 11.2**). Here's a quick rundown of these options:

Page break before each occurrence: Choosing this checkbox places a page break right before the selected part. Examples might include using it for a Trailing Grand Summary, Title Header, Header, or Body.

Page break after every __ occurrence: Choosing this checkbox places a page break after x instances of the selected header. You set the number of instances. Examples might include selecting a body or footer part where you've created a layout in which x records will fit on a page.

Restart page numbers after each occurrence: Use this checkbox if, for example, you want to group a subsummary of records together and restart the page numbers after each subsummary.

Allow part to break across page boundaries: By default, FileMaker will try to keep a part on a single page. Use this checkbox if you do *not* want to keep a part on the same page or when the body is simply too large to fit on a single page.

Discard remainder of part before new page: This option can only be used if you've also checked *Allow part to break across page boundaries.*

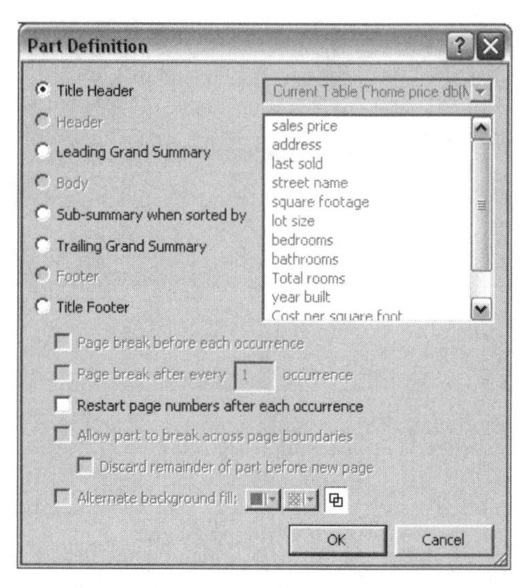

Figure 11.57 The Part Definition dialog box lets you change a part's definition, plus control page breaks and numbering related to that part.

Table 11.2

Page Break and Numbering Options

In the Part Definition Dialog Box Choose	For Use With These Layout Parts
Page break before each occurrence	Subsummary (if sorted by body) Trailing subsummary Trailing grand summary
Page break after every x occurrences	Leading grand summary Subsummary (if sorted by body) Trailing grand summary
Restart page numbers after each occurrence	Title header Header Leading grand summary Subsummary (if sorted by body) Footer
Allow part to break across page boundaries	Leading grand summary Subsummary (if sorted by body) Trailing grand summary
Discard remainder of part before new page	Leading grand summary Subsummary (if sorted by body) Trailing grand summary

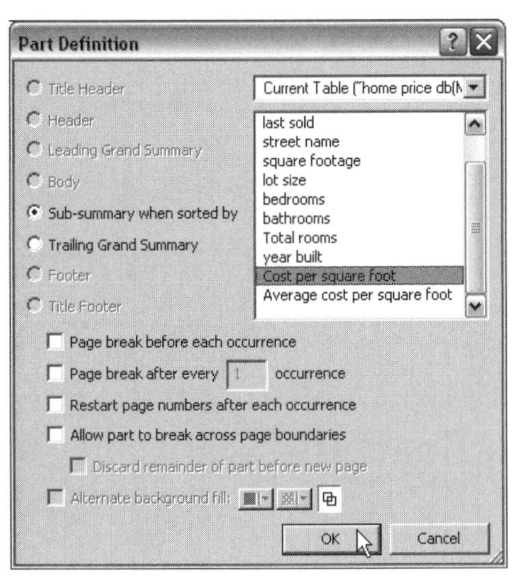

Figure 11.58 If you create a subsummary part, use the right-hand list to pick a field and click *OK*.

To change a part type or break field:

1. Make sure you're in Layout mode (Ctrl L in Windows, ⌘ L on the Mac). Double-click on the label of the part you want to change.
2. When the Part Definition dialog box appears, choose a part type from the left-side list.

   If you want to change the field used by a subsummary part (called a break field by FileMaker), click the *Sub-summary when sorted by* button and then make a new field selection in the right-hand list (**Figure 11.58**).
3. Click *OK*. The part type changes.

To paginate layout parts:

1. Make sure you're in Layout mode (Ctrl L in Windows, ⌘ L on the Mac). Double-click on the label of the part you want to change.
2. When the Part Definition dialog box appears, select the appropriate checkbox among the page break/page numbering choices in the lower part of the dialog box. See **Table 11.2** for more information on which page breaks and numbering schemes work best with various layout parts.
3. When you're done making your changes, click *OK*.

Working with Fields in Layouts

When you're working with layouts remember: *Adding* a field to a *layout* isn't the same thing as *creating* a field for the *database*. Layouts are simply differing views of the same data. Add a layout or delete a layout—either way the database itself isn't changed. The same notion applies when adding a field to a layout: It's just a view of a field that's already been created within the database.

For information on how to create a brand new field, see *To define a field* on page 96. Once you've created a field, you can easily add it to a new layout directly without having to define it again. In fact, it's common while designing a layout to discover that you need to define a new field. Just keep straight the difference between defining fields for the database versus adding a field to a layout and you'll be fine.

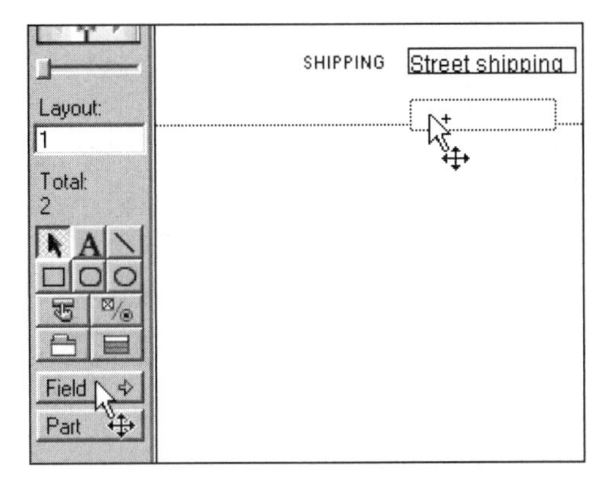

Figure 11.59 To add an already defined field to a layout, click on the status area's *Field* button and drag the resulting field to where you want it.

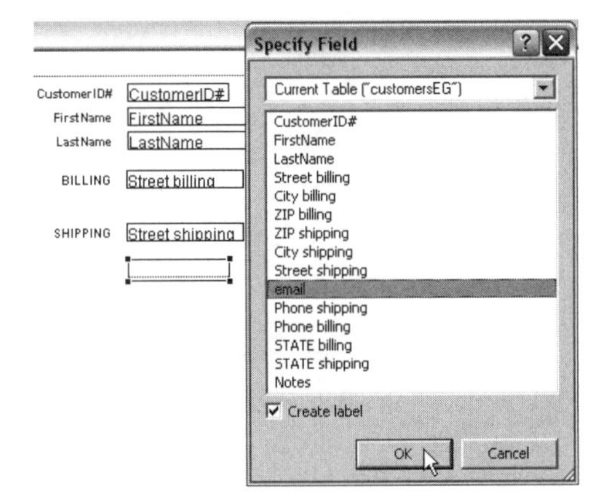

Figure 11.60 Selecting the *Field* button opens the Specify Field dialog box, allowing you to select a field definition (and add its name if you leave the bottom box checked).

To add a field to a layout:

1. To add *already defined* fields to a layout, click on the *Field* button in the left-hand Layout status area and drag the resulting field where you want it within the layout (**Figure 11.59**).
2. When the Specify Field dialog box appears, click on a name for the new field (**Figure 11.60**). You can add a field defined in another database by clicking on the *Current Table* pop-down menu above the field list and navigating to the database with the desired field.
3. If you want a field label to appear in the layout, also check the *Create label* box below the list.
4. Click *OK*. The layout reappears with the added field. If you want to further format the field, see *Formatting Fields or Objects* on page 203.

✔ Tip

- If you want to redefine the just-added field, stay in Layout mode and just double-click on the field. The Specify Field dialog box reappears, allowing you to pick another field definition.

To delete a field from a layout:

1. Make sure you're in Layout mode (Ctrl L in Windows, ⌘ L on the Mac). Select the field you want to delete by clicking it.
2. Press Delete.

✔ Tip

- Remember: Deleting a field from a layout merely removes it from that layout. The data and field still exist in the *database* and, so, can be used in other layouts as you need them.

Resizing fields

Sometimes you create a field and only later realize that it is too small for the intended text (**Figure 11.61**). In that case, the text will be cut off. Resizing solves the problem.

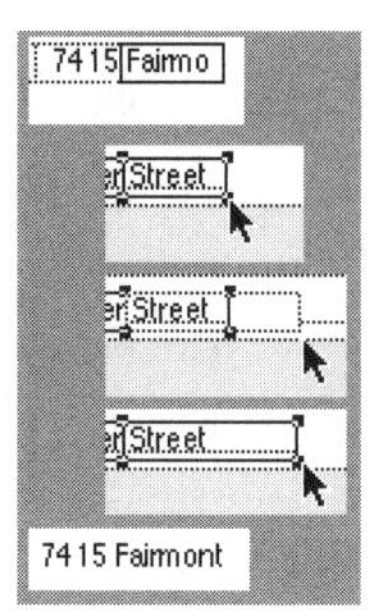

Figure 11.61 To resize a field in Layout mode, click on the field and drag a corner. Once back in Browse mode (bottom), the field's text is no longer cut off.

To resize a field:

1. Switch to Layout mode (Ctrl L in Windows, ⌘ L on the Mac).
2. Click on the field you want to resize and hold down your cursor. The corners of the field become small black boxes, known as handles.
3. Drag the handles to make the field larger or smaller. When it reaches the size you want, release the cursor.
4. Switch back (Ctrl B in Windows, ⌘ B on the Mac) and you'll see that all the field's text now shows. Getting the field big enough may require some toggling between Layout and Browse modes to check your progress.

✔ Tip

- To cleanly enlarge a field horizontally or vertically, click on the field and press Shift just before you drag the handle. The field then only expands in the direction you first drag it, whether it's horizontal or vertical.

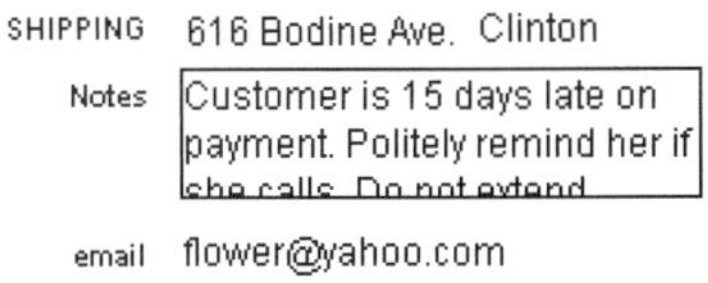

Adding scroll bars to large text fields

Sometimes enlarging a field isn't practical, either because your layout doesn't have the room or because the field has so much text that it would overwhelm the rest of the layout (**Figure 11.62**). In such cases, adding a scroll bar to the text field is the best approach—or perhaps add a separate tab for notes, as explained on page 191.

To add a scroll bar:

1. Switch to Layout mode (Ctrl L in Windows, ⌘L on the Mac) and double-click the field to which you want to add a scroll bar (**Figure 11.63**).
2. When the Field/Control Setup dialog box appears, the field already will be selected, so just click *Include vertical scroll bar* (**Figure 11.64**). Click *OK* to close the dialog box.
3. Back in Layout mode, the field now has a scroll bar. Switch to Browse mode and you'll see that the scroll bar not only allows you to scroll through all the text but also offers an immediate visual cue that there's more text than what shows (**Figure 11.65**).

Figure 11.62 Consider adding a scroll bar when a field has too much text to fit within your layout.

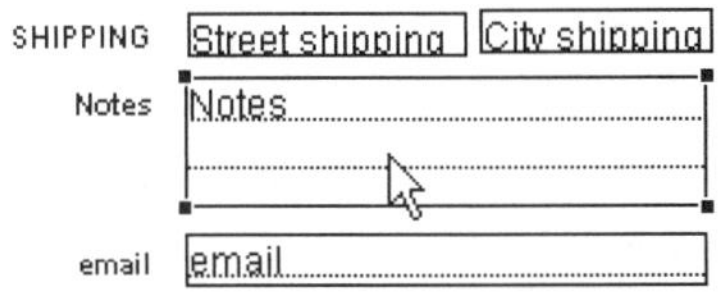

Figure 11.63 Switch to Layout mode, then double-click on the field you want to add the scroll bar to.

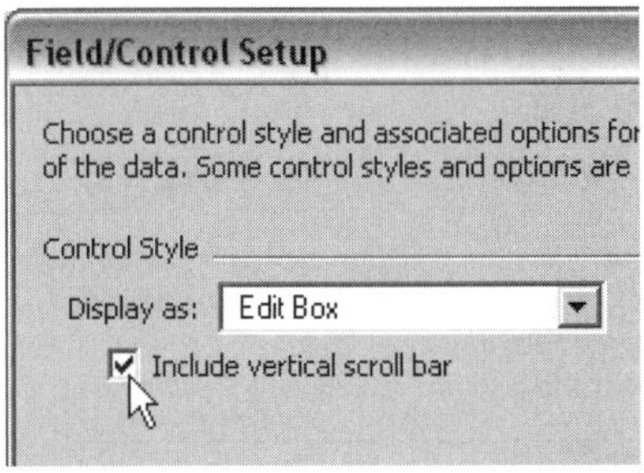

Figure 11.64 In the Field/Control Setup dialog box, check *Include vertical scroll bar*, then click *OK* to close the dialog box.

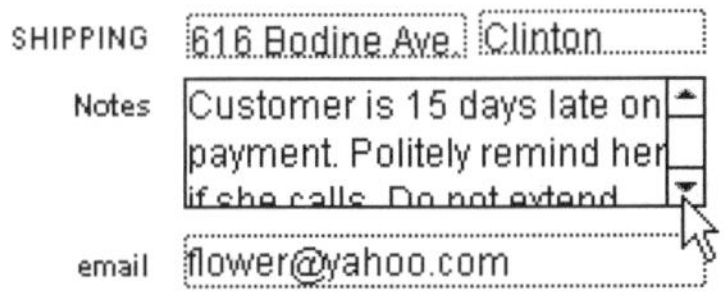

Figure 11.65 The field after a scroll bar is added.

To set the field tab order:

1. Switch to Layout mode (Ctrl L in Windows, ⌘ L on the Mac), then choose Layouts > Set Tab Order.
2. The Set Tab Order dialog box appears, along with a series of numbered arrows indicating the current tab order for your fields (**Figure 11.66**).

   If you want to just slightly alter the order, click on the tab number you want to change and type it in (left, **Figure 11.67**). If you assign No. 1 to an arrow, you'll also need to renumber the original No. 1 arrow (right, **Figure 11.67**).

   To completely change the order, click *Remove* in the Set Tab Order dialog box (top, **Figure 11.68**). That eliminates all the tab numbers (bottom, **Figure 11.68**). Then click the arrows in the order you want the tab order set.
3. When you're done, click *OK* to close the dialog box.

✔ Tip

- Each layout can have its own tab order, allowing you to customize each layout for its intended users.

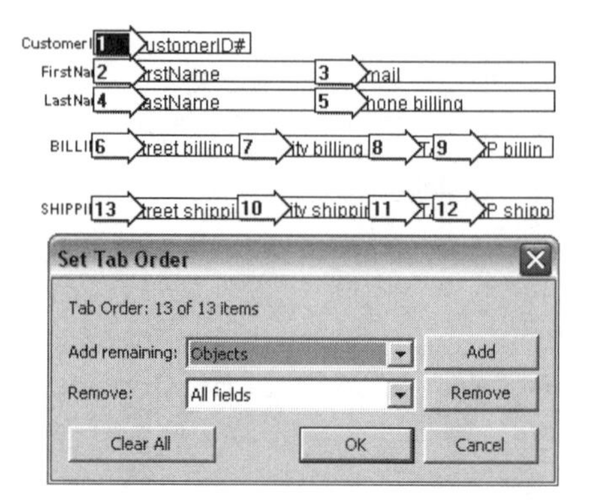

Figure 11.66 When the Set Tab Order dialog box appears, a series of numbered arrows indicate the current tab order for your fields with the first highlighted.

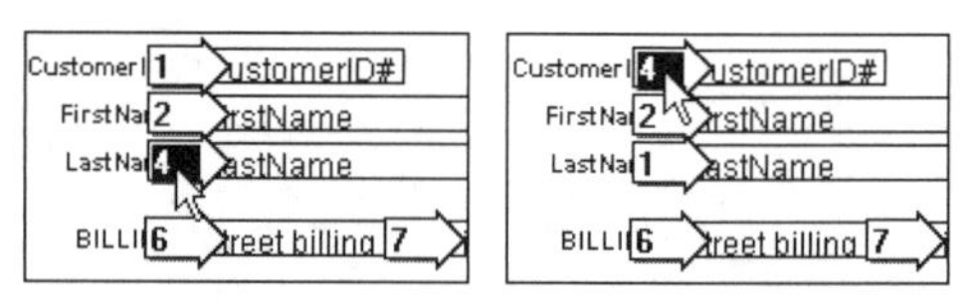

Figure 11.67 Click the box you want to renumber (left). Type in a new number, then click the next box you want to renumber (right).

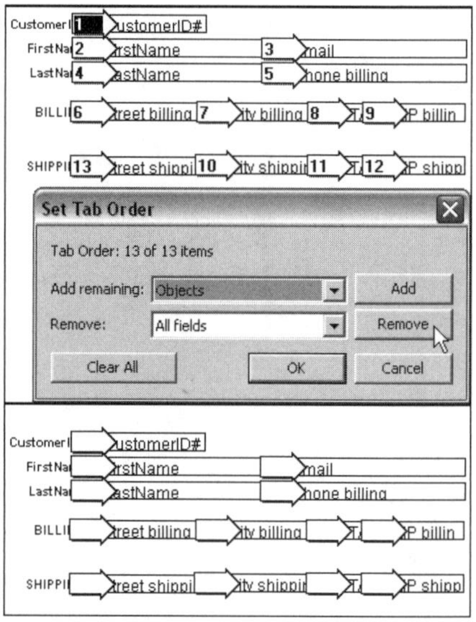

Figure 11.68 To completely change the order, click *Remove* (top). That eliminates all the tab numbers (bottom) and lets you click the arrows in the new order you want.

Working with Objects in Layouts

Whether it's text, a field, a field name, or a graphic, FileMaker treats each as a separate object that can be selected, moved, rearranged, and grouped. Most of these functions reside under the Arrange menu, which appears only when you're in Layout mode. These objects also can be graphically embellished with shading, borders, and fills via the tools in the Layout status area. For more information on using graphics with objects, see *Working with Graphics* on page 212.

Tabbed layouts, a new FileMaker layout object, makes it easy to present data in an easy-to-read fashion (**Figure 12.1**). See *Using Tabbed Layouts* on page 191.

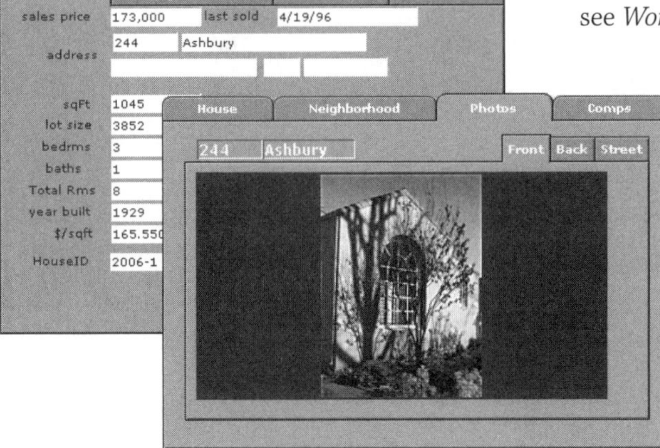

Figure 12.1 FileMaker's new tabbed layouts make it easy to present lots of information in an easy-to-read format.

While FileMaker makes it easy to move individual objects around a layout, it also allows you to *group* objects and then treat them as a single object. By creating groups of groups, you can organize pieces of a layout into units that speed your work.

By default, FileMaker displays objects in the order they were created, with the most recent atop (or in front of) the earlier objects. Sometimes in designing a layout, it's useful to stack objects atop each other to create a special effect, such as the appearance of a three-dimensional object. While each object remains a separate object, rearranging the stack order changes the overall appearance.

To make it easier to build layouts, FileMaker comes with built-in rulers, T-Squares, and grids. For more information, see *Using Layout Guides* on page 186.

✔ Tip

- You may find it faster when arranging and grouping objects to use FileMaker's Arrange toolbar (**Figure 12.2**). To turn it on, choose View > Toolbars > Arrange.

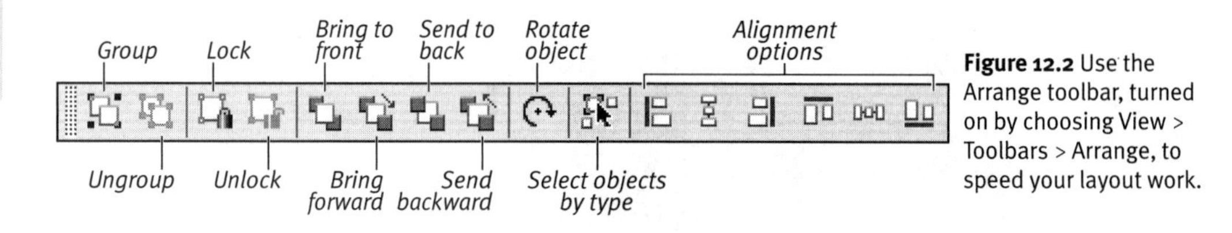

Figure 12.2 Use the Arrange toolbar, turned on by choosing View > Toolbars > Arrange, to speed your layout work.

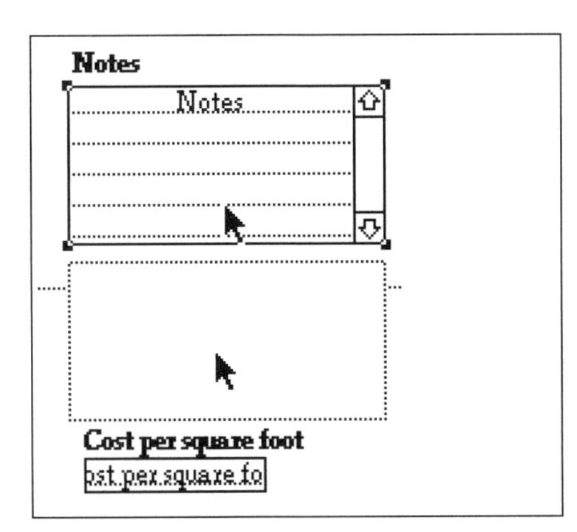

Figure 12.3 To move an object within a layout, click on it and drag it. A dotted outline of the object appears as you move the object.

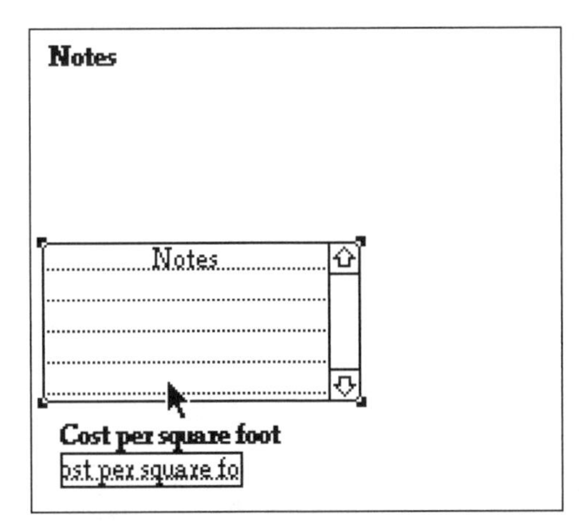

Figure 12.4 Once you've dragged an object to where you want it, release the cursor.

To move an object within the same layout:

1. Switch to Layout mode (Ctrl L in Windows, ⌘L on the Mac), then select the object by clicking on it with your cursor. Keep pressing your cursor and drag the object to its new location in the layout. A set of dotted lines marks the object's position as you drag it (**Figure 12.3**).

   If you want to ensure that the object only moves horizontally (or vertically), hold down Shift as you drag it.
2. Once you put the object where you want it, release the cursor (**Figure 12.4**). The object now appears in the new location within the layout.

✔ Tip

- While the field moved in the above example, the "Notes" field label did not. That's because the label is a separate object. While you can move more than one object at a time by Shift-clicking on several objects before dragging them, *grouping* such objects often makes more sense because things like field labels automatically tag along when you move a field. See *To group objects* on page 181.

To move an object to another layout:

1. Switch to Layout mode (Ctrl L in Windows, ⌘L on the Mac), then select the object by clicking on it with your cursor.
2. Choose Edit > Cut (Ctrl X in Windows, ⌘X on the Mac).
3. Switch to the other layout and choose Edit > Paste (Ctrl V in Windows, ⌘V on the Mac).
4. Once the object appears in the layout, use your cursor to move it exactly where you want it.

To copy an object:

1. Switch to Layout mode (Ctrl L in Windows, ⌘ L on the Mac), then select the object by clicking on it with your cursor.
2. Choose Edit > Duplicate (Ctrl D in Windows, ⌘ D on the Mac).
3. Use your cursor to move the duplicated object to where you want it.

To delete an object:

1. Switch to Layout mode (Ctrl L in Windows, ⌘ L on the Mac), then select the object by clicking on it with your cursor.
2. Press Delete. If you deleted the wrong object, choose Edit > Undo (Ctrl Z in Windows, ⌘ Z on the Mac).

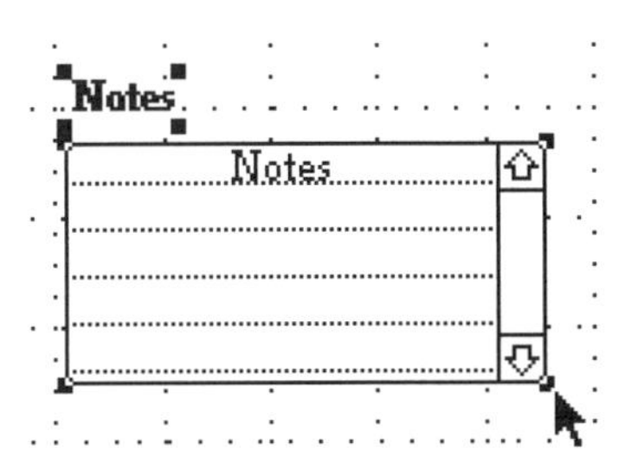

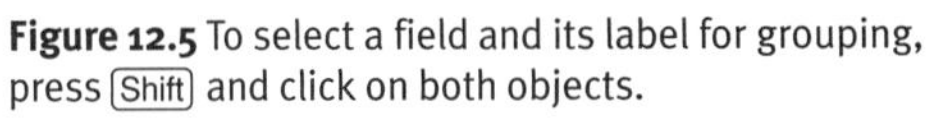
Figure 12.5 To select a field and its label for grouping, press [Shift] and click on both objects.

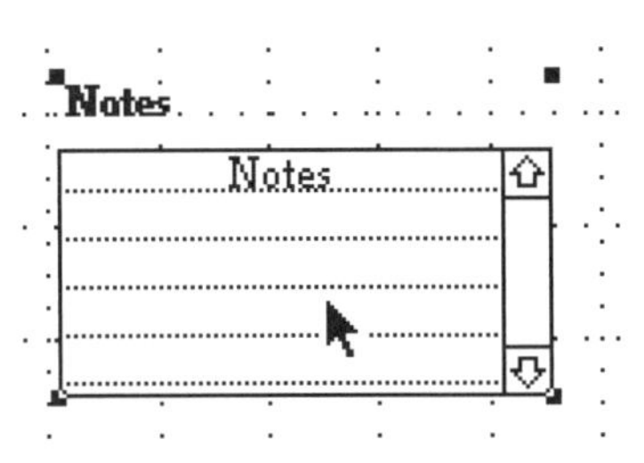

Figure 12.6 Once they're grouped, the field and its label become one object, as indicated by the single set of handles at the object's corners.

Grouping objects

By default, FileMaker treats each item added to a layout as a separate object. But sometimes there can be great advantage to having multiple objects treated as a single object (grouping). For example, if you use labels for fields, grouping the label with the field ensures that they stay together when you move a field within a layout. Similarly, it can speed up your layout work to group related topic fields and then move them to a new spot with a single click-and-drag.

To group objects:

1. Switch to Layout mode ([Ctrl][L] in Windows, [⌘][L] on the Mac), then select the first object by clicking on it with your cursor.
2. Hold down [Shift] while you continue clicking on the objects you want to group together (**Figure 12.5**).
3. Choose Arrange > Group or use your keyboard: [Ctrl][R] in Windows, [⌘][R] on the Mac. The previously individual objects now become a single object (**Figure 12.6**).

✔ Tip

- You can create subgroups within larger groupings. For example, create a group of just two objects (a field label with its field) before grouping that field with other fields. That way, if you later decide to ungroup the fields, you'll still have the field name grouped with its field.

To ungroup objects:

1. Make sure you're in Layout mode (Ctrl L in Windows, ⌘ L on the Mac), then Shift-click the objects you no longer want grouped.
2. Choose Arrange > Ungroup or use your keyboard: Ctrl Shift R in Windows, Shift ⌘ R on the Mac. The selected objects will no longer be grouped (see *Tip* for exceptions).

✔ Tip

- If you have created subgroups within a group, you'll have to repeat the Ungroup command at each level to fully break up those groupings.

To lock layout objects:

1. Make sure you're in Layout mode (Ctrl L in Windows, ⌘ L on the Mac), then select the pieces of the layout you want to protect from accidental changes by holding down Shift as you click on each object.
2. Choose Arrange > Lock or use your keyboard: Alt Ctrl L in Windows, Option ⌘ L on the Mac.

To unlock layout objects:

1. Make sure you're in Layout mode (Ctrl L in Windows, ⌘ L on the Mac), then hold down Shift as you click on the objects you want to unlock.
2. Choose Arrange > Unlock or use your keyboard: Shift Alt Ctrl L in Windows, Shift Option ⌘ L on the Mac.

✔ Tip

- When creating groups, if one object is locked, all the grouped objects become locked as well.

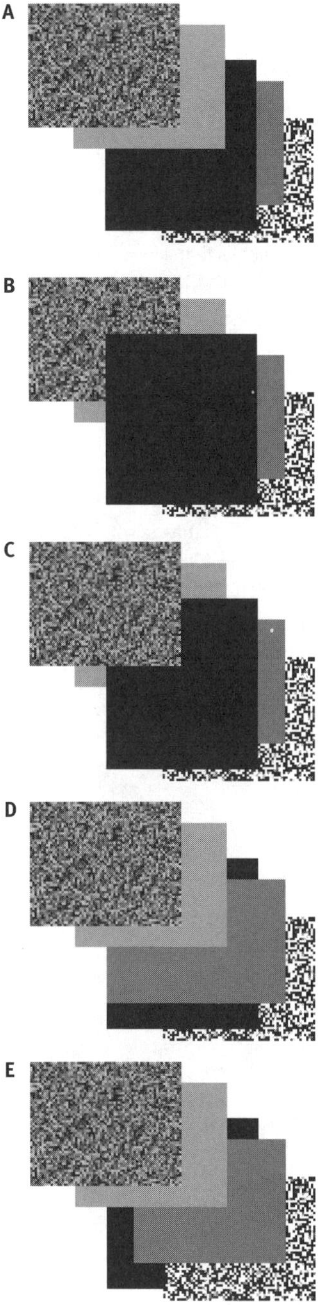

To change the stack order of objects:

1. Switch to Layout mode (Ctrl L in Windows, ⌘ L on the Mac), then select the object you want to move by clicking on it with your cursor.

2. From the Arrange menu, choose one of four commands: Bring to Front, Bring Forward, Send to Back, or Send Backward. The closer an object lies to the front (or top) of the stack, the more of it will be visible. By selecting and moving various objects, you can manipulate the arrangement to your satisfaction (**Figure 12.7**).

   - **Bring to Front** (Alt Ctrl [in Windows, Option ⌘ [on the Mac): Use this command to bring the selected object to the very front (or top) of the stack.

   - **Bring Forward** (Shift Ctrl [in Windows, Shift ⌘ [on the Mac): Use this command to bring the selected object forward one layer.

   - **Send to Back** (Alt Ctrl] in Windows, Option ⌘] on the Mac): Use this command to send the selected object to the very back (or bottom) of the stack.

   - **Send Backward** (Shift Ctrl] in Windows, Shift ⌘] on the Mac): Use this command to send the selected object back one layer.

Figure 12.7 **A** Initially, the black square lies in the middle of the stack order. **B** Brought to the front. **C** Brought forward one layer from its initial position. **D** Sent back one layer from its initial position. **E** Sent to the back.

Rotating objects

Because each field, label, and graphic within FileMaker is treated as an object, you're free to rotate them to make a layout more compact, less cluttered, or just more eye-grabbing. FileMaker limits you to rotating objects in 90-degree increments. If you need more precise control, create the object within a true graphics program and then import it into FileMaker.

To rotate an object:

1. Switch to Layout mode (Ctrl L in Windows, ⌘ L on the Mac), then select the object you want to rotate by clicking on it with your cursor (**Figure 12.8**).
2. Choose Arrange > Rotate or use your keyboard: Alt Ctrl R in Windows, Option ⌘ R on the Mac. The Rotate command moves an object 90 degrees clockwise (**Figure 12.9**).

✔ Tips

- Repeat the Rotate command to continue spinning an object in 90-degree increments until it reaches the position you want.
- If you prefer, press and hold your cursor on the selected object's "handles"—the small black squares on its periphery—then rotate it directly.

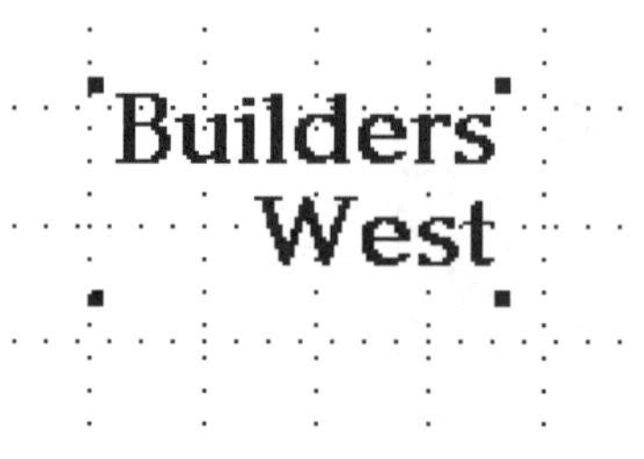

Figure 12.8 To rotate an object, first select it while in Layout mode, then choose Arrange > Rotate.

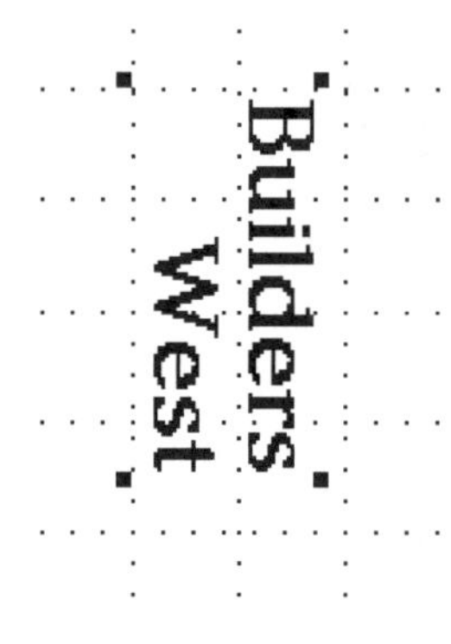

Figure 12.9 The Rotate command spins the object clockwise in 90-degree increments. Repeat the command to spin the object 180 and 270 degrees.

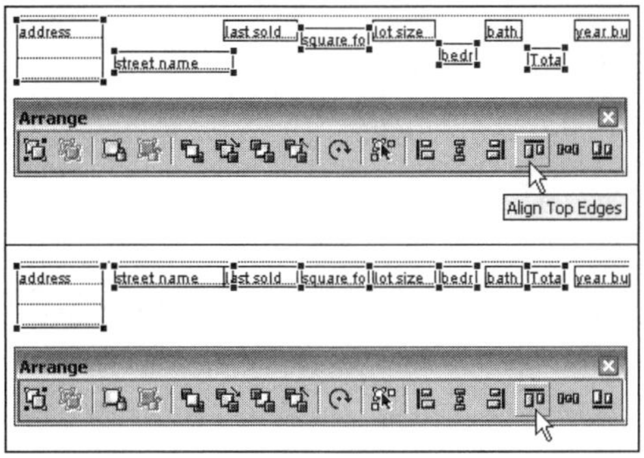

Figure 12.10 After selecting the objects, click one of the alignment buttons in the Arrange toolbar (top). The objects are realigned based on your choice (bottom).

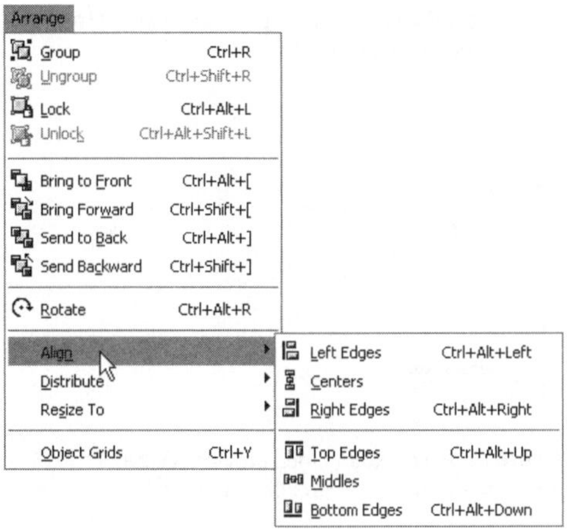

Figure 12.11 You can also realign objects by choosing Arrange > Align and choosing from the submenu.

Aligning objects

Your layout will be easier to read and look more professional if you vertically or horizontally align fields, labels, and groups of fields as much as possible.

To align objects:

1. Switch to Layout mode (Ctrl L in Windows, ⌘L on the Mac), then select the objects you want to align by holding down Shift and clicking on them with your cursor.
2. Click one of the alignment buttons in the Arrange toolbar (top, **Figure 12.10**). The selected objects are realigned based on your choice (bottom, **Figure 12.10**).

✔ Tip

- If you don't want to bother with the Arrange toolbar, you can choose Arrange > Align and choose from the submenu (**Figure 12.11**).

Using Layout Guides

FileMaker's various layout guides are strictly optional but you'll find that they make it much easier to create professional layouts. You can use them while you're creating a layout or to go back and tidy up previous work. Here's a quick rundown on how each guide functions:

Text Ruler: Provides a horizontal measure in inches, pixels, or centimeters (**Figure 12.12**).

Graphic Rulers: Provides horizontal and vertical rulers in inches, pixels, or centimeters (**Figure 12.13**).

Ruler Lines: Provides a matrix of horizontal and vertical dotted lines to help position layout objects. The matrix can be set in inches, pixels, or centimeters (**Figure 12.14**).

T-Squares: Provides an intersecting horizontal line and vertical line, which can be moved to guide the positioning of layout objects (**Figure 12.15**).

Object Grids: Provides an invisible grid whose measurement units can be adjusted. When Object Grids is on, layout objects "snap" to the nearest grid line.

Size Palette: Provides a set of number entry boxes that help you precisely position layout objects (**Figure 12.16**).

Figure 12.12 The Text Ruler lets you choose your measurement units and includes icons for choosing fonts, alignments, and tabs.

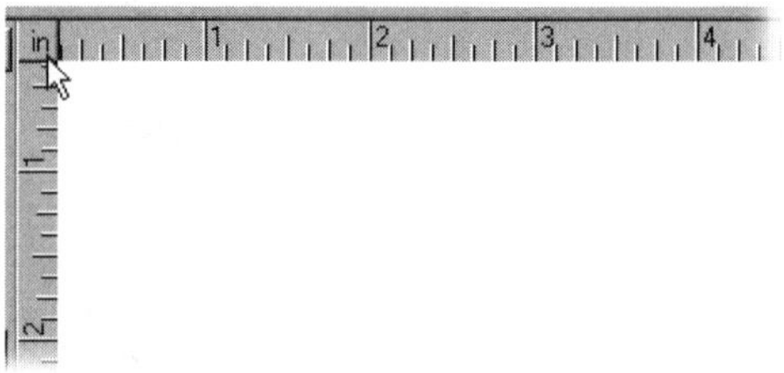

Figure 12.13 The measurement units for Graphic Rulers, which aid horizontal and vertical placement of the selected object, can be changed via the Layouts menu.

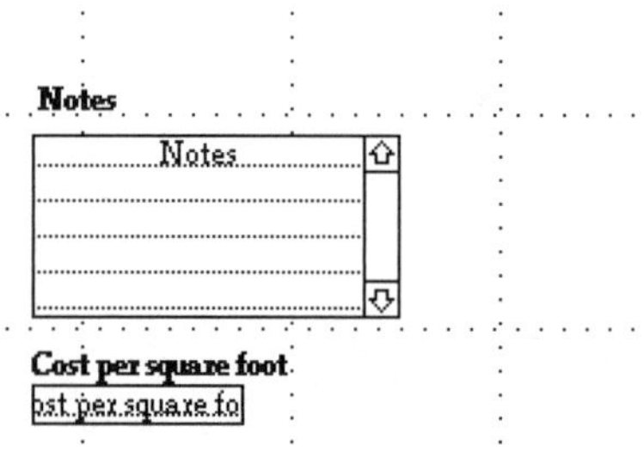

Figure 12.14 The Ruler Lines provide a visible matrix to help position layout objects.

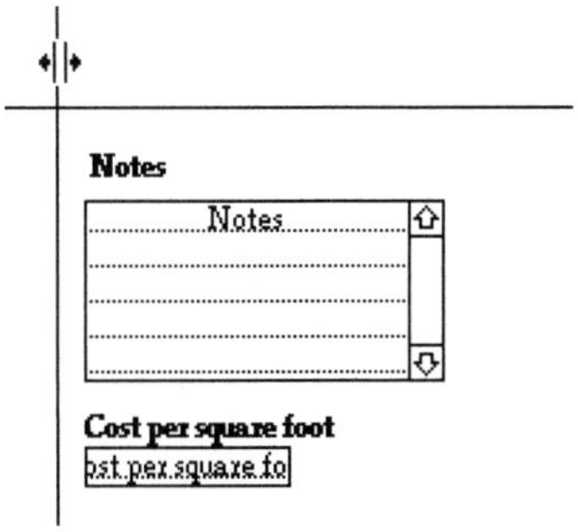

Figure 12.15 The T-Squares option provides a horizontal and a vertical line that extends across the entire layout—easing alignment of multiple objects.

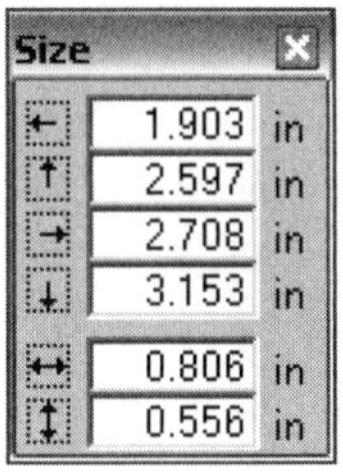

Figure 12.16 The Size palette allows you to precisely position layout objects via the numeric entry boxes.

To use the Text Ruler:

1. Make sure you're in Layout mode (Ctrl L in Windows, ⌘ L on the Mac), then choose View > Text Ruler.
2. Use the ruler or, if you have it turned on, the various text icons in the Text Formatting toolbar to adjust selected text as you desire. For more information on text formats, see *Formatting Fields or Objects* on page 203.
3. To hide the ruler, choose View > Text Ruler again.

To use the Graphic Rulers:

1. Make sure you're in Layout mode (Ctrl L in Windows, ⌘ L on the Mac), then choose View > Graphic Rulers. To adjust the measurement units used, click the upper-left corner where the horizontal and vertical rulers meet to cycle through the choices: inches, centimeters, or pixels. For more information, see *To change ruler and grid units* on page 190.
2. To hide the graphic rules, choose View > Graphic Rulers again.

To use Ruler Lines:

1. Make sure you're in Layout mode (Ctrl L in Windows, ⌘ L on the Mac), then choose View > Ruler Lines. To adjust the measurement units used, see *To change ruler and grid units* on page 190.
2. To hide the rulers, choose View > Ruler Lines again.

To use T-Squares:

1. Make sure you're in Layout mode (Ctrl L in Windows, ⌘L on the Mac), then choose View > T-Squares. To adjust the placement of the T-Square lines, click and hold your cursor, then drag the line where you want it (**Figure 12.17**).
2. To hide the T-Squares, choose View > T-Squares again.

To use Object Grids:

1. Make sure you're in Layout mode (Ctrl L in Windows, ⌘L on the Mac), then choose Arrange > Object Grids (Ctrl Y in Windows, ⌘Y on the Mac). To adjust the measurement units used and the fineness of the grid, see *To change ruler and grid units* on page 190.
2. To turn off Object Grids, choose Arrange > Object Grids again.

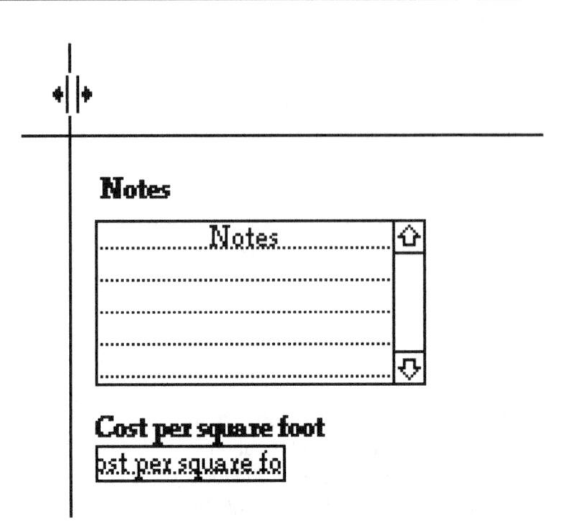

Figure 12.17 Adjust the placement of the T-Square lines by clicking on a line and dragging it.

To use the Size palette:

1. Make sure you're in Layout mode (Ctrl L in Windows, ⌘ L on the Mac), then select the object you want to position by clicking on it with your cursor.
2. Choose View > Object Size.
3. Once the Size palette appears (**Figure 12.18**), make sure you're working in the measurement unit you prefer: inches, pixels, or centimeters. To adjust the palette's measurement units, see *To change ruler and grid units* on the next page.
4. Type in the measurements you want in the Size palette's number entry boxes. When you're done, press Enter in Windows, Return on the Mac. The object is resized based on your entry.

✔ Tip

- Use the Size palette while click-dragging an object to position a layout object *exactly* where you want it. Just select your object, open the Size palette, and click-drag the object while keeping an eye on the palette's measurements.

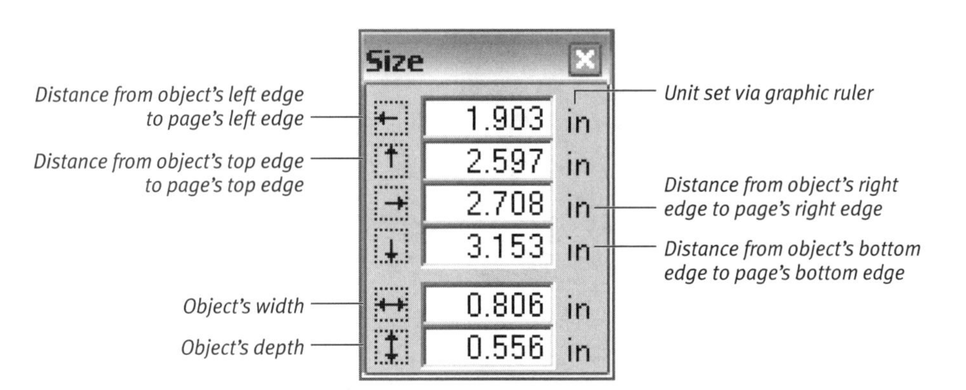

Figure 12.18 The Size palette provides details on the position—and dimensions—of a selected object.

Changing ruler and grid units

FileMaker lets you set the ruler and grid to measure the layout and its items in inches, pixels, or centimeters.

To change ruler and grid units:

1. To change the units, choose Layouts > Set Rulers.
2. The Set Rulers dialog box appears. It includes two pop-down menus (**Figure 12.19**). The top one sets the *Units* used by the Graphic rulers, Ruler lines, the Object Grids, and the Size palette. The second pop-down menu, *Grid spacing*, controls the fineness of the Object Grids' mesh of horizontal and vertical lines. Make your adjustments to one or both pop-down menus and click *OK*.

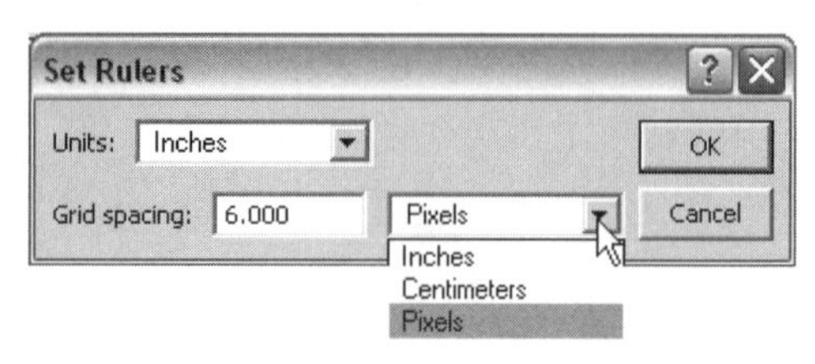

Figure 12.19 The Set Rulers dialog box includes two pop-down menus: one for ruler units and one for controlling the fineness of the Object Grids' mesh.

Using Tabbed Layouts

Tabbed layouts mimic the familiar tabs of paper file folders (or many FileMaker dialog boxes for that matter). As you switch from tab to tab, the layout shows different fields—making them a great way to present lots of information in a single layout without crowding the fields.

To add tabbed layouts:

1. Make sure you're in Layout mode (Ctrl L in Windows, ⌘ L on the Mac), then use the pop-down menu just above the book icon to select the layout that you want to use as the starting point for your tabbed layout.

2. When the layout appears, choose Layouts > Duplicate Layout and while nothing changes onscreen, FileMaker makes a copy of the layout dubbed [*originalname*]+*copy*. Choose Layouts > Layout Setup and when the Layout Setup dialog box appears, rename the layout copy to make its function obvious. In our example, we use *Tabbed for Sales* (**Figure 12.20**).

3. You may want to select all the fields and labels (Ctrl A in Windows, ⌘ A on the Mac) and drag them away from where you want to put the tabs (**Figure 12.21**).

4. Click the Tab Control tool, then click in the layout and drag the pointer until it reaches the general shape and size you want (**Figure 12.22**).

(continued)

Figure 12.20 After duplicating the layout, give it a name that makes its function obvious.

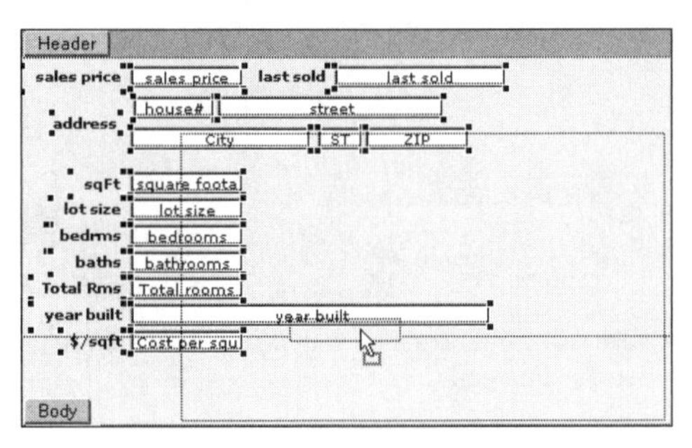

Figure 12.21 To make room for the tabs, select all the existing fields and drag them down the page.

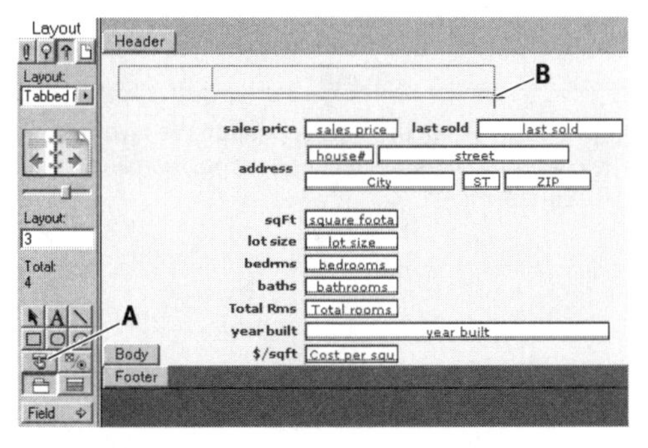

Figure 12.22 Click the Tab Control tool (**A**), then click in the layout and drag the pointer until it reaches the general shape and size you want (**B**).

5. Release the cursor and the Tab Control Setup dialog box appears (top, **Figure 12.23**).
6. Type the name of your first tab in the *Tab Name* text box and click *Create* (bottom, **Figure 12.23**).
7. Repeat step 6 until you've created as many tabs as you need, then click *OK* to close the dialog box (**Figure 12.24**).
8. When the tabs appear on the layout, use the corner handles to reposition and resize them as needed (**Figure 12.25**).

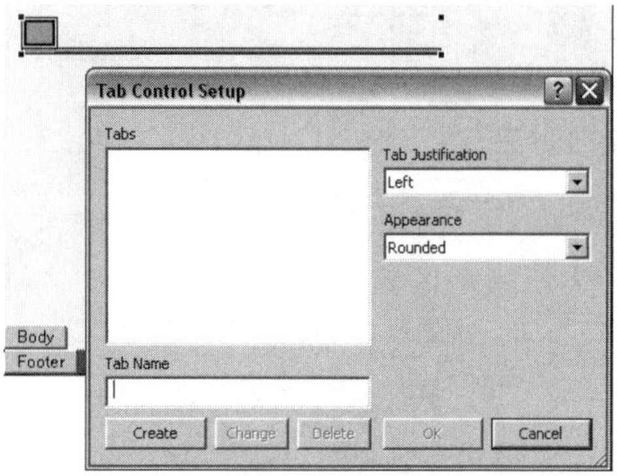

Figure 12.23 When the Tab Control Setup dialog box appears, click in the *Tab Name* window to create your first tab. Once you type in a name, click *Create* to save it.

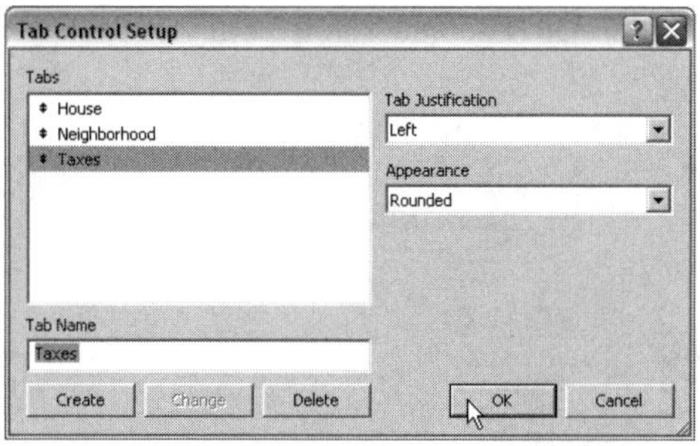

Figure 12.24 After creating your last tab, click *OK* to close the dialog box.

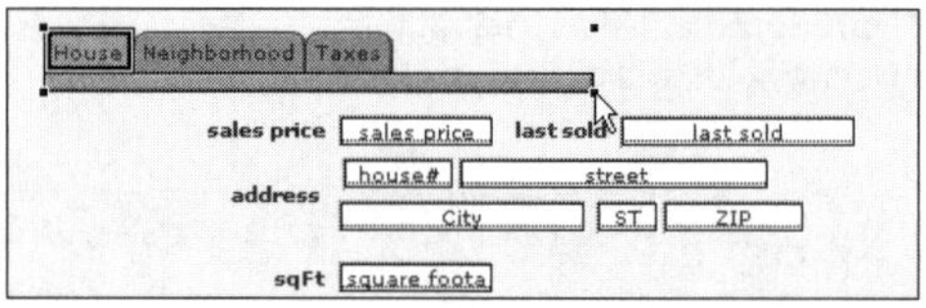

Figure 12.25 When the tabs appear on the layout, use the corner handles if you need to reposition and resize them.

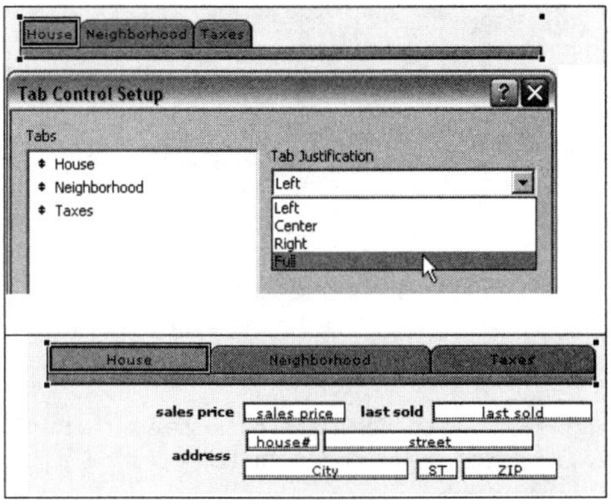

Figure 12.26 To run the tabs full width, double-click the layout object and choose *Full* in the *Tab Justification* drop-down menu (top). Once you close the dialog box, the tabs widens to fill the space (bottom).

9. If you need to change the alignment of the labels, double-click the tabs and make a new choice in the *Tab Justification* drop-down menu (top, **Figure 12.26**). Click *OK* to close the database and see the changes (bottom, **Figure 12.26**). (In our example, *Full* is used to stretch the tabs across the width of the field.

✔ Tips

- In step 2, you don't have to duplicate a layout before adding tabs. It's just a way to avoid messing up an existing layout as you learn how best to use tabs.
- Add new tabs any time by double-clicking the tabs and following steps 6–7. The other tabs automatically resize to make room for the new tab.

To change the tab labels:

1. Make sure you're in Layout mode (Ctrl L in Windows, ⌘L on the Mac). Double-click the tabs to open the Tab Control Setup dialog box.
2. Select a label in the *Tabs* list, then type a new name for it in the *Tab Name* text box, and click *Change* and the selected label is renamed (**Figure 12.27**).
3. Close the dialog box by clicking *OK*. The tabs reappear with the new label applied (**Figure 12.28**).

✔ Tip

- You also can use the Tab Control Setup dialog box to change the shape of the *Appearance* of the tabs from rounded to squared. And, as you saw in step 7 on page 192, you can change the *Tab Justification*.

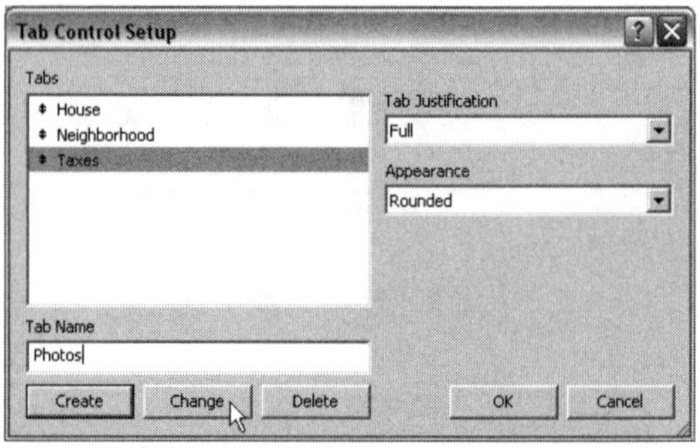

Figure 12.27 To change a label name, select it in the *Tabs* list, type in a new name, and click *Change*.

Figure 12.28 After closing the dialog box, the tab's new name appears.

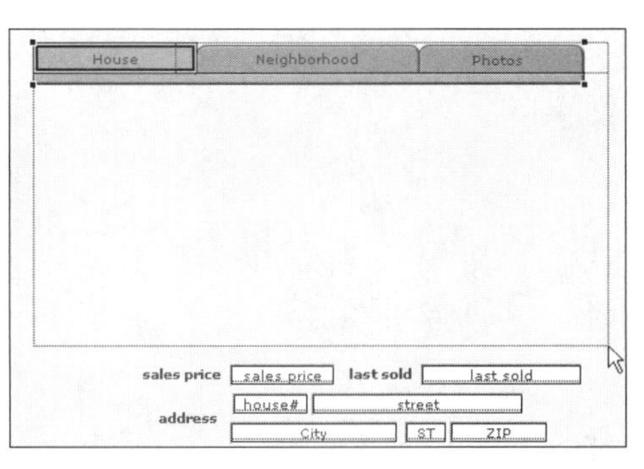

Figure 12.29 To make room for the fields in the new tabs, click and drag a corner handle to enlarge the tabbed layout object.

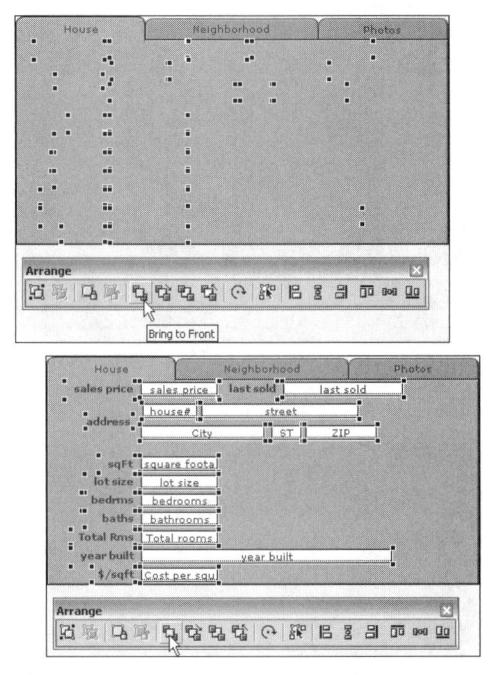

Figure 12.30 Select the fields you want from the original, non-tabbed portion of your layout and drag them into the selected tab (top). Click the Bring to Front button to move the fields to the top of the stack where they can be seen (bottom).

To add content to the tabs:

1. Make sure you're in Layout mode (Ctrl L in Windows, ⌘ L on the Mac). To make room for the fields you want to add to the new tabs, click and drag a corner handle to enlarge the tabbed layout object (**Figure 12.29**).
2. Select the tab in which you want the fields to appear. Select any fields you want to use from the original, non-tabbed portion of your layout and drag them into the selected tab. (In our example, we're putting *all* of the original fields into the first tab.) But because the tabbed layout object is newer than the original fields, it sits higher in the stack order and covers up the fields (top, **Figure 12.30**). With the original fields still selected, click the Bring to Front button in the Arrange toolbar and the fields move to the top of the stack order where they can be seen (bottom, **Figure 12.30**).
3. To see how the tab looks with data in the fields instead of labels, switch to Browse mode (Ctrl B in Windows, ⌘ B on the Mac) (**Figure 12.31**).

(continued)

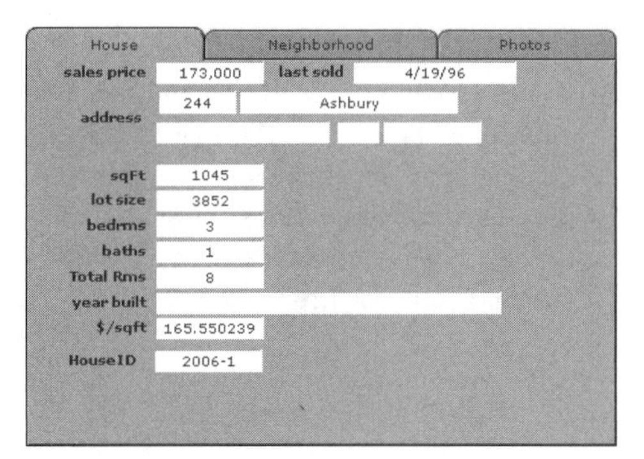

Figure 12.31 To see how the tab looks with data in the fields instead of labels, switch to Browse mode.

4. Switch back to Layout mode (Ctrl L in Windows, ⌘ L on the Mac) and click one of the *empty* tabs (*Photos* in our example) (**Figure 12.32**).

5. To generate *new* fields in the *current database* for placement in the selected tab, choose File > Define > Database (Ctrl Shift D in Windows, Shift ⌘ D on the Mac). When the Define Database dialog box appears, click the *Fields* tab and follow the steps to define fields as explained on page 96.

   or

   To add fields from *another related database*, choose File > Define > Database (Ctrl Shift D in Windows, Shift ⌘ D on the Mac). When the Define Database dialog box appears, click the *Relationships* tab and follow the steps to create a relationship as explained on page 132. You then follow steps 1–3.

✔ Tips

- To give yourself more room on the layout to rearrange the original fields and the new tabs, click the body part's bottom edge and drag it way down the screen. Once you finish rearranging everything, you can resize the body to a more appropriate compact size.
- You can even put a tabbed layout inside another tabbed layout (**Figure 12.33**). In our example, the photos are pulled from a separate database of house photos linked to the home prices database by a House ID# match field (**Figure 12.34**).

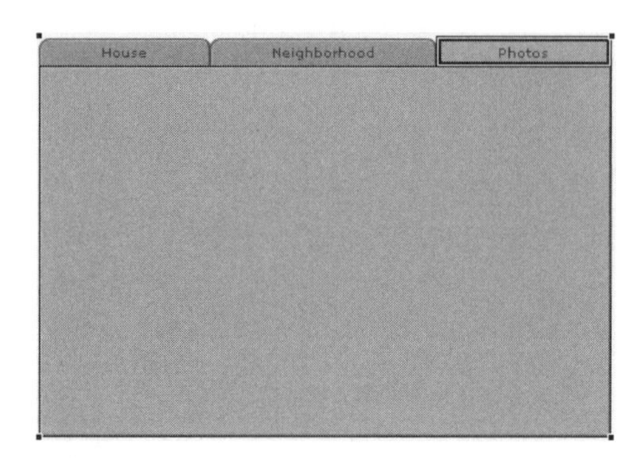

Figure 12.32 Switch back to Layout mode and click one of the *empty* tabs (*Photos* in our example).

Figure 12.33 If used with caution, you can pack even more into a layout by creating tabs *within* tabs.

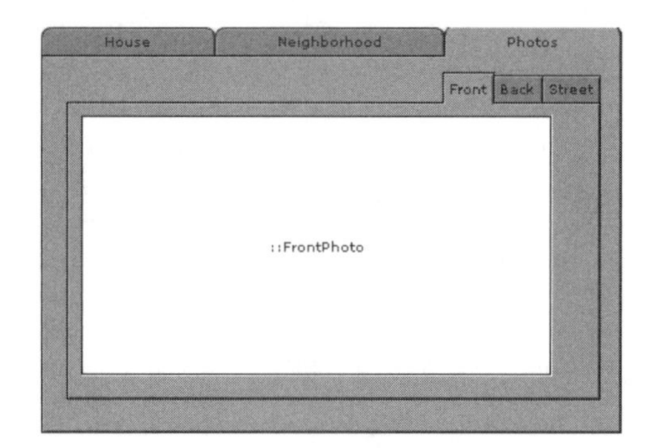

Figure 12.34 As the :: (double colon) indicates, you can display data from related files within tabs.

LAYOUT FORMATTING AND GRAPHICS

Once you've done the basic construction for a layout—the parts, fields, and objects covered in the previous chapter—you're ready to add the formatting and graphics that will make your database visually inviting. Whether it's choosing suitable fonts or adding a color graphic, this often time-consuming work can spell the difference between a so-so database that's little used or a professional-grade product with immediate appeal.

Working with Text

Quite often you'll find yourself working with text in a two-step process: You'll add text for the information it provides and then later go back to style the text by choosing special fonts or colors. This section deals with the first step. For information on styling *individual* blocks of text, see *Formatting Fields or Objects* on page 203. To set *database-wide* text defaults, see *To set formatting defaults* on page 200.

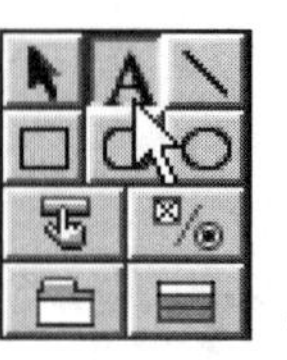

Figure 13.1 Click on the Text tool in the Layout status area to add text.

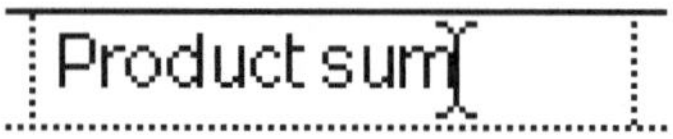

Figure 13.2 An I-beam cursor marks your text-insertion spot.

To add text to a layout:

1. Make sure you're in Layout mode (Ctrl L in Windows, ⌘ L on the Mac), then click the Text tool in the left-hand status area (**Figure 13.1**).
2. Click in the layout where you want the text and start typing. An I-beam cursor marks your progress (**Figure 13.2**).

✔ Tip

- Because creating a text label for a field has no effect on the actual field name, you can create different labels in different layouts for the same field. The sales force, for example, may have an in-house name for something that the accounting folks call something else entirely. By creating a sales layout and an accounting layout—each with its own labels—everyone's happy, even though the field's *actual* name remains the same.

To select text:

1. In either Layout mode (Ctrl L in Windows, ⌘ L on the Mac) or Browse mode (Ctrl B in Windows, ⌘ B on the Mac), click on the text you want to select. If you want to select an entire word, double-click. To select a full line of text, triple-click on it.
2. Once you've selected the text, you can:
   - Delete it (press Delete).
   - Cut it for pasting elsewhere (Ctrl X in Windows, ⌘ X on the Mac).
   - Replace it with other text (type in the new text or paste selected text from elsewhere).
   - Change its attributes, such as its font, size, or style (see following pages).

Setting Format Defaults

Default formats apply to fields and objects across the *entire* database. (To set attributes for *individual* fields and objects, see *Formatting Fields or Objects*, on page 203.) At times, you may want to set format defaults up front to save you the bother of formatting every time you create a new field. Other times, setting formats field by field may be exactly what you want to do. FileMaker, as usual, lets you do either.

Setting some basic *database-wide* defaults early on, however, gives you a foundation to build on. As you work along and find you want to change the format for an *individual* field or object differently, you can then use specific choices within the Format menu (**Figure 13.3**).

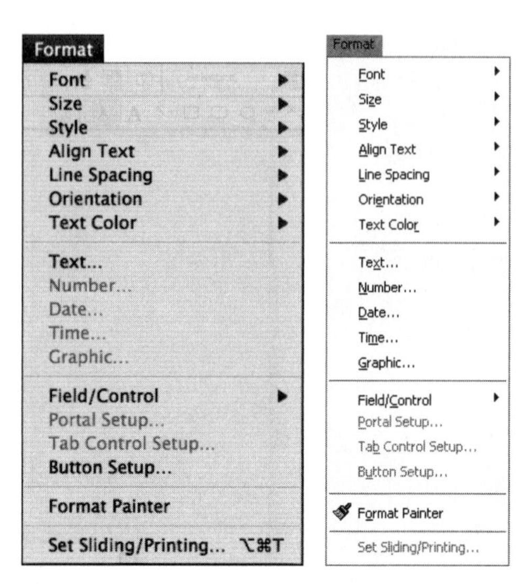

Figure 13.3 Depending on what you've selected, you can use the Format menu to set individual fields or database-wide defaults.

To set formatting defaults:

1. Make sure you're in Layout mode (Ctrl L in Windows, ⌘ L on the Mac) with *nothing* selected (otherwise some of the Format menu's choices are unavailable, signified by them being grayed out).
2. Under the Format menu, choose any of the five middle items (Text, Number, Date, Time, Graphic) to set the default formatting. Examples of each of your selections will appear in that dialog box's sample area. Here's the rundown on each:

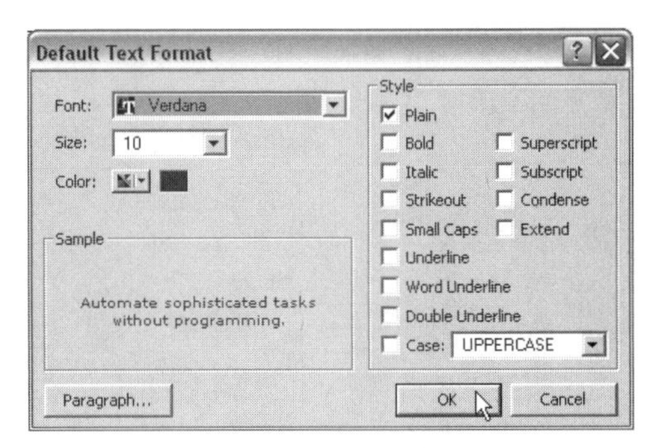

Figure 13.4 Use the Default Text Format dialog box to set the font, text size, color, and style.

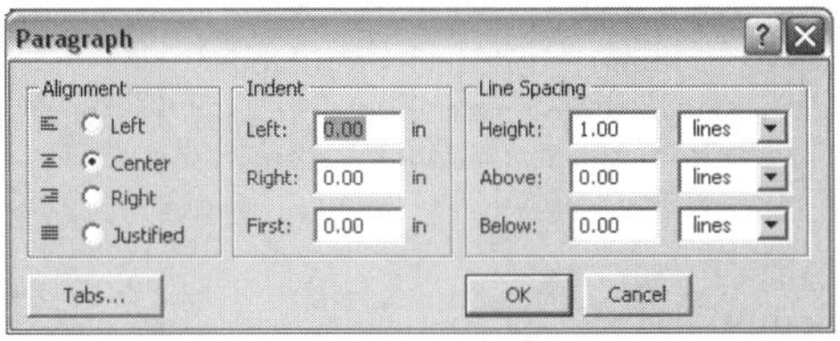

Figure 13.5 The Paragraph dialog box, reached via the Default Text Format dialog box, lets you set text alignment, indents, and line spacing.

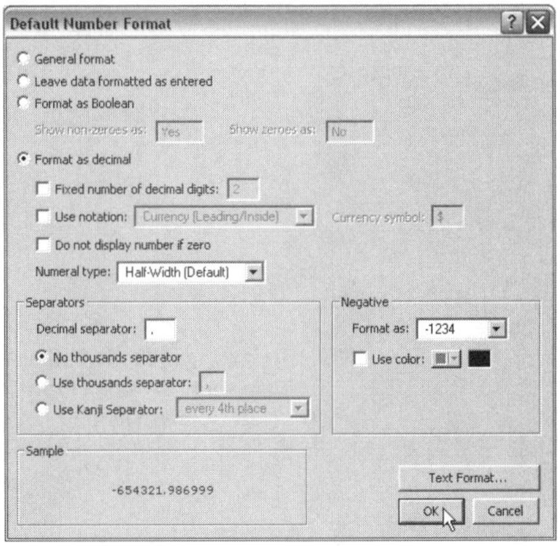

Figure 13.6 Use the Default Number Format dialog box to control the appearance of field numbers.

Default Text Format: With this dialog box (**Figure 13.4**), you can set the default *Font, Size, Color*, and *Style*. By clicking on the lower-left *Paragraph* button, you'll reach the Paragraph dialog box (**Figure 13.5**) where you can set the default alignment, indents, and line spacing for text. Finally, by clicking on the *Tabs* button in the Paragraph dialog box, you'll reach the Tabs dialog box. See *To set text tabs* on page 206.

Default Number Format: Within this dialog box (**Figure 13.6**), you can set the default to *General Format, Leave data formatted as entered, Format as Boolean* (Yes-No, True-False), plus control how many decimals you want showing, set a currency symbol to precede numbers (an unlikely database-wide choice unless every number field in the database deals with money), what sort of decimal separator you want (if any), and how negative numbers are displayed. The lower-right *Text Format* button, by the way, takes you back to the Text Format dialog box. Sorry, you can't use it to set a different font for numbers only: If you go back and change the text settings, they'll change in all default fields.

(continued)

Default Date Format: Within this dialog box (top, **Figure 13.7**), you can choose to *Leave date formatted as entered*, *Format as* (with six different date formatting options) (**Figure 13.8**), or click the *Custom* radio button to reach still more choices (bottom, **Figure 13.7**).

Default Time Format: Within this dialog box (**Figure 13.9**), you've got another zillion choices on time formats. Who knew there were so many?

Default Graphic Format: Within this dialog box (**Figure 13.10**), you can use the three pop-up menus to control how graphics are cropped and fitted within your field's frame. Use the *Sample* window to see how the various options are displayed.

3. When you're done making your default choices, click *OK*. Repeat to set other format defaults.

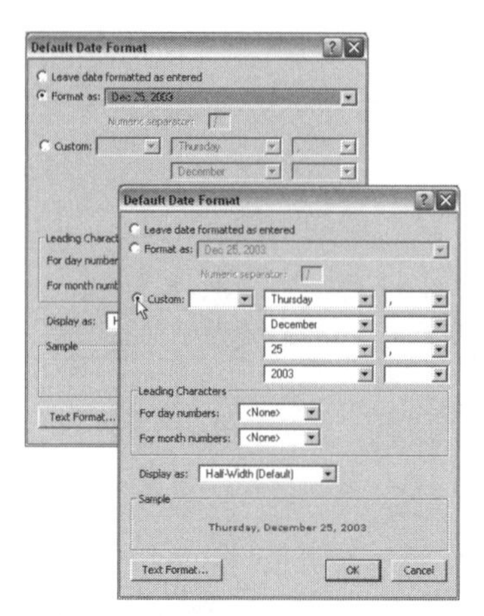

Figure 13.7 Use the Default Date Format dialog box to choose six standard options (top) or click *Custom* for even more choices (bottom).

Figure 13.8 The *Format as* pop-up menu offers six date format choices.

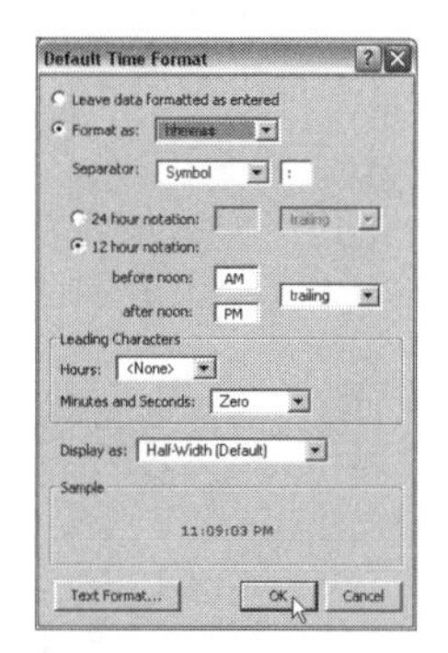

Figure 13.9 Use the Default Time Format dialog box to select from a myriad of options.

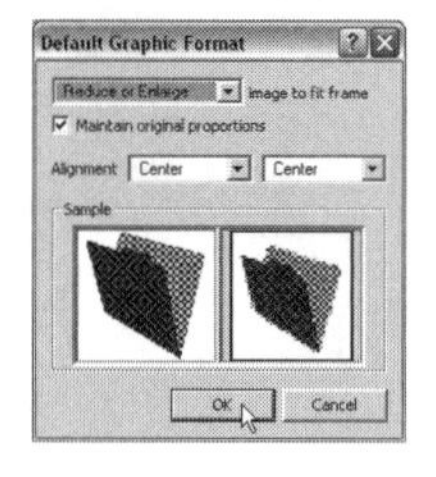

Figure 13.10 Use the Default Graphic Format dialog box to control cropping and fitting. The sample window previews the options.

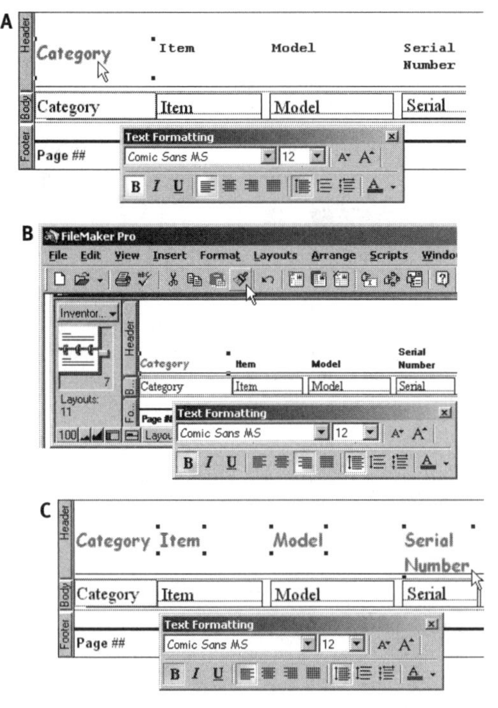

Figure 13.11 Select the field whose formatting you want to use (**A**), click the icon to activate the Format Painter (**B**), and click the field you want formatted. Click and drag to format several fields at once (**C**).

Figure 13.12 After using the Format Painter, the formatting of the *Category* label field has been applied to the *Item*, *Model*, and *Serial Number* label fields.

Formatting Fields or Objects

This section shows you how to change *individual* fields or objects. If you're looking to set format defaults for the entire database, see *To set formatting defaults*, on page 200.) You can, by the way, format several fields at the same time—as long as you're setting the same attribute in each field, such as text. The Format Painter makes it much simpler to format fields or objects.

Using the Format Painter

Anyone who has ever used the Format Painter in Microsoft Office will instantly recognize FileMaker's own Format Painter, which works identically. The Format Painter lets you apply nearly all the attributes of a text field or graphic object to other text fields or graphic objects. You cannot, however, apply text attributes to objects and vice versa.

To use the Format Painter:

1. Make sure you're in Layout mode (Ctrl L in Windows, ⌘L on the Mac), then select the field or object whose formatting you want to use (the source field) (**A**, **Figure 13.11**).
2. Click the Format Painter icon, which is part of the Standard toolbar, to activate the Format Painter (**B**, **Figure 13.11**).
3. Click the field or object to which you want to apply the formatting (the target field). Click and drag if you want to select several fields to format simultaneously (**C**, **Figure 13.11**). Release the cursor and the formatting is applied (**Figure 13.12**).

(continued)

✔ Tips

- If you change your mind midway through the process, press Esc to deactivate the Format Painter. The Format Painter's brush-shaped cursor returns to the customary arrow shape.
- Having the Text Formatting toolbar visible (View > Toolbars > Text Formatting) lets you see which text attributes are currently selected. This makes it much easier to know if you've actually selected the source field.
- The Format Painter uses the same steps to apply attributes from one object to another (**Figure 13.13**).
- The Format Painter also can apply attributes to fields or objects in any other open database. Arrange the databases so that both windows are visible, then click the field or object whose formatting you want to use, click the Format Painter icon, and click the other database's field or object (**Figure 13.14**).
- While the Format Painter is a great way to apply multiple text attributes, it's limited to attributes available in the Text Formatting toolbar. For applying attributes not found in the toolbar, such as Strikeouts, Indents, and Tabs, see *Setting multiple text attributes* on the next page.

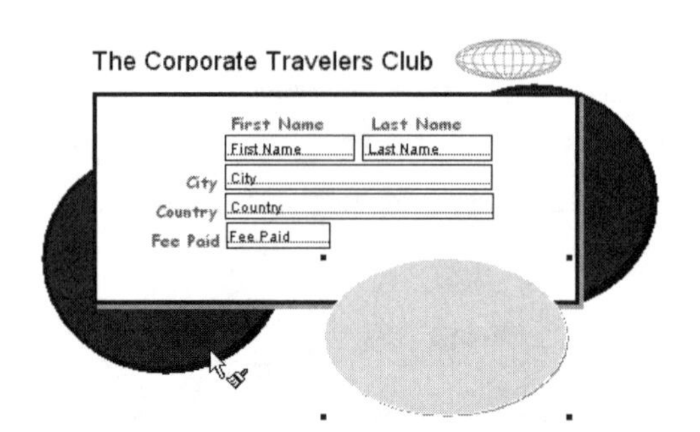

Figure 13.13 Formatting objects with the Format Painter works just as it does for formatting text fields. Here, the right circle's formatting has been applied to the left circle.

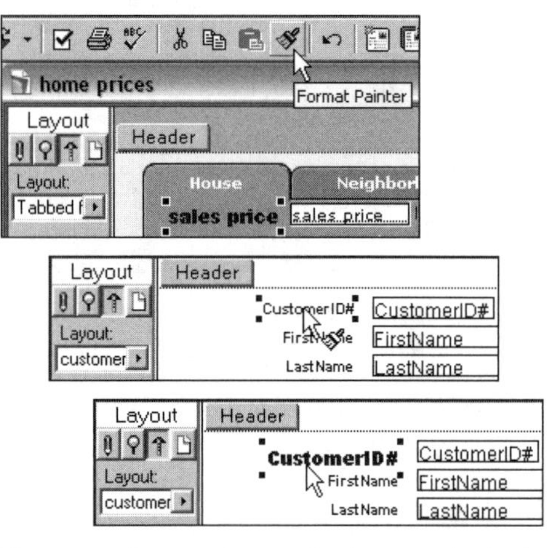

Figure 13.14 By arranging two databases so that both windows are visible, the Format Painter can apply attributes from one to the other.

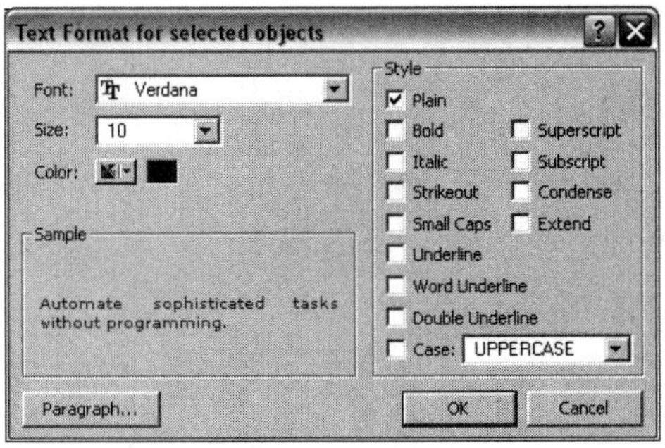

Setting multiple text attributes

This approach can save you time if you want to change, say, a font's size and style at the same time.

To set several text attributes at once:

1. Select your text and choose Format > Text.
2. When the Text Format dialog box appears (**Figure 13.15**), use the drop-down menus and checkboxes to select the *Font*, *Size*, *Color*, and *Style* of your text. To set the alignment, indentation, or line spacing of text, click the *Paragraph* button in the lower left.
3. Once the Paragraph dialog box appears (**Figure 13.16**), you can set the text *Alignment*, *Indent*, and *Line Spacing*.
4. When you're done, click *OK* to close the Paragraph dialog box, then click *OK* again to close the Text Format dialog box.

✔ Tip

- It's often quicker to format text using the Text Formatting toolbar (**Figure 13.17**). To see it, choose View > Toolbars > Text Formatting.

Figure 13.15 The Text Format dialog box lets you set multiple text attributes, including paragraph formatting via the lower-left button.

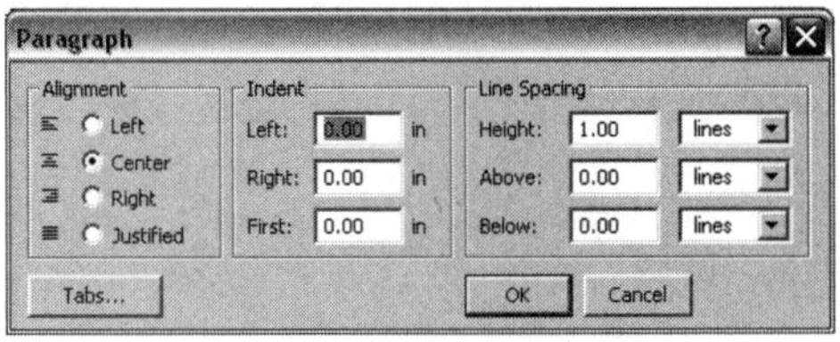

Figure 13.16 The Paragraph dialog box lets you set text alignment, indentation, and line spacing.

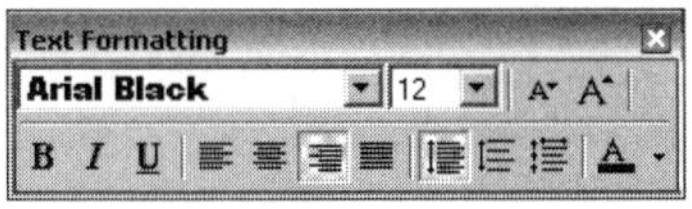

Figure 13.17 Use the Text Formatting toolbar for quick access to most of the text formatting controls.

To set text tabs:

1. Select the text for which you want to set tabs and choose Format > Text.
2. When the Text Format dialog box appears (**Figure 13.15**), click the *Paragraph* button in the lower left. When the Paragraph dialog box appears (**Figure 13.16**), click the *Tabs* button.
3. When the Tabs dialog box appears (**Figure 13.18**), the current tab settings, if there are any, appear in the upper-left window. To change them, select one with your cursor and type in a new position number, and click *Set*.
   - To create a new tab, choose a *Type* in the upper-left panel, type in the position number, and click *New*.
   - To start over, click *Clear*.
   - To set a decimal tab, click the *Align on* radio button. If you want to use something other than a period, type it into the adjacent entry box.
   - Fill characters appear between tabbed items (usually dashes or periods). Type in your choice.
4. When you're done, click *OK*.

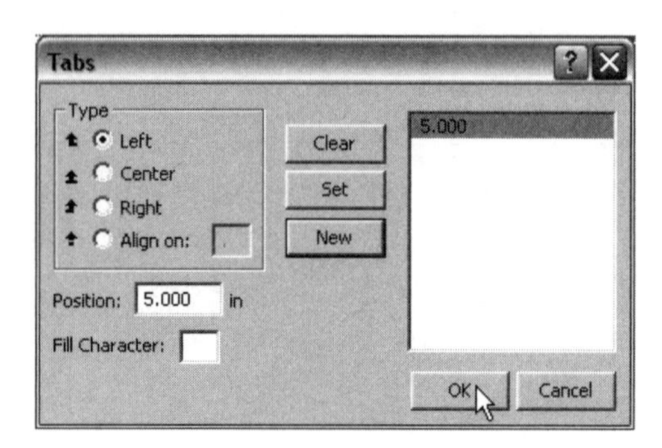

Figure 13.18 The Tabs dialog box lets you change existing tabs or create new ones.

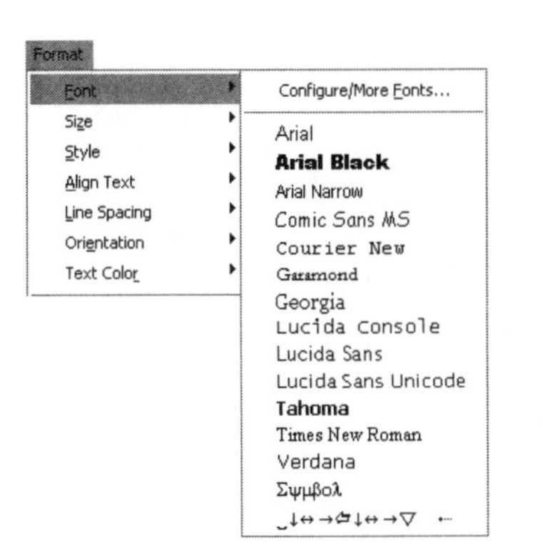

Figure 13.19 Choose Format > Font to quickly apply any font to your selected text.

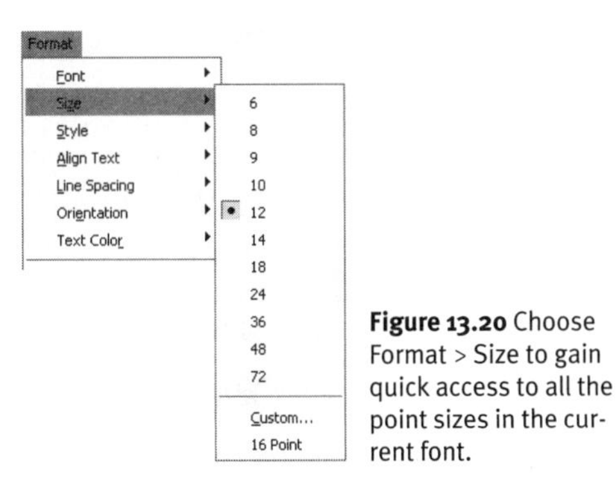

Figure 13.20 Choose Format > Size to gain quick access to all the point sizes in the current font.

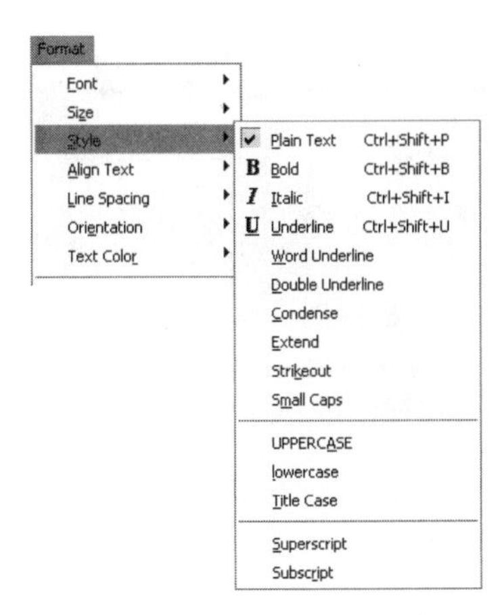

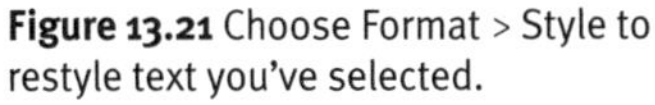

Figure 13.21 Choose Format > Style to restyle text you've selected.

To choose a font:

1. Select the text to which you want to apply another font. To select multiple fields or objects, just press Shift as you click on each field or object.
2. Choose Format > Font (**Figure 13.19**). When the drop-down menu of fonts appears, drag your cursor to the font you want and release the cursor. The selected text changes to the newly selected font.

To choose a text size:

1. Select the text or field containing text you want to change. To select multiple fields or objects, just press Shift as you click on each field or object.
2. Choose Format > Size (**Figure 13.20**). When the drop-down menu of text sizes appears, drag your cursor to the size you want and release the cursor. The selected text changes size.

To choose a text style:

1. Select the text or field containing text you want to change. To select multiple fields or objects, just press Shift as you click on each field or object.
2. Choose Format > Style (**Figure 13.21**). When the drop-down menu of text styles appears, drag your cursor to the style you want and release the cursor. Since text can have multiple styles (bold with italic with underline), continue using the drop-down menu until you've applied all the desired styles.

To align text:

1. Select the text or field containing text you want to change. To select multiple fields or objects, just press Shift as you click on each field or object.
2. Choose Format > Align Text (**Figure 13.22**). When the drop-down menu of alignment choices appears, drag your cursor to the alignment you want and release the cursor. The alignment of the selected text reflects your new choice.

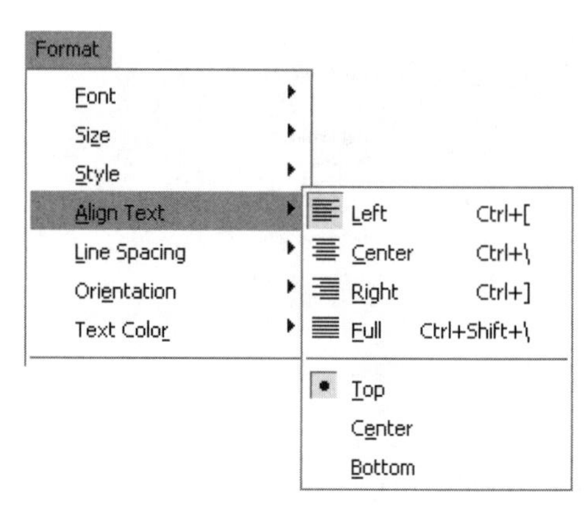

Figure 13.22 Choose Format > Align Text for quick access to alignment options without having to open a dialog box.

To choose line spacing:

1. Select the text or field containing text you want to change. To select multiple fields or objects, just press Shift as you click on each field or object.
2. Choose Format > Line Spacing (**Figure 13.23**). When the drop-down menu of spacing choices appears, drag your cursor to the one you want and release the cursor.

   If single or double line spacing won't do, choose Custom, which opens the Paragraph settings dialog box (**Figure 13.24**).
3. Use the Line Spacing section to set your line *Height* and the spacing *Above* and *Below* the line. The drop-down menus for each allow you to make your spacings based on the number of lines, inches, pixels, or centimeters.
4. Once you're ready, click *OK*.

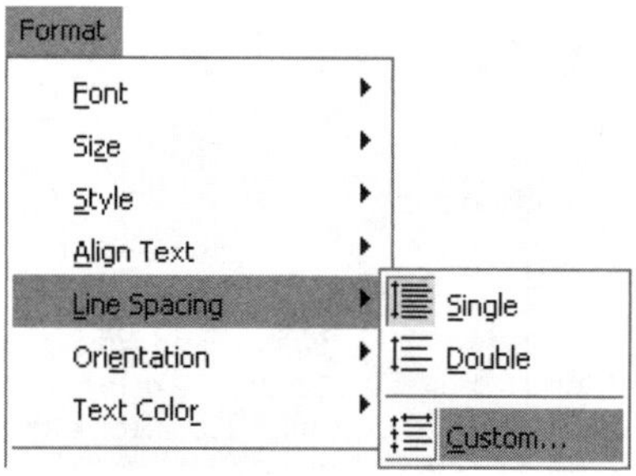

Figure 13.23 Choose Format > Line Spacing to apply single, double, or custom spacing.

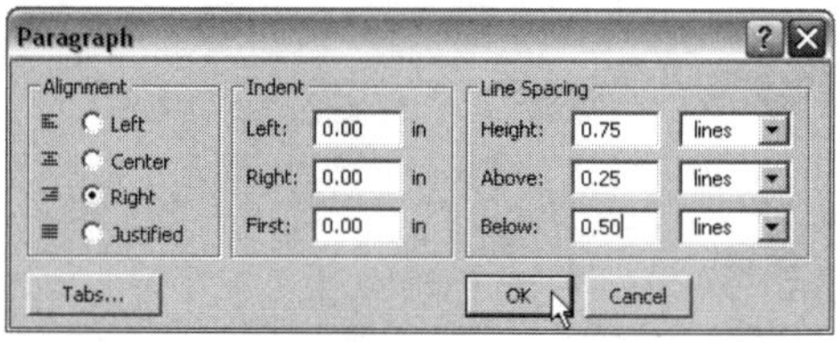

Figure 13.24 Custom line spacing is handled within the Paragraph dialog box.

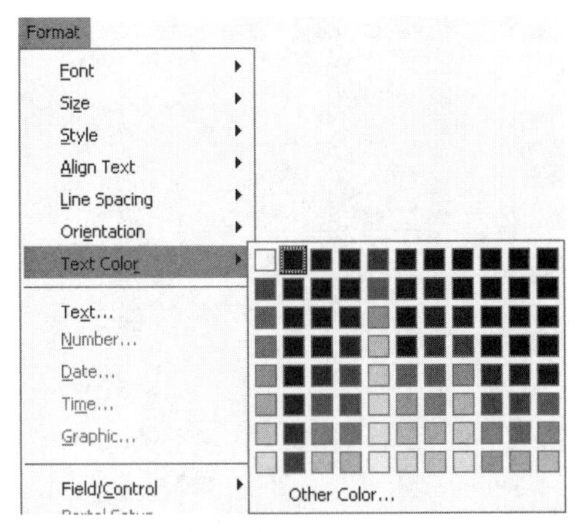

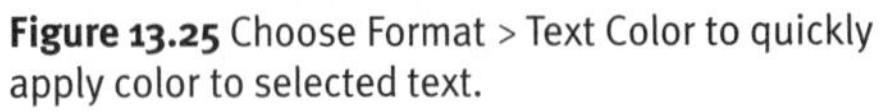

Figure 13.25 Choose Format > Text Color to quickly apply color to selected text.

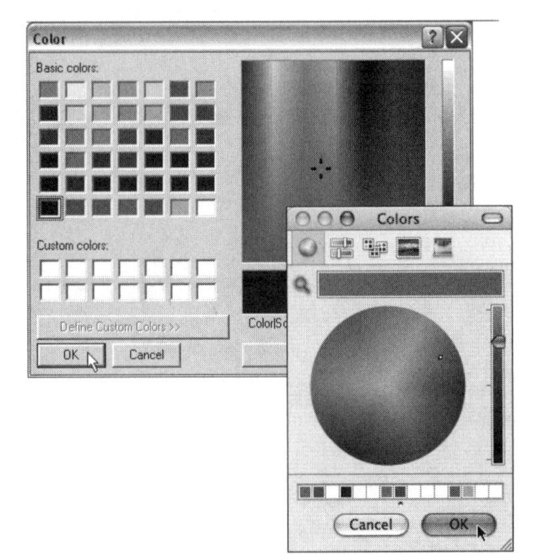

Figure 13.26 Use Windows' Color dialog box (top) or the Mac's Color Picker (bottom) to choose a custom text color.

To choose a text color:

1. Select the text or field containing text you want to change. To select multiple fields or objects, just press Shift as you click on each field or object.
2. Choose Format > Text Color (**Figure 13.25**). When the submenu of colors appears, drag your cursor to the one you want, and release the cursor. The text changes to the color you've chosen.

✔ Tip

- If you want to use a custom color, choose *Other Color* in step 2, and use the dialog boxes that appear to pick your color (**Figure 13.26**). When you're done, click *OK* and the new color is applied.

To format a number field:

1. Make sure the field you want to format is, in fact, a number-type field. (You can check in the Define Fields dialog box: Ctrl Shift D in Windows, Shift ⌘ D on the Mac.)
2. Choose Format > Number, which opens the Number Format dialog box (**Figure 13.27**).
3. Make your choices (for specifics on the dialog box, see step 2 of *To set formatting defaults*, on page 200). Click *OK*.

To format a date field:

1. Make sure the field you want to format is a date-type field. You can do this by checking the Define Fields dialog box: Ctrl Shift D in Windows, Shift ⌘ D on the Mac.
2. Choose Format > Date, which opens the Date Format dialog box (**Figure 13.28**).
3. Make your choices (for specifics on the dialog box, see step 2 of *To set formatting defaults*, on page 200). Click *OK*.

✔ Tip

- While the *Format as* pop-up menu still includes a two-digit year choice, it's best to use the four-digit year formats.

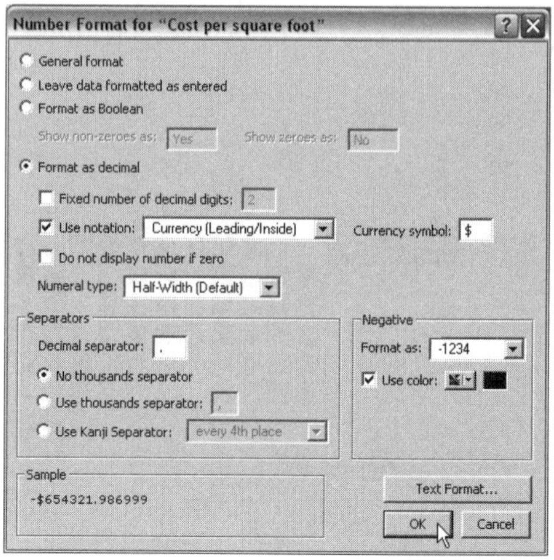

Figure 13.27 The Number Format dialog box's settings are applied to number fields you've selected or used to set *default* number settings if no field is selected.

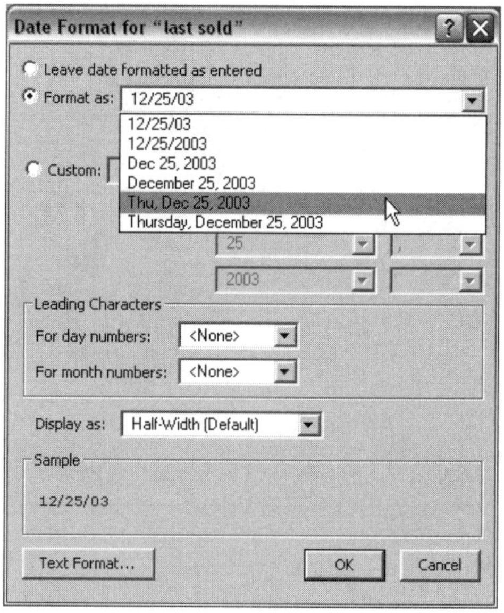

Figure 13.28 The Date Format dialog box's settings are applied to selected date fields or used to set *default* date settings if no field is selected.

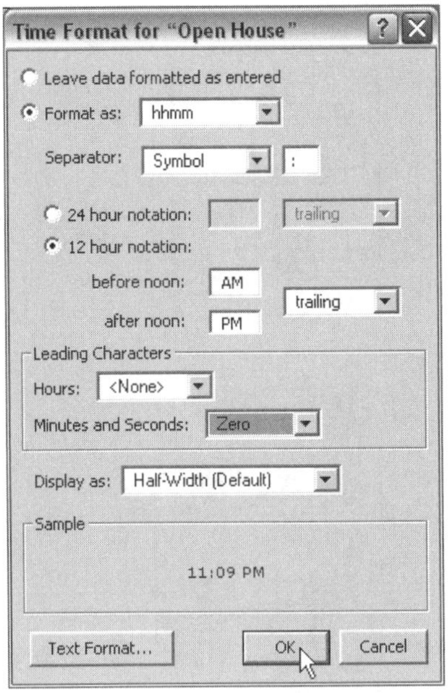

Figure 13.29 The Time Format dialog box's settings are applied to selected time fields or used to set *default* time settings if no field is selected.

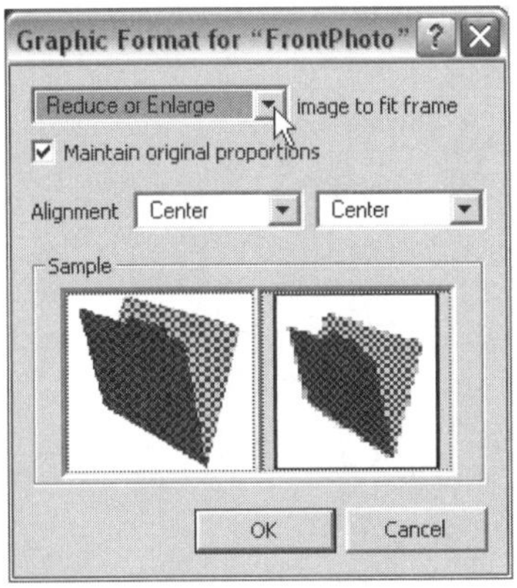

Figure 13.30 The Graphic Format dialog box's settings are applied to selected graphics or used to set *default* graphic settings if no field is selected.

To format a time field:

1. Make sure the field you want to format is a time-type field. You can do this by checking the Define Fields dialog box: Ctrl Shift D in Windows, Shift ⌘ D on the Mac.
2. Choose Format > Time, which opens the Time Format dialog box (**Figure 13.29**).
3. Make your choices (for specifics on the dialog box, see step 2 of *To set formatting defaults*, on page 200). Click *OK*.

To format a graphic field:

1. Make sure the field you want to format is a container-type field, which is the only kind that can accept a graphic (see page 94). You can do this by checking the Define Fields dialog box: Ctrl Shift D in Windows, Shift ⌘ D on the Mac.
2. Choose Format > Graphic, which opens the Graphic Format dialog box (**Figure 13.30**).
3. Make your choices, using the three pop-up menus to control the placement of the graphic within its field, then click *OK*.

Working with Graphics

The Layout status area includes a powerful collection of tools for adding graphic interest and emphasis to your layouts (**Figure 13.31**).

Pointer Tool: Use this tool to select or resize fields and objects.

Text Tool: Though it's nestled amid the draw tools, this tool's really for, well, text. See *Working with Text* on page 198 for more information.

Line Tool: Use this tool with the Pen Tools to create lines of varying width, color, and pattern.

Shape Tools (rectangle, rounded rectangle, oval): Use the three tools with the Fill Tools to create shapes of varying colors and patterns. Also see *To change the stack order of objects* on page 183 for information on how to arrange overlapping shapes.

Button, Field/Control Tools: By adding buttons, you can link them to commons scripts, such as opening another database or printing a particular report. See *To add a button* on page 220. Use the Field/Control Tool to add or change fields. See *Defining Fields* on page 93.

Tab Layout, Portal Tools: Tabbed layouts make it easy to present lots of data in an easy-to-read fashion. See *Using Tabbed Layouts* on page 191. Portals are views of data from other databases. See *To define a portal* on page 139.

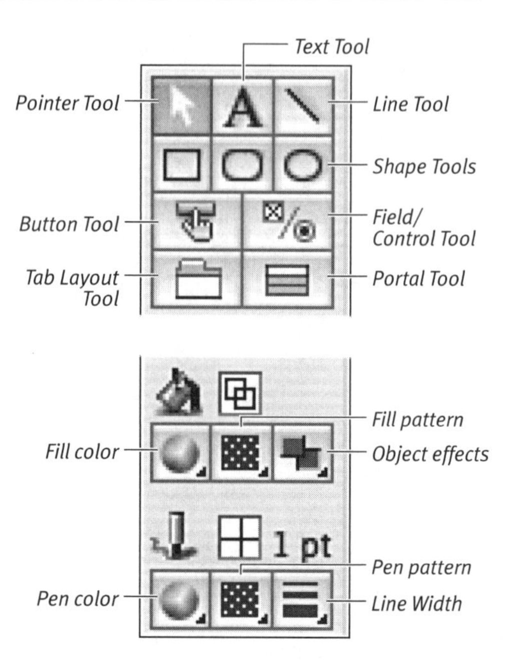

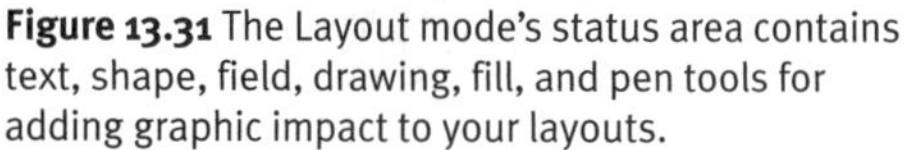

Figure 13.31 The Layout mode's status area contains text, shape, field, drawing, fill, and pen tools for adding graphic impact to your layouts.

View of current fill settings
Fill color
Object effects
Fill pattern

Figure 13.32 The Fill Tools control colors and patterns for shapes.

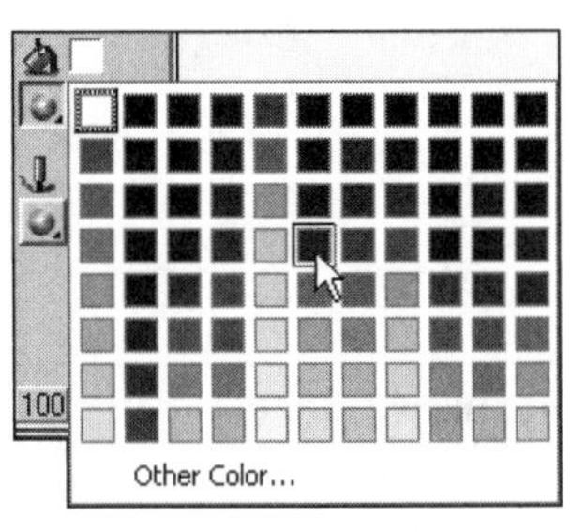

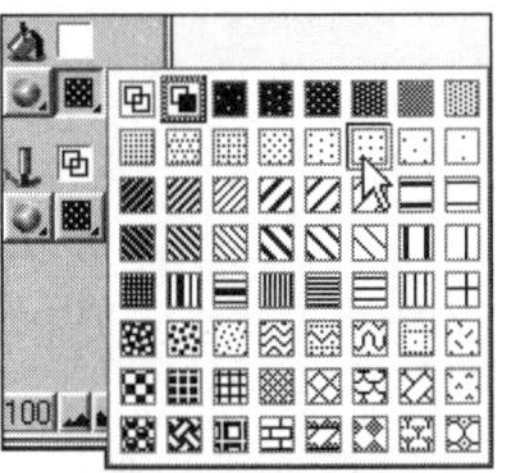

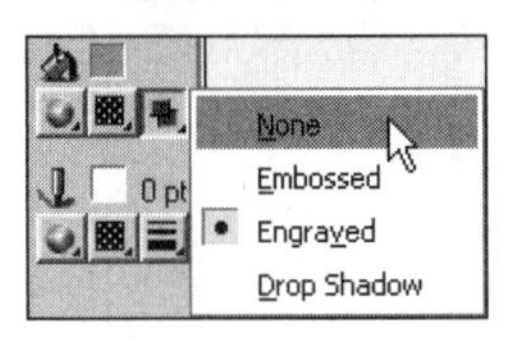

Figure 13.33 Use the drop-down menus to reach the fill colors, patterns, and effects.

Fill Tools (color, pattern, object effects): Use these three tools (**Figure 13.32**) with the Shape Tools. Each offers a variety of choices via their drop-down menus (**Figure 13.33**). The Object Effects tool lets you easily add some visual flourishes previously confined to full-fledged graphics programs.

Pen Tools (color, pattern, line width): Use this trio of tools (**Figure 13.34**) with the Line Tool. Like the Fill Tools, these three tools operate via drop-down menus (**Figure 13.35**).

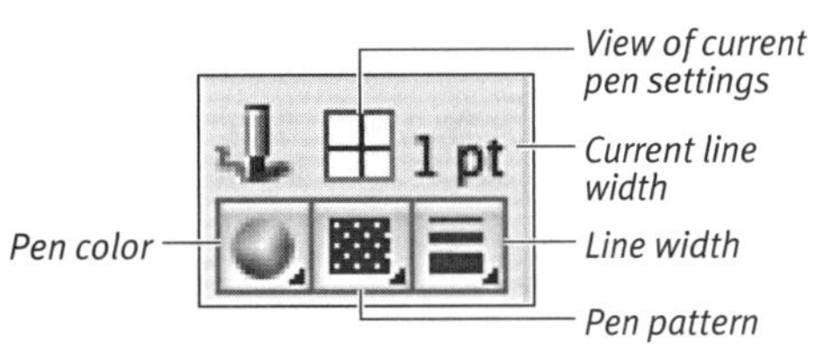

Figure 13.34 The Pen Tools control line colors, patterns, and widths.

Other Color...

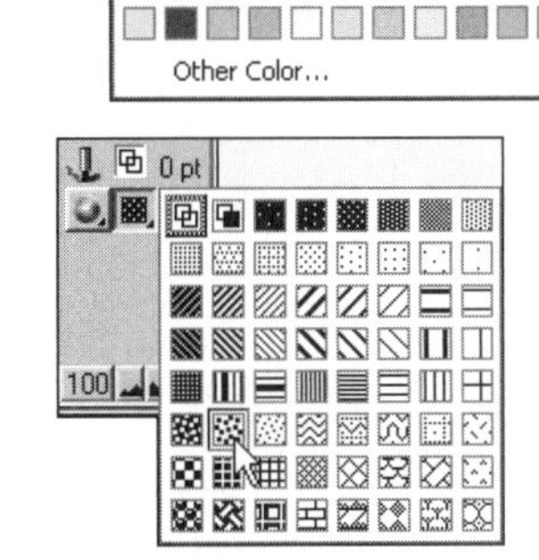

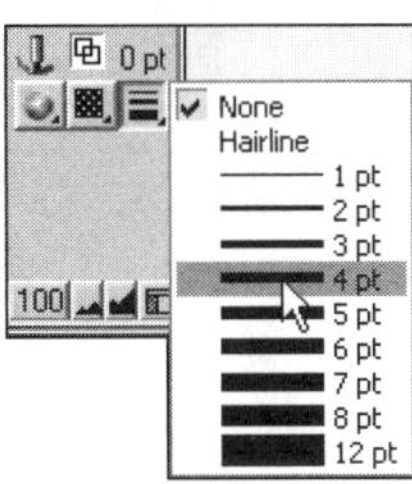

Figure 13.35 Use the drop-down menus to choose line colors, patterns, and widths.

WORKING WITH GRAPHICS

To select a drawing tool:

- Switch to Layout mode (Ctrl L in Windows, ⌘ L on the Mac), then click on the tool of your choice. When it's active, it becomes gray (left in **Figure 13.36**).

✔ Tips

- It's easy to accidentally unselect a tool. To keep it selected until you deliberately click on another tool, double-click the tool and the icon's outline turns white to indicate it's locked on (right in **Figure 13.36**).
- To toggle between any tool and the Pointer tool, press Enter (the one by the numeric keypad).

To draw an object:

1. Switch to Layout mode (Ctrl L in Windows, ⌘ L on the Mac), then click on the drawing tool of your choice: Line, Rectangle, Rounded Rectangle, or Oval.
2. Click with your cursor where you want the shape to begin and drag the cursor to where you want the shape to end. See **Table 13.1**, *FileMaker's Object Drawing Tools*, for more details.

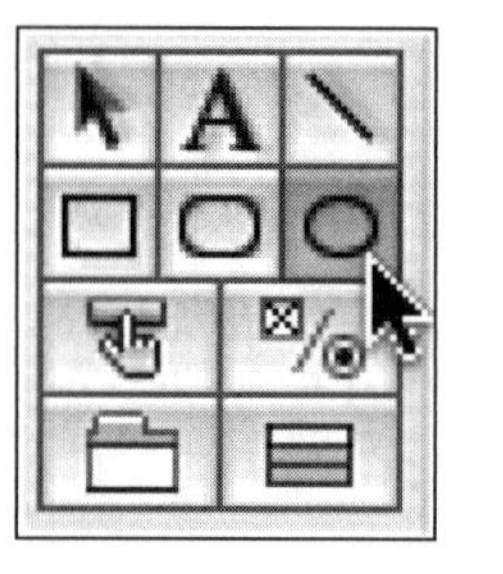

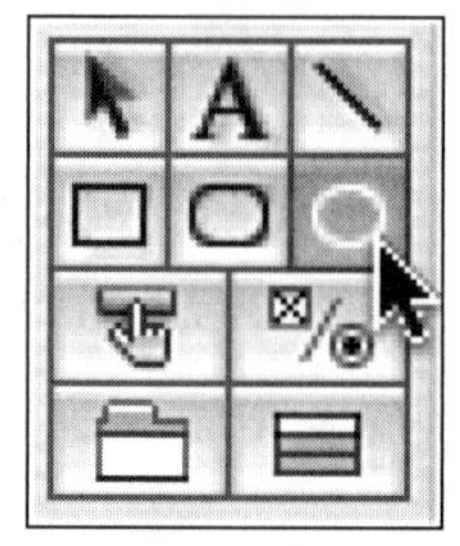

Figure 13.36 When a tool's selected it shows a black line on a dark gray background (left); when it's locked the line turns white (right).

Table 13.1

FileMaker's Object Drawing Tools

Tool Icon	Shape	Action
(line icon)	Line	Select Line Tool. Click on start point, and press cursor until end point reached.
	Horizontal, vertical, or 45-degree line	Select Line Tool. Press Alt (Windows) or Option (Mac) while clicking on start point, and dragging cursor until end point reached.
(rectangle icon)	Rectangle	Select Rectangle Tool. Click on start point and drag cursor until rectangle is the size you want.
	Square	Select Rectangle Tool. Press Alt (Windows) or Option (Mac) while clicking on start point, and dragging cursor until square is the size you want.
(rounded rectangle icon)	Rounded rectangle	Select Rounded Rectangle Tool. Click on start point and drag cursor until rectangle is the size you want.
(oval icon)	Oval	Select Oval Tool. Click on start point and drag cursor until oval is the size you want.
	Circle	Select Oval Tool. Press Alt (Windows) or Option (Mac) while clicking on start point, and dragging cursor until circle is the size you want.

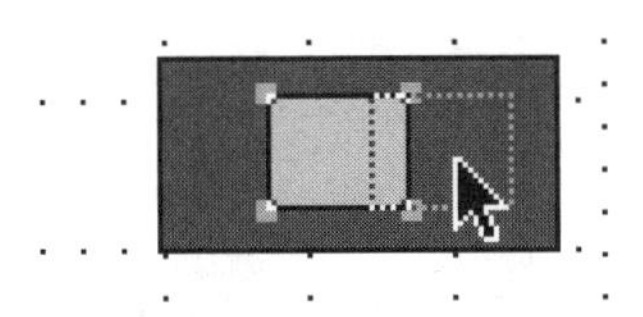

Figure 13.37 To move an object, click on it with the Pointer Tool and drag it. A dotted outline marks your progress.

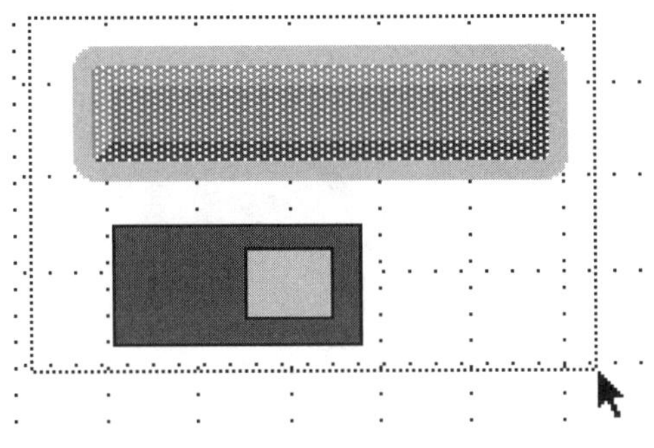

Figure 13.38 Click and drag the Pointer Tool to select multiple objects.

To select and move an object:

1. Make sure you're in Layout mode (Ctrl L in Windows, ⌘ L on the Mac), then click on the object. To select multiple objects, hold down Shift before clicking on the objects.

2. Small squares appear on each corner of the object to let you know it's been selected. Continue holding down your cursor and drag the object where you want it. A dotted outline of the object marks your movement until you release the cursor (**Figure 13.37**).

✔ Tips

- You also can select multiple objects with the Pointer Tool by pressing and holding down the cursor, then dragging the resulting square to include the objects (**Figure 13.38**).

- To select everything in a layout, use the Select All keyboard command (Ctrl A in Windows, ⌘ A on the Mac).

To deselect an object:

- Simply click your cursor anywhere within the layout or select a tool other than the Pointer Tool within the tool palette.

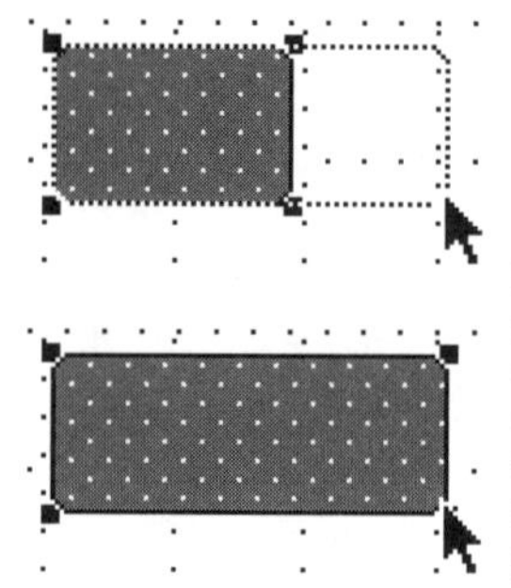

Figure 13.39 To resize an object, grab on the corner handles and drag until it reaches the size you want. A dotted outline marks your progress.

To resize an object:

1. Select the Pointer Tool, then click on the object.
2. Handles (small black squares) appear at the object's corners. Click on any handle and drag it to reshape the object. A dotted outline of the object's new shape marks your movement until you release the cursor (**Figure 13.39**).

✔ Tip

- If you want more precision in resizing an object (such as making its size identical to other objects), use the Size palette: Click on the object, then choose View > Object Size, and use the palette to enter measurements for the object. When done, press Enter in Windows, Return on the Mac. The selected object assumes the sizing you entered.

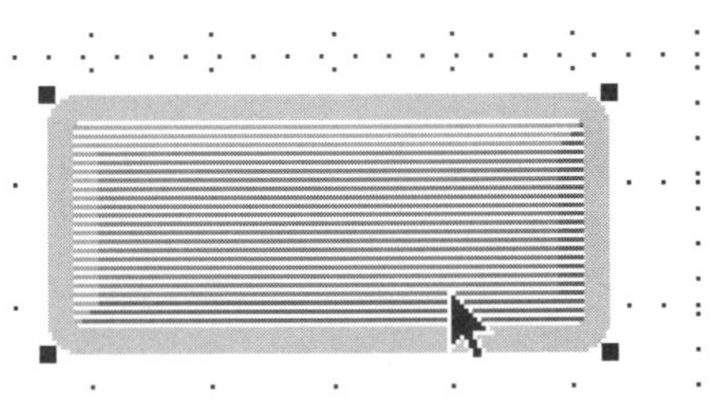

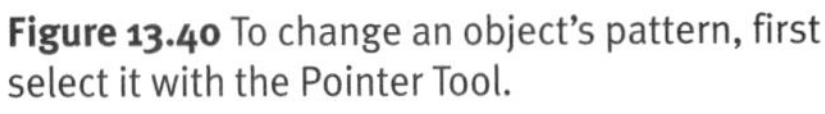

Figure 13.40 To change an object's pattern, first select it with the Pointer Tool.

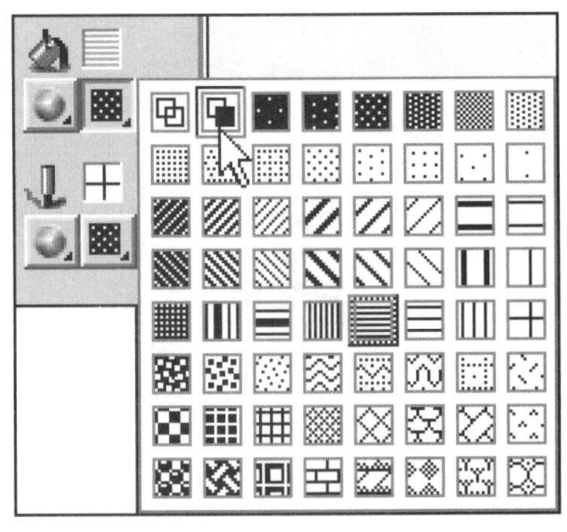

Figure 13.41 Use the Fill Tool's pattern drop-down menu to select a new pattern. The arrow marks the new solid choice; the striped box by the bucket icon marks the previous pattern.

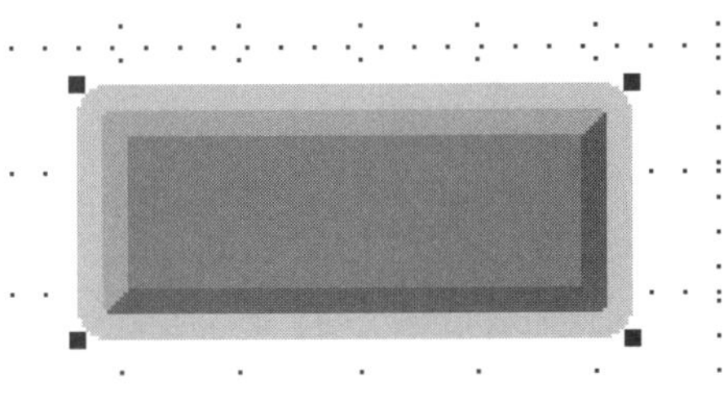

Figure 13.42 The object with its new solid pattern.

Changing fill colors, patterns, and effects

Setting a fill color, pattern, or effect is like setting a default: You start by making sure *nothing* is selected.

To set or change an object's fill color, pattern, or effect:

1. To change an object's *existing* fill color or pattern, select the object using the Pointer Tool (**Figure 13.40**).
2. Now click on one of the Fill tools to select a color, pattern, or effect (**Figure 13.41**).
3. When the tool's drop-down menu appears, drag your cursor to the choice you want and release the cursor. The fill is applied to the object (**Figure 13.42**).

✔ Tip

- If you want to start all over on the pattern, select the object and then click the transparent pattern, found in the upper-left corner of the pop-down choices.

Changing lines

Setting the pen color, pattern, or width is like setting a default: You start by making sure nothing is selected.

To set or change line color, pattern, or width:

1. To change an existing line, select it using the Pointer Tool (**Figure 13.43**).
2. Now click on any of the Pen tools that control color, pattern, or line width (**Figure 13.44**).
3. When the tool's drop-down menu appears, drag your cursor to the line style choice you want and release the cursor. The selected line changes to reflect your choice (**Figure 13.45**).

✔ Tip

- Use the pen color to change the border color of objects (fields use a separate process; see *To set or change field borders, fills, and baselines* on the next page). Just select the object and click the pen color drop-down menu to make your choice.

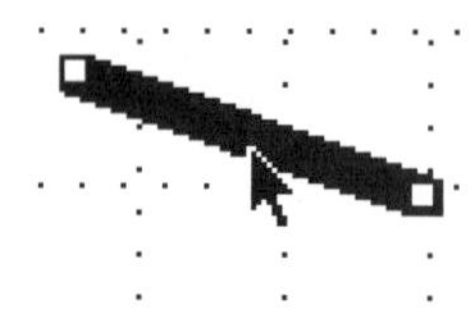

Figure 13.43 To change a line's width, first select it with the Pointer Tool.

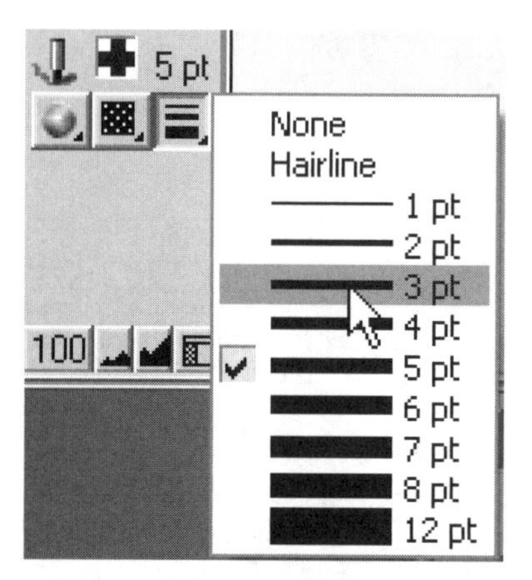

Figure 13.44 Use the Pen Tool's line-width drop-down menu to select a new line width. The check marks the previous line width.

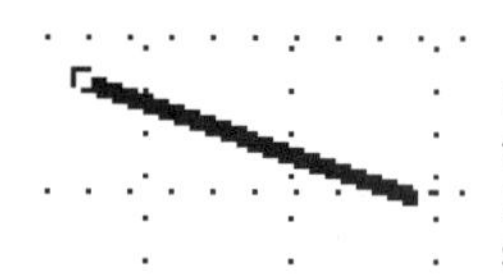

Figure 13.45 After using the drop-down menu, the line assumes its new, sleek look.

Figure 13.46 When the Field Borders dialog box first opens, the lower-left drop-down menu is already set to *Borders*.

Figure 13.47 Choose *Fill* from the Field Borders dialog box's drop-down menu to control field color and pattern.

Figure 13.48 Choose *Baselines* from the Field Borders dialog box's drop-down menu to control the baseline pattern and weight.

Changing borders, fills, and baselines

To set the defaults for field borders, fills, or baselines, first make sure nothing is selected.

To set or change field borders, fills, and baselines:

1. To change an existing field's borders, fills, or baselines, first select it using the Pointer Tool. This procedure applies to fields only, not other objects.
2. Choose Format > Field/Control > Borders (Ctrl Alt B in Windows, Option ⌘ B on the Mac)
3. When the Field Borders dialog box appears (**Figure 13.46**), use the lower-left drop-down menu to set the borders, fill, or baselines.

   In setting field borders, the four upper-left boxes control the boundary around the field. The results of your choices appear in the upper-right *Sample* area. Checking *Text baselines* places horizontal lines within fields containing multiple lines of text. Checking *Between repeating values* separates repeating field entries with lines.

   In setting field fills (**Figure 13.47**), use the two button-shaped, drop-down menus just to right of *format* to set the color and the pattern. In our example, we've selected a dark color, which is shown in the *Sample* area.

   In setting field baselines (**Figure 13.48**), use all three button-shaped, drop-down menus just to right of *format* to set the color, pattern, and line weight.
4. When you've made your choices, click *OK*.

Using Buttons with Scripts

FileMaker makes it easy to add buttons to layouts, to which you can then attach scripts. Such buttons are treated as layout objects, meaning you can use all the formatting tricks covered in the rest of this chapter.

To add a button:

1. Make sure you're in Layout mode (Ctrl L in Windows, ⌘L on the Mac) and select a layout via the pop-up menu.
2. Click the Button Tool within the Layout status area (**Figure 13.49**), then use your cursor to draw a button within the layout. Release the cursor when the button reaches the size you want (**Figure 13.50**).
3. When the Button Setup dialog appears, select a script step from the left-hand list (**Figure 13.51**). Set options for the script step, if any, using the *Specify* button in the *Options* panel. Not every step will offer the same options, and steps grayed out in the list don't apply to your particular button.
4. If you want, change the *Button Style* from the default *Rectangular button* to the *Rounded button*. Leave *Change to hand cursor over button* selected to help cue users that the button triggers an action. Click *OK* to close the dialog box.

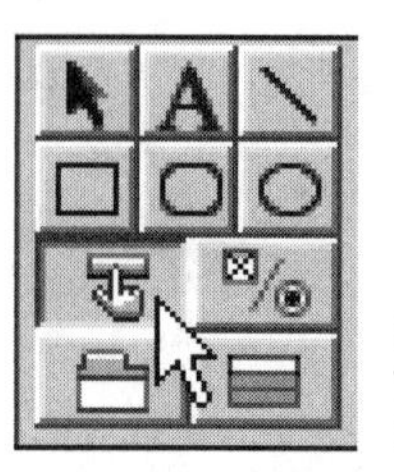

Figure 13.49 Click the Button Tool to add a script-linked button to a layout.

Figure 13.50 Click and drag the cursor in the layout to create a button.

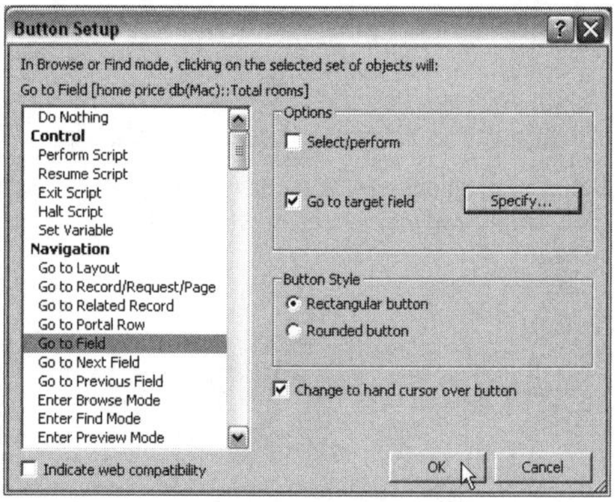

Figure 13.51 Use the Button Setup dialog box to assign a script and shape to the button.

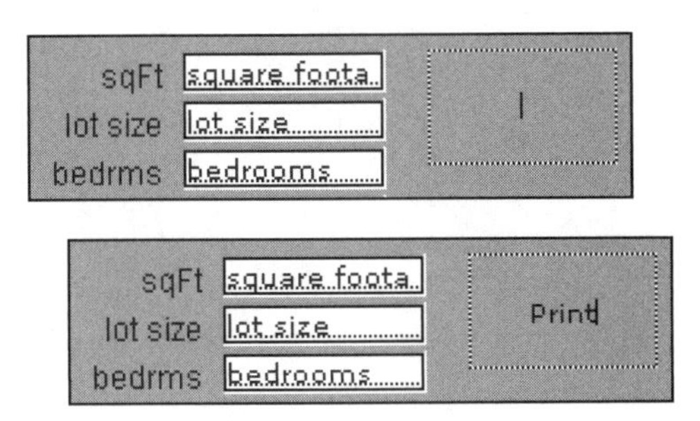

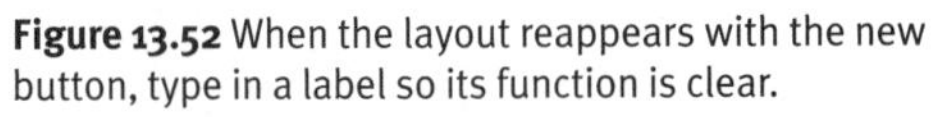

Figure 13.52 When the layout reappears with the new button, type in a label so its function is clear.

Figure 13.53 Format the button's text and appearance using the steps covered in *Working with Graphics* (top). Switch to Browse mode to see the final appearance (bottom).

5. When the layout reappears with the new button, type in a label for it at the I-beam cursor (**Figure 13.52**). When you're done, click anywhere outside the button.
6. Format the button's appearance using the steps covered in *Working with Graphics* on pages 212–220 (top, **Figure 13.53**). Switch to Browse mode (Ctrl B in Windows, ⌘ B on the Mac) and your button is ready for action (bottom, **Figure 13.53**).

✔ Tips

- If you've never used scripts, don't let the many scripting options available in the Button Setup dialog box put you off. Some of the most useful scripts—triggering a sort, switching to another layout, printing a report—are easy to set up and will save you lots of time.
- Generally, you don't want buttons to appear on printouts, so switch to Layout mode and select the button. Choose Format > Set Sliding/Printing. In the Set Sliding/Printing dialog box, check *Do not print the selected objects* and click *OK* to apply the change and close the dialog box.

Copying or deleting a button

Copying a button duplicates not just the graphic but the linked script as well.

To copy or delete a button:

1. Switch to Layout mode (Ctrl L in Windows, ⌘ L on the Mac) and with the Pointer Tool, click on the button to select it.
2. To copy the button, use the Copy command (Ctrl C in Windows, ⌘ C on the Mac), move to the layout where you want the button to appear, and paste it in place (Ctrl V in Windows, ⌘ V on the Mac).
3. To delete the button, simply press Delete or ←Backspace.

To resize or move a button:

1. Switch to Layout mode (Ctrl L in Windows, ⌘ L on the Mac) and with the Pointer Tool, click on the button to select it.
2. To resize the button, simply hold down the cursor and drag one of the button's corner handles to the size you want.

   To move the button, click on its center and drag the button where you want it.

To change a button's definition:

1. Switch to Layout mode (Ctrl L in Windows, ⌘ L on the Mac) and double-click the button.
2. When the Button Setup dialog box appears, change the steps or option choices as desired. Click *OK* to apply the changes and close the dialog box.

Part V

Sharing & the Web

CHANGING FORMATS

No software program is an island. In fact, FileMaker can import and export data in dozens of formats—including all your old files created with earlier versions of FileMaker. It's easier than ever to work with Microsoft Excel and Adobe Acrobat PDF (Portable Document Format) files. Records created using FileMaker 7 use the very same format as FileMaker 8, but legacy files created with FileMaker versions 3–6 also can be converted without problems. This chapter also covers how to recover data if a FileMaker file should ever become damaged.

Working with Excel and PDF Files

Sometimes you or co-workers need to see FileMaker data in spreadsheet form or want to sift through some Microsoft Excel numbers using FileMaker. Moving in either direction's no problem: FileMaker 8 can quickly generate Excel-compatible files or read data created by Excel. Similarly, you can move Adobe PDF (Portable Document Format) files in and out of FileMaker with ease. Additionally, it's just as easy to email the Excel or PDF file to others. This section focuses on saving (exporting) FileMaker data in the Excel and PDF formats. For more on importing those formats into FileMaker see *To import data for a new FileMaker database* on page 235.

To save or email records for Excel:

1. Before you export the FileMaker database, use FileMaker's Find and Omit commands to expand or narrow the Found Set to just the records you'll want. Use FileMaker's Sort command to then put the records in the order you want them to appear initially in Excel (**Figure 14.1**).
2. In Browse, Layout, or Preview mode, choose File > Save/Send Records As > Excel.
3. When the Save Records As Excel dialog box appears, use the *Save As* text window to clearly name the file (leave the `.xls` suffix as is) and use the *Where* drop-down menu to navigate to the folder in which you'll save the file (**Figure 14.2**). Use the *Save* drop-down menu to choose whether to save the *Records being browsed* or (less often) only the *Current Record*.

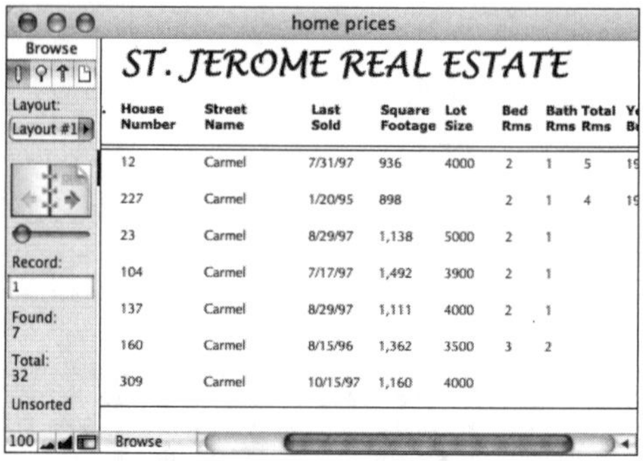

Figure 14.1 Before exporting a FileMaker database, use the Find, Omit, and Sort commands to order the records as you want them to appear in Excel.

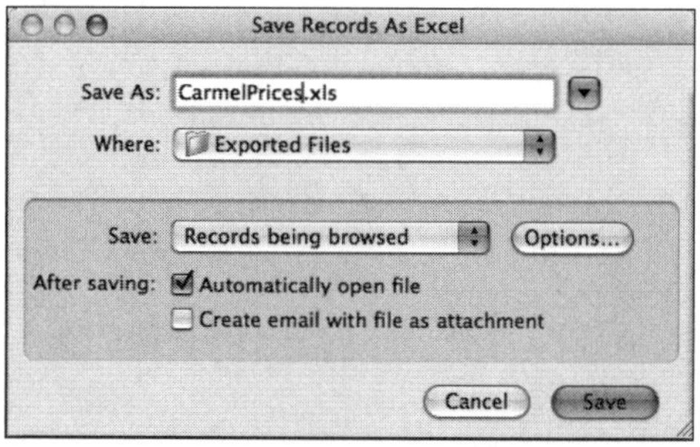

Figure 14.2 Use the *Save As* text window to name the file and the *Where* drop-down menu to navigate to the folder in which you'll save the file.

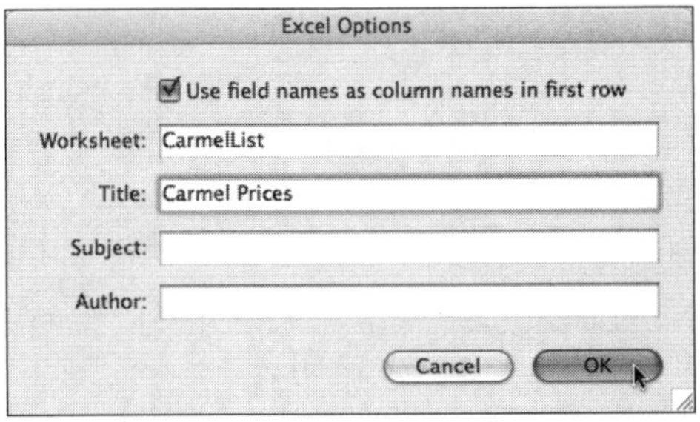

Figure 14.3 By default, *Use field name as column names in first row* is selected in the Excel Options dialog box. Adding a *Worksheet* name helps you identify the data once it's opened in Excel.

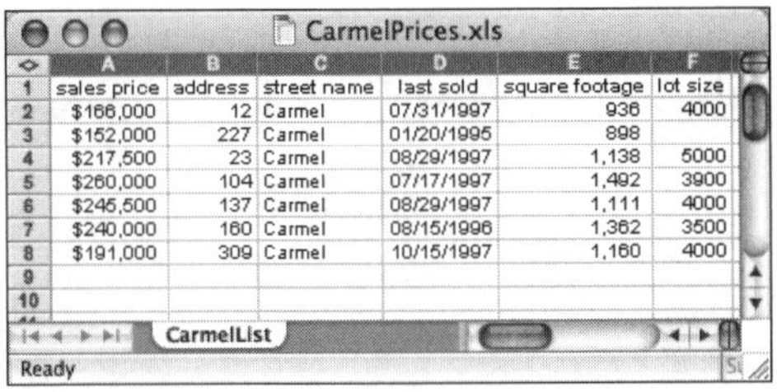

Figure 14.4 If you selected *Automatically open file* in step 5, the new file opens in Excel.

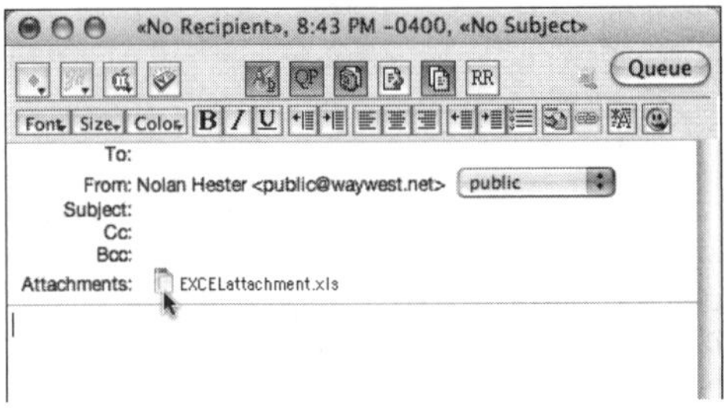

Figure 14.5 If you selected *Create email* in step 5, your default email program generates a new blank message with the Excel file attached.

4. To set how the records appear within Excel, click *Options* to open the Excel Options dialog box (**Figure 14.3**). By default, *Use field name as column names in first row* is selected. Deselect the box if you want no column names to appear. Name the *Worksheet* using the first text box; use the other three based on your needs. Click *OK* to return to the Save Records As dialog box.

5. Back in the Save Records As dialog box, you can select the first checkbox to *Automatically open file* in Excel once it's saved.

   or

   Select the second checkbox to *Create email with* [an Excel] *file as attachment* (**Figure 14.2**).

   or

   Select both boxes to open the file in Excel *and* create a new email with an Excel attachment.

6. Once you make your choices, click *Save* to close the dialog box. If you selected *Automatically open file* in step 5, the new file opens in Excel (**Figure 14.4**). If you selected *Create email...*, your default email program generates a new blank message with the Excel file attached (**Figure 14.5**).

To save records as PDF:

1. Before you export the FileMaker database, use FileMaker's Find and Omit commands to expand or narrow the Found Set to just the records you'll want. Use FileMaker's Sort command to then put the records in the order you want them to appear in the PDF.
2. In Browse, Layout, or Preview mode, choose File > Save/Send Records As > PDF.
3. When the Save Records As PDF dialog box appears, use the *Save As* text window to clearly name the file (leave the `.pdf` suffix as is) and use the *Where* drop-down menu to navigate to the folder in which you'll save the file (**Figure 14.6**). Use the *Save* drop-down menu to choose whether to save the *Records being browsed* or (less often) only the *Current Record.*
4. To set how the records appear in a PDF, click *Options* to open the PDF Options dialog box where the *Document* tab is selected by default (**Figure 14.7**). Fill in the text windows as needed; note that the bottom area lets you set which pages print and how they are numbered. If you want more control over the PDF's appearance, see Tips on the next page. Click *OK* to return to the Save Records As dialog box.
5. Back in the Save Records As dialog box, you can select the first checkbox to *Automatically open file* in your default PDF viewer once it's saved.

   or

   Select the second checkbox to *Create email with* [a PDF] *file as attachment.*

   or

   Select both boxes to open the file as a PDF *and* create a new email with a PDF attachment.

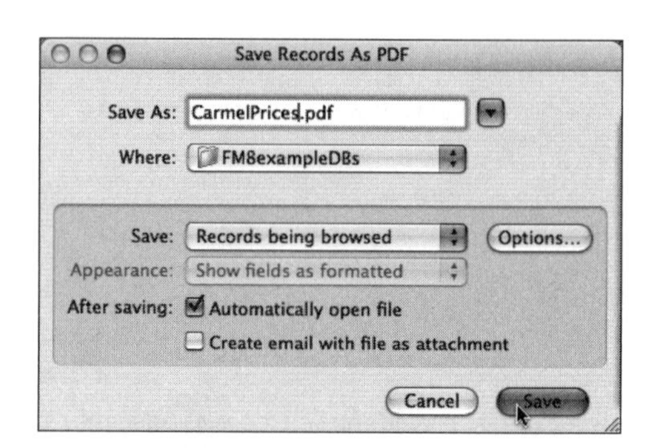

Figure 14.6 Use the *Save As* text window to name the file and the *Where* drop-down menu to navigate to the folder in which you'll save the file. To set how the records appears in a PDF, click *Options*.

Figure 14.7 In the PDF Options dialog box, the *Document* tab is selected by default. Use the top half to add identifying details; the bottom half to control which pages print.

Figure 14.8 The PDF version preserves the layout and data of the original FileMaker document.

Figure 14.9 Save just the layout without data, by setting the *Save* drop-down menu to *Blank Record* and choosing an option in the *Appearance* drop-down menu.

Figure 14.10 Use the *Security* tab to control who can open, edit, and print the PDF document.

Figure 14.11 The *Initial View* tab gives you precise control over how the PDF document appears when first opened.

6. Once you make your choices, click *Save* to close the dialog box. If you selected *Automatically open file* in step 5, the new file opens in your default PDF viewer (**Figure 14.8**). If you selected *Create email...*, your default email program generates a new blank message with the PDF file attached.

✔ Tips

- In step 3, you can save just the FileMaker layout without data by setting the *Save* drop-down menu to *Blank Record* and then choosing one of three options in the *Appearance* drop-down menu (**Figure 14.9**). This is handy if, for example, you want to get someone's reaction to a layout and its fields—without needing to include the data.
- In step 4, you can use the *Security* tab to require a password from anyone opening the PDF document (**Figure 14.10**). You also can control whether the document can be printed or changed.
- Also in step 4, you can use the *Initial View* tab to control the PDF document's appearance when it first opens (**Figure 14.11**). There may be times when you want to exert this level of control. But take a minute to consider whether you really need to override the PDF viewer settings of the recipient.

Exporting FileMaker Data

It's easy to export FileMaker records for applications besides Excel and PDF viewers—in fact many of the steps are identical. Just remember that the target application (the one in which you'll open the exported file) must be able to read one of the formats listed in **Table 14.1** on page 234.

To export FileMaker records:

1. Before you export the FileMaker database, use FileMaker's Find and Omit commands to expand or narrow the Found Set to just the records you'll want. Use FileMaker's Sort command to then put the records in the order you want them to appear within the receiving document.
2. In Browse mode (Ctrl B in Windows, ⌘B on the Mac), choose File > Export Records.
3. When the Export Records to File dialog box appears, type in a name for the file and navigate to the folder where you want to store it. Use the *Type* drop-down menu to select a file format accepted by the application to which you're exporting (**Figure 14.12**).
4. Use the *After saving* checkboxes to select *Automatically open file* in the target application, or *Create email with file as attachment*, or both (**Figure 14.13**). Click *Save* after making your choice.

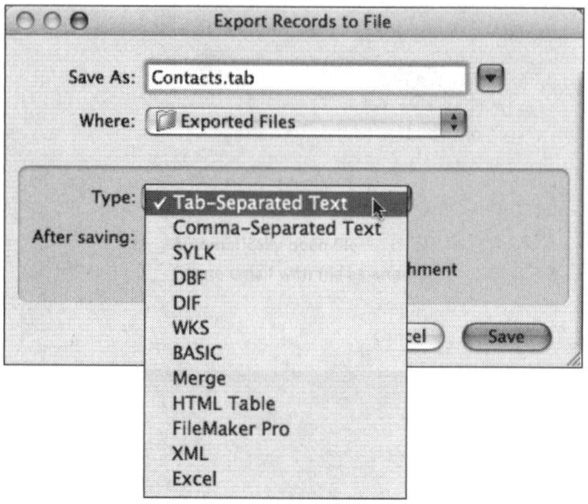

Figure 14.12 Name the exported file, set where it'll be saved, and use the *Type* pop-up menu to pick a compatible format for your target application.

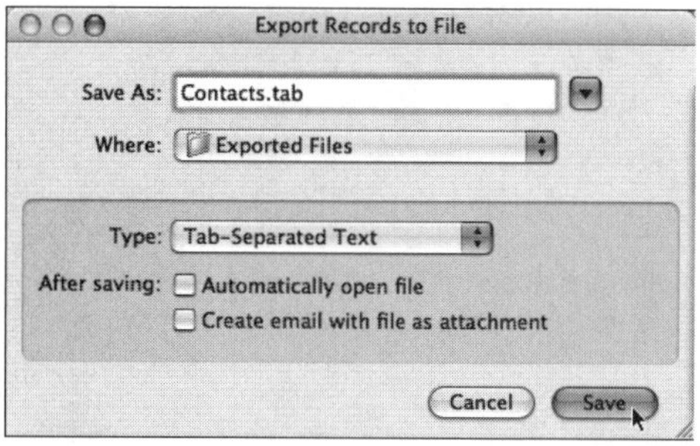

Figure 14.13 Use the *After saving* checkboxes to open the file automatically in the target application, create an email attachment, or both.

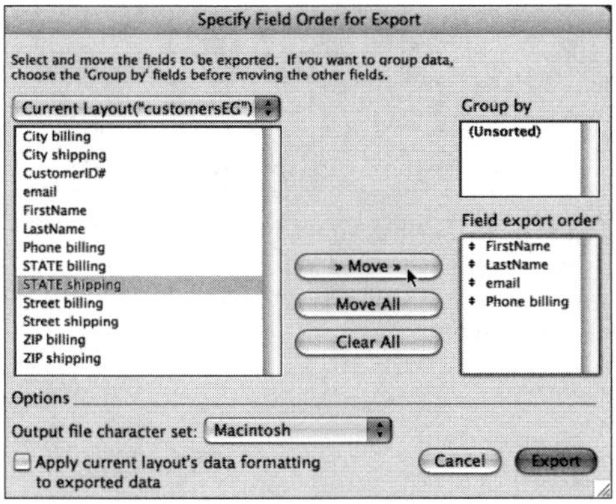

Figure 14.14 Use the Specify Field Order for Export dialog box to pick and order the FileMaker fields you're exporting.

Figure 14.15 FileMaker exports the data in your chosen format: tab-separated text in our example open in a no-frills text editor.

5. When the Specify Field Order for Export dialog box appears, the left-hand list automatically displays the fields in the *Current Layout* (**Figure 14.14**). If that layout does not contain all the fields you want to export, use the *Current Layout* drop-down menu to select *Current Fields* (also see first Tip).

6. After selecting fields in the left-hand list, click the center *Move* button to place them in the right-hand list of fields to be exported. To export all the fields, click *Move All*. If you change your mind and want to remove a field from the right-hand list, select it and click *Clear*.

7. Once you've moved all the fields you want to export into the right-hand list, click and drag the double-arrows next to each field to rearrange the list's export order.

8. Select *Apply current layout's data formatting to exported data* if, for example, you want to preserve particular text, number, or currency formats you already created for the fields you're exporting. Do not make the selection if you just want to export the raw, unformatted data.

9. Click *Export*. FileMaker then places the data into a file based on your chosen format, which you open in your other application (in our example, a no-frills text editor) (**Figure 14.15**).

(continued)

✔ Tips

- In step 5, thanks once again to FileMaker's improved relational abilities, you also can use the drop-down menu to grab fields from any related file or table. For more information on using relational databases, see page 125.
- Also in step 5, if you're exporting records containing subsummary data, other applications may not be able to handle FileMaker's summary fields directly. Take the extra step of selecting in the left-hand list any summary fields, then click inside the *Group by* window to select a subsummary, and click *Move*. The field is added to the right-hand *Field export order* list. (See *Using Calculation and Summary Fields* on page 119.)
- The Specify Field Order for Export dialog box includes an option to ease cross-platform exports. Click the *Output file character set* drop-down menu and choose the platform or character coding system for the operating system (**Figure 14.16**).
- Not every export format can handle the multiple values contained in FileMaker's repeating fields. Work around this by cloning the original file that contains the repeating fields (see *To save a copy of a database file* on page 37). Then divide the repeating field data into separate records by selecting *Splitting them into separate records* within the Import Options dialog box (see *Using Repeating Fields* on page 112).

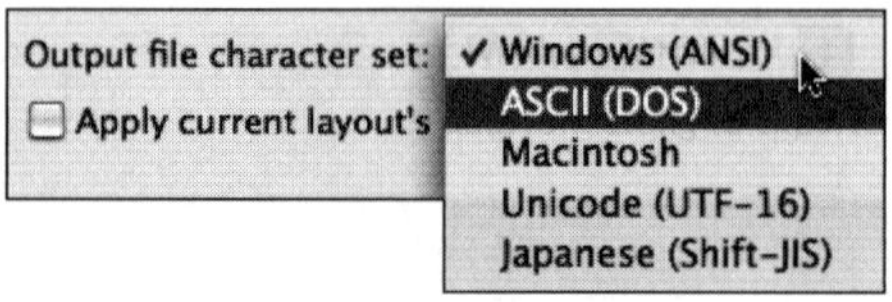

Figure 14.16 Use the *Output file character set* drop-down menu to ease font mapping problems when exporting to other platforms or character coding systems.

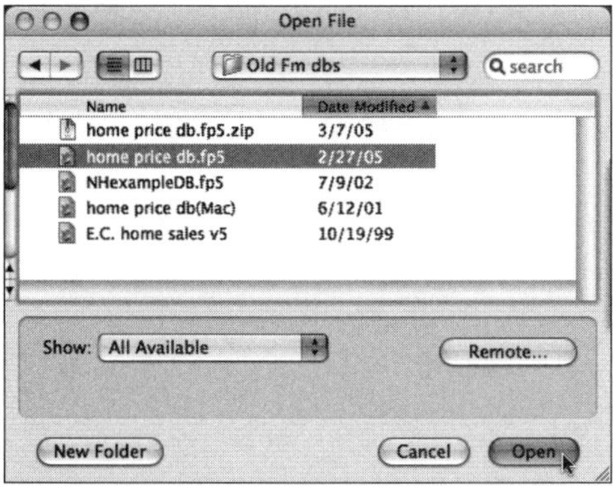

Figure 14.17 Navigate to the file created using an earlier version of FileMaker and click *Open*.

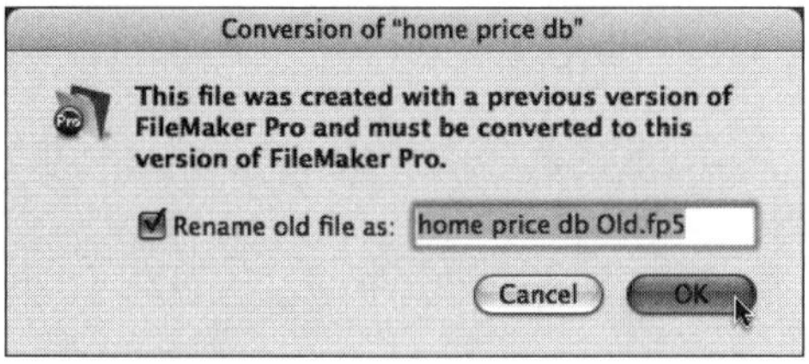

Figure 14.18 Before converting a previous-version file, FileMaker automatically renames it by adding *Old* to the name.

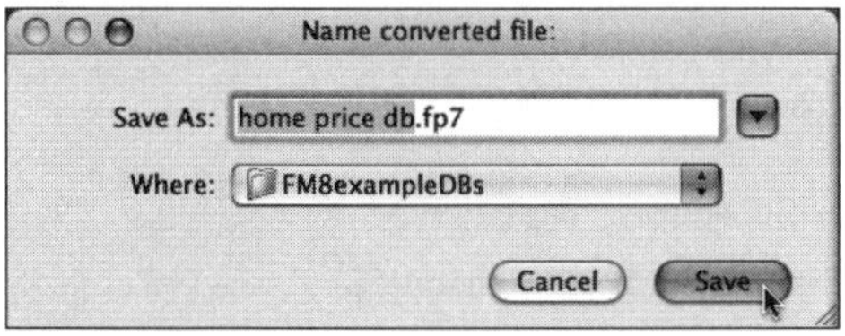

Figure 14.19 By default FileMaker applies the original file's name to the .fp7 version. Rename it if you like, then click *Save*.

Converting Earlier FileMaker Data

Versions 7 and 8 of FileMaker both use the .fp7 format, so there's no need to convert FileMaker 7 files before working on them within FileMaker 8. Any files created with earlier versions of FileMaker, however, first need to be converted to the .fp7 format.

To convert files from FileMaker versions 3–6:

1. While running FileMaker 8, choose File > Open (Ctrl O in Windows/⌘ O on the Mac) and navigate to the file created using an earlier version of FileMaker. Once you find it, click *Open* (**Figure 14.17**).
2. A dialog box appears, alerting you that the older *original* file will be converted and automatically renamed by adding *Old* to its name (**Figure 14.18**). Unless you want to type in another name, click *OK*.
3. The Name converted file dialog box appears and by default applies the original file's name to the .fp7 version (**Figure 14.19**). Rename it if you like, then click *Save* to close the dialog box.
4. A progress bar appears *briefly* as FileMaker converts the old database. The new version of the file then appears in Browse mode, ready for use in FileMaker 8.

Importing Data into FileMaker

Moving data into FileMaker boils down to converting your original source document to a file format that FileMaker can handle. (See **Table 14.1**, *Using FileMaker with Other File Formats*, below.) When importing, you have two basic choices: move the data into a new FileMaker database (sometimes called *converting* data) or move it into an *existing* FileMaker database. If your destination file is an existing FileMaker database, you'll also need to decide whether to add to the existing records, replace all the records, or just update any changed records. To import an Excel or PDF file into FileMaker, see *To import data for a new FileMaker database* on the next page. These same steps can be used with any of compatible formats listed in **Table 14.1**.

Table 14.1

Using FileMaker with Other File Formats

File Extension	Format	What FileMaker Can Do With Format
.fp7	FileMaker	Import data from FileMaker 3 or later) Export to FileMaker 7 or 8
.tab or .txt	Tab-separated text	Exchange data with almost any application
.csv or .txt	Comma-separated values; Comma-separated text	Exchange data with BASIC programs and dBASE
.slk	SYLK	Exchange data with spreadsheet applications
.dif	DIF	Exchange data with spreadsheet applications, such as VisiCalc
.wk1 or .wks	WKS	Exchange data with Lotus 1-2-3. FileMaker can import both formats but only exports .WK1
.bas	BASIC	Exchange data with Microsoft BASIC programs
.mer	Merge	Combine Merge file data with main file text to create form letters
.htm or .html	HTML	Export FileMaker data as HTML table
.DBF	DBF	Exchange data with dBASE III and dBASE IV
.XLS	Excel	Import data from Microsoft Excel
	ODBC	Import as ODBC, serve FileMaker data.
.XML	XML	Import and export XML data.

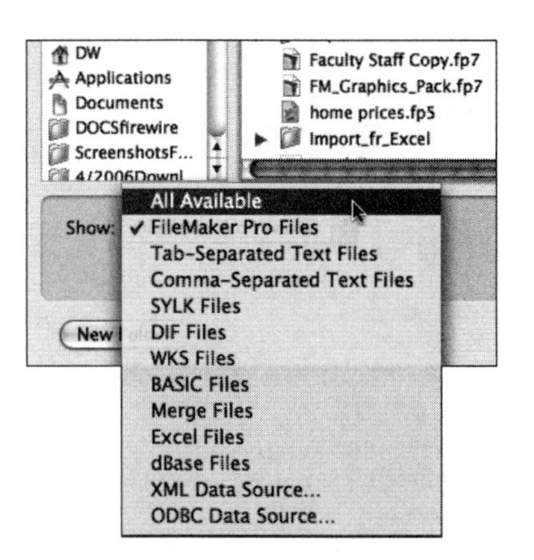

Figure 14.20 Use the Open File dialog box's *Show* pop-up menu to pick a format for the incoming data.

Figure 14.21 Navigate to the folder where the source file is stored, select it, and click *Open*. In our example, we use an old Excel file.

Figure 14.22 If an Excel file contains more than one worksheet (spreadsheet), FileMaker asks you to choose one.

To import data for a *new* FileMaker database:

1. First make a copy of your original data. Now, open your source file using its original application and save it in one of the formats listed in **Table 14.1** on page 234. Close the source file and quit the original application.
2. Launch FileMaker and choose File > Open (Ctrl O in Windows/⌘ O on the Mac).
3. When the Open File dialog box appears, use the *Show* drop-down menu to switch from *FileMaker* (the default) to *All Available* or the specific format used by the file you are importing (**Figure 14.20**).
4. Navigate to the folder where the source file is stored, select it, and click *Open* (**Figure 14.21**). (In our example, we're using an old Excel file.)
5. If you're converting an Excel file that contains more than one worksheet (spreadsheet), FileMaker asks you which one to use (**Figure 14.22**). Select the worksheet you want and click *Continue*.

(continued)

6. If the spreadsheet includes named ranges, FileMaker also lets you specify which one you want to use. Select the range you want and click *OK*. Another dialog box asks whether to treat the spreadsheet's column headings as *Field names* or *Data* (**Figure 14.23**). Make your choice—in most cases, *Field names*—and click *OK*.

7. A dialog box appears and automatically adds *Converted* to the file's name (**Figure 14.24**). Change the name as you wish, navigate to the folder where you want it stored, and click *Save*.

8. Once the new file opens (the time required depends on the file's size), the original source data appears in the FileMaker database (top, **Figure 14.25**).

✔ Tip

- If there's lots of data within the other application document that you won't need in the FileMaker database, it's easier to weed it out using the original application *before* you import it into FileMaker.

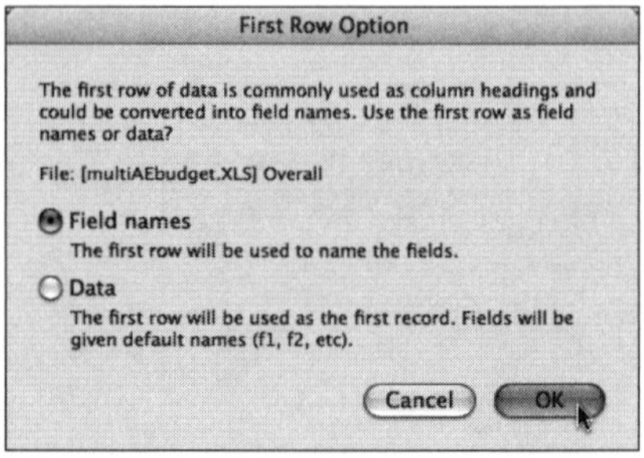

Figure 14.23 If you're converting a spreadsheet, FileMaker asks whether to treat the column headings as *Field names* or *Data*.

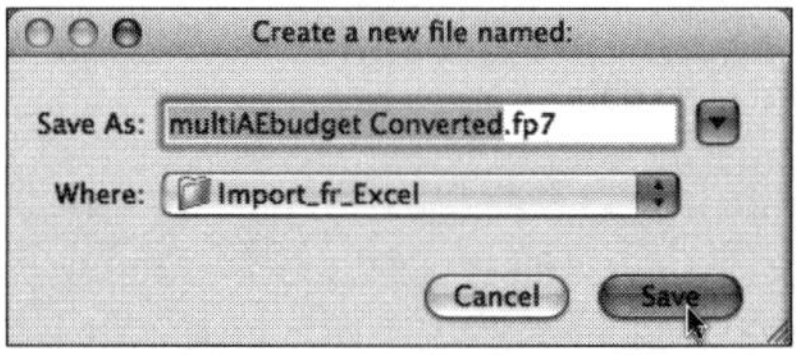

Figure 14.24 FileMaker automatically uses the original file name, and adds the word *Converted*. Rename if you like, then click *Save*.

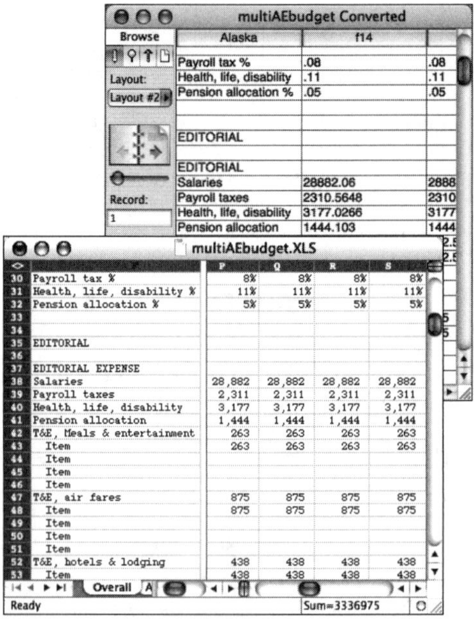

Figure 14.25 The data, and even some of the layout, of the original Excel spreadsheet (lower left) ports cleanly over to FileMaker (upper right).

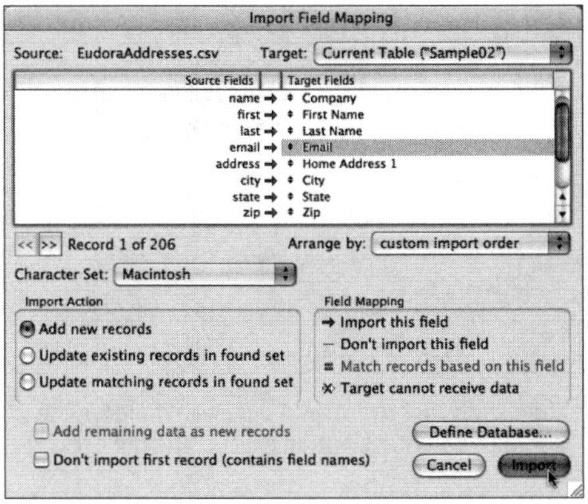

Figure 14.26 The Import Field Mapping dialog box gives you precise control over the data imported—and its order.

To import data into an *existing* FileMaker database:

1. Make backup copies of your original data *source* file (the one you're importing data from) and the FileMaker *destination* file (the one you're importing the data into).
2. Open your source file using its original application and save it in one of the formats listed in **Table 14.1** on page 234. Close the source file and quit the application.
3. Launch FileMaker and make sure you're in Browse mode (Ctrl B in Windows/ ⌘B on the Mac). Open the FileMaker database into which you want to import data (Ctrl O in Windows, ⌘O on the Mac). If you'll be replacing particular records, use FileMaker's Find, Omit, and Sort commands to expand or narrow the Found Set to only the records you'll be replacing.
4. Now, choose File > Import Records > File.
5. Navigate to the folder where the source file is stored, select it, and click *Open*.
6. When the Import Field Mapping dialog box appears, the *Source* file is listed in the upper left (a `.csv` file of Eudora addresses) and the *Target* in the upper right (Sample02, a FileMaker database of just nine contacts) (**Figure 14.26**). Check to see if the *Source Fields* listed on the left are properly matched with the *Target Fields* names on the right. If there's a mismatch, reorder the right-hand fields by clicking each one and dragging it to match its counterpart on the left. To double-check the matchups, click the << and >> buttons to see if the actual data lines up with the proper fields.

(continued)

7. To control individual field imports, click the icon in the center column to allow (➡) or block (—) importing. (FileMaker automatically sets the other two icons: the (≡) indicating match fields and the (✖) indicating a source–target mismatch by type or permissions.)

8. To add a new field to the FileMaker database, click the lower-right *Define Database* button and create the needed field.

9. Use the *Import Action* panel's radio buttons to set whether you want the source data to *Add* or *Update* the records already in the FileMaker database.

10. Once you've tweaked the source-to-database mapping to your satisfaction, click *Import*. Depending on your files, the Import Options dialog box appears, asking how you want to treat auto-enter and repeating fields (**Figure 14.27**). Make your choices and click *Import*.

11. FileMaker displays the imported records in Browse mode, along with an Import Summary dialog box of how the records and fields were handled (**Figure 14.28**). Click *OK* to close the dialog box and begin using your expanded database.

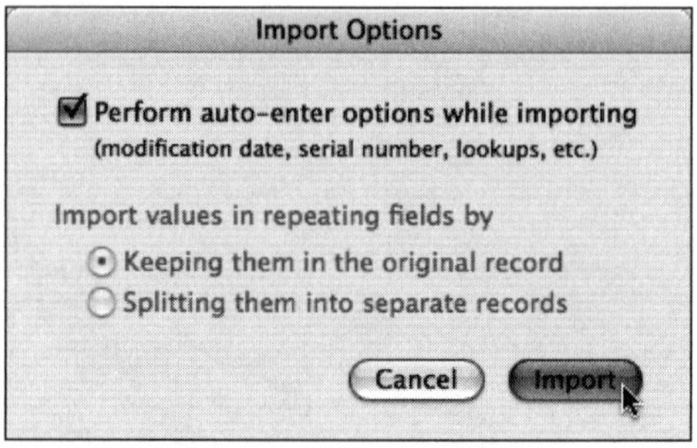

Figure 14.27 In most cases, you'll want to leave the *Perform auto-enter...* option checked before clicking *Import*.

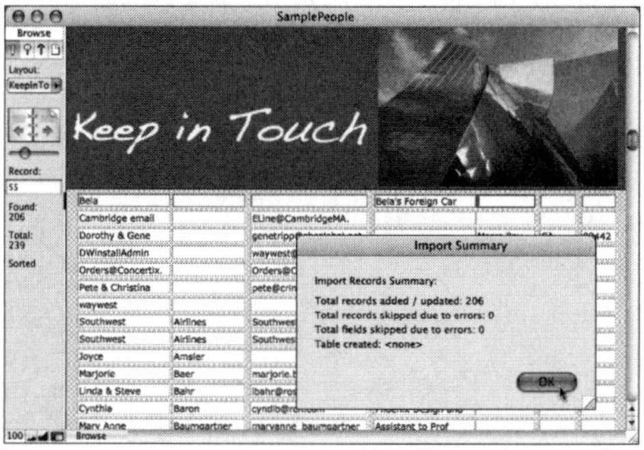

Figure 14.28 FileMaker displays the imported records in Browse mode, along with an Import Summary dialog box of how the records and fields were handled.

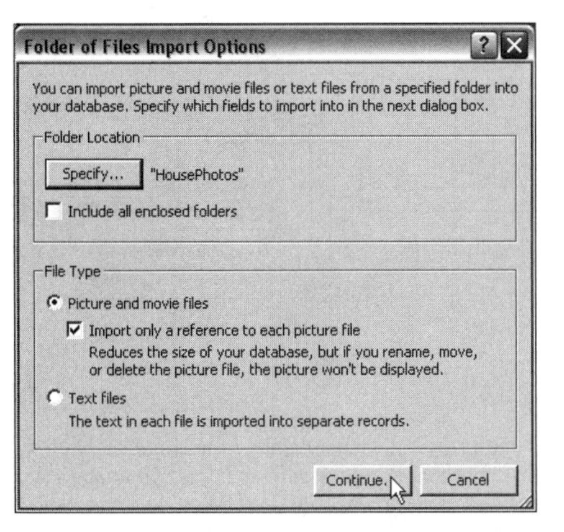

Figure 14.29 When the Folder of Files Import Options dialog box appears, click *Specify* to pick a particular folder, and choose a *File Type* (pictures and movies or text).

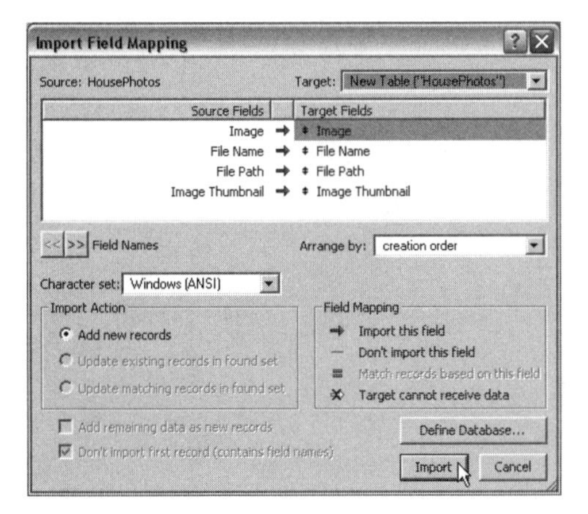

Figure 14.30 If there's a mismatch between the left-hand and right-hand field names, use the *Arrange by* pop-up menu or click and drag the right-hand fields.

To import a folder of files (graphics or text):

1. Open the FileMaker database into which you'll be importing the files.
2. Choose File > Import Records > Folder.
3. When the Folder of Files Import Options dialog box appears, click *Specify* and navigate to the folder whose contents you want to import (**Figure 14.29**).
4. When the import options dialog box reappears, you can check *Include all enclosed folders* if you also want to import files inside folders within the main folder. (By default, the box is not checked.)
5. In the lower half of the dialog box (**Figure 14.29**), choose the *File Type* you want to import: *Picture and movie files* or *Text files*. If importing picture or movie files, consider checking *Import only a reference to each picture file* to keep the database's size from growing too large. For more on importing a folder of graphics, see the *Tips*. Once you've made your choices, click *Continue*.
6. When the Import Field Mapping dialog box appears (**Figure 14.30**), check that the field names listed in the *Source Fields* list match those in the *Target Fields* list. If none of the fields match, use the *Target* drop-down menu to locate the correct target fields. At that point, the names may be the same but in the wrong order. If so, use the *Arrange by* pop-up menu to choose *matching names*, which should fix the problem. Otherwise, click and drag to reorder the right-hand list of fields.

(continued)

7. Make sure the *Import Action* radio button is set to the desired choice. If this is the first time you've imported this folder's files, *Add new records* is chosen by default. You also have the option of replacing or updating previously imported files—just make sure that's what you want because either choice overwrites the earlier files. Once you've made your choice, click *Import*.

8. FileMaker displays the newly imported records in Browse mode, along with an Import Summary dialog box of how the records and fields were handled (**Figure 14.31**). Click *OK* to close the dialog box.

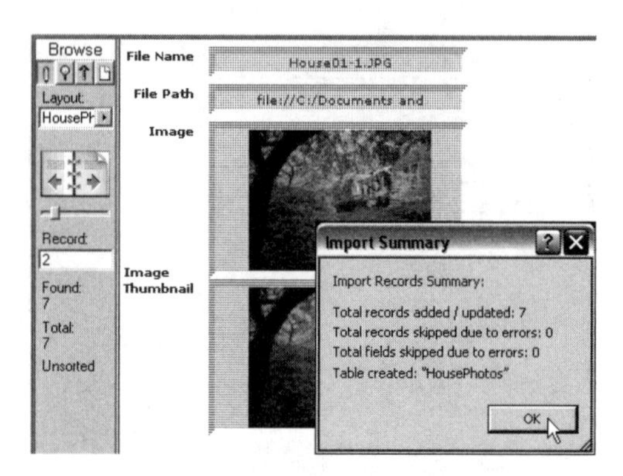

Figure 14.31 FileMaker displays the imported photos in Browse mode, along with an Import Summary dialog box of how the records and fields were handled.

✔ Tips

- FileMaker can import the most commonly used graphic formats (GIF, TIFF, JPEG, and EPS) plus a bunch of others.
- If you import just a reference to a graphic, FileMaker imports a space-saving thumbnail of the original (source) graphic, plus the file path back to the original. This allows you to click the FileMaker thumbnail and see the original. Just make sure you put the source graphic in a long-term storage spot before starting the import process; if you move it later on, FileMaker cannot find the original and displays an error message.

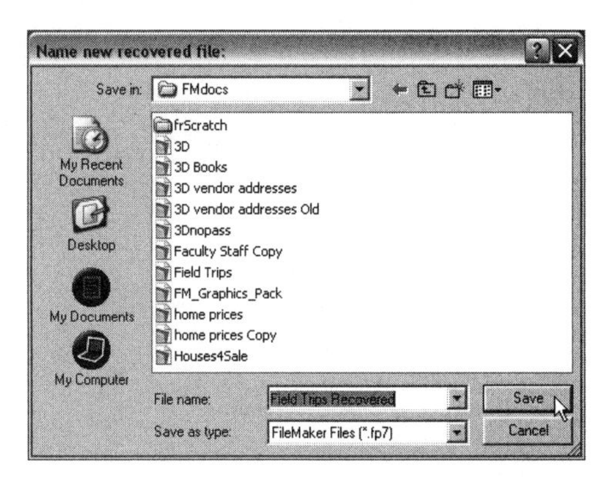

Figure 14.32 When it opens a damaged file, FileMaker automatically adds *Recovered* to its previous name. Change the name if you wish, then click *Save*.

FileMaker Pro

Recovery is complete. During recovery:

364K Bytes were salvaged.
0 whole records were skipped.
0 field values were skipped.
0 lost field definitions were rebuilt.

If you have further problems with this file, call FileMaker, Inc. Technical Support.

OK

Figure 14.33 May the news always be this good: FileMaker provides a detailed report on how many records, fields, and values were recovered.

Recovering Damaged Files

A file can become damaged from any number of causes: a sudden power loss, hard drive crash, or corrupted bit of software. Most of the time, if you close and reopen the file, FileMaker performs what it calls a consistency check and everything works fine. If that doesn't work, you try to rescue the file with FileMaker's Recover command.

To recover a damaged file:

1. If you suspect that the file's been damaged, close it immediately (Ctrl W in Windows, ⌘ W on the Mac).
2. Choose File > Recover.
3. In the Open Damaged File dialog box, navigate your way to the damaged file. Click *Open*.
4. When the Name new recovered file dialog box appears, FileMaker by default adds the word *Recovered* to the end of the file's old name (**Figure 14.32**). If you like, type in another name. Click *Save*.
5. As it runs through a number of steps to recover the file, a progress bar appears briefly. When FileMaker's done, a status report dialog box appears—hopefully with good news (**Figure 14.33**). Click *OK* to close the dialog box and return to your work.

SHARING

Using a mix of accounts and privileges, FileMaker lets you control precisely which people can share which files. The quick and dirty way to control access is to use FileMaker's predefined privilege sets, as explained on page 246. As you create files, you can assign full, edit, or read-only privileges to each one. If you're the only one using FileMaker or you're working in a very small group, that may be all you need.

If you're working in an organization with more than five people, however, you'll quickly see that you need more specific controls. One reason is to protect the data from getting deleted or mangled. Another reason: to control who can see sensitive information such as salaries.

In teasing out the difference between accounts and privileges, think of it this way: Accounts link files to the *identities* of individuals or groups. Privilege sets link files to *actions* (viewing, adding, and changing records) and determine which actions can be taken.

By default, each file automatically has two basic accounts: Admin and Guest. So you could quickly set a general level of access for all files by defining the rights of the Admin and Guest accounts. In the long run, however, it's probably better to create individual accounts for identification purposes and then separate privilege sets based on certain common actions. In that sense, privileges offer more flexibility since you can control access at the file, layout, or even individual field level.

For example, consider that job functions in any organization change less often than the people doing those jobs. In the long run, your system may be easier to manage if you create privilege sets tied to certain actions based on levels of needed access. You then can create individual accounts for each person, which you then tie to various privilege sets. If a person changes departments, you can simply link her account to a new set of privileges. If a person leaves the company, it's easy to cancel all privileges for his account without having to rework any privilege sets.

Table 15.1

Network Rights: Hosts vs. Guests

Party	Has Right To
Host Only	Change file user status or close shared file
	Define, delete, change access rights or groups
	Define fields or change field definitions
	Save file copies (with Save a Copy command)
	Reorder layouts
Any User (One at a time)	Edit record or layout
	Define, change value lists
	Define, change own passwords
	Define, change relationships
	Open ScriptMaker dialog box
Any User (Any time)	Find, sort, browse records
	Export, import records
	Choose a page setup and print
	Switch layout view or mode
	Check spelling

Networking with FileMaker

FileMaker's networking abilities make it easy for PCs and Macs to share the same FileMaker database file. Inevitably, layouts will not look exactly the same on each platform. And since the Windows and Mac operating systems use different default fonts—and render them at 96 dpi on Windows and 72 dpi on Macs—text may also appear a bit differently. In some cases, this will force you to add a bit more space to tight Mac-generated layouts used on Windows machines. But, overall, the FileMaker match across platforms is pretty close. Since FileMaker 8 sticks with the .fp7 format introduced with FileMaker 7, anyone on the network using version 7 or newer can access the same files.

To *host* a file simply means being the first user to open a shared FileMaker file. Anyone opening the file after the host is considered a *guest*. The host can set access rights and make file changes that guests cannot. For details, see **Table 15.1**, *Network Rights: Hosts vs. Guests*. FileMaker's network access privileges, by the way, are not the same as the access rights set by your computer's operating system. For information on setting Web access to FileMaker, see *Publishing on the Web* on page 265.

File sharing is set file by file using the FileMaker Network Settings dialog box. When a host needs to make substantial changes to a file, sharing must be turned off (see **Table 15.1**, *Network Rights: Hosts vs. Guests*) and guest users temporarily are denied access to the file. Once the host finishes the modifications, the file can again be shared. A file can be shared by no more than five users at any one time. To share it with more users than that you need to use FileMaker Server Advanced or share it over the Web (see *Publishing on the Web* on page 265).

To share a file as host:

1. Open the file you want to share (Ctrl O in Windows, ⌘ O on the Mac).
2. Choose Edit > Sharing > FileMaker Network (Windows) or FileMaker Pro > Sharing > FileMaker Network (Mac) (**Figure 15.1**). When the FileMaker Network Settings dialog box appears (**Figure 15.2**), make sure the file you want to share is selected in the *Currently open files* list and select *On* next to *Network Sharing*.
3. In the *Network access to file* panel, select *All users*.

   or

   Select *Specify users by privilege set*, click *Specify*, and in the Specify users by privilege set dialog box, select one of three sets: *Full Access*, *Data Entry Only*, or *Read-Only Access* (**Figure 15.3**). Click *OK* to apply the privileges and close the dialog box.
4. Back in the FileMaker Network Settings dialog box, click *OK* to close it and activate sharing.

✔ Tips

- In step 3 if *No users* is selected, guests won't be able to open the file—even if Network Sharing is set to *On*.
- Read-Only Access is just what it sounds like: users can see files but not change them. Data Entry Access is similar except that users can create, change, and delete FileMaker records. The Full Access set does all that, plus lets users change layouts, value lists, and scripts. Though their access powers differ, all three choices allow sharing.

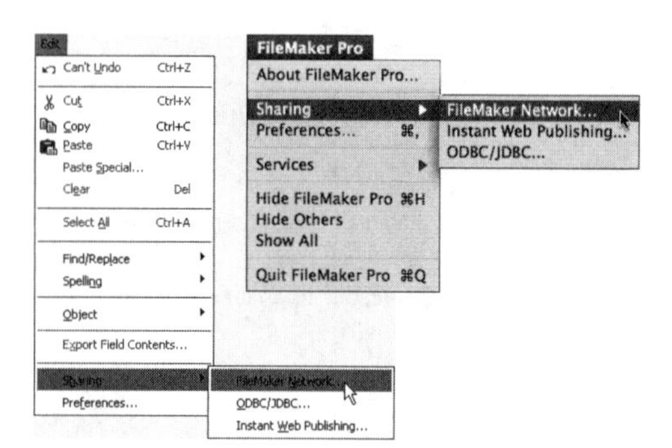

Figure 15.1 To turn FileMaker file sharing on or off, choose Edit > Sharing > FileMaker Network (Windows) or FileMaker Pro > Sharing > FileMaker Network (Mac).

FileMaker Network Settings
FileMaker Network Settings
Turn on Network Sharing to share your open files using TCP/IP.
Network Sharing: Off On
TCP/IP Address: 192.168.1.104; 192.168.2.114
File access via FileMaker Network
Currently open files
home price db.fp7
Network access to file
File: "home price db.fp7"
All users
Specify users by privilege set (Specify...)
No users
Don't display in Open Remote File dialog
This file is being used by 0 users. To send users a message, click the Send Message button.
Send Message... Cancel OK

Figure 15.2 To share a file, make sure the file you want to share is selected in the *Currently open files* list and select *On* next to *Network Sharing*.

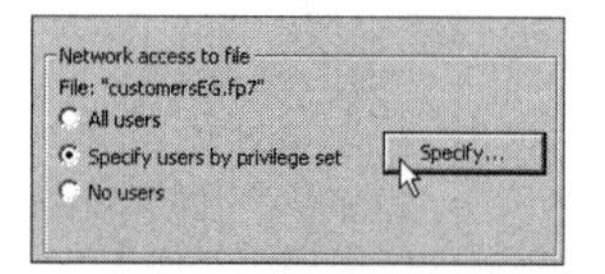

Specify users by privilege set
Users are granted access via their privilege set. Only active accounts can access this file. Use the Define Accounts and Privileges window to activate additional accounts.
Enable access via FileMaker Network

On	Privilege Set	Active accounts
☐	[Full Access]	Admin
☐	[Data Entry Only]	
☑	[Read-Only Access]	

OK Cancel

Figure 15.3 Select *Specify users by privilege set* and click *Specify* (top). In the Specify users by privilege set dialog box, select one of three sets: *Full Access*, *Data Entry Only*, or *Read-Only Access* (bottom).

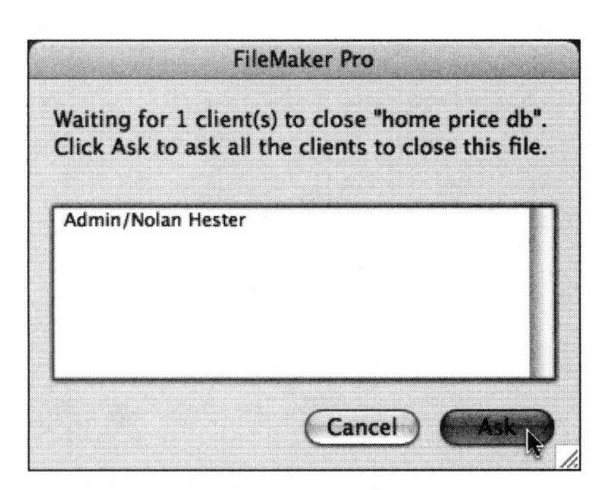

Figure 15.4 When you try to sharing a file being used by others, click *Ask* to alert guests that you want to close the file.

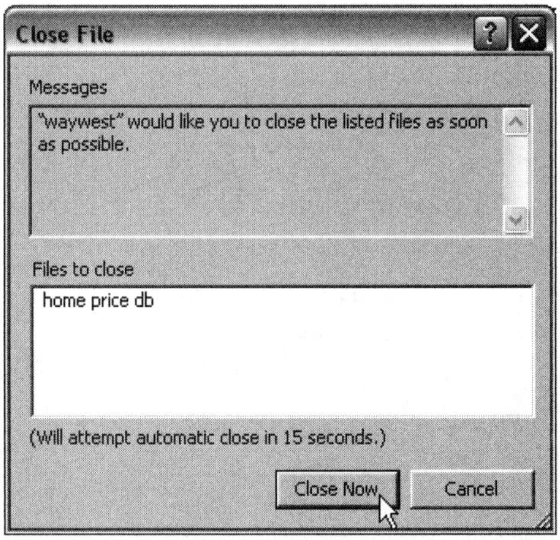

Figure 15.5 When guests using an about-to-be-closed file receive a message from the host, they can click *Close Now* to close the file immediately or *Cancel* to leave it open until they're done.

To close a shared file as host:

1. If you're hosting the file, close it (Ctrl W in Windows, ⌘W on the Mac).
2. A dialog box appears listing other users of the file (**Figure 15.4**). Click *Ask*.
3. Guest users will be alerted to close the file (**Figure 15.5**). If all the guests click *Close Now*, the file closes immediately on the guest and host machines. If a guest clicks *Cancel*, FileMaker leaves the file open until the guest closes it. If a guest doesn't respond, FileMaker automatically closes the file in 30 seconds.

To stop sharing a file but leave it open:

1. If you need to work on a shared database and therefore need to stop sharing the file but leave it open for your own work, choose Edit > Sharing > FileMaker Network (Windows) or FileMaker Pro > Sharing > FileMaker Network (Mac).
2. When the FileMaker Network Settings dialog box appears, select a file in the *Currently open files* list and click *Send Message* (**Figure 15.6**).
3. When the message dialog box appears, type your message in the text window and click *OK* (top, **Figure 15.7**). All guests using the database immediately receive your message (bottom, **Figure 15.7**).
4. Once all guests close the shared file, change *Network Sharing* to *Off* for that file (**Figure 15.8**). The file will no longer be visible over the network but will remain open on your computer so that you can work on it. Remember to turn file sharing back on after you finish maintenance work on the file.

✔ Tip

- In step 4, once all guests close the file the message at the bottom of the FileMaker Network Settings dialog box changes to *This file is being used by 0 users* (**Figure 15.9**).

Figure 15.9 After all guests close the file, the message in the FileMaker Network Settings dialog box changes to *This file is being used by 0 users.*

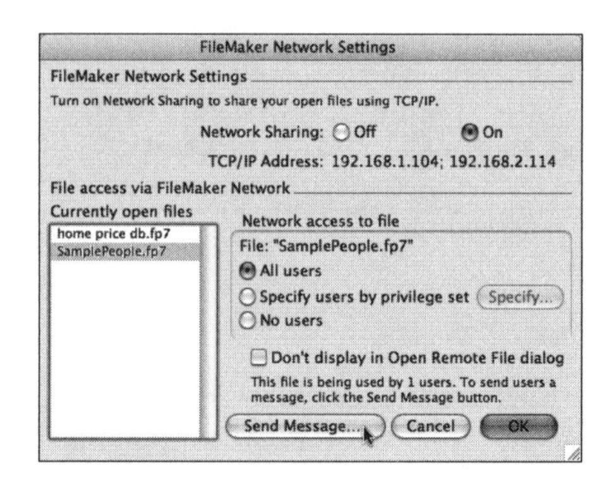

Figure 15.6 To stop sharing a file but leave it open, select a file in the *Currently open files* list and click *Send Message.*

Figure 15.7 Type your message in the text window and click *OK* (top) and guests using the database immediately receive your message (bottom).

Figure 15.8 Once all guests close the shared file, change *Network Sharing* to *Off* for that file.

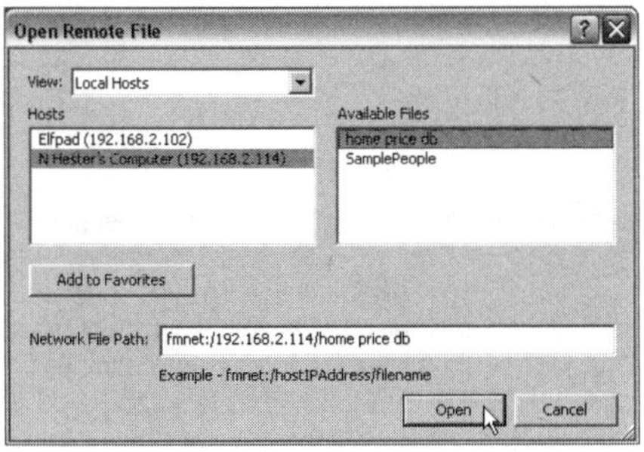

Figure 15.10 In the Open Remote File dialog box, set the *View* drop-down menu to *Local Hosts*, select a computer from the *Hosts* list, and then select the database you need in the *Available Files* list.

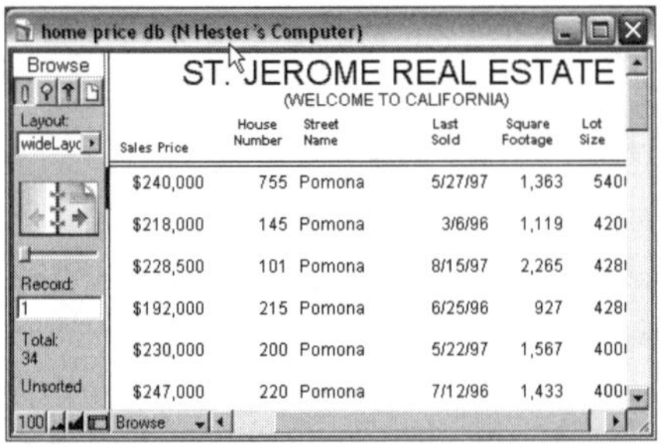

Figure 15.11 The shared database opens with the host computer listed in parentheses in the title bar.

Figure 15.12 The *Add to Favorites* feature lets you give a nickname to a host computer and set your view to only see the databases you need.

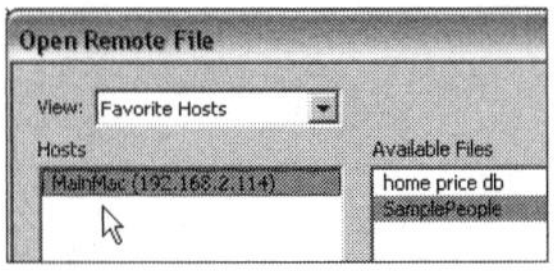

Figure 15.13 Back in the Open Remote File dialog box, set *View* to *Favorite Hosts* to see your customized view.

To open a file as a guest:

1. Choose File > Open Remote or use your keyboard (Ctrl Shift O in Windows, Shift ⌘ O on the Mac).
2. When the Open Remote File dialog box appears, set the *View* drop-down menu to *Local Hosts* (**Figure 15.10**). In the left-hand *Hosts* list, select the computer where the shared database resides, then in the right-hand *Available Files* list, select the database you need.
3. Click *Open* and the shared database opens with the host computer listed in parentheses in the title bar (**Figure 15.11**). Depending on your access privileges, you can then view, add, or edit records. See *Setting Accounts and Privileges* on the next page.

✔ Tips

- In step 2, if the host computer is listed in the Open Remote File dialog box but none of the shared databases appear, check the host computer's sharing and firewall settings. They may be set to block guests.
- In step 2, if you regularly connect to the same host computer or the same databases, click *Add to Favorites* to open the Edit Favorite Host dialog box (**Figure 15.12**). Give a nickname to the host computer, set your view to only see the databases you need, and click *Save*. Back in the Open Remote File dialog box, set *View* to *Favorite Hosts* to see your customized view (**Figure 15.13**).
- In step 2, if you need to use the Hosts Listed by LDAP, get the required server settings from your network administrator.
- Unless the host has closed or stopped sharing a file you recently used, you can reopen it by choosing File > Open Recent and choosing it from the submenu.

Setting Accounts and Privileges

As explained on page 246, FileMaker includes three predefined privilege sets, Read-Only Access, Data Entry Only, and Full Access. These make it easy to create quick-and-dirty access controls. FileMaker also includes two default accounts, Guest with Read-Only Access and Admin with Full Access. To get the best combination of security and flexibility, however, you really should create privilege sets and accounts tailored to your needs.

Creating Accounts

Only users with Full Access privileges can define a password other than their own. By default, the Admin account comes with Full Access privileges, so you need to protect it with a master password. This master password is a key part of creating a secure FileMaker network since it keeps anyone else from having full privileges unless you deliberately grant them. Guest, the other default account, offers Read-Only Access to files but you need to activate it first. At that point, you can begin creating individual accounts. Aside from the master password, passwords are set based on the level of access needed, which can run the gamut. For details, see **Table 15.2**, *Access Privileges*.

Table 15.2

Access Privileges

Check	To Let Users
Access the entire file	Do any task using a master password. Only choice that grants right to define, change, or delete passwords. Also grants right to change field or group definitions, and document preferences.
Browse records	View record data
Print records	Print any records
Export records	Export any records, copy a found set, enable Web Companion sharing
Override data entry warnings	Enter data even if it doesn't match preset entry options
Design layouts	Create and change layouts
Edit scripts	Create and change scripts
Define value lists	Create and change value lists
Create records	Create new records and enter data
Edit records	Change data in records
Delete records	Delete any records

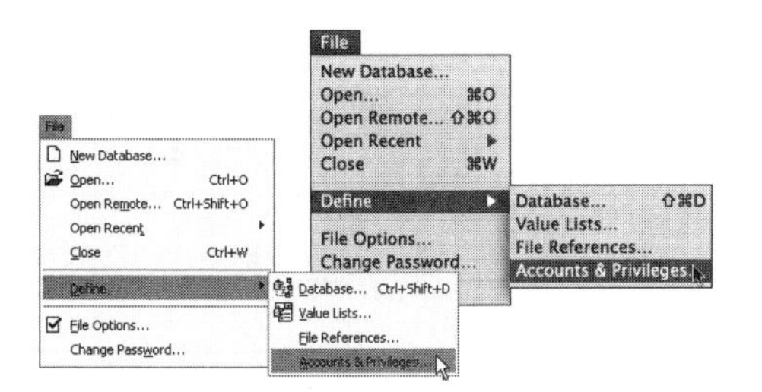

Figure 15.14 To create a password, choose File > Define > Accounts & Privileges.

Figure 15.15 With the *Accounts* tab active, select the *Admin* account and click *Edit*.

Figure 15.16 In the Edit Account dialog box, type a password into the *Password* text box. Be sure to write it down for safekeeping.

Figure 15.17 The last step requires that you type in the name of the *Full Access Account* (*Admin* unless you changed it) and the *Password* you just chose.

To create a password for the Admin account:

1. Open any file and turn file sharing off. Choose File > Define > Accounts & Privileges (**Figure 15.14**).
2. When the Define Accounts & Privileges dialog box appears, the *Accounts* tab is automatically selected (**Figure 15.15**). Select the *Admin* account and click *Edit*.
3. In the Edit Account dialog box, type a password into the *Password* text box (**Figure 15.16**). Write it down somewhere safe because you cannot bypass the password once it's entered. Click *OK* to close the dialog box.
4. When the Define Accounts & Privileges dialog box reappears, click *OK* to close the dialog box.
5. When the Confirm Full Access Login dialog box appears, type in the name of the *Full Access Account* (*Admin* unless you changed it) and the *Password* you chose in step 3 (**Figure 15.17**). Click *OK* to close the dialog box and apply the password protection. Remember to turn File Sharing back on for the file you turned off in step 1.

✔ Tip

- Passwords can include up to 31 characters, can include spaces, and are case sensitive. For example, *WayWest* will not be accepted in place of *waywest*. If you haven't already written it down, do so now.

To activate the Guest account:

1. Open any file and choose File > Define > Accounts & Privileges.
2. When the Define Accounts & Privileges dialog box appears, the *Accounts* tab is automatically selected (**Figure 15.15**). Find the line for the *[Guest]* account and select the *Active* box (**Figure 15.18**). Click *OK* to close the dialog box.
3. When the Confirm Full Access Login dialog box appears, type in the name of the *Full Access Account* (*Admin* unless you changed it) and the *Password* you chose in step 3 on the previous page. Click *OK* to close the dialog box and apply the activation. The *Guest Account* option now is available at login for files assigned the Read-Only privilege set (**Figure 15.19**). (For more information, see *Creating Privilege Sets* on page 259.)

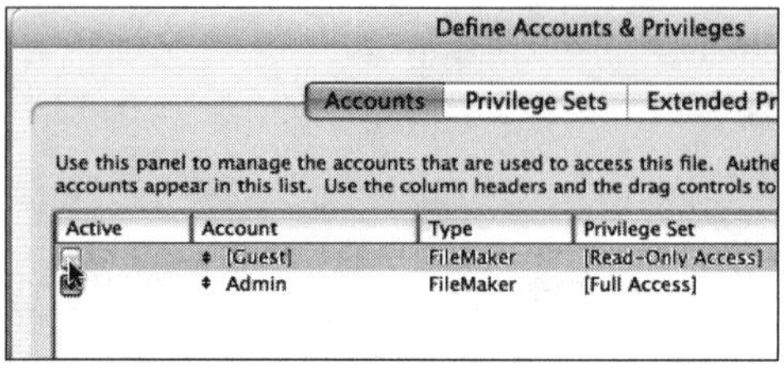

Figure 15.18 Find the line for the *[Guest]* account and select the *Active* box.

Figure 15.19 The *Guest Account* option appears at login for files assigned the Read-Only privilege set.

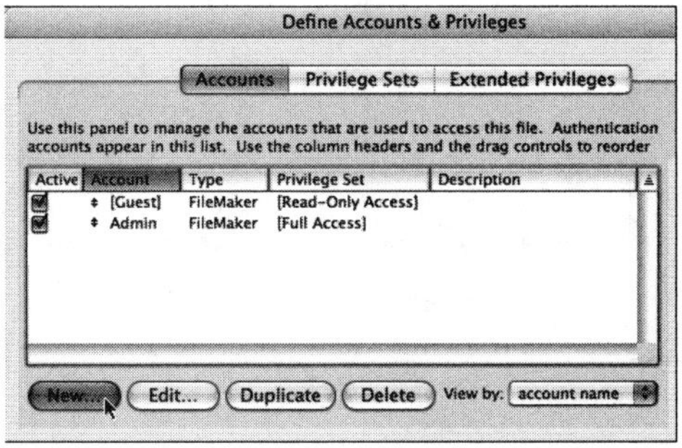

Figure 15.20 To create user accounts, make sure the *Accounts* tab is automatically selected and click *New*.

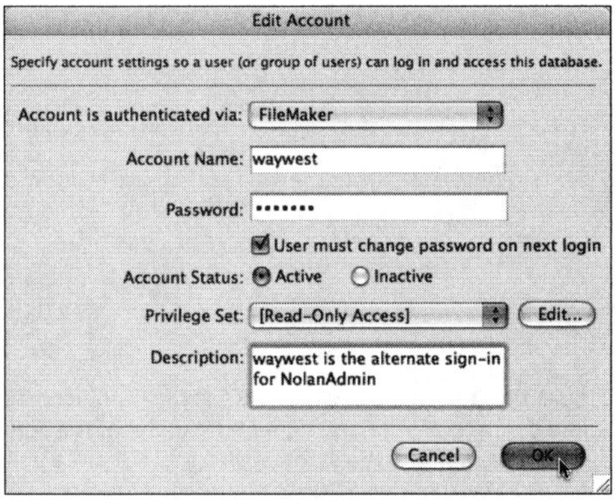

Figure 15.21 Use the *Account Name* and *Password* text windows to create a new account.

To create user accounts:

1. Open any file and choose File > Define > Accounts & Privileges.
2. When the Define Accounts & Privileges dialog box appears, the *Accounts* tab is automatically selected. Click *New* (**Figure 15.20**).
3. When the Edit Account dialog box appears, use the *Account Name* and *Password* text windows to create a new account (**Figure 15.21**).
4. If you're creating an individual user account, select *User must change password on next login* (see third Tip). Make sure that *Active* is selected.
5. For now, use the *Privilege Sets* drop-down menu to choose one of FileMaker's three predefined privilege sets, for safety's sake probably *Read-Only Access*. (Once you create customized privilege sets on page 259, you can come back and change this to the appropriate set.) Click *OK* to close the dialog box.

(continued)

6. The new account is now listed in the Define Accounts & Privileges dialog box (**Figure 15.22**). Click *OK* to close the dialog box.

7. When the Confirm Full Access Login dialog box appears, type in the name of the *Full Access Account* (*Admin* unless you changed it) and the *Password* you chose in step 3 on page 253 (**Figure 15.23**). Click *OK* to close the dialog box and create the account.

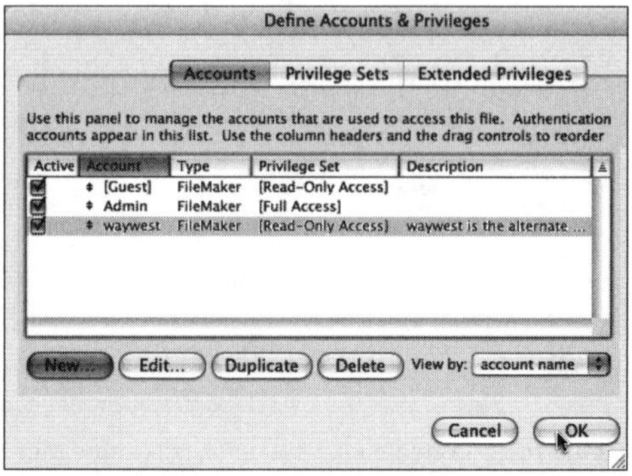

✔ Tips

- In step 3, unless your records sit on an external server, leave the default setting as *Account is authenticated via* set to *FileMaker*.

- In step 3, if you're setting up accounts for individual users, make the *Account Name* the same as the person's User Name (as shown in Edit > Preferences > General on Windows, File > Preferences > General on the Mac). That way, users only have to type in their password since FileMaker automatically fills in the Account Name.

Figure 15.22 The new account is added to the list of accounts.

Figure 15.23 As always, when the Confirm Full Access Login dialog box appears, type in the name of the *Full Access Account* and the *Password*.

- In step 4, assuming you're creating accounts for each user (the preferred approach), the beauty of selecting *User must change password on next login* is that it creates the best of both worlds: Each user can create a truly private password, yet you as the administrator still can control which files and actions that account can access through privilege sets. If you're creating a *shared* account do not select *User must change password on next login.* That's because one user could create a password that no one else sharing the account would know.
- As with creating databases and relationships back in Chapter 10, this business of creating accounts and privilege sets can turn into a tail-chasing affair of which comes first. It's inevitable that as you create accounts—and then switch over later to creating privilege sets—you'll realize you need to create yet another of one or the other. It's not a problem. If you're working in the Define Accounts & Privileges dialog box, just click the *Accounts* or *Privilege Sets* tab to switch over and make the addition.

Changing an account password or privileges

Only users who know the master password can change the password or privileges for an account other than their own. After you create customized privilege sets later in this chapter (see page 259), you may want to come back and change the privileges of some individual accounts.

To change account passwords:

1. Open any file and choose File > Define > Accounts & Privileges.
2. When the Define Accounts & Privileges dialog box appears, the *Accounts* tab is automatically selected. Select the account whose password you want to change and click *Edit* (**Figure 15.24**).
3. When the Edit Account dialog box appears, type a new password into the *Password* text box (**Figure 15.25**). Deselect *User must change password on next login* (otherwise, why bother changing it). Click *OK* to close the dialog box.
4. When the Define Accounts & Privileges dialog box reappears, click *OK* to close the dialog box and apply the password change.
5. When the Confirm Full Access Login dialog box appears, type in the name of the *Full Access Account* (*Admin* unless you changed it) and the *Password* you chose in step 3 on page 253. Click *OK* to close the dialog box and apply the password change.

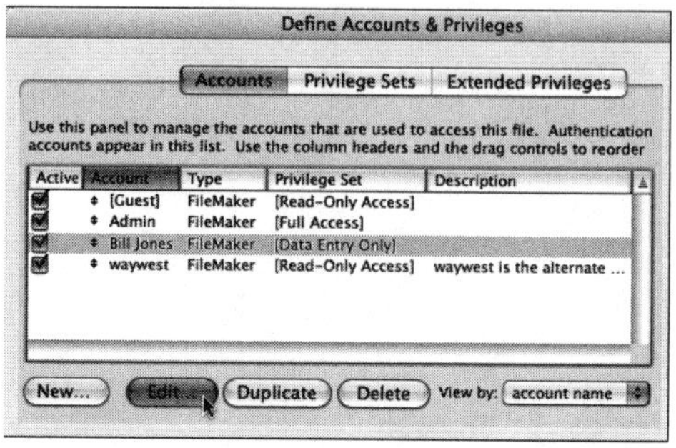

Figure 15.24 To change any account, select it in the list and click *Edit*.

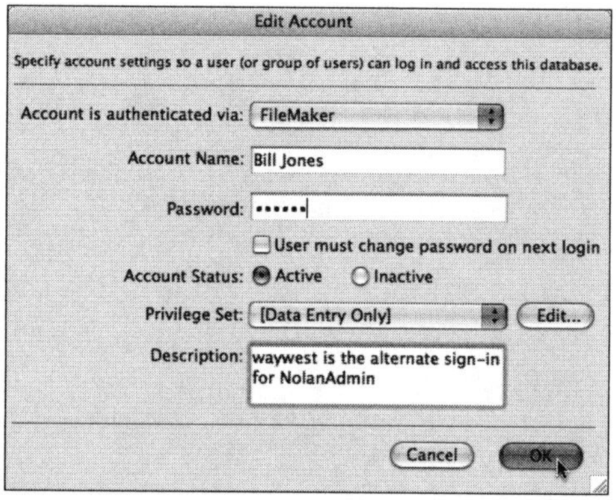

Figure 15.25 Type the new password into the *Password* text box and click *OK*.

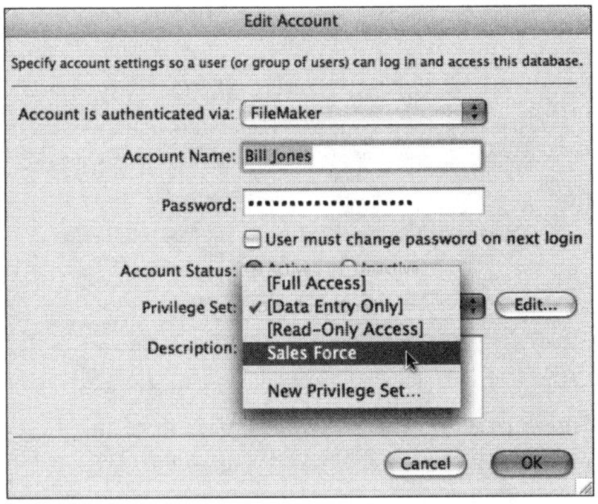

Figure 15.26 To change an account's privileges, make a selection in the *Privilege Set* pop-up menu.

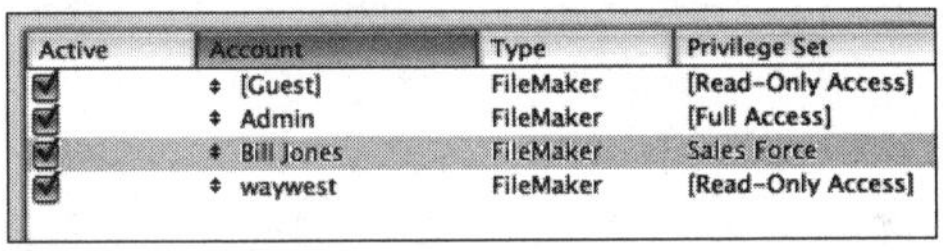

Figure 15.27 When the Define Accounts & Privileges dialog box reappears, the account's *Privilege Set* is updated.

To change account privileges:

1. Open any file and choose File > Define > Accounts & Privileges.
2. When the Define Accounts & Privileges dialog box appears, the *Accounts* tab is automatically selected. Select the account whose privileges you want to change and click *Edit* (**Figure 15.24**).
3. When the Edit Account dialog box appears, click the *Privilege Set* drop-down menu and choose another set (**Figure 15.26**). Click *OK* to close the dialog box.
4. When the Define Accounts & Privileges dialog box reappears, the account's *Privilege Set* is updated (**Figure 15.27**). Click *OK* to close the dialog box and apply the change.
5. When the Confirm Full Access Login dialog box appears, type in the name of the *Full Access Account* (*Admin* unless you changed it) and the *Password* you chose in step 3 on page 253. Click *OK* to close the dialog box and apply the password change.

Duplicating or deleting accounts

After creating an account, you can generate variations by duplicating the first account and then editing it. When people leave the organization, delete their old accounts.

To duplicate accounts:

1. Open any file and choose File > Define > Accounts & Privileges.
2. When the Define Accounts & Privileges dialog box appears, the *Accounts* tab is automatically selected. Select the account you want to copy and click *Duplicate* (**Figure 15.28**). A copy of the account is added to the dialog box and named [*original name*]+*Copy* (**Figure 15.29**). You can then click *Edit* to make any changes to the copy or click *OK* to close the dialog box.
3. When the Confirm Full Access Login dialog box appears, type in the name of the *Full Access Account* (*Admin* unless you changed it) and the *Password* you chose in step 3 on page 253. Click *OK* to close the dialog box.

To delete accounts:

1. Open any file and choose File > Define > Accounts & Privileges.
2. When the Define Accounts & Privileges dialog box appears, the *Accounts* tab is automatically selected. Select the account you no longer need and click *Delete*. The account is removed from the list (**Figure 15.30**). Click *OK* to close the dialog box.
3. When the Confirm Full Access Login dialog box appears, type in the name of the *Full Access Account* (*Admin* unless you changed it) and the *Password* you chose in step 3 on page 253. Click *OK* to close the dialog box.

Figure 15.28 Quickly generate variations of an account by selecting it and clicking *Duplicate*.

Figure 15.29 A copy of the selected account is added to the list.

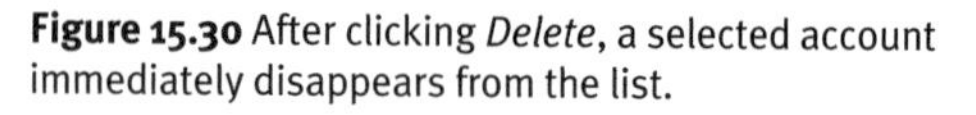

Figure 15.30 After clicking *Delete*, a selected account immediately disappears from the list.

Figure 15.31 To create a privilege set, switch to the *Privilege Sets* tab and click *New*.

Figure 15.32 Use the *Privilege Set Name* and *Description* text windows to create a first privilege set based on the particular needs of a group of people.

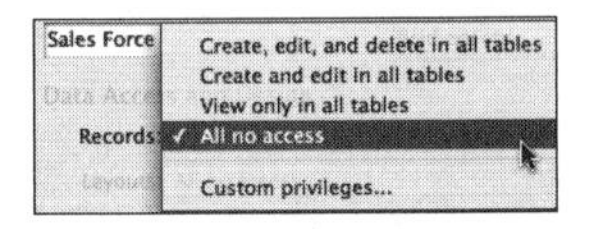

Figure 15.33 Use the *Records* pop-up menu to select among four basic options or select *Custom privileges*.

Figure 15.34 The pop-up menus for *Layouts*, *Value Lists*, and *Scripts* offer the same sets of options.

Creating Privilege Sets

FileMaker offers an incredible—and at times intimidating—level of control over the access granted by different privilege sets. In fact, using custom privileges, you can control access right down to the individual fields. Before plunging into customizing everything, however, get your feet wet by creating basic privilege sets that include such commonly needed powers as printing or exporting records.

To create privilege sets:

1. Open any file using an account with Full Access (typically the *Admin* account) and choose File > Define > Accounts & Privileges.
2. When the Define Accounts & Privileges dialog box appears, the *Accounts* tab is automatically selected. Select the *Privilege Sets* tab and click *New* (**Figure 15.31**).
3. When the Edit Privilege Set dialog box appears, use the *Privilege Set Name* and *Description* text windows to create a first privilege set based on a group of people who need a particular level of access. In our example, we've created a *Sales Force* set for out-of-office agents (**Figure 15.32**). By default, a new set initially has few privileges.
4. Begin with the *Data Access and Design* area to decide what privileges this access group should have. Use the *Records* pop-up menu to select among four basic options or select *Custom privileges* to create a unique privilege (**Figure 15.33**). Use the *Layouts*, *Value Lists*, and *Scripts* pop-up menus to pick among the options that they all share: three basic ones and a custom one (**Figure 15.34**).

(continued)

5. Use the *Other Privileges* section to control whether the group can, for example, print or export records (**Figure 15.35**). Leave as is the only checkbox selected by default (*Disconnect user from FileMaker Server when idle*). Use the *Available menu commands* drop-down menu to control whether users of this file see *All* FileMaker commands, those for *Editing only*, or a *Minimum* set.

6. In the *Extended Privileges* section (**Figure 15.36**), *Access via FileMaker Network* is selected already if the file's Network Sharing is on (see page 246). Unless you need to swap data with external enterprise-level database servers, leave everything else unchecked. If you need to share FileMaker data over the Web (controlled by *Access via Instant Web Publishing*), that's covered separately on page 266 in Chapter 16.

7. When you finish making all your selections in the Edit Privilege Set dialog box, click *OK* to close it (**Figure 15.37**).

8. When the Define Accounts & Privileges dialog box reappears, the new privilege set lists no active accounts (**Figure 15.38**). To link accounts to this new privilege set, click the *Accounts* tab and see *To change account privileges* on page 257. When you're done, click *OK* to close the dialog box.

9. When the Confirm Full Access Login dialog box reappears, type in the name of the *Full Access Account* (*Admin* unless you changed it) and the *Password* you chose in step 3 on page 253. Click *OK* to close the dialog box and apply all the changes.

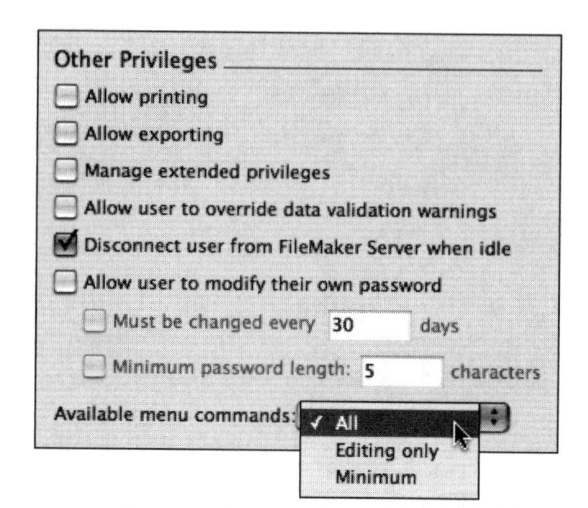

Figure 15.35 Use the *Other Privileges* section to control whether the group can do such things as print or export records.

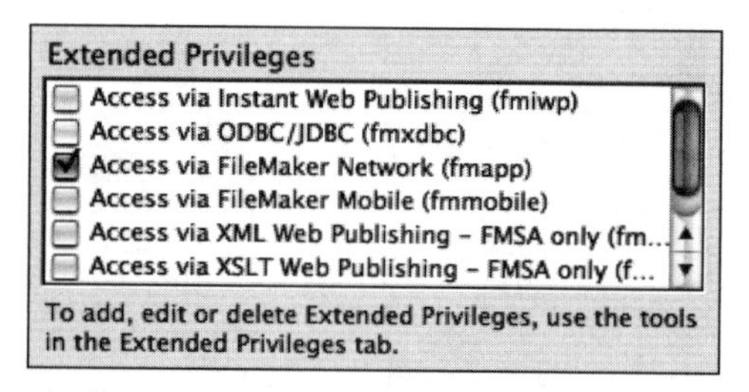

Figure 15.36 In the *Extended Privileges* section, *Access via FileMaker Network* is already selected if Network Sharing is on.

Figure 15.37 When you finish making all your selections in the Edit Privilege Set dialog box, click *OK* to close it.

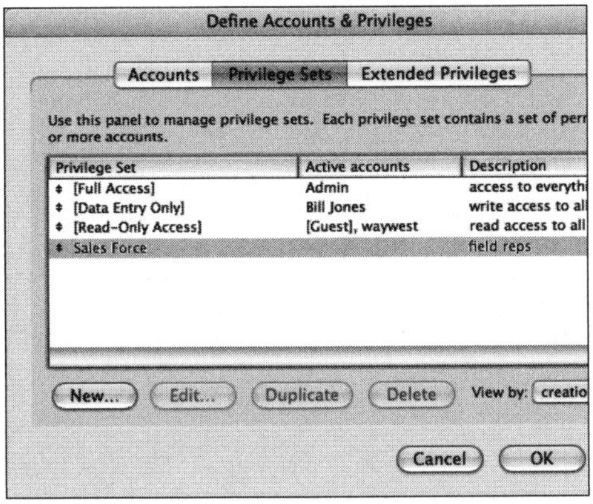

Figure 15.38 Initially, the new privilege set has no *Active accounts*. To assign some, switch to the *Accounts* tab.

✔ Tips

- Prior to FileMaker version 7, you had to turn off file sharing to change privileges. That's no longer necessary and anyone using an affected file can complete their work undisturbed. The changes take effect the next time any user logs in.
- In step 5, consider selecting two additional checkboxes: *Allow user to modify their own password* and *Must be changed every _ days*. Your network files will be more secure if users occasionally must pick a new password. But go easy: any more frequent than every 30 days can be a bother for users.
- The *Extended Privileges* section of the Edit Privilege Set dialog box controls how users share data (**Figure 15.36**). Think of them as the power behind the throne: you'll seldom encounter them but it helps to know they're there. One such privilege enables FileMaker's Instant Web Publishing to share data through a Web browser. Another lets you exchange data with a mainframe by way of ODBC (Open Database Connectivity) or JDBC (Java Database Connectivity).

To change a privilege set:

1. Open any file using an account with Full Access (typically the *Admin* account) and choose File > Define > Accounts & Privileges.
2. When the Define Accounts & Privileges dialog box appears, the *Accounts* tab is automatically selected. Click the *Privilege Sets* tab.
3. Select the privilege set you want to change and click *Edit.*
4. In the Edit Privilege Set dialog box, you can rename the set as well as change its access privileges as explained in the previous section. When you're done, click *OK* to close the dialog box.
5. When the Define Accounts & Privileges dialog box reappears, you can either select another privilege set to edit or click *OK* to close the dialog box.
6. When the Confirm Full Access Login dialog box reappears, type in the name of the *Full Access Account* (*Admin* unless you changed it) and the *Password* you chose in step 3 on page 253. Click *OK* to close the dialog box and apply all the changes.

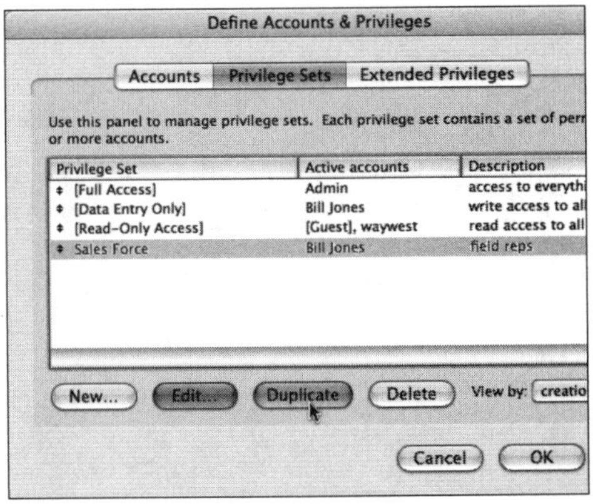

Figure 15.39 Generate other privilege sets you may need by selecting one from the list and clicking *Duplicate*.

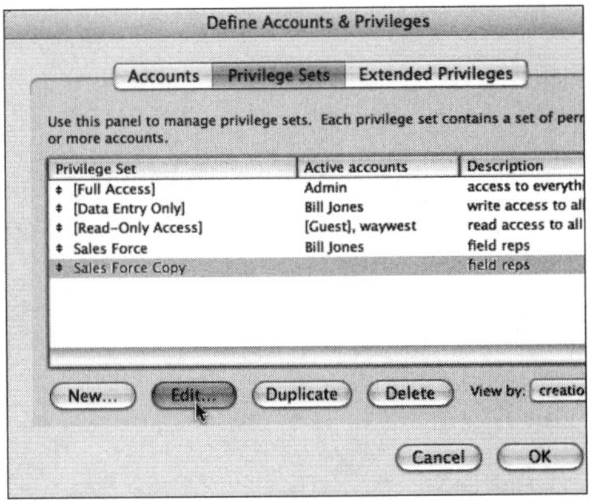

Figure 15.40 Once you create a copy, click *Edit* to begin customizing its privileges.

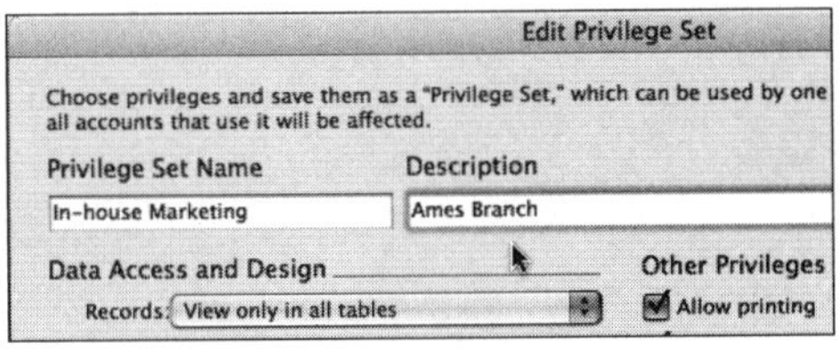

Figure 15.41 When the Edit Privilege Set dialog box appears, start by renaming the copy and providing quick description.

Duplicating or deleting privilege sets

Once you go through the trouble of creating a privilege set exactly as you want it, you can quickly generate other sets you may need by duplicating the first and then editing the duplicates. As time passes and your needs change, prune out old privilege sets by deleting them.

To duplicate a privilege set:

1. Open any file using an account with Full Access (typically the *Admin* account) and choose File > Define > Accounts & Privileges.
2. When the Define Accounts & Privileges dialog box appears, the *Accounts* tab is automatically selected. Click the *Privilege Sets* tab.
3. Select the privilege set you want to copy and click *Duplicate* (**Figure 15.39**). A copy of the selected privilege appears in the list and is automatically selected (**Figure 15.40**).
4. Click *Edit* and the Edit Privilege Set dialog box appears where you can begin modifying the privileges for use with another group (**Figure 15.41**). To finish, see step 4 of *To change a privilege set* on the previous page.

To delete a privilege set:

1. Open any file using an account with Full Access (typically the *Admin* account) and choose File > Define > Accounts & Privileges.
2. When the Define Accounts & Privileges dialog box appears, the *Accounts* tab is automatically selected. Click the *Privilege Sets* tab.
3. Select the privilege set you no longer need and click *Delete* (**Figure 15.42**). The selected privilege disappears from the list.
4. Click *OK* to close the dialog box and when the Confirm Full Access Login dialog box reappears, type in the name of the *Full Access Account* (*Admin* unless you changed it) and the *Password* you chose in step 3 on page 253. Click *OK* to close the dialog box and apply the change.

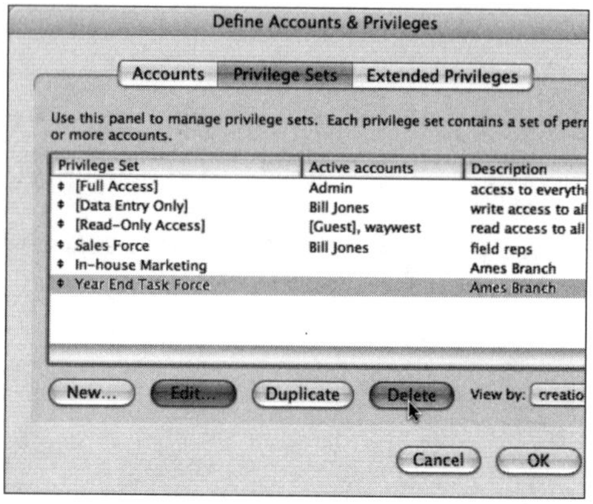

Figure 15.42 Select the privilege set you no longer need and click *Delete*.

Publishing on the Web

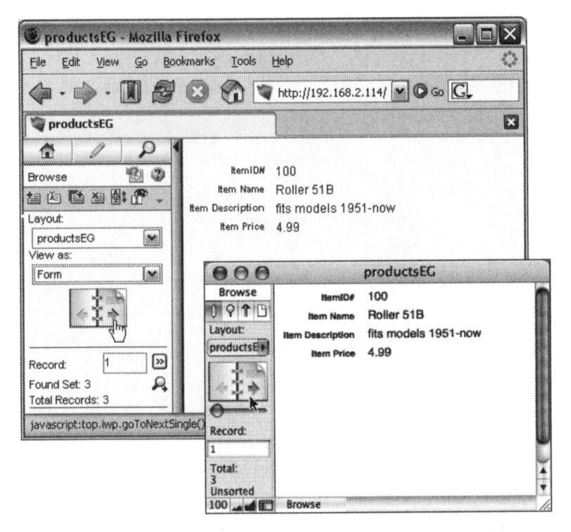

Figure 16.1 Records open in a Web browser (top left) look and work almost identically to those opened within FileMaker itself (bottom right).

Using a Web browser to work with shared FileMaker records feels very similar to working with them within FileMaker itself (**Figure 16.1**). Thanks to script-driven buttons embedded in the layouts created by FileMaker's Instant Web Publishing, Web users can search records, update information, sort tables, and so on. Of course, the records are visible and open only to those users to whom you've granted permission. Permissions are set file by file using a mix of accounts and associated privilege sets, which work just like those you set up in Chapter 15 for inhouse networking. (See in *Sharing* on page 243.)

Sharing with Instant Web Publishing

Up to 10 files can be shared over the Web simultaneously by five different users. For any more than that, you'll need FileMaker Server Advanced (a $749 retail upgrade beyond FileMaker Pro 8).

To share files over the Web:

1. Open the FileMaker files you want to share (Ctrl O in Windows, ⌘ O on the Mac).
2. Choose Edit > Sharing > Instant Web Publishing (Windows) or FileMaker Pro > Sharing > Instant Web Publishing (Mac) (**Figure 16.2**).
3. When the Instant Web Publishing dialog box appears, set the *Instant Web Publishing* radio button to *On* (**Figure 16.3**).
4. Select a file in the *Currently open files* list, select *Specify users by privilege set*, and click *Specify*.
5. When the Specify users by privilege set dialog box appears, select the *On* button beside each *Privilege Set* you want to have Web access to this file (**Figure 16.4**). Click *OK* to close the dialog box.
6. When the Instant Web Publishing dialog box reappears, select another file you want to share from the *Currently open files* list and repeat steps 4–5 (**Figure 16.5**).
7. When you finish setting the privileges for each open file, click *OK* to close the dialog box and allow those files to be shared.

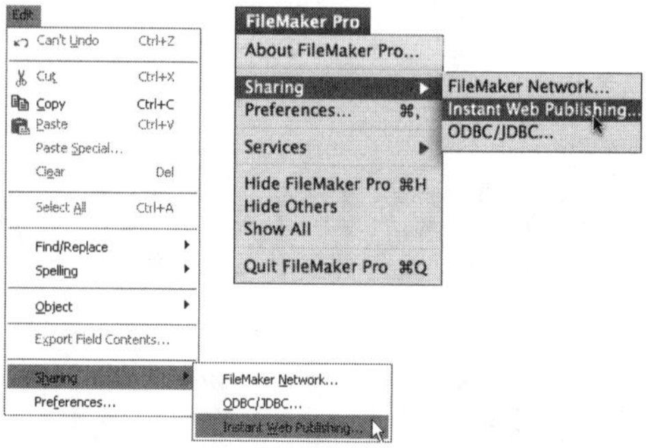

Figure 16.2 To share a file over the Web, choose Edit > Sharing > Instant Web Publishing (Windows) or FileMaker Pro > Sharing > Instant Web Publishing (Mac).

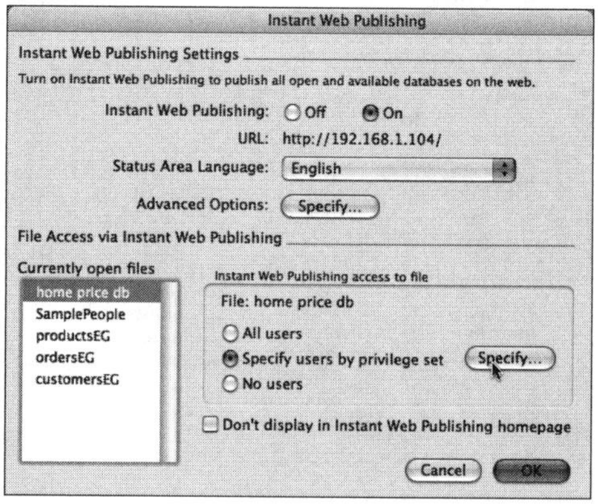

Figure 16.3 In the Instant Web Publishing dialog box, set the *Instant Web Publishing* radio button to *On*, make a selection in the *Currently open files* list, and click *Specify* to choose a privilege set.

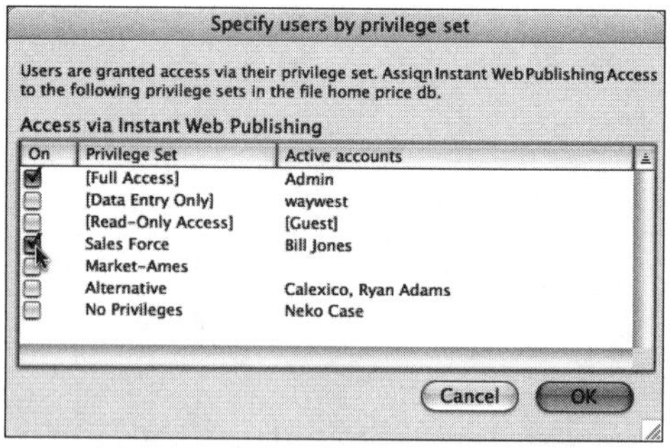

Figure 16.4 Select the *On* button beside each *Privilege Set* you want to have Web access to the file.

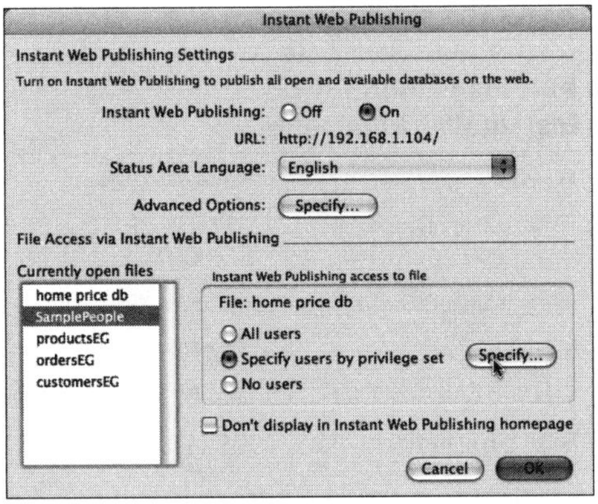

Figure 16.5 If there are other files you want to share, select them in the *Currently open files* list and repeat the previous steps.

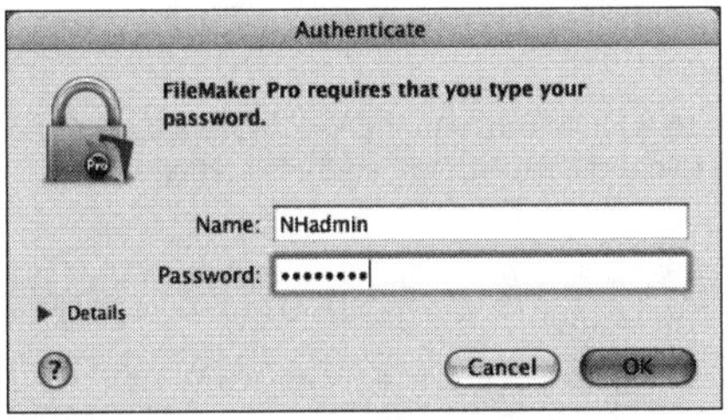

Figure 16.6 Depending on your setup, FileMaker may ask for your Admin *Password* before letting you turn on Web sharing.

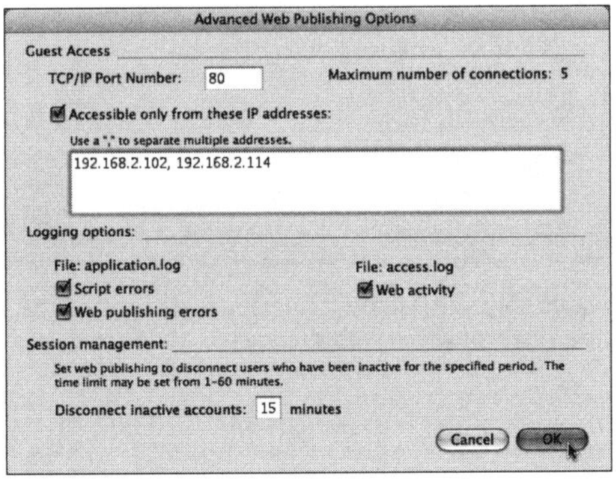

Figure 16.7 To limit Web sharing to particular computers, use the Advanced Web Publishing Options dialog box to enter specific IP addresses.

✔ Tips

- Depending on your setup, you may see an alert dialog box at the beginning of step 3 (**Figure 16.6**). Just type in your *Password*, click *OK* and the Instant Web Publishing dialog box appears.
- In step 4 if *No users* is selected, the file can't be opened over the Web—even if sharing is set to *On*.
- In step 5, for more information on creating and using privilege sets, see *Setting Accounts and Privileges* on page 250.
- At the bottom of the Instant Web Publishing dialog box, there's a checkbox for *Don't display in Instant Web Publishing homepage*. Why would you use it? Suppose you have several *relational* databases that feed data to each other using portals or lookups. To work together for your Web users, they all need to be shared over the Web even if your users work directly in only one or two of them. Instead of showing users a potentially confusing list of all these files, the checkbox hides the ones they don't need to open.
- In the Instant Web Publishing dialog box, you can further limit access to any selected file by clicking the *Specify* button next to *Advanced Options*. When the Advanced Web Publishing Options dialog box appears, type in the IP addresses for the computers you want to have access to the files (**Figure 16.7**). No other computers will have access to this file. Click *OK* to close the dialog box and return to the Instant Web Publishing dialog box.
- To turn off Web sharing, close the file on the host computer.

Using Files Over the Web

Make sure you've created the necessary accounts and privilege sets for users to access files over the Web. (See *Setting Accounts and Privileges* on page 250). You'll also need to tell users the IP (Internet Protocol) address for where the files are stored. Users' Web browsers need to support CSS (Cascading Style Sheets), since Instant Web Publishing depends on it for displaying the files properly over the Web. For details, see **Table 16.1**, *Browsers Supporting Instant Web Publishing.*

To open a file over the Web:

1. Make sure that Web sharing has been turned on for each of the FileMaker databases you want to open (See *To share files over the Web* on page 266.)
2. Launch your Web browser and in the *Address* or *Location* text window, type the URL or IP address where the file is being hosted (`http://192.168.1.104/` in our example, though yours may be different) (**Figure 16.8**). Press Enter (Windows) or Return (Mac).
3. The Instant Web Publishing Database Homepage appears, displaying all the open databases for which you have activated Web sharing (**Figure 16.9**). Click the FileMaker file you want to open.

Table 16.1

Browsers Supporting Instant Web Publishing

BROWSER	OPERATING SYSTEM
Firefox 1.0 or higher	Windows XP or 2000, Mac OS X 10.1 or higher
Internet Explorer 6.0 or higher	Windows XP or 2000
Safari 1.1	Mac OS X 10.2
Safari 1.2 or 1.3	Mac OS X 10.3
Safari 2.0 or higher	OS X 10.4 or higher

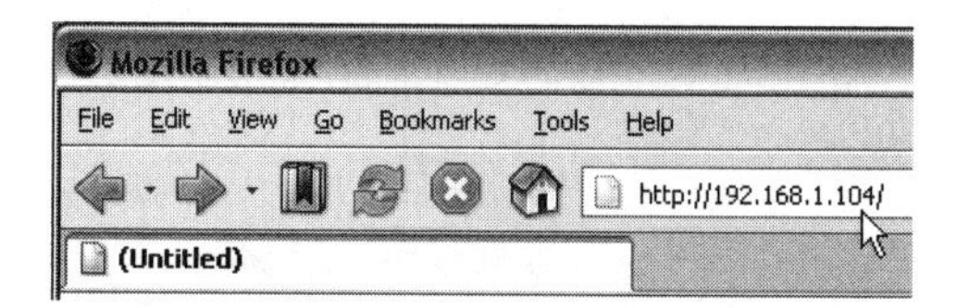

Figure 16.8 Once Web sharing is activated, a user just needs to enter the URL or IP address in their browser.

Figure 16.9 The Database Homepage displays all the open files for which Web sharing has been activated.

FileMaker Instant Web Publishing - Mozilla Firefox
File Edit View Go Bookmarks Tools Help
http://192.168.1.104/
FileMaker Instant Web Publishing
Instant Web Publishing
Open database "SamplePeople" with:
Guest Account
Account Name and Password
Account Name: Admin
Password: ************
Login Cancel
Done

Figure 16.10 Before you can actually see a file, you must login using your FileMaker account name and password.

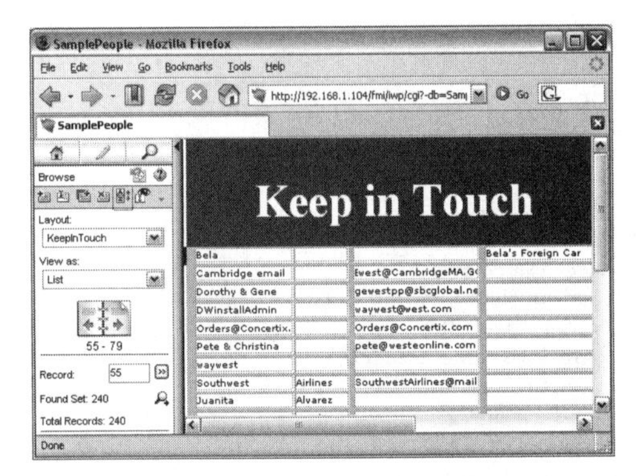

Figure 16.11 Files shared over the Web look remarkably like those seen by users running FileMaker itself.

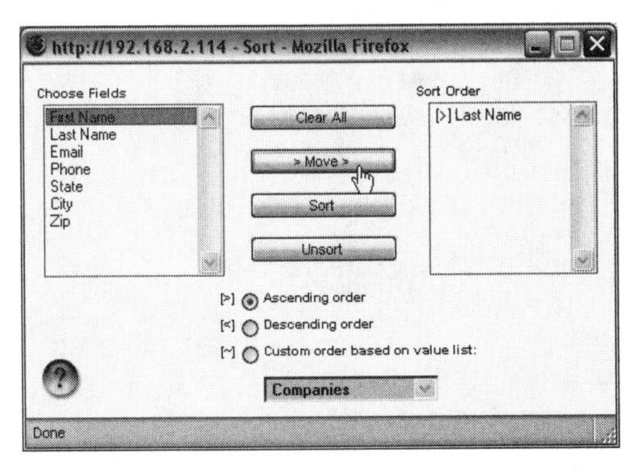

Figure 16.12 Instant Web Publishing mimics FileMaker's regular windows as in this example of a Web-based Sort dialog box.

4. If the page is password protected (and it should be), you have to enter an *Account Name* and *Password* before clicking *Login* (**Figure 16.10**).
5. The file appears, looking very similar to how it might appear to anyone actually running FileMaker (**Figure 16.11**).
6. Choose any button in the left-hand panel to trigger hidden scripts that closely mimic what you'd see running FileMaker directly on your computer (**Figure 16.12**).
7. When you're done working on the file, close the browser window or tab. What could be easier?

INDEX

D

G

H

M

N

O

P

Q

R

S

T

U

V

W

X

Y

Z